Technology Tools for Students with Autism

Technology Tools for Students with Autism
Innovations that Enhance Independence and Learning

edited by

Katharina I. Boser, Ph.D.,
Glenelg Country School
Individual Differences in Learning Association
Clarksville, Maryland

Matthew S. Goodwin, Ph.D.,
Bouvé College of Health Science and
College of Computer and Information Science
Northeastern University
Boston, Massachusetts

and

Sarah C. Wayland, Ph.D.
Center for Advanced Study of Language
University of Maryland College Park

·P A U L·H·
BROOKES
PUBLISHING CO.®

Baltimore • London • Sydney

Paul H. Brookes Publishing Co.
Post Office Box 10624
Baltimore, Maryland 21285-0624
USA

www.brookespublishing.com

Typeset by Cenveo Publisher Services, Columbia, Maryland.
Manufactured in the United States by
Sheridan Books, Inc., Chelsea, Michigan.

The individuals described in this book are composites or real people whose situations have been masked and are based on the authors' experiences. Names and identifying details have been changed to protect confidentiality.

Selected clip art © 2013 Jupiterimages Corporation.
Cover art ©istockphoto/ma_rish.

Library of Congress Cataloging-in-Publication Data

The Library of Congress has cataloged the printed edition as follows:
Boser, Katharina I. (Katharina Irene)
  Technology tools for students with autism : innovations that enhance independence and learning /
by Katharina I. Boser, Ph.D., Matthew S. Goodwin, Ph.D., and Sarah Wayland, Ph.D.
    pages   cm
  Includes bibliographical references and index.
  ISBN 978-1-59857-262-9 (hardcopy : alk. paper)
  ISBN 978-1-59857-553-8 (EPUB3)

  1. Autistic children—Education. 2. Educational technology. I. Title.

  LC4717.B67 2013
  371.9—dc23   2013016306

British Library Cataloguing in Publication data are available from the British Library.

2017   2016   2015   2014   2013

10   9   8   7   6   5   4   3   2   1

Contents

About the Editors

Katharina I. Boser, Ph.D., received her B.A., M.A., and Ph.D. from Cornell University in developmental psychology and cognitive science and wrote her dissertation about the early development of child language. She completed postdoctoral work at the University of Maryland studying language rehabilitation using computing technologies for patients with aphasia. In 2000, she joined the research faculty at Johns Hopkins University School of Medicine in Cognitive Neurology, where until 2005 she studied language training with low-verbal subjects and cognition (number representation, memory, and visual attention) in children with autism. She has conducted research on social robots and is involved in usability research with technology companies developing computer software for use with children with autism and other cognitive and/or learning issues. She was a board member and later cochair of the Innovative Technologies for Autism initiative for Autism Speaks until 2011. Dr. Boser is president of Individual Differences in Learning, an educational nonprofit in Maryland that provides professional development to teachers and parents regarding brain-based teaching techniques and innovative technologies for students with a range of cognitive impairments, including autism and twice exceptionality. She presents at many national and international conferences on autism technology research and cognition and advocates for universal design for learning and 21st-century learning and teaching at state and national levels. Since the fall of 2011, she has been a technology coordinator for the Glenelg Country School in Ellicott City, Maryland.

Matthew S. Goodwin, Ph.D., is an assistant professor at Northeastern University with joint appointments in the Bouvé College of Health Sciences and College of Computer & Information Science, where he coadministers a new doctoral program in personal health informatics. He is a visiting assistant professor and the former director of clinical research at the MIT Media Lab. Goodwin serves on the executive board of the International Society for Autism Research, is chair of the Autism Speaks Innovative Technology for Autism initiative, and has adjunct associate research scientist appointments at Brown University. Goodwin has over 15 years of research and clinical experience at the Groden Center working with children and adults on the autism spectrum and developing and evaluating innovative technologies for behavioral assessment and intervention, including telemetric physiological monitors, accelerometry sensors, and digital video and facial recognition systems. He received his B.A. in psychology from Wheaton College and his M.A. and Ph.D., both in experimental psychology, from the University of Rhode Island. He completed a postdoctoral fellowship in affective computing in the Media Lab in 2010.

Sarah C. Wayland, Ph.D., is a senior research scientist at the University of Maryland's Center for Advanced Study of Language and a faculty affiliate in the Special Education Program in the College of Education. She has worked on issues pertaining to language for over 25 years, first at Brandeis University, where she earned a Ph.D. in Cognitive Psychology, and then at Northeastern University, the University of Maryland School of Medicine, and now at the University of Maryland College Park. She was not in academia for all that time; for over a decade she worked in industry designing those annoying telephone voice systems everyone loves to yell at.

Active in the local disability community, she has helped organize numerous conferences designed to help parents and professionals learn more about ways to help their children with disabilities. She is on the executive committee of the Individual Differences in Learning Association and has been a board member of the Special Education Citizens' Advisory Committee of Prince George's County, Maryland, since 2007. She comoderates GT-Special, an international Listserv for parents of twice-exceptional children (children who are both gifted and learning disabled), and is a member of the Gifted and Talented with Learning Disabilities (GT/LD) Network. She is also a Parents' Place of Maryland PEP (Parents Encouraging Parents) leader of Prince George's County, Maryland.

Dr. Wayland lives with her wonderful husband and their two fabulous boys in Riverdale Park, Maryland.

Contributors

Gregory D. Abowd, D.Phil., is Regents' and Distinguished Professor in the School of Interactive Computing at the Georgia Institute of Technology. He received the degrees of M.Sc. and D.Phil. in computation from the University of Oxford. Dr. Abowd leads a research group interested in human-centered applications of mobile and ubiquitous computing technologies, with an emphasis on home and health. He was a leader in establishing the importance of computing technology to address a variety of challenges linked to autism and has published widely on this topic and assisted in the development of commercial solutions. He is Fellow of the Association of Computing Machinery (ACM). In 2009, he was awarded the ACM Eugene Lawler Humanitarian Award for his research efforts.

Rosa I. Arriaga, Ph.D., is a developmental psychologist in the School of Interactive Computing and Director of Pediatric Research for the Health Systems Institute at Georgia Institute of Technology. Her emphasis is on using psychological theory and methods to address fundamental topics of human–computer interaction. Current research interests in the area of health include how technology and crowd sourcing can aid individuals with autism spectrum disorders and their caregivers, how mobile solutions can improve chronic care management, and how lab-based technologies can be scaled and deployed to broaden their impact.

Emma Ashwin, Ph.D., received her undergraduate degree in psychology at the University of Cambridge in 2003 and subsequently began work as a research assistant at the Autism Research Centre (ARC) in Cambridge, England. She then completed a Ph.D. in the ARC, investigating fetal hormonal effects on social and emotional development and the effects on later brain function and structure. She is currently a research scientist at Bath University, England.

Simon Baron-Cohen, Ph.D., Director of the Autism Research Centre (ARC) in Cambridge, England, is Professor of Developmental Psychopathology at the University of Cambridge and Fellow at Trinity College, Cambridge. He holds degrees in Human Sciences from New College, Oxford, a Ph.D. in Psychology from University

College, London, and an M.Phil. in Clinical Psychology at the Institute of Psychiatry. He is Director of the Cambridge Lifespan Asperger Syndrome Service, a clinic for adults with suspected autism. He is author or editor of numerous books for both scholarly audiences and parents and teachers and is author of the DVD-ROM *Mind Reading*, nominated for a BAFTA for Best Off-Line Learning. He is also editor-in-chief of the online open access journal *Molecular Autism*. He has received awards from the American Psychological Association, the British Association for the Advancement of Science, and the British Psychological Society for his research into autism, which currently is focused on testing the "extreme male brain" theory. He has been president of the Psychology Section of the BA and vice president of the International Society for Autism Research as well as the National Autistic Society.

Katharine P. Beals, Ph.D., holds a Ph.D. in linguistics from the University of Chicago and worked for 5 years as a senior software engineer in the Natural Language group of Unisys Corporation before joining the University of Pennsylvania Graduate School of Education and Drexel University School of Education. Her research interests include language acquisition, educational software, and the education of children with autism. She has presented posters at the Autism Association of America and International Meeting for Autism Research conferences and has published articles and book chapters on computational linguistics, pragmatics, and autism. She is also the architect of the GrammarTrainer software program, a comprehensive English grammar curriculum for children on the autistic spectrum, as well as the author of *Raising a Left-Brain Child in a Right-Brain World* (Shambhala, 2009), a book that addresses issues facing children with autism who are in educational settings. Finally, she is the parent of a 16-year-old boy on the autistic spectrum.

Bonnie Beers, M.A., earned her B.A. in English literature and secondary education from Duke University, and her M.A. in special education from The George Washington University. She has taught students with learning disabilities and was the high school division director for the Multiple Learning Needs program for students with developmental disabilities at Ivymount School in Rockville, Maryland. She is currently the secondary coordinator of the Model Asperger Program, where she is also in charge of curriculum development for middle and high school. She has taught courses and given countless presentations in the areas of literacy, math, language, and emotion management.

Chris Bendel earned his B.M. in music, concentrating in education, at Virginia Commonwealth University. He has been at Ivymount School in Rockville, Maryland, for 5 years, 4 as a teacher in the classroom, and most recently serving as educational and assistive technology specialist. His research interests include finding ways to leverage technology to meet the needs of all types of learners, both functionally and academically, and finding effective ways to incorporate technology into a universal design for learning framework. He strives to find ways to connect students to the lessons and supports they require in and outside of the classroom to help encourage "always-on" learning.

Alise Brann, Ed.S., Research Analyst at AIR, has more than a decade of experience in educational and assistive technology. Her current project for the Center for Technology Implementation is PowerUp WHAT WORKS, which focuses on advancing teaching and learning through technology in inclusive classrooms. She has written several online articles including, "Students with Disabilities in Charter Schools," "Using Technology to Support Struggling Students in Science," "Captioned Media: Literacy Support for Diverse Learners," an "Ask the Tech Expert" column, and a chapter in *Breakthrough Teaching and Learning: How Educational and Assistive Technologies Are Driving Innovation* (Gray & Silver-Paculla, eds., Springer, 2011). She received her Ed.S. in assistive technology and her M.S. Ed. in special education from Simmons College in Boston.

Jed R. Brubaker, M.A., is a Ph.D. candidate in informatics at the Donald Bren School of Information and Computer Sciences at the University of California, Irvine. His research focuses on social computing and human–computer interaction. He holds an M.A. in communication, culture, and technology from Georgetown University and a B.S. in psychology from the University of Utah.

Christopher R. Bugaj, M.A., CCC-SLP, is a founding member of the Assistive Technology Team for Loudoun County Public Schools in Virginia. He is the coauthor of *The Practical (and Fun) Guide to Assistive Technology in Public Schools*, published by the International Society on Technology in Education. He hosts the A.T.TIPSCAST (http://www.attipscast.com), a multi-award-winning podcast featuring strategies to differentiate learning. He is the author of ATEval2Go (http://www.bit.ly/ateval2go), an application for iPad that helps professionals perform consultations and evaluations, and also coproduces the popular Night Light Stories podcast (http://www. nightlightstories.net), which features original stories for children of all ages.

Jessica Gosnell Caron, M.S., CCC-SLP, graduated from MGH Institute of Health Professions in 2007 with a master's in communication science disorders. Since 2008, she has been a speech-language pathologist in the Augmentative Communication Program at Children's Hospital, Boston. Her clinical focus includes assessment and intervention for children and adults who present with complex communication needs; with special interest in high-tech users of augmentative and alternative communication (AAC). She has published articles on the topic of using iDevices and applications, including "Apps: An Emerging Tool for SLPs" (*ASHA Leader*, 2011) and "There Isn't Always an App for That" (*Perspectives Journal*, 2011). She has lectured nationally and internationally on the topic of high-tech AAC and has taught graduate-level courses in augmentative communication at both Mass General Institute of Health Professions and Northeastern University.

Kelley Challen-Wittmer, Ed.M., CAS, has, since 2004, facilitated programming for individuals with autism spectrum disorders (ASDs). After receiving a master's degree and certificate of advanced study in counseling from Harvard Graduate

School of Education, Challen-Wittmer spent several years at Massachusetts General Hospital's Aspire Program, founding an array of life and career skills development programs. She currently works as Director of Transition Services at NESCA, a private neuropsychology practice in Newton, Massachusetts, where she oversees transition planning, consultation, evaluation, and training services. Challen-Wittmer specializes in ASDs, including Asperger syndrome, adolescent transition, college and career counseling, and social and life skill development.

Yvel Cornel Crevecoeur, Ph.D., is an in-residence 2012–2013 Boston College and CAST postdoctoral fellow and an assistant professor of special education in the Department of Leadership & Special Education at The City College of New York. He is interested in designing and evaluating universal learning environments that include accessible instructional materials for learners at the pre-K–12 and post-secondary levels who experience learning difficulties, especially individuals with diverse cultural and linguistic backgrounds. He has also worked with at-risk learners as a probation officer for the Florida Department of Juvenile Justice.

Yvonne Domings, Ed.M., is Director of Online Learning and Instructional Designer at CAST, where she developed the Building Comprehension Through Social Understanding (BCSU) instructional approach to improve reading comprehension for students with autism spectrum disorder (ASD) by addressing the autism-specific deficits in theory of mind and imaginative play. She holds a master's degree from Harvard University in mind, brain, and education. Prior to working at CAST, she spent several years helping teachers broaden regular education curricula to encompass the academic, social, and behavioral needs of students with ASD. She has shared her expertise in the educational and affective needs of students with autism in teacher professional development programs.

Ofer Golan, Ph.D., is a senior lecturer and chair of the Clinical Child Psychology Program at Bar-Ilan University, Israel. His research involves clinical and developmental aspects of autism spectrum conditions (ASC), focusing especially on the use of technology and multimedia to enhance emotion recognition, expression, and understanding in individuals with ASC. Past and current technology for ASC projects include Mindreading (http://www.jkp.com), *The Transporters* video series (http://www.thetransporters.com), and ASC-Inclusion (http://www.asc-inclusion.eu).

Tracy Gray, Ph.D., Managing Director at the American Institutes for Research, directs the Center for STEM Education and Innovation. She leads PowerUp WHAT WORKS, an innovative online learning platform that provides tools and resources to strengthen teaching and learning enhanced by technology for struggling learners. She led two additional projects funded by the U.S. Department of Education, Office of Special Education Programs, National Center for Technology Innovation (NCTI) and the Center for Technology Implementation in Education (CITEd). Dr. Gray has authored numerous publications and recently coedited *Breakthrough Teaching* *and Learning: How Educational and Assistive Technologies Are Driving Innovation* (Springer, 2011), with Dr. Heidi Silver Pacuilla. Dr. Gray was a vice president for the Morino Institutes, where she led the Youth Learn initiative. She was the first chief operating officer and acting deputy director for the Corporation for National and Community Service, which launched Americorps. She received her Ph.D. and M.A. from Stanford University. Dr. Gray lives with her husband in Washington, D.C., and is the mother of two daughters.

Joan L. Green, M.A., CCC-SLP, the founder of Innovative Speech Therapy, is a licensed and certified speech-language pathologist with many years' experience helping children and adults who have communication, cognitive, literacy, and learning challenges. She received her undergraduate and graduate education and training at Northwestern University. She has developed a unique effective approach to therapy that empowers individuals, families, and professionals with state-of-the-art local and online therapy, coaching, and training programs. She authored *Technology for Communication and Cognitive Treatment: The Clinician's Guide* and *The Ultimate Guide to Assistive Technology in Special Education: Resources for Education, Intervention, and Rehabilitation* (Innovative Speech Therapy, 2007). She offers an informative free e-newsletter at http://www.innovativespeech.com to more than 7,000 recipients. These newsletters highlight affordable technology treasures such as iPad apps and interactive online sites as well as strategies for success. In 2008, Green received the Most Outstanding Contribution to the Field Award from the Maryland Speech-Language-Hearing Association.

Melissa A. Hartman, Ed.D., is currently a special education supervisor for Loudoun County Public Schools in Virginia. She consults around the country providing professional development and training on universal design for learning as a member of the faculty cadre at CAST. She completed her dissertation research on students with Asperger syndrome at The George Washington University and for more than 20 years has worked with students on the autism spectrum and their families. She has been an adjunct professor at several local universities, teaching classes on curricula and methods, consultation, and special education. Her work has been published in *Teaching Exceptional Children*. She loves to model and share new technology with her colleagues and teachers. Professional interests include transition, technology integration, professional development, and school leadership.

Gillian R. Hayes, Ph.D., is an associate professor at the University of California, Irvine, Donald Bren School of Information and Computer Sciences where she designs, develops, and deploys unobtrusive data collection and management technologies that empower people to use collected data to address real human needs in sensitive and ethically responsible ways. She directs the Social and Technological Action Research group and is affiliated with the Laboratory for Ubiquitous Computing and Interaction, the Intel Science and Technology Center for Social Computing, the Center for Autism Research and Treatment, the Center for Ethnography, the Center for Biomedical Informatics, the Center for Research on Information

Technology & Organizations, the California Institute for Telecommunications and Information Technology, and the Institute for Genetics and Bioinformatics. She is a fellow in the University of California Center for Collaborative Research for an Equitable California and serves as Director of Technology Research at the Center for Autism and Neurodevelopmental Disorders of Southern California and Chief Technology Officer for Tiwahe Technology.

Stephen W. Hosaflook, M.Ac., has a B.S. in marketing from Rochester Institute of Technology and a master's in accounting from Kennesaw State University. He is Chief Executive Office of Tiwahe Technology, a high-tech design and consulting firm specializing in autism and other assistive and educational technologies. Along with Dr. Hayes, he created Technology in the Workplace workshops, which instruct students on using technology as they transition into the work force.

Felicia Hurewitz, Ph.D., is the director of the Drexel Autism Support Program, which uses peer-mediated support to help students with autism spectrum disorder navigate the college experience. After receiving her doctorate in psychology from the University of Pennsylvania, Dr. Hurewitz was a postdoctoral scholar at the Rutgers University Institute for Research in Cognitive Science, and then a professor of psychology at Drexel University. She has received a number of research awards, including a National Academy of Education/Spencer Foundation postgraduate fellowship and an Innovative Technology grant from Autism Speaks. Dr. Hurewitz is interested in developing and evaluating new models for assessing and educating children and adults with autism, especially through the use of such technologies as iPad applications and through peer or employer mentorship. Dr. Hurewitz also recently founded Edment Consulting to assist schools, families, and providers with creating new educational and transition opportunities.

Brooke Ingersoll, Ph.D., received her Ph.D. in experimental psychology from the University of California, San Diego. She is currently an assistant professor of psychology at Michigan State University (MSU), where she directs the MSU Autism Research Laboratory. Her research is focused on the development and evaluation of social communication interventions for children with autism spectrum disorder (ASD). Her current work, funded by the Department of Defense's Autism Research Program and Autism Speaks, involves the development of online methods for teaching parents of children with ASD to promote their child's social communication.

Julie A. Kientz, Ph.D., is an assistant professor in the department of Human Centered Design and Engineering at the University of Washington. Dr. Kientz's primary research areas are in the fields of human-computer interaction, ubiquitous computing, and health informatics. She directs the Computing for Healthy Living and Learning Lab, which focuses on designing, developing, and evaluating future computing applications in the domains of health and education. In particular,

Dr. Kientz has worked on designing and evaluating mobile, sensor, and collaborative applications for people with sleep disorders, parents of young children, and individuals with autism. Her primary research methods involve human-centered design, technology development, and a mix of qualitative and quantitative methods.

Corinna E. Lathan, PE, Ph.D., is the founder of AnthroTronix, an engineering product development company including the AT KidSystems brand, which develops computer interfaces and educational software for children with disabilities. She is also the founder of Keys to Empowering Youth, a science and technology mentoring program for junior high school girls, and a board member of Engineering World Health, which supports the emergence of health care technology in the developing world. Dr. Lathan was a governor appointee to the Task Force on the Universal Design for Learning, whose work led to Maryland's State Department of Education Regulation 13A.03.06. Dr. Lathan received her B.A. in biopsychology and mathematics from Swarthmore College and an S.M. in aeronautics and astronautics and Ph.D. in neuroscience from MIT.

Minna Levine, Ph.D., OTR/L, President of SymTrend, has a B.S. in occupational therapy from the University of Pennsylvania and a Ph.D. in psychology from Brandeis University. She was principal or coinvestigator on three small-business research grants from the National Institute of Mental Health for the development of electronic diary software for use by teens with Asperger syndrome and their caregivers and by professionals and families doing behavioral observations with young children with autism. Dr. Levine works with researchers and clinicians developing self-monitoring tools for individuals with chronic pain, neurological issues, depression, and anxiety.

Dorothy Lucci, M.Ed., CAGS, has over 30 years' experience in the field of autism and is a national consultant specializing in program design and inclusion of individuals diagnosed with autism spectrum disorder. She has conducted research at Boston University Medical Center and the University of Connecticut, been Director of the Autism Support Center, and worked as a school psychologist and general and special education teacher. Currently, she is Director of Aspire, a program at Massachusetts General Hospital, Boston. She is a consultant to SymTrend and a member of the Board of Directors of the Asperger's Association of New England. Her publications are in academic journals, the *ASQ Quarterly*, and a book chapter in *The Exceptional Brain* (Obler & Fein, Eds., Guilford Press, 1988). In 2007 she was nominated to Marquis Who's Who in American Education. In 2010 she was a senior investigator at the Mind and Life Summer Research Institute: Education, studying Developmental Neuroscience and Contemplative Practices: Questions, Challenges and Opportunities.

Donald Scott McLeod, Ph.D., has been on staff at Boston's Massachusetts General Hospital since 1990. He became Aspire's Executive Director in January 2003 after acting as Associate Director for 10 years. Dr. McLeod received his doctorate in clinical psychology from Boston University. He is a clinical instructor in psychology at Harvard Medical School. Dr. McLeod consults with schools about supporting students with autism spectrum disorder in the classroom, school, and greater community. He is a member of the Board of Directors of the Asperger's Association of New England.

Marek Michalowski, Ph.D., earned his B.A. and M.S. in computer science and psychology from Yale University and a Ph.D. in Robotics from Carnegie Mellon University, with a thesis entitled, *Rhythmic Human–Robot Social Interaction.* He has conducted psychological research into autism, nonverbal interaction, and social development using Keepon Pro, a teleoperable social robot. He cofounded BeatBots with Dr. Hideki Kozima, the designer of Keepon, to commercialize their robots in order to support further research and development of therapeutic tools. He oversaw the development of the My Keepon toy, launched in Toys 'R' Us in 2011, and designed the Zingy character featured in UK-based EDF Energy's "Feel Better Energy" advertising campaign. He has appeared on the *Today Show* to discuss the use of robots in autism therapy. He has won numerous National Science Foundation grants, the Smiley Award, a *Popular Science* Best of Toy Fair Award, and a Maker Faire Editor's Choice Award.

Kathryn Nagle, M.Ed., earned her B.A. at Sarah Lawrence College, concentrating in art conservation chemistry, and went on to receive her M.Ed. in secondary chemistry education, focusing on the application of universal design for learning principles to increase student success. She works as the middle and high school science teacher in the Model Asperger Program (MAP), where she also acts as the supervisor of, and provides curriculum support to, the elementary science teachers. In addition to her teaching responsibilities, she is the technology coordinator for MAP, working with students and staff to integrate assistive technology and electronic executive function supports into the everyday classroom.

Nazneen is a Ph.D. student at the School of Interactive Computing at Georgia Tech. She is advised by Dr. Gregory D. Abowd and Dr. Rosa I. Arriaga. She is a researcher in the field of ubiquitous computing and human–computer interaction. Her research interests are in developing technologies for children with autism and their caregivers. Nazneen's current research is on designing capture and access technologies for in-home behavioral data collection and sharing. Her work has been published in the *Journal of Personal and Ubiquitous Computing, ASSETS, Pervasive Health,* and *CHI.* She was the recipient of the Bill George Fellowship Award in 2010.

Nigel Newbutt, Ph.D., is a senior lecturer at Bath Spa University (England) in digital cultures. His research interests are in the areas of autism, technology, and the sociology of technology. His Ph.D. was completed at University College Dublin, Ireland, where he investigated the views of young people with autism and their engagement with a virtual world. His research to date has focused on participatory input and user-centered design approaches, as well as a qualitative approach to gathering data. His work sees him engaged in classrooms, working with children and teachers to design and develop virtual worlds to help provide a platform that in many ways helps to create a setting where social communication can be explored.

Mark E. Nichols, M.Ed., is the supervisor of assistive technology/digital IEPs and Lead Digital Rights Manager for accessible instructional materials in Loudoun County Public Schools (LCPS), Virginia. His inspiration began in 1981 when his sister was born with cerebral palsy. Fabricating switches and programming communication devices at a young age laid the foundation for his career. He attended Lynchburg College, Virginia, where he received a B.A. in special education and psychology, and then George Mason University for his M.Ed. in assistive technology. As a founding member of the LCPS Assistive Technology team, he helped develop and support various cutting-edge professional development strategies. He was the recipient of the 2012 Virginia Society for Technology in Education Leader of the Year Award and the 2012 Lynchburg College M. Carey Brewer Alumni Award.

Linda J. O'Neal, M.A., received her bachelor's degree in psychology from the University of Southern California and earned her master's degree in special education from California State University, Los Angeles. She has served as Transition Specialist for the Irvine Unified School District for the past 26 years, including oversight of the Career Link Program. Her responsibilities include coordinating employment and transition planning efforts for secondary students. She also writes and administrates local, state, and federal career development grants. For the past 20 years, she has also been a part-time faculty member at Chapman University, where she teaches special education teacher credentialing courses.

Sarah Parsons, Ph.D., is Head of the Centre for Social Justice and Inclusive Education at the University of Southampton, England. Since completing a Ph.D. in developmental psychology at the University of Nottingham, she has researched the use of innovative technologies for children with autism and the experiences of children with disabilities and their families. She was a partner on the European FP7-funded COSPATIAL project (2009–2012), which explored the use of collaborative technologies for supporting social skills for children with autism. She is currently a partner on the ESRC-funded SHAPE project (2012–2013), which works closely with school practitioners to identify ways of using interactive technologies in the classroom.

Patricia Kelly Ralabate, Ed.D., joined CAST as Director of Implementation in September 2011 and currently teaches bilingual and special education policy courses for The George Washington University Graduate School of Education and Human Development. Previously, she served as a Boston College postdoctoral fellow-in-residence at CAST, working on universal design for learning leadership issues. As Senior Policy Analyst for special and gifted education for the National Education

Association, she was Principal Editor of *The Puzzle of Autism*, an educator guide on autism spectrum disorder (ASD). She also worked for 25 years with many students with ASD as a speech-language pathologist in Connecticut public schools.

Corina Ratz, M.A., graduated with her master's in counseling from The Chicago School of Professional Psychology. She joined the Applied Professional Practice team as the associate director in January 2011. Prior to this, for the last 4 years she had been practicing as a bilingual family therapist at the Pediatric Developmental Center with Advocate Illinois Masonic Medical Center. There, she worked primarily with Spanish-speaking families who were seeking help for their children with a history of developmental problems associated with behavioral difficulties. Previously, Ratz worked as a child therapist on the Child and Adolescent Psychiatry Unit at Chicago's Children's Memorial Hospital.

Charlotte Safos is Vice President and Chief Operating Officer of AnthroTronix. She also serves as Vice President and General Manager of AT KidSystems, the manufacturer, marketer, and distributor of educational and health products developed by AnthroTronix. She is responsible for the daily operations of the company and contributes to strategic planning and direction, research and development efforts, business development, and new product development. Prior to joining AnthroTronix, Safos worked for the United Cerebral Palsy Association, a national disability organization. She was responsible for development and management of projects for children and adults with disabilities.

Carole Samango-Sprouse, Ed.D., studies the relationship between the brain and behavior and its impact on school performance in children with sex chromosome variations, autism spectrum disorder, neurogenetic disorders including neurofibromatosis–type1, and developmental dyspraxia, among other conditions. She is Director of the Neurodevelopmental Diagnostic Center for Young Children, located near Annapolis, Maryland. In addition, she is an associate clinical professor of pediatrics at The George Washington University and is on staff at Children's National Medical Center in Washington, D.C. She presently serves on the steering committee of the Autism Genetic Resource Exchange, an organization that fosters neurobiological research about children with autism. Dr. Sprouse has published more than 80 articles about the neurocognitive capabilities of children who are atypical.

Howard C. Shane, Ph.D., is an associate professor of otolaryngology at Harvard Medical School and the director of the Center for Communication Enhancement and the Autism Language Program at Boston Children's Hospital. He has designed more than a dozen computer applications used widely by persons with disabilities and holds two U.S. patents. Dr. Shane has received Honors of the Association Distinction and is a fellow of the American Speech and Hearing Association. He is the recipient of the Goldenson Award for Innovations in Technology from the United Cerebral Palsy Association and has authored numerous papers and chapters on severe speech impairment, lectured throughout the world on the topic, and produced numerous computer innovations enjoyed by persons with complex communication disorders.

Rita Shewbridge, M.S., is currently employed as a design engineer at AnthroTronix. She received her M.S. in tangible interaction design from Carnegie Mellon University and is now pursuing a Ph.D. in human-centered computing at the University of Maryland, Baltimore County. Her research interests are in rehabilitation and assistive technologies.

Andrea Tartaro, Ph.D., received her Ph.D. in technology and social behavior, a joint Ph.D. in the areas of computer science and communication studies, from Northwestern University. As part of her graduate work, she designed and evaluated technology interventions with social group programs for children with autism. She is currently an assistant professor of computer science at Furman University in Greenville, South Carolina, and previously taught computer science at Union College in Schenectady, New York. She also has a B.A. in computer science from Brown University, an M.A. in instructional technology from Teachers College, Columbia University, and an M.S. in computer science from Northwestern University.

Allison Wainer, M.A., is a graduate student in clinical psychology at Michigan State University. She is interested in disseminating autism spectrum disorder (ASD) interventions in community settings. Her current work, funded by a fellowship from Autism Speaks, is focused on the development and evaluation of an online parent-training program that teaches parents of children with ASD to support their child's imitation skills.

Simon Wallace, Ph.D., completed his undergraduate and postgraduate degrees at the University of London. He has conducted research across a variety of fields, including genetic phenotyping, cognitive neuroscience, diagnosis, and technology interventions. In 2008 he left academic research to work for Autism Speaks as Director of Scientific Development in Europe and since 2011 as Research Director for Autistica. Prior to his leaving research, Dr. Sarah Parsons and he researched the usefulness of virtual reality tools (an immersive room and a desktop computer system) in the future education of children with autism.

Monica Adler Werner, M.A., is the director of the Model Asperger Program at the Ivymount School in Rockville, Maryland. In that capacity she has spearheaded the development of a social learning curriculum that emphasizes problem solving, self-advocacy, and self-regulation while keeping students on track academically. She has coauthored *Unstuck and On Target* (Paul H. Brookes Publishing Co., 2011), an evidence-based curriculum to enhance cognitive flexibility and problem solving in students with Asperger syndrome. She is the coauthor of several papers and posters about working with children with Asperger syndrome or high-functioning autism.

She has an undergraduate degree from the University of Pennsylvania and her master's degree from Johns Hopkins.

Michael T. Yeganyan, M.S., has degrees in information and computer science from the University of California, Irvine, Donald Bren School of Information and Computer Sciences. His M.S. thesis focused on the design, development, and evaluation of an innovative tool for special education classrooms that combined the functionality of visual schedules, choice boards, and a token-based reward system in a distributed touchscreen system for both students and teachers. Previously, he worked at Intel and Experian. He currently resides in Los Angeles and is a mobile developer at ISBX.

Foreword

How I wish today's technology had been available when I was in school! But it wasn't. Faced with a teaching environment of lectures and schoolbooks, with everyone doing the same work, in the same classroom, on the same schedule, at the same pace, I failed at high school. Eventually, I dropped out.

Yet I wasn't a failure everywhere. My father taught at the local university, and their labs were open to me night and day. Instead of a rigidly defined teaching plan, they offered me my pick of texts and the freedom to read them any time, night or day. There were no teachers standing at the blackboard to lecture me, but there were always grad students to answer my questions, however strange they might have seemed. Best of all, though, was the technology. Because I wasn't a kid who learned just by reading. I learned by reading and doing, in concert, and technology was what made the doing fun.

The engineering labs were full of test equipment and circuitry. I could read how a radio worked, then put a radio receiver on the bench and actually test it with the books and manuals beside me. By reading, experimenting, and asking questions, I honed in on new knowledge quickly, efficiently, and in the way that worked best for me. In the space of 18 months, I taught myself as much electrical engineering as many people learn in 6 years of college.

That's what happens when you take a kid with special interests, unusual focus, and concentration—all hallmarks of autism—and place him in an environment where he can immerse himself as deeply as he wants, as long as he wants. It's a powerful thing, something that's all too rare in our public schools today.

I didn't know how effectively I'd educated myself at the time because I had no way to know what any other engineer might know. Even today, I've never tried a point-by-point comparison of knowledge. However, in the working world, that doesn't matter anyway: employers want results, not test scores. When it came to efficient designs that worked, it's clear that I was just as effective as many engineers with postgraduate educations in the field.

The sound effects and live sound reinforcement I created with that knowledge have entertained millions, and people continue watching and listening today, thirty-some years later. My work has certainly stood the test of time, and it's all the validation any engineer could ask for.

Yet I was a total failure in school, and for that I blame the absence of technology, as well as a lack of self-educational freedom. Teaching someone like me by the book just doesn't work, and when something catches my fancy, making me hold back for the 99% of the class that needs to go slower drives me crazy. At the same time, I was behind my classmates on many ordinary-seeming topics, and there's no reason for them to wait for me.

Unfortunately, there was no way for a kid like me to run ahead and immerse himself in his special interest without the technology to back him up. That's still true today, and it's important because there are still plenty of young geeks who learn by doing and at their own pace.

For those kids, as with me, technology helps in many areas:

- Computers make it possible to search out and track information, which can be useful for monitoring, observing, and analyzing behavior—something that can help people with autism spectrum disorder (ASD) with social awareness in a "metacognitive" way.

- Mobile devices allow us to to connect without the "distraction" of social stimuli that often make it hard for people with ASD to interact face to face.

- Computers can be programmed to do things, whether that means creating music, directing a machine tool, or driving a motorized telescope to sweep the sky.

- Dedicated devices allow us to actually make things and have those hands-on experiences that are so important. Making things can encompass a tremendous range, from woodworking to car repair and almost anything a craftsman or technician can build or repair.

Technology helps in a vitally important way: People with autism have, as a group, a strong need for logic, regimentation, and order. We often have trouble relating to other humans, whose logical failings are well known. That makes some of us perfectly suited to engage computers, the supreme incarnation of logical, regimented, and orderly behavior.

Kids that fail miserably engaging other children may find great success in a world of machines. Machines don't trick us, lie, or make fun of us when we don't understand. They just sit there. That may be frustrating to an ordinary kid, but it's a great comfort to any child who's been teased, bullied, and tricked by unreliable and manipulative classmates.

I'd like to mention one final benefit of technology in the classroom: When kids use technology to communicate, the device erases disabilities that might otherwise be visible and humiliating. When all the answers are typed or spoken into the computer, every student's paper or audio response is as readable and understandable as any other. Some may choose to use accessibility functions such as speech-to-text to have the computer type out their wishes, desires, answers, and ideas. Penmanship and other barriers to written productivity no longer present a handicap for the student. Kids who have trouble speaking face to face communicate through the keyboard or by using a microphone as effectively as anyone else. Someone who is socially crippled by the inability to read expressions and body language is just like anyone else reading text on a screen or listening and typing or speaking answers to a computer or mobile device.

So far, I've limited myself to ways in which students can use technology to enhance their own learning experience. However, teachers will not only facilitate their *students'* learning when they bring new interactive learning technologies into the classroom but also facilitate *their own* path to learning. When teachers adopt new technology, the benefits to them may be even greater. New technologies will also connect teachers with colleagues and students hundreds and even thousands of miles away. Online classrooms are already transforming student collaboration. Machines may not make teachers smarter—yet—but they sure will make them seem that way!

All this has just scratched the surface of what technology can do for us. Now, you are about to a read an entire book that will expand on the subject beyond my wildest childhood dreams.

So read on.

John Elder Robison

Foreword

A few years ago, a mother approached me after I gave a lecture on autism and shared a story about her teenage son who has autism spectrum disorder (ASD). She described to me the frustration she and her son had experienced because of his difficulty in communicating his needs and wishes. Her son was minimally verbal. For years, every month or so, her son would become extremely agitated, making it clear that he was searching for something, but she was unable to figure out what he wanted. Recently, her son had been introduced to an application (app) that could be readily used on a mobile tablet computer as a means of communication. Something clicked. Soon, he was using the keyboard to tell her about his desires and needs. For one thing, he wanted to watch a certain videotape she had shown him years before. Could she find it for him? Indeed she did, and finally he was able to enjoy what he had been searching for all those years. Even more exciting, however, was the effect this new technology was having on his ability to function in school. His mother explained that he was now able to spend a good deal of his time with his age-mates and that there were a number of subjects in which he was excelling. It was a bonus that having these apps available on devices such as tablets or smartphones added to the "cool" factor and attracted positive attention from his peers.

As chief science officer of Autism Speaks, the leading science and advocacy organization for autism, I hear more and more of these stories about the transformative effect of technology from families and people affected by ASD. Technology is changing the way that people with ASD interact, communicate, and connect with the world. As a result, it is also changing how we think about autism as we discover hidden talents and capabilities that are revealed only when the right technology is provided. These stories just scratch the surface of how technology is influencing the world of autism treatment and research.

The three editors of *Technology Tools for Students with Autism: Innovations that Enhance Independence and Learning* are extremely well qualified to summarize the rapidly developing field of technology-based tools for students with autism. As recognized leaders in this field, Matthew S. Goodwin and Katharina I. Boser have headed the Autism Speaks Innovative Technology for Autism (ITA) initiative for over a decade, helping shape Autism Speaks research direction and training in the area of technology for people with autism. Sarah C. Wayland has worked for many years on methods for promoting language development and more recently in the area of using visual feedback technology for teaching social skills. Together, they bring complementary perspectives and expertise in the areas of cognitive and social development, language, education, intervention, and data capture and analysis.

To my knowledge, there is no other book available for individuals with ASD that captures the state of the field of technology-based learning tools. This book is written in a practical and easy-to-understand way that will make it especially useful for teachers, families, and persons with ASD from toddlerhood through adulthood. The book covers a wide range of important and practical topics, beginning with a review of federal, state, and philanthropic policies that support research and technology development as well as innovation to improve services for children with autism, including the guidelines and initiatives that are shaping how technology is used in the classroom.

A broad overview of a variety of new tools is provided, including technologies to facilitate expressive and receptive language, social skills, peer relations, emotion regulation, executive function, reading, and employment. The tools described include more established technologies such as using visual cues and visual supports, as well as more novel approaches like gaming, virtual environments, sensors, and robotics.

Section V on data collection tools—with Chapter 12 aptly titled "No More Clipboards!"—will be welcomed by teachers, parents, and clinicians. With the backbone of behavioral interventions resting on good data collection, these tools can revolutionize how information is collected, analyzed, stored, and shared. A particularly important feature of these tools is the ability to coordinate care among teachers, clinicians, and parents. This kind of coordinated care is essential for children with autism but often difficult to realize without a feasible, mobile means of shared communication. Also to be welcomed is a section targeted at teachers, schools, and school districts to help them make informed decisions about what types of technology they should invest in and the advantages and disadvantages of different approaches.

A discussion of distance learning technologies is particularly timely because these approaches are increasingly recognized as the best way to enhance professional training throughout the world. With an estimated prevalence of 1 in 88 individuals affected by ASD worldwide, there is an urgent and great need to provide access to evidence-based treatments and services in remote and underserved regions of the world.

A challenge of similar scale is meeting the needs of adults with autism. Although great strides have been made in providing early behavioral intervention and educational programs, many adolescents and adults struggle to get the support they need. Technologies that can support independent living and employment will help fill this gap. Thus, the section on technologies for adults with autism is a particularly valuable part of this book.

Autism spectrum disorder is often referred to as a public health crisis, in large part because of the great unmet need for appropriate interventions, services, and support for individuals struggling with ASD throughout the life span. As this book illustrates, technology has opened the door to a new set of scalable tools that can help address this challenge and help people with ASD live the most productive and satisfying lives possible.

Geraldine Dawson, Ph.D.
Chief Science Officer, Autism Speaks
Research Professor of Psychiatry, University
of North Carolina at Chapel Hill

Preface

This volume originated from, and is dedicated to, a number of researchers, educators, parents, and individuals on the autism spectrum who believe that technology can meaningfully improve education and quality of living. Since roughly 2005, beginning with Matthew S. Goodwin and Katharina I. Boser's board membership on the Innovative Technology for Autism (ITA) initiative at Autism Speaks, and Sarah C. Wayland and Katharina I. Boser's involvement with teachers and students through human computer interaction workshops and universal design for learning (UDL) advocacy, we have all felt the desire to relay the important message that technologies for autism need to reach a wider audience. This volume represents the outcome of that desire and is guided by three goals. First, we sought to assemble a volume in which a number of experts from a variety of disciplines came together to share, and thus better understand, current and future innovative approaches to the use of technology for persons with autism spectrum disorder (ASD). Second, we hoped that in writing for teachers and clinicians, as well as designers and computer scientists, we might encourage more interdisciplinary collaboration. Third, we felt it was important to include people on the autism spectrum in the writing and execution of this volume. Many of our authors have children or are themselves diagnosed with ASD and thus have intimate connections with the content of this volume. By including commentary and input from John Elder Robison and Stephen Shore, we hoped to make evident our deep connection with stakeholders from the community.

Encouraging collaboration is tied to the need for better interdisciplinary research. There is a need for more research on long-term efficacy and therapeutic and learning benefits, as well as drawbacks, of the use of technologies in the field. However, this is a complex, constantly evolving, and highly interdisciplinary field where innovations often happen more quickly than research can keep up. Collaboration and interdisciplinary research are essential to moving the field forward. The difficulty and paucity of well-designed and well-conducted research in this emerging field of technological assessment and intervention are well documented. One way to overcome these barriers is to encourage more empirical evaluations that include multiple small-subject studies that can be used to attract research funding that can replicate and extend the findings in larger samples. In addition, the negative stigma of tools like virtual reality and robotics, and now mobile technologies, is still very real in academic settings, where the line between learning and games is often blurred. Such technologies are often viewed as toys rather than legitimate learning tools. Our goal in facilitating collaborative research is to shift the prevailing view of technologies in the research community so that technologies are seen not as toys or distractions but, rather, as important research and therapeutic tools. We also wish to emphasize that developing technologies for ASD is intended not to replace the expertise and skill of professionals but to augment, enhance, and extend their impact and reach.

The goal of educating, facilitating, and documenting the power of technologies for individuals with ASD is one that Katharina I. Boser and Matthew S. Goodwin have been working on for many years, most notably through their membership, and later as chairs, of Autism Speaks's ITA. Through these roles, and with a number of key colleagues, identified in the Acknowledgments, we organized workshops, talks, and poster presentations at professional conferences. We guest-edited and contributed to special issues on technology in both autism and computer science journals. We also distributed grants to fund technology-focused research and to support undergraduate and graduate courses dedicated to technology and autism at Berkeley, Georgia Institute of Technology, Massachusetts Institute of Technology, Northwestern University, University of Southern California, and University of Toronto. Sarah C. Wayland was a community mentor for our technology and autism design competition held through Core77 in 2010 and since 2008 has been involved in innovative technologies through her research investigating the efficacy of a technology tool, the Conversation Clock, for teaching teens with autism the art of conversation. Sarah and Katharina have advocated for UDL in Maryland and through workshops and lectures at the Human Computer Interaction Lab and in the Department of Education at University of Maryland, College Park.

Creating and demonstrating the personal connection between technologies and users who benefit is our third goal. We each have a personal connection in addition to the connection through children and adults with ASD with whom we have worked. Using computerized systems to research best practices in training language and symbol learning, Katharina I. Boser worked with low-verbal children at Johns Hopkins University. Her prior work with patients with aphasia used many of the same techniques. Having worked as a researcher and teacher of students with a range of cognitive and social abilities, as well as being a parent of a twice-exceptional student, she continues to believe in technology's equalizing power. Matthew S. Goodwin spent 15 years working at the Groden Center in Rhode Island throughout his graduate work at the University of Rhode Island and postdoctoral work at the MIT Media Lab. His work there involved exploring, developing, and evaluating technologies that used wireless physical activity and physiological sensing and digital facial expression detection systems for use by children and adults with ASD. Sarah C. Wayland has two wonderful boys with autism; her struggle to help them function in a world that is not always friendly to people with autism has given her a deeper understanding of the challenges and how to address them. Her work advocating for her own children has translated into an active role in the local autism advocacy community. Both Sarah C. Wayland and Katharina I. Boser have been involved in providing resources to parents and teachers in the Southern Maryland area through a nonprofit organization called Individual Differences in Learning, a group that focuses on student strengths rather than weakness.

The technologies described in the chapters of this volume play to the strengths of students with autism. It is our hope that the approaches described herein will allow future researchers, teachers, clinicians, and developers to shape a positive future for us all.

Finally, in an effort to keep this book as current as possible, we would like to invite you to let us know if you find a web address that is not functioning or are aware of any product or company name changes that should be updated in the book. Please e-mail us at techtoolsforautism@gmail.com and we will review and post updates on the Brookes Publishing web site for all customers to access: http://www.brookespublishing.com/boser.

Note: There is debate in the publishing community regarding capitalization of the word "internet." APA guidelines are to capitalize it, but that seemed like capitalizing the name of a public utility, e.g., Electricity or Water. It feels old-fashioned, which isn't the aesthetic we were aiming for in this book. For this reason, we chose not to capitalize the word "internet."

Acknowledgments

The three of us are indebted to the following people, without whom this volume would not have been possible: Portia Iversen, Jon Shestack, Sophia Colamarino, Dan Gillette, Therese Finazzo, Gregory Abowd, Justine Cassell, Charles "Skip" Rizzo, Yoram Bonneh, Michelle Dawson, Amanda Baggs, John Elder Robison, Stephen Shore, Temple Grandin, Simon Wallace, Olga Solomon, Khai Truong, Geri Dawson, Andy Shih, Paul Law, Rob Ring, Maria Dixon, Karrie Karahalios, Tony Bergstrom, and Felicia Hurewitz. These are people who inspired and advocated for us, consulted with us, and in a variety of forms participated in the development of technology, research, and education for persons with autism spectrum disorders.

We also acknowledge the contributions of our editors at Brookes, Rebecca Lazo and Steve Plocher, as well as all the contributions of the authors of the chapters in this volume.

To Bryan, Alexander, and Emma Booth,
who have understood and encouraged this important
effort, and Ruth and Otmar Boser for their support and love
K.I.B.

To Alan Thompson, Oliver Thompson, and
Justin Wayland and my mom and dad, Susan and Bob Wayland,
who always believe in me, the power of which cannot be overestimated
S.C.W.

To Sage, Sophia, and Emmeline for being
such a loving and supportive family, and to my two
dear Charlies, who delightfully broadened my concept of humanity
M.S.G.

Perspectives from an Adult with Autism Spectrum Disorder

THE EARLY DAYS...
AUTISM, COMPUTERS, AND DIAGNOSIS

The convergence of computers and individuals with autism is amazing on a number of levels. First is the timeliness of when computers and autism began to enter public consciousness. The Atanasoff–Berry Computer (ABC) was conceived in 1937 and successfully tested in 1942. Just a year later, in 1943, the U.S. Army engaged John Mauchly and J. Presper Eckert to develop the Electronic Numerical Integrator And Computer (ENIAC), later popularized as a "Giant Brain" in 1946.

It was that same year Dr. Leo Kanner wrote his seminal paper "Autistic Disturbance of Affective Contact," ushering in awareness of autism as another condition of humankind. A year later, in 1944, while the Mark-I (with its 50-foot crankshaft) was completed by Harvard professor Howard Aiken, Hans Asperger published a paper in Austria about a population of children having a widely varying skill set, who, with proper education, could make great contributions to society. After this paper's translation into English in 1981 by Lorna Wing, children with this condition were identified by the name of the author, Asperger syndrome.

Given the uneven skill set that hallmarks many persons with autism, the diversity of the autism spectrum may very well exceed that of the general population. Computers are wonderful devices for persons on the autism spectrum, accommodating to their needs so that they can do great things using their computer.

In addition to ushering in the invention of the resister-transistor logic (RTL) and the first integrated circuit on a single chip, 1961 was the year I was born, after a quick labor, and it was reported that I looked like an egg at 24 hours of age. In 1963, I was struck with what I call the *autism bomb*, or regressive autism, where I lost functional communication, had meltdowns, withdrew from the environment, and, in short, became significantly autistic.

That year also heralded the first interactive, real-time computer drawing system, developed by Ivan Sutherland, called the Sketchpad. Although my parents had a year to go before getting my diagnosis of autism, it might have been helpful to me at that time to have a graphically based device such as an iPad to help me communicate. The evolution of this and other graphical user interfaces that are included in the myriad augmentative and alternative communication (AAC) devices we have today—the iPad and other tablets with Proloquo2go and other communication-based applications (apps)—would have been great to have as well.

The year 1964 brought along two important events: the IBM System/360 for the computer world and a diagnosis of being on the autism spectrum for me. As bright as the world looked for IBM and the use of computers at that time, the future appeared dim for me. Fortunately, my parents refuted calls for institutionalization by professionals who had "never seen a child who was so sick" and implemented their own version of what we would today refer to as a home-based early intervention program.

SCHOOL, WATCHES, ACADEMICS, AND GETTING ALONG

By the time I was 4 years old, speech had begun to return and I was admitted to the center that initially recommended institutionalization. I was reevaluated, and instead of being considered psychotic, atypically developing, with strong autistic tendencies, I was upgraded to "neurotic." Things were looking up.

At that time I discovered the wonderful world of watch motors. Using a sharp kitchen knife, I would pop off the back and turn the little screw holding the motor to the stem used to wind up the spring. The casing would fall away, admitting me to a miniature wonderland that could be explored, disassembled, and then put back together, sometimes with innards from a different watch. Often the timekeeping gods were with me, and the watch continued to function or even returned to functionality after it was put back together.

My parents encouraged this interest by providing me with all sorts of other devices to explore. Clock radios, television sets, and other electronic equipment were most fascinating to me. Had I known about the work of Dr. Ted Hoff in the development of the first integrated circuit chip containing both the arithmetic logic unit and control unit in 1974, I would have done anything to get my hands on one of those to view with a microscope.

Entering regular school kindergarten at age 6, I was a complete social and academic catastrophe. Saying the letter B repeatedly did not endear me to my classmates, and I was almost a grade behind in most of my subjects. Had the learning technologies—never mind the concepts—for teaching hidden curriculum existed as they do today in low-tech paper-and-ink form or in such high-tech apps as those found on the iPad and other devices, I would have had a much greater chance at learning appropriate behavior with my classmates and gotten along with them much better. Today's software focusing on helping people with autism recognize emotions would have been very helpful as well.

Educationally, the techniques for developing academic accommodations would have helped greatly in my learning math, reading comprehension, writing, and other activities school-age children are expected to do. As is true for many persons on the autism spectrum, I found penmanship a great challenge. I lived in fear of walking into a classroom only to find a paragraph or two on the board, which meant we were expected to copy the text by hand. By the time I got through a sentence, everyone else was done and on to the next task. Similarly, copying definitions from the dictionary and engaging in creative writing during class were challenging as well.

Instead of being considered just a slow writer, with the benefits of today's technology I would have thrived. The accommodation of a keyboarding input device would have helped me greatly in getting my thoughts on paper instead of being "output bound" by the proprioceptive and motor control requirements of writing by hand.

Although I loved to read, comprehension remained a challenge. Today we know that using visual mind maps (whether on paper or on a computer) can be very helpful in structuring a procedure for students with disabilities to draw meaning out of text. On a related note, I remember refusing to answer questions to a reading exercise because I just knew that the world was not contained on the back of a large turtle. My studying all the books on astronomy from the school library told me otherwise.

Fortunately, things were better in middle school because I finally realized that using words instead of sound effects from the environment really helped with social interaction. I was also able to engage in my special interest of music by joining the band. On the other hand, engaging with computers would have to wait until high school, where there were two teletypes and a futuristic dot matrix DecWriter linked to a PDP 11 in the high school across town.

Upon entering high school, I found my attempts to take the computer course to learn programming in BASIC were thwarted by scheduling conflicts. Not letting that get in my way, I would spend much of my free time hanging around that lab absorbing what I could of the programming language. However, only students taking a class could get an account enabling them to use the computer. The challenge of gaining access to the computer was easily solved by helping students who were taking the course log into their own account; this I did in return for gaining their permission and password. Many hours were spent using and programming the computer to do such tasks as calculating gear ratios for my bicycle.

THE ADULT WORLD OF HIGHER
EDUCATION, WORK, COMMUNITY, AND RELATIONSHIPS

College was a utopia for me. Bullies had fallen by the wayside, and courses were more interesting. If I wanted to ride my bicycle at midnight, I could find someone just as strange as I was to come along. The computer courses, such as systems analysis and design, were fascinating; so much so that I taught this course several times at the college level before obtaining my current job as assistant professor of special education. However, it was the mid- to late 1980s, when personal computers (then called microcomputers) were merely in their infancy (read "expensive") and owning one remained a fantasy.

The year 1984 was not like *1984* in that the first Apple Macintosh was released, revolutionizing how the end-user interacted with their machines. However, it was not until 1989 that I finally got my first computer, a Macintosh SE, for the unbelievably low sum of $2,410. It took a few weeks to integrate the machine into my schema before I used it—to write a 10-page paper for a master's level course in music education. Previously, my protocol had been to write several drafts by hand before typing the final copy. Using the program WriteNow, I worked on my paper... and suddenly it was done! I finished in about a third of the time it would have taken in the past.

I felt as if I had cheated because the paper was done so quickly. These days we take for granted the facility computers provide in terms of developing writing projects from conception to completion.

Whether working as an accountant completing trial balances and reports, teaching college-level courses in computer literacy and systems analysis and design, or, as in the present, using and educating future teachers on using cyber tools for special education, computers have been pervasive in my life. The work in this book is seminal in that it addresses the many barriers to the use of computers in education, employment, and life in general. More iPads and other devices sit idle and gather dust because educators need to be taught how to use the hardware and software before they can apply this knowledge on their students' behalf.

Dating was always a mystery to me. Although there is no computer software that can provide direct support in this area, having a better understanding of the hidden curriculum and recognizing emotions would have helped me greatly. Perhaps I would have understood, in my undergraduate days, a woman saying, "I really like hugs and backrubs" meant more than a source of deep pressure that I craved. By the time I got to graduate school, I had pretty much done my own study on nonverbal communication and dating, yet I remained clueless. However, by graduate school, my research in this area helped me to understand that a woman hugging, kissing, and holding my hand all at about the same time should not be mistaken for her intention to become a Temple Grandin squeeze machine! That woman became my wife (for now over two decades).

THE FUTURE

Bode's law of computers doubling processing power every 18 months suggests that computers will become more pervasive throughout our lives in ways that have yet to be imagined. Through mindful research and education, as you are about to read in this book, we can pave the way for enabling these machines to empower all of us to lead fulfilling and productive lives to our greatest potential.

Stephen Shore, Ed.D.
Assistant Professor of Special Education,
Adelphi University

Stephen Shore is an assistant professor at the Ammon School of Education at Adelphi University, where he teaches courses in special education and autism. He focuses his research and teaching on matching preferred practices to the needs of persons with autism.

In addition to working with and talking about life on the autism spectrum, Dr. Shore presents and consults internationally on educational and social inclusion as well as on adult issues pertaining to relationships, employment, advocacy, and disclosure as discussed in his numerous books, articles, and DVDs.

Nonverbal and diagnosed at age 2 and 1/2 with "atypical development and strong autistic tendencies," he was recommended to be institutionalized, but his parents rejected his institutionalization in favor of parent-based intensive early intervention and support.

President Emeritus of the Asperger's Association of New England and former board member of the Autism Society, Dr. Shore serves on the boards of the Language and Cognitive Development Center, Asperger Syndrome and High Functioning Autism Association, the Autism Services Association, and other autism-related organizations.

Overview

Policy, Research, and Implementation Support

Katharina I. Boser

■ ■

Our book on 21st century tools for students with autism necessarily begins with an exploration of national (and international) policies on the use of innovative technology in the context of a variety of services and environments in which those services are delivered. These introductory chapters also direct us to the centrality of universal design for learning (UDL) as a framework for both low- and high-tech interventions for students with disabilities that can be adopted across a variety of settings. Chapters 1 and 2 provide us with not only a legal and policy but also an education and research framework within which to understand the necessity of these tools for students with autism spectrum disorder (ASD) as well as for other students with related disabilities.

Through the lens of policy trends and initiatives, Tracy Gray and Alise Brann's "What Is Driving Innovative and Assistive Technology Solutions in Autism Services?" provides an overview of the federal and philanthropic policies that support research, technology development, and innovation to improve services for children with autism. They examine the important impact of U.S. Department of Education guidelines and state-level initiatives that are driving educational change and reform through a variety of service delivery models, including public, charter, and online schools; tele- and virtual therapy; game-based learning; and immersive environments. State and district implementation trends that affect students with autism are also explored, from mainstreaming to district technology policies and staff development support. Finally, they discuss the role that technology can play to help communities to transition youth and support their integration into the workplace, civic life, and further education. Case stories of innovative service delivery models and "bright spots" of autism services are included as sidebars to illustrate possible practices and implementation successes.

In "Universal Design for Learning: Meeting the Needs of Learners with Autism Spectrum Disorders," Yvonne Domings, Yvel Cornel Crevecoeur, and Patricia Kelly Ralabate, experts from CAST, explain how universal design for learning—an innovative framework for curriculum and instructional design—addresses the learning needs of students with ASD. Domings, Crevecoeur, and Ralabate elucidate the UDL approach to developing learning experiences, an approach that changes the perspective from learner to environment, when pointing to the existence of a disability. The authors suggest tools intended to reduce barriers in the environment within the UDL framework. Domings, Crevecoeur, and Ralabate highlight and describe ways in which students with ASD can become expert learners in UDL environments. The authors discuss the importance of high expectations through tight goals with flexible means of achievement, scaffolding, and support. Detailed examples of UDL implementation for students with ASD in classroom settings are provided through two cases: voice volume and reading comprehension. Each case reviews teaching with technology strategies specific to the area of impairment; these strategies incorporate the three main domains of UDL: providing multiple forms of 1) representation, 2) expression for increased access to information and increased output (respectively), and 3) ways to motivate and engage.

Both chapters in this section provide an important backdrop against which to read the chapters in each of our following sections (i.e., classroom tools, language and literacy, data management, social regulation and emotion understanding, teacher training, and work transition). They highlight the importance of a variety of such new tools as gaming, virtual environments, sensors, and robotics in the ongoing and changing tools that clinician and educators are adopting for successful intervention. This overview stresses the ways in which typical interventions for the main areas of impairment in autism, including language, social regulation and emotion understanding, and executive function can be assisted by innovative tools and the educators who adopt them.

What Is Driving Innovative and Assistive Technology Solutions in Autism Services?

■ ■

Tracy Gray and Alise Brann

Autism spectrum disorders (ASDs) can manifest in many different ways, with symptoms ranging from mild to severe. Addressing the needs of children and adults with autism requires "sophisticated educational and therapeutic approaches" (Interagency Autism Coordinating Committee [IACC], 2010). These approaches include specialized instruction and support from professionals as well as access to technology devices and systems that offer additional means of building connections for the individual. In both cases, the field has been evolving as policy changes increasingly focus on autism. This heightened focus includes interventions and services combined with technological advances that redefine how supports and instruction can be provided.

In this chapter, we provide an overview of the policies that affect the work carried out by professionals from a variety of fields. These professionals address the behavioral, emotional, academic, health care, and employment needs of individuals with ASDs. In addition, we provide an overview of emerging technology trends as they relate to service delivery, school district implementation, and transition to the community.

OVERVIEW OF POLICY

Government agencies, research centers, and advocacy groups are recognizing the immediate need to attend to the many issues related to autism services. From basic research to implementation challenges, new initiatives are raising awareness,

---

We wish to acknowledge the contribution of Heidi Silver-Pacuilla, Ph.D., in the development of this chapter.

asking new questions, and creating new solutions. In this section, we will examine policy trends in the United States related to educational and assistive technology (AT) for individuals with autism.

Policy Trends in the United States

There has been a steady climb in the total public school enrollment of students with autism from 0.3% in 1998 to 0.7% in 2009 (U.S. Department of Education, National Center for Education Statistics [NCES], 2011), with the majority of these children served in mainstream classrooms for at least part of the school day (Fuchs, Fuchs, & Stecker, 2010). This mainstreaming is in response to the requirements of two major pieces of legislation: the Individuals with Disabilities Education Improvement Act of 2004 (IDEA 2004; PL 108-446) and Section 504 of the Rehabilitation Act of 1973 (PL 93-112). Under these laws, students with disabilities must be provided with a free and appropriate public education in the least restrictive environment possible. A general education classroom is considered the least restrictive environment by default, although the requirements of a free and appropriate public education may be met with a continuum of placement options, up to and including the provision of special education and related services in a substantially separate environment.

■ ■

EARLY IDENTIFICATION OF CHILDREN WITH AUTISM SPECTRUM DISORDERS

Research has shown that early identification and intervention are critical elements in improving outcomes for children with autism spectrum disorders. Learn the Signs. Act Early, a campaign launched by the Centers for Disease Control and Prevention, is an example of a large-scale public health effort geared toward improving early identification of children with ASD. The campaign web site (http://www.cdc.gov/ncbddd/actearly/index.html) includes resources, guides, and information for families, and names of health care providers and early childhood educators. It has the goal of ensuring that everyone involved in the care of young children is capable of recognizing appropriate developmental milestones and how delays in development may be early signs of autism.

■ ■

Expanding awareness of autism and ASDs, coupled with concerns about rising rates of diagnosis, have put increased pressure on policy makers and researchers to address the needs of children and adults with ASD. In 2006, the U.S. Congress passed the Combating Autism Act (CAA; PL 109-416), which authorized nearly $1 billion for autism research, public health programs, early intervention, and other treatment services (IACC, 2010); CAA reauthorization was submitted at the end of 2010 (Autism Votes, 2011a). The Combating Autism Reauthorization Act of 2011 (CARA; PL 112-32), provided significant funding for the Centers for Disease Control and also authorized the creation of the Interagency Autism Coordinating Committee (IACC), which coordinates the various federal agencies involved in autism education, treatment, and research. Additional legislation, the Autism Services and Workforce Acceleration Act (S. 850), introduced in April 2011 to coincide with Autism Awareness Month, aimed to build upon CARA and address the unique needs of adults with autism by authorizing funding for research, treatment, and services (Association of University Centers on Disabilities, 2011).

An additional piece of legislation, the Patient Protection and Affordable Care Act (PPACA; PL 111-148), has several provisions that can affect children, youth, and young adults with ASD and related disorders. Provisions addressing preexisting conditions, lifetime benefit caps, and conditions under which an insurance company can drop coverage could all benefit individuals with autism, who frequently have significant health care costs (Association of Maternal & Child Health Programs [AMCHP], 2012; Autism Speaks, 2013).

COORDINATION OF FEDERAL AGENCIES

Recognizing that services and support for people with autism are needed across the life span, and in areas related to health, learning, community, employment, and relationships, the Interagency Autism Coordinating Committee (IACC) coordinates the efforts of numerous federal agencies: the Department of Health and Human Services (HHS), the Administration for Children and Families (ACF), the Centers for Medicare and Medicaid Services (CMS), the Centers for Disease Control and Prevention (CDC), the Health Resources and Services Administration (HRSA), the National Institutes of Health (NIH), the Office on Disability (OD), the Substance Abuse and Mental Health Services Administration (SAMSHA), and the Department of Education (ED; IACC, 2010).

State Initiatives

Other major policies affecting autism services include major state-level initiatives to require private health insurance plans to provide coverage of evidence-based, medically necessary autism treatments to both children and adults. Prior to 2011, 25 states had enacted autism insurance reform laws; an additional 14 states had introduced insurance reform bills (Autism Votes, 2011b). Such autism advocacy organizations as Autism Speaks, Autism Votes (a project of Autism Speaks), and The Autism Society have been key players in moving these pieces of legislation forward, and they are continuing to push for expanded coverage at both the state level and the federal level.

As provisions of the PPACA roll out into 2014, states will be responsible for creating health insurance exchanges. Although 18 states have thus far indicated their intentions to include coverage for behavioral therapies for individuals with ASD, it remains to be seen how these insurance exchanges will affect health care coverage for these populations (AMCHP, 2012; Autism Speaks, 2013). In addition, there has been increased attention to the need for professional development and certification programs that prepare teachers to address the needs of students with autism. These programs focus on understanding the characteristics of students with ASD, learning effective behavior strategies for students with ASD, and completing additional fieldwork. An example of a state's efforts to address this need can be found in California, where the Teacher Corps has partnered with local school districts to provide training to approximately 25,000 veteran teachers who currently hold a special education credential. State regulations by the California Commission on Teacher Credentialing required teachers who work with students with ASD to hold an autism authorization certification. In an effort to ensure teachers were able to meet these requirements before the deadline, alternative certification programs worked closely with school districts to provide autism authorization certification programs for each school district, creating an expedient pathway for currently credentialed teachers to become certified.

EMERGING TECHNOLOGY TRENDS

The National Center for Technology Innovation (NCTI) housed at the American Institutes for Research has been tracking trends in educational technology and AT for the past decade. The trends indicate a decided shift toward portable, networked, customizable, and multitasking technology solutions with touch interfaces that are mirroring consumer technology development (Gray, Silver-Pacuilla, Brann, Overton, & Reynolds, 2011).

AUGMENTATIVE AND ALTERNATIVE COMMUNICATION APPS COMBINE PORTABILITY, CUSTOMIZABILITY, AND TOUCH TO PROVIDE STATE-OF-THE-ART COMMUNICATION SOLUTIONS

Proloquo2Go

Augmentative and alternative communication (AAC) apps represent a noteworthy example of how consumer technology developments are pushing the boundaries of assistive technology toward devices that are cheaper, more portable, more customizable, and capable of performing multiple tasks. One such app, Proloquo2Go (for the iPad, iPhone, and iPod Touch) has garnered significant attention since its release in 2009. Proloquo2Go uses the tagline "AAC in Your Pocket" and takes advantage of advances in consumer technology to offer an alternative to the traditional bulky and expensive dedicated AAC device. With over 8,000 symbols, support for text and symbol communication, and options for customization and expansion, Proloquo2Go has become a popular choice for parents, caregivers, and educators working with children with communication difficulties, including those with ASD. Although dedicated AAC devices may still be necessary for many students and in many situations, the rise of the AAC app demonstrates what may be possible as consumer and assistive technologies continue to advance.

In this section, we will explore how these emerging technology trends may affect students with ASD. We will discuss the recent research that supports the idea that technology can have educational and therapeutic benefits for people with ASD (Bellini & Akullian, 2007; Bölte, Golan, Goodwin, & Zwaigenbaum, 2010; Economic and Social Research Council, 2012; Golan, LaCava, & Baron-Cohen, 2007). Further, we will examine the emerging research to determine which features are most effective for specific populations and specific tasks (Gray, Silver-Pacuilla, Overton, & Brann, 2010). Throughout the chapter, we highlight key areas where the innovative use of technology can benefit children and adults with ASD.

Portability

Developments in processing speeds and increasingly portable technologies have changed the way people live, work, shop, and play. Commonly owned devices that can fit in a pocket are capable of taking pictures, giving directions, looking up information, taking video, sending e-mail, playing games, and surfing the internet, all in addition to making phone calls. The trend toward portability has a number of implications for people with ASD:

- Smaller, more portable devices mean smaller, less intrusive communication methods and less stigma; the majority of people these days are using some type of electronic device.

- Fully portable AT software goes wherever the user goes—school, home, library, work, or a friend's house (Gray et al., 2011).

- GPS-enabled devices allow people with ASD who may struggle with directions or feel disoriented by unfamiliar locations to carry maps in their pocket, increasing their independence. Such devices also enable monitoring of individuals where safety is an issue.

- Portable MP3 players or video players can be preloaded with social stories and audio prompts that can be played back in specific situations to provide on-the-go support.

- Alerts and reminders can be programmed into even a basic cell phone, covering everything from upcoming appointments to behavior prompts.

The emergence of AT in the "cloud" where computing resources (hardware and software) are available in a remote location and accessible over a network (typically the internet), represents a new option for AT users looking for highly portable solutions. Though still in the early stages, AT in the cloud allows users to access the features and options they need most on any computer or device, wherever they go. The Global Public Inclusive Infrastructure (GPII, 2011; http://www.gpii.net) project is an example of domestic and international organizations working together to think about how AT features and capabilities might be shifted into the cloud. Instead of requiring users with disabilities to set up preferences and features on computers at work, school, home, and the library, the goal of the GPII is to build "accessibility and extended usability directly into the internet's infrastructure" (GPII, 2011). A cloud-based structure that increases AT portability would potentially remove the barriers to access wherever technology is found; by simply logging in to their personal profile, individuals could "use the access features they need anywhere, anytime, on any device" (Kelley, 2011).

Though AT in the cloud is still in the early stages, many developers are working on more portable options for their AT software. A proposed priority on inclusive cloud and web computing, released for public comment in January 2013 by the National Institute on Disability and Rehabilitation Research (NIDRR), indicates the likelihood of increased federal funding in this area (NIDRR, 2013).

Convergence of Mainstream and Assistive Technology

Technological convergence is defined as the transformation of various technological systems to a single platform to perform multiple tasks. One challenge historically to state-of-the-art AT has been that assistive devices have not always kept up with consumer electronics in terms of options available (e.g., wireless access, Bluetooth). For example, in the early 2000s, although mainstream cell phones were improving in terms of processing power and capabilities, many AAC devices had not yet followed suit with similar features and functionality (DeRuyter, McNaughton, Caves, Bryen, & Williams, 2007). Today, handheld communication devices demonstrate how state-of-the-art AT is taking shape through converged platforms. Many mainstream devices, such as smart phones or touchscreen tablets, bring together ATs and options that were once available only on separate platforms. In addition to using these types of devices for communication, students with autism can access a number of different applications to support and accompany them through their day-to-day activities.

The shift toward convergence in mainstream technology and AT—with AT features being integrated in mainstream devices, and vice versa—is a critical milestone in promoting accessibility and independence for users with disabilities. This integration has resulted in increased affordability and access for people with disabilities. Further, this easy and reliable access to mainstream technology reduces "digital exclusion," which is often a reality for individuals with autism and other disabilities (DeRuyter et al., 2007).

Just a few years ago, each communication device, scheduler, prompt, and navigation system required its own device; now, converged platforms afford students with autism, their teachers, and their parents the convenience of powerful solutions. At the same time, applications designed for people with disabilities are crossing over into the mainstream, blurring the distinctions between AT and consumer technologies (Fuchs et al., 2010). Most of us now use ATs every day without thinking about it: text-to-speech on the GPS, voice-activated dialing on our cell phones, and touch screens to access information (Gray et al., 2010). Applications originally designed for people with disabilities are increasingly recognized as presenting solutions for the wider consumer market (Jana, 2009).

Customizability

Trends in consumer technology reflect an increasing market demand for customizability: Most users demand devices and tools that can be modified to fit their needs and goals. This trend, as well as the expectations of consumers, is leading to innovations in AT, leveraging options and platforms to build AT devices that can be configured to meet the unique needs of individuals. Educational technology and AT software and devices now commonly provide options for creating flexible goals, materials, assessments, and activities that accommodate learner differences. For example, interfaces can allow the user to adjust and arrange the visual and audio components of a software program according to his or her preferences; new technologies can now allow individuals to create customized, situation-specific communication systems quickly and easily.

Touch Interface

In the last several years, a flurry of news stories has emerged declaring the iPad or the iPod Touch as "miracles" for children with autism. Beyond the hype, however, these stories represent an important shift in how we create and use AT tools. Research on these new technologies is in the initial stages, although initial results and anecdotal reports seem positive. However, touch screen overlays have long been used to provide computer access to users with disabilities, so it is reasonable to assume that touch interfaces on mainstream devices (iPad, iPod Touch, tablet PCs, etc.) could be beneficial for a number of different populations. These developments are critical for several reasons. First, the use of an iPod Touch and an inexpensive AAC application can put a completely customizable communication device in the hands (and pocket) of a child with ASD for approximately $500. This cost is less than 10% of a full-featured AAC device, making an iPod Touch or iPad an attractive option for families or individuals looking for a flexible solution for communication.

In addition, for young people, an iPhone may be less stigmatizing than carrying a bulky AAC device. For individuals on the autism spectrum who struggle to hold a pen or pencil, touch interfaces may make drawing and writing more accessible. Finally, some early research with touch and multitouch interfaces has indicated that such interfaces may have social benefits, including enhancement of social, communicative, and language development in individuals with ASD, especially when working together on a task (Farr, Yuill, & Raffle, 2010; Gal et al., 2009; Ploog, Scharf, Nelson, & Brooks, 2013). These devices may not be appropriate for every user or every situation, but the trend toward more natural interfaces (touch, gesture recognition) signal positive developments in technologies for individuals with autism.

SERVICE DELIVERY MODELS

The varying avenues of service delivery for children and young adults with autism can play a critical role by helping to disseminate best practices, providing valuable resources to parents and caregivers, helping parents to recognize early signs of developmental delays, and ensuring that parents and professionals have access to needed tools and resources. In this next section, we highlight several service delivery models (public, charter, and online schools; virtual therapy; and game-based learning and immersive environments) and how the research and policy landscape is affecting the provision of services for people with autism.

Schools

Families raising a child with autism often face many challenges: educational, legal, financial, emotional, and medical. Families of children with ASD are more likely than families of children with other special health care needs to experience gaps in their insurance coverage. Nearly half of these families indicate that their existing health care coverage is not sufficient to meet their child's needs, compared to approximately one third of families with other special health care needs (AMCHP, 2012; Autism Speaks, 2013). Frequently, families must pay out-of-pocket for any services, such as speech and language therapies, or occupational therapy that is not covered by insurance or through publicly funded programs (AMCHP, 2012; IACC, 2010). In addition, even when these services are covered, families may encounter benefit caps and lifetime limits on coverage. As students move through the school system and transition into employment, vocational programs, or further education, parents and caregivers may feel overwhelmed and unsure about available options. Provisions under the PPACA related to benefit caps, preexisting conditions, and extended coverage for young people on their parents' plan may address some of these issues moving forward, but the implications are not yet clear.

The policy landscape related to special education in schools generates a push-pull between parents and educators over what constitutes "appropriate" services under IDEA and Section 504 of the Rehabilitation Act of 1973 and what the school is willing and able to provide (Smith, 2008). At a minimum, services for a child with autism may cost as much as $20,000 per year, with more intensive intervention programs pushing costs into the range of $100,000 per student (Ganz, 2007; Smith, 2008). The financial cost of educating a child with autism is a challenge for cash-strapped schools and can lead to disproportionate numbers of children with autism converging on those school districts that provide quality services. This situation often causes further burden on the local school districts. Students with autism are more likely than their peers to receive out-of-district placements, furthering costs to the district (Smith, 2008). In addition, many parents with the means to do so move to areas with well-respected autism programs, increasing the number of students with autism in a particular district (Winerip, 2010). We examine specific challenges and opportunities for service delivery in public, charter, and online schools.

Public Schools Though school districts tend to show considerable variation in their programs for students with autism, they are positioned to play a valuable role in providing needed services. Policies related to funding, care, resources, and dissemination of information vary widely by state (IACC, 2010), and a more cohesive approach to service delivery is needed. Still, public schools have the capacity to provide critical, time-sensitive, and research-based interventions early on in a child's academic career. Schools can best meet the needs of the thousands of children with ASD when they have access to the latest research, resources for funding, and links to outside organizations for partnership and information sharing. Changes to policy, infrastructure, and the research-to-practice landscape can help ensure that public schools are an active partner in helping families with diagnosis, assessment, care, and support; resolving medical issues; and linking interventions in school and home.

Charter Schools As part of the public education system, charter schools must abide by the same federal special education laws and regulation as public schools; in practice, the provision of special education services in charter schools can vary widely (Ahearn, 2001; Rhim & Kowal, 2008). This difference in service delivery can be due to a number of factors, complicating how charter schools are viewed for the purposes of federal regulations (IDEA). For example, depending upon state law, a charter school may be considered a separate local education authority (LEA) or may be considered linked to an existing LEA. The degree of linkage with an existing LEA varies; thus charters may share responsibility for special education services or may be solely responsible for service provision.

Partnerships and allocations of responsibility can vary widely between states and even within states. As a result, there may be confusion about who is legally responsible for providing special education services (Ahearn, 2001; Mead, 2008; Rhim & Kowal, 2008). If the charter school is considered its own LEA, then it is ultimately responsible for the costs associated with special education. However, for schools that are part of a larger LEA, lack of clarity can affect how funds and staff are allocated for special education; for example, if a charter school thought that the LEA was responsible for special education services, the school may not have budgeted for hiring necessary staff or providing necessary AT devices. Although charter schools may serve many students with special needs, questions have been raised about possible underenrollment of students with disabilities. As a result, some charter schools may have disproportionately fewer students with special needs than do the local public schools (Ahearn, 2001; Hehir, 2010). In addition, charters can face unique challenges because they may not have the centralized support and resources of a large district. Early on, many charters may explicitly or implicitly turn away students with special needs because they may lack the infrastructure to provide quality services. Further, some fledgling charter schools may not be in a position to absorb the high costs associated with educating children with more severe disabilities (Batdorff, Maloney, May, Doyle, & Hassel, 2010; Estes, 2004).

In some states, charter schools have not been required to demonstrate special education capacity prior to authorization, meaning that authorizing bodies may be unaware or lack understanding of key federal, state, and local regulations related to students with special needs (Lange, Rhim, & Ahearn, 2008; Mead, 2008). Because of these issues, there have been concerns about the quality of special education in some charter schools because a lack of expertise, staff, and available resources can adversely affect the schools' abilities to provide services to students with ASD and other disabilities (Estes, 2009; Hehir, 2010).

Online Schools   Online and virtual schools are emerging as a potential opportunity for delivering differentiated instruction that responds to the wide variety of needs of individuals with ASD. According to policy proceedings on virtual K–12 public education, "Virtual schools that cater to individual students' unique learning needs are aligned with the intent of IDEA and have the potential to open new educational opportunities to children with disabilities" (Müller, 2010).

Little is known about how virtual schools are serving students with disabilities (Müller, 2010). Virtual schools may face the same challenges as charter schools with regard to legal identity and determining roles and responsibilities in providing special education and related services, compounded by difficulties in providing special education services, conducting IEP meetings, and ensuring that federal disability requirements are met within a virtual environment (Müller, 2010). An additional complication is that special education law was written before online classrooms and virtual schools became commonplace, so policy has not yet caught up to the new educational landscape.

Although there are some concerns around virtual special education services, key elements of virtual schools may make them particularly well suited to providing learning opportunities for students with disabilities. Virtual schools and online learning environments tend to offer individualized programming, opportunities for parental involvement, frequent feedback, and multimodal presentation formats (Müller, 2010). These critical features of online learning echo the literature on best practices in special education and individualizing instruction to meet the needs of diverse learners. Research on virtual schools for students with disabilities is ongoing, so it remains to be seen whether this environment will prove to be successful in meeting the needs of these students.

Emerging Service Delivery Options

For most young people with ASDs, schools will remain the primary avenue of service delivery. Additional services may be provided through local hospitals or locally based speech or occupational therapists. However, service provision is generally limited by geographic proximity; diagnosis, intervention, and treatments can vary widely depending on location. In these situations, emerging service delivery options may hold the key to leveraging innovative technologies (e.g., mobile devices, touch interfaces, robotics, gesture recognition) to create games, tools, devices, and software for children and adults with ASD.

Virtual Therapy, Teletherapy, and Telemedicine   Tele- or virtual therapy can provide a possible solution to the difficulties faced by children from linguistically, geographically, and other diverse groups in gaining access to assessment, services, diagnosis, and early intervention. Often, evidence-based interventions are not available, or there is a lack of service providers with requisite training to implement these practices effectively (IACC, 2010), so provision of some therapies or interventions virtually may help ensure that all students with ASD have access to best practices. Differences in prevalence of ASD and related resources across geographic areas within the United States, as well as in other English-speaking countries, can result in significant variation in the types of services and support that are available, including medical treatments, parental supports, respite care, transition resources, and AT support (IACC, 2010). Online schools have demonstrated that it is possible to provide some related services virtually (e.g., occupational therapy, speech therapy) but that not all these services are suited to virtual therapy (Müller, 2010). However, teletherapies can be part of a larger service delivery plan and can help overcome barriers posed by distance or inaccessibility (Polovoy, 2008).

Game-Based Learning   Recent research in the field has shown that many types of interactive technology, games, robotic toys, and other technology tools may be used successfully as part of a treatment plan for children with autism (Carey & Markoff, 2010; Dautenhahn & Werry, 2004). Building upon what is known about how children with autism learn, many of these immersive environments or game-based learning tools allow for unstructured, child-based learning of social interactions, appropriate behavior, and other key skills (Dautenhahn & Werry, 2004). Video games and other multimedia can also be used successfully to model appropriate and desired behaviors, as well as to teach specific skills, in particular social skills (Center for Implementing Technology in Education [CITEd], 2008; Gal et al., 2009). (See the Using Multimedia Technology to Teach Social Skills sidebar for more information on games and multimedia for social skill instruction).

USING MULTIMEDIA TECHNOLOGY TO TEACH SOCIAL SKILLS

Most children learn the skills needed for social interaction in the course of normal development. However, for students with ASD, research has shown that social skills should be taught explicitly through the use of modeling and role playing (DeGeorge, 1998; Elksnin & Elksnin, 2000; Peterson, Young, Salzburg, West, & Hill, 2006), with a goal of helping students learn to generalize social skills across varied situations. Generalization can be supported through a focus on desired skills using a variety of teaching methods, authentic contexts, and role playing incorporated throughout the school day (DeGeorge, 1998; Elksnin & Elksnin, 2000; Waltz, 1999). Technology tools and multimedia can be excellent choices for supporting social skill instruction. Many people with ASDs are visual learners, and thus videos, simulations, virtual environments, pictures, and other multimedia can be extremely effective teaching tools (CITEd, 2008; Parsons, 2006). The use of multimedia, simulations, virtual environments, and other technology tools can complement such common social skill activities as role playing, social stories, observing peer behavior, social skill autopsies, and preteaching skills prior to a new social experience (Canney & Byrne, 2006).

Immersive or virtual environments are another area of gaming technology that shows promise for children and young adults with ASD. Because students with autism and ASD tend to learn and generalize best when taught in as authentic situations as possible, many researchers are using simulations and immersive environments to allow the user with ASD to practice skills in a "real-life" environment (CITEd, 2008; Elksnin & Elksnin, 2000). An additional benefit is that these immersive environments are safe in that students can practice the desired skill repeatedly, without fear of making errors (CITEd, 2008; Parsons, Leonard, & Mitchell, 2006). Although research on these tools is still limited, initial results do suggest that performing a task in an immersive or virtual environment may boost performance of that task in the real world (CITEd, 2008; Parsons, 2006; Parsons et al., 2006).

PROMISING PRACTICE: IMMERSIVE ENVIRONMENTS

TeachTown

TeachTown is a system incorporating therapeutic curricula aimed at children with autism and other special populations developmentally aged 2–7. It is designed to build receptive language, cognitive, and academic abilities and social interaction skills. The basics of TeachTown include on-computer lessons, off-computer activities, data tracking of student progress, note taking during sessions to update team members, and synchronization of therapies and updates in curricula.

Through the NCTI Technology in the Works award program, TeachTown, the Los Angeles Unified School District and California State University, Los Angeles, collaborated to further test the system's ability to make a difference in the lives of children through disciplined data collection.

Data derived from the standardized assessments deployed in the Whalen et al. (2010) study showed that the students using the program made very significant gains in language and cognitive areas, as well as in specific skills like the identification of body parts. According to the findings, it is clear that the program has been motivating and engaging, contributing to a positive and productive learning environment in the classroom. The results were profound enough that the Los Angeles Unified School District continued the study beyond its initial phase, and incorporated the former control groups into treatment with TeachTown.

SCHOOL DISTRICT IMPLEMENTATION TRENDS

The lines between special and general education are "blurring" (Fuchs et al., 2010). As more students are served in general education classrooms, special educators shift to a role of collaborator, and services are being delivered in new ways. In this section on school implementation trends, we discuss inclusion and pull-out models, as well as staff development needs and the implications of universal design for learning (UDL) and AT tools in mainstream classrooms.

Interventions and Placement

Targeted interventions are critical for school-age children with autism, particularly because many children may spend all or part of their day in the general education classroom (CITEd 2008; IACC, 2010). Communication and social interaction may be of particular importance, especially because students who "are not socially compe-tent are unable to take full advantage of the peer learning situations presented" in the classroom (CITEd, 2008). With a shift toward more inclusive placements, many general education teachers will need to become more familiar with social and life skills instruction, as well as such common interventions as speech therapy (Elksnin & Elksnin, 2000). When students are unable to interact appropriately with their peers or engage in learning opportunities, they cannot be said to be fully included. However, many schools may be unsure how to provide these needed services within the context of the inclusive classroom.

Staff Development Support

Differences in policy, available resources, and training have led to disparities in the numbers of students diagnosed with ASD, as well as in the types of therapies and interventions they receive (IACC, 2010). Schools can play a key role in ameliorat-ing these differences by helping their teachers to bridge the research-to-practice gap. There is a significant need for quality professional development for classroom teachers to help them understand ASD, as well as improved coordination among parents, pediatricians, and autism service providers (Howroyd, 2009). Health care and other early care and education providers may not have received training in rec-ognizing the early warning signs of an ASD and thus need training and support to help them become a key component of the diagnosis process. As such, all staff who interact with young children (teachers, nurses, early care providers, and others) should receive professional development on autism, including information about the complex and variable nature of ASDs and how methods used with these chil-dren may differ from those employed with other children with disabilities (How-royd, 2009).

Implications of Universal Design for Learning

The UDL approach provides a blueprint for creating instructional goals, meth-ods, materials, and assessments that work for all students; it is not a single, one-size-fits-all solution but, rather, flexible approaches that can be customized and adjusted for individual needs. This framework has gained recognition over the past decade as a viable approach to meeting the needs of students with disabili-ties. It received a significant boost in national support when it was written into the reauthorization of the Higher Education Opportunity Act of 2008 (PL 110-315) as a teaching practice all preservice teachers should learn. This national support brought UDL out of the special education realm, where it has long been recog-nized as a framework for meeting multiple needs and providing access to the general curriculum, and into the mainstream. It remains imperative, however, to continue to advocate for AT when required to best support individuals' unique needs and to emphasize the continuum of technology solutions that exists, rang-ing from the universal to the highly specialized (Rose, Hasselbring, Stahl, & Zabala, 2005).

The UDL approach offers guidance for teachers to address the challenges posed by the diverse needs of their students in terms of providing flexible instructional materials, techniques, and strategies. This support is particularly relevant for teachers who seek to differentiate instruction to meet the range of needs presented by students with ASD.

TRANSITION TO THE COMMUNITY

The inclusion of more students with autism in every school, community, and region has challenged organizations to put programs and supports in place to assist youth and their families to bridge the world of school to the world of work, independent living, and community engagement. As learning opportunities for young people with autism improve, the question becomes, How can members of this population best be served as they progress to adulthood? In this section, we examine the trends in planning for inclusion of youth and adults with ASD in the community and accommodating their needs.

Self-Determination

The goal of self-determination for students in special education has grown to take on new meanings as students are mainstreamed and included in new settings. Expanding the concept and curriculum of self-determination is critical to post-school success and a demonstrated component of successful transitions (Wehmeyer, Palmer, Soukup, Garner, & Lawrence, 2007). A critical element of the transition planning process is the involvement of the young person with ASD and his or her family, to the degree possible. Involving the student can help ensure that transition plans incorporate his or her needs, interests, and desires for the future, and various technologies can be helpful in facilitating this involvement (IDEA Partnership, n.d.; Morningstar, Lattin, & Sarkesian, 2009). Transition planning enables youth on the autism spectrum to gain experience with setting goals, finding resources in their communities, and becoming advocates for themselves (Morningstar et al., 2009; Wehmeyer et al., 2007).

Workplace

The evolving model of supported employment shows positive results for individuals with disabilities to secure and keep work in the general public workspace with a job coach or other specific support (West et al., 2002). Technology supports can also facilitate access to meaningful employment. These supports may include technologies in the workplace that enable productivity, such technologies as text-to-speech, speech-to-text, word prediction, and calendar programs. Other technologies may include the use of reminders and alerts (using mobile phones), prompts and guidelines for specific situations loaded onto an MP3 player, or the use of social stories and videos that a young adult can call up to remind himself or herself how to approach different employment tasks and activities. As young people with autism transition out of school and into the workforce, there is a critical need for training in employment-based social skills. These skills are essential for effective interviewing, sociability, and daily interactions with co-workers; however, the repetition and consistency needed for generalization mean that teaching these skills can be time consuming and expensive. Simulation technologies can help by allowing students with autism to work through social skills modules at their own pace, repeating them as often as necessary.

■ ■

PROMISING PRACTICE: SIMULATIONS FOR SOCIAL SKILLS

Social Simentor

Simulations allow youth and young adults with autism spectrum disorder (ASD) to practice social interactions in a safe, nonthreatening space with no consequences for mistakes or missteps. Unlimited opportunities for repetition, consistency, and adjustable pace are other key benefits of simulation technologies. One such program is Social Simentor, which employs a virtual "mentor" and role playing to teach soft skills that are necessary in the workplace.

This tool builds upon many of the inherent benefits of technology tools—self-paced work, repetition, progress monitoring—to create a series of intensive training simulations around a variety of common workplace themes (e.g., interviewing, talking on the phone, interacting with co-workers). Virtual simulations like Social Simentor can provide critical support for one-to-one social skill instruction and help ease the training burdens for service providers. These tools offer step-by-step instructions that enable students of many levels to be able to utilize the software on their own and receive targeted, constructive feedback based on their responses and actions.

Research on Social Simentor is in the early stages, although initial results have been positive. With a National Center for Technology Innovation Tech in the Works grant, the Social Simentor team conducted a case study to examine the effects of the software on a small group of treatment students with cognitive disabilities (including students with ASD) compared to a control group without cognitive disabilities (Baney, Hirsch, & Casey, 2010). Both groups conducted mock interviews with volunteers from local human resource organizations. After two and one-half weeks of using Social Simentor, the treatment population received higher ratings on "hireabilty" from interviewers than did the higher-functioning control population.

■ ■

Civic and Community Life

A key part of transition is preparing and instructing students for community involvement (Wehman, 2013), including direct instruction in actual performance. Finding friends, leisure activities, and community events should all be key elements of transition planning. One of the promising practices in this area is the use of virtual and tele-field trips and simulations, which provide early and safe steps for this community-based instruction. In addition, how technology can support an individual's healthy lifestyle and leisure activities is an area of active development and study (Rose, 2010; Yang & Foley, 2011). The technology may include adaptive devices or equipment that can help a young person with ASD participate in recreational activities. It may also include video games, played alone or with peers.

CONCLUSION

Concurrent with the apparent increase in the prevalence of children with ASD, there is a growing trend for more government and legislative action to address the needs of these children, their families, and communities. Increased funding has resulted in a growing body of research that provides valuable insight into best practices to address the emotional, behavioral, educational, and employment needs of these individuals. Further, the ongoing development of technology tools and resources has enabled a growing number of children and adults with ASD to become more engaged in classrooms to benefit from learning experiences.

REFERENCES

Ahearn, E. (2001). Public charter schools and children with disabilities. *ERIC Digest E609*. Arlington, VA: ERIC Clearinghouse on Disabilities and Gifted Education. Retrieved from http://www.ericdigests.org/2002-2/public.htm

Association of Maternal & Child Health Programs (AMCHP). (2012, February). *The Affordable Care Act and children and youth with autism spectrum disorder and other developmental disabilities* (AMCHP Issue Brief). Retrieved from http://www.hdwg.org/sites/default/files/AMCHP-Issue-Brief-ACAandCYwithASD-DD.pdf

Association of University Centers on Disabilities. (2011). *Autism Workforce Act* [Press release]. Retrieved from http://www.aucd.org/template/news.cfm?news_id=6500&parent=311&parent_title=Autism&url=/template/page.cfm?id%3D311

Autism Services and Workforce Acceleration Act of 2011, S 850, 112th Cong. (2011).

Autism Speaks. (2013). *Autism benefits lagging under federal health care reform.* Retrieved from http://www.autismspeaks.org/advocacy/advocacy-news/autism-benefits-lagging-under-federal-health-care-reform

Autism Votes. (2011a). *Combating Autism Reauthorization Act (CARA-S.4044) of 2010.* Retrieved from http://www.autismvotes.org/site/c.frKNI3PCImE/b.6376831/k.ACFC/CARA.htm

Autism Votes. (2011b). *State initiatives* [Map]. Retrieved from http://www.autismvotes.org/site/c.frKNI3PCImE/b.3909861/k.B9DF/State_Initiatives.htm

Baney, L., Hirsch, L.W., & Casey, C. (2010). *Social Simentor: Assessment of an e-learning assistive technology tool.* Retrieved from National Center for Technology Innovation, http://www.nationaltechcenter.org

Batdorff, M., Maloney, L., May, J., Doyle, D., & Hassel, B. (2010). *Charter school funding: Inequity persists.* Muncie, IN: Ball State University. Retrieved from http://www.bsu.edu/teachers/media/pdf/charterschfunding051710.pdf

Bellini, S., & Akullian, J. (2007). A meta-analysis of video modeling and video self-modeling interventions for children and adolescents with autism spectrum disorders. *Exception Children, 73*(3), 264–287.

Bölte, S., Golan, O., Goodwin, M.S., & Zwaigenbaum, L. (2010). What can innovative technologies do for autism spectrum disorders? *Autism, 14*(3), 155–159.

Canney, C., & Byrne, A. (2006). Evaluating Circle Time as a support to social skills development: Reflections on a journey in school-based research. *British Journal of Special Education, 33*(1), 19–24.

Carey, B., & Markoff, J. (2010, July 10). Students, meet your new teacher, Mr. Robot. *New York Times.* Retrieved from http://www.nytimes.com/2010/07/11/science/11robots.html

Center for Implementing Technology in Education (CITEd). (2008). *Multimedia instruction of social skills.* Retrieved from http://www.cited.org/index.aspx?page_id=154

Combating Autism Act of 2006, PL 109-416, 42 U.S.C. §§ 201 et seq. (2006).

Combating Autism Reauthorization Act of 2011, PL 112-32, 42 U.S.C § 201 et seq. (2011).

Dautenhahn, K., & Werry, I. (2004). Towards interactive robots in autism therapy. *Pragmatics & Cognition, 12*(1), 1–35.

DeGeorge, K.L. (1998). *Using children's literature to teach social skills.* Retrieved from http://www.ldonline.org/article/6194

DeRuyter, F., McNaughton, D., Caves, K., Bryen, D.N., & Williams, M.B. (2007). Enhancing AAC connections with the world. *Augmentative and Alternative Communication, 23*(3), 258–270.

Economic and Social Research Council (ESRC). (2012, November 29). Technology use in the classroom helps autistic children communicate. *ScienceDaily.* Retrieved from http://www.sciencedaily.com/releases/2012/11/121129093329.htm

Elksnin, L.K., & Elksnin, N. (2000). *Teaching parents to teach their children to be prosocial.* Retrieved from http://www.ldonline.org/article/6036

Estes, M.B. (2004). Choice for all? Charter schools and students with special needs. *Journal of Special Education, 37*(4), 257–267.

Estes, M.B. (2009). Charter schools and students with disabilities: How far have we come? *Remedial and Special Education, 30*(4), 216–224.

Farr, W., Yuill, N., & Raffle, H. (2010). Social benefits of a tangible user interface for children with autistic spectrum conditions. *Autism, 14*(3), 237–252.

Fuchs, D., Fuchs, L.S., & Stecker, P.M. (2010). The "blurring" of special education in a new continuum of general education placements and services. *Exceptional Children, 76*(3), 301–323.

Gal, E., Bauminger, N., Goren-Bar, D., Pianesi, F., Stock, O., Zancanaro, M., & Tamar Weiss, P.L. (2009). Enhancing social communication of children with high-functioning autism through a co-located interface. *Artificial Intelligence and Society, 24*(1), 75–84.

Ganz, M.L. (2007). The lifetime distribution of the incremental societal costs of autism. *Archives of Pediatric Adolescent Medicine, 161*(4), 343–349.

The Global Public Inclusive Infrastructure. (2011). *Home.* Retrieved from http://www.gpii.net

Golan, O., LaCava, P.G., & Baron-Cohen, S. (2007). Assistive technology as an aid in reducing social impairments in autism. In R.L. Gabriels & D.E. Hill (Eds.), *Growing up with autism: Working with school-age children and adolescents* (pp. 124–142). New York, NY: Guilford Press.

Gray, T., Silver-Pacuilla, H., Brann, A., Overton, C., & Reynolds, R. (2011). Converging trends in educational and assistive technology. In T. Gray & H. Silver-Pacuilla (Eds.), *Breakthrough teaching and learning: How educational and assistive technologies are driving innovation* (pp. 5–24). New York, NY: Springer.

Gray, T., Silver-Pacuilla, H., Overton, C., & Brann, A. (2010). *Unleashing the power of innovation for assistive technology.* Washington, DC: American Institutes for Research.

Hehir, T. (2010, January 27). Charters: Students with disabilities need not apply? *Education Week, 29*(19), 18–19, 21.

Higher Education Opportunity Act of 2008 PL 110-315, 20 U.S.C. § 1400 *et seq.* (2008).

Howroyd, C. (2009). *Autism professional development: 5 steps to success.* AutismPro

Whitepaper. Retrieved from http://www.autismpro.com

IDEA Partnership. (n.d.). *Secondary transition collection.* Retrieved from http://www.ideapartnership.org/index.php?option=com_content&view=article&id=1485

Individuals with Disabilities Education Improvement Act (IDEA) of 2004, PL 108-446, 20 U.S.C. § 1400 *et seq.* (2004).

Interagency Autism Coordinating Committee, Department of Health and Human Services (IACC). (2010). *2010 strategic plan for autism spectrum disorder research* (NIH Publication No. 10-7573). Retrieved from http://www.iacc.hss.gov

Jana, R. (2009, September 24). How tech for the disabled is going mainstream. *Business Week.* Retrieved from http://www.businessweek.com/magazine/content/09_40/b4149058306662.htm

Kelley, M. (2011, June 25). *ALA annual 2011: Helping disabled patrons gain access through the cloud.* Retrieved from http://www.libraryjournal.com/lj/communityala/891140-448/ala_annual_2011_helping_disabled.html.csp

Lange, C.M., Rhim, L.M., & Ahearn, E.M. (2008). Special education in charter schools: The view from state education agencies. *Journal of Special Education Leadership, 21*(1), 12–21.

Mead, J.F. (2008). *Charter schools designed for children with disabilities: An initial examination of issues and questions raised* [Special report]. Alexandria, VA: National Association of State Directors of Special Education. Retrieved from http://www.uscharterschools.org/specialedprimers

Morningstar, M.E., Lattin, D.L., & Sarkesian, S. (2009). It's more than just the law: People make it happen. *Transition Coalition.* Retrieved from http://www.transitioncoalition.org/transition/tcfiles/files/docs/peopleMakeItHappen_8-20091250526573.pdf/peopleMakeItHappen_8-2009.pdf

Müller, E. (2010). *Virtual K–12 public school programs and students with disabilities: Issues and recommendations* [Policy Forum Proceedings document]. Alexandria, VA: National Association of State Directors of Education. Retrieved from http://www.projectforum.org

National Institute on Disability and Rehabilitation Research. (2013). Inclusive cloud and web computing. *Federal Register, 78*(10), 2919–2923. Retrieved from http://www.

gpo.gov/fdsys/pkg/FR-2013-01-15/html/2013-00577.htm

Parsons, L.D. (2006). Using video to teach social skills to secondary students with autism. *Teaching Exceptional Children, 39*(2), 32–38.

Parsons, S., Leonard, A., & Mitchell, P. (2006). Virtual environments for social skills training: Comments from two adolescents with autistic spectrum disorder. *Computers in Education, 47*(2), 188–206.

Patient Protection and Affordable Care Act of 2009, PL 111-148, 42 U.S.C. § 18001 *et seq.* (2010).

Peterson, L.D., Young, K.R., Salzberg, C.L., West, R.P., & Hill, M. (2006). Using self-management procedures to improve classroom social skills in multiple general education settings. *Education and Treatment of Children, 29*(1), 1–21.

Ploog, B., Scharf, A., Nelson, D., & Brooks, P.J. (2013). Use of computer-assisted technologies (CAT) to enhance social, communicative, and language development in children with autism spectrum disorders. *Journal of Autism and Developmental Disorders, 43*(2), 301–322.

Polovoy, C. (2008, June 17). Audiology telepractice overcomes inaccessibility. *The ASHA Leader.* Retrieved from http://www.asha.org/Publications/leader/2008/080617/080617c.htm

Rehabilitation Act of 1973, PL 93-112, 29 U.S.C. §§ 701 *et seq.* (1973).

Rhim, L., & Kowal, J. (2008). *Demystifying special education in charter schools.* Alexandria, VA: National Association of State Directors of Education. Retrieved from http://www.uscharterschools.org/specialedprimers

Rose, D.H., Hasselbring, T.S., Stahl, S., & Zabala, J. (2005). Assistive technology and universal design for learning: Two sides of the same coin. In D. Edyburn, K. Higgins, & R. Boone (Eds.), *Handbook of special education technology research and practice* (pp. 507–518). Whitefish Bay, WI: Knowledge by Design.

Rose, T. (2010). Leisure and recreation. In J. McDonnell & M.L. Hardman (Eds.), *Successful transition programs: Pathways for students with intellectual and developmental disabilities* (2nd ed., pp. 217–240). Thousand Oaks, CA: Sage Publications.

Smith, F. (2008, March 19). Educators deal with the growing problem of autism. *Edutopia.* Retrieved from http://www.edutopia.org/autism-school-special-needs

U.S. Department of Education, National Center for Education Statistics. (2011). *Digest of education statistics, 2010* (NCES 2011-015), Chap. 2.

Waltz, M. (1999). *Pervasive developmental disorders: Finding a diagnosis and getting help.* Arlington, TX: Future Horizons, Inc.

Wehman, P. (2013). *Life beyond the classroom: Transition strategies for young people with disabilities* (5th ed.). Baltimore, MD: Paul H. Brookes Publishing Co.

Wehmeyer, M., Palmer, S., Soukup, J., Garner, N., & Lawrence, M. (2007). Self-determination and student transition planning knowledge and skills: Predicting involvement. *Exceptionality, 15*, 31–44.

West, M., Hill, J.W., Revell, G., Smith, G., Kregel, J., & Campbell, L. (2002). Medicaid HCBS waivers and supported employment pre– and post–Balanced Budget Act of 1997. *Mental Retardation, 40*(2), 142–147.

Whalen, C., Moss, D., Ilan, A.B., Vaupel, M., Fielding, P., Macdonald, K., … Symon, J. (2010). Efficacy of TeachTown: Basics computer-assisted intervention for the Intensive Comprehensive Autism Program in Los Angeles Unified School District. *Autism, 14*, 179–197.

Winerip, M. (2010, August 1). A school district that takes the isolation out of autism. *New York Times.* Retrieved from http://www.nytimes.com/2010/08/09/education/09winerip.html?ref=education

Yang, S., & Foley, J. (2011). Exergames get kids moving. In T. Gray & H. Silver-Pacuilla (Eds.), *Breakthrough teaching and learning: How educational and assistive technologies are driving innovation* (pp. 87–110). New York, NY: Springer.

Universal Design for Learning

Meeting the Needs of Learners with Autism Spectrum Disorders

▪ ▪

Yvonne Domings, Yvel Cornel Crevecoeur, and Patricia Kelly Ralabate

These are exciting times. New digital technologies are developing in ways that were impossible to envision in the 1990s. These developments have had a huge impact on peoples' lives—on the availability of information and our ability to connect with each other. Digital technologies have also had a huge impact on the learning sciences and the way teaching and learning are viewed. Simultaneously, digital technologies have made developing flexible, high-quality learning experiences much quicker and easier. At CAST, we believe these new developments have the potential to change the way educators are able to help a larger number of learners, including those with autism spectrum disorders (ASDs),[1] reach their full potential. This chapter explains how universal design for learning (UDL)—an innovative framework for curriculum and instructional design—addresses the needs of learners with ASDs in classrooms. We share two instructional examples that apply UDL to the development of literacy skills and social and emotion understanding, areas that can be particularly challenging for learners with ASD. In addition, we present a different approach to developing learning experiences, one that views the learning environment as "disabling" rather than viewing the learner as disabled. Finally,

---

[1] We acknowledge the current debate in the autism community regarding the accepted practice of using person-first language. Although we agree with the point made by autism self-advocates that autism is part of their individuality and therefore should not be separated in language like a disorder or disability, we also feel that universal design for learning (UDL) focuses on barriers in the curriculum and how these barriers "disable" learners. In this regard, we prefer to focus first on individual learners and avoid labels. When it is necessary to refer to a group, we use person-first language to maintain the focus on individual learners and their interactions within learning environments.

tools are recommended that benefit learners with ASD by reducing barriers in the environment.

CURRENT VIEWS OF LEARNING

The modern learning sciences leverage such digital technologies as fMRIs and PET scans, which enable researchers to view the brain while an individual is learning and performing tasks. Digital imaging has revealed two very consistent findings: 1) that learners are highly variable and 2) that learning is highly dependent on the context (Fischer & Bidell, 2006; Rose & Fischer, 2009; Siegler, 1994; van Geert & Fischer, 2009). As a result of these new understandings, the learning sciences have undergone a dramatic shift from traditional linear perspectives of the way learning occurs (i.e., that all individuals progress through the same series of stages during learning) toward a much more dynamic view of learners and the learning process (i.e., that learning happens in the interaction of the individual and the learning context).

Learners Are Highly Variable

Modern learning sciences have consistently found that learners are highly variable. Some of this variability is individual. Every person is unique based on his or her individual genes (nature) and on his or her experiences over time (nurture). In other words, the combination of the two (nature and nurture) means that there are inherent differences among learners in how they think and act as well as fluctuations in performance within individuals as they interact in different environments. Variability in how people learn is a result of the interaction of genetic makeup and experiences (Fischer & Bidell, 2006; Grigorenko & Sternberg, 1997). The bottom line is that the way an individual interacts with and processes experiences will vary and will have a tremendous influence on the way he or she learns.

Learning Is Highly Dependent on the Context

Another consistent finding from the learning sciences is that learning is highly dependent on the learning context (e.g., Fischer & Bidell, 2006; Grigorenko & Sternberg, 1997; van Geert & Fischer, 2009). A person may be very talented when learning in one context, yet be challenged to learn in another. A person's ability is a function of the interaction between the person's skills or knowledge (his or her internal resources) and the requirements in the environment (demands).

Enabling learning means offering appropriate challenges by ensuring demands are high enough to require the learner to push himself or herself beyond his or her current repertoire of skills and understanding. However, demands cannot be so high that they overwhelm the learner's ability to achieve the instructional goal. It is also important to reduce or eliminate those demands in the environment that are unnecessary. If a learner does not immediately possess the internal resources required to perform well in the learning environment, an educator should provide supports and scaffolds to reduce excessive demands without reducing expectations. Supports include but are not limited to glasses, braille, or communication boards that the learner may always need; whereas such scaffolds as concrete prompts, cuing, hand-over-hand assistance, coaching, or modeling can be progressively reduced or removed as the learner begins to demonstrate proficiency.

Consider a basic example to contextualize possible scaffolds before we delve deeper into the needs of learners with ASD: A learner who does not understand Spanish will not learn well in a classroom where the teacher is speaking only Spanish. That learner does not have the internal resources (understanding of Spanish) or the external resources (translation) to meet the demands of the learning environment. If the goal is to master Spanish, the learner may come to understand Spanish over time from being exposed to the language in the classroom. However, it is also almost certain that he or she will fall behind the rest of the learners in other content areas if language translation is not available while the student develops an understanding of Spanish. In other words, if the external resources or scaffolds (e.g., translation of content, vocabulary support) are not provided while the student is developing an ability to understand Spanish (i.e., the student's internal resources), he or she will fail to learn other content areas and may even appear disabled.

Understanding learner variability, minimizing unnecessary demands within the context, and providing options are ways to positively affect not only a learner's perceived ability but also, over the long run, a learner's potential to learn and succeed in life (Luria, 1976). If educators do not do these things, some learners will certainly fall behind.

Variability in Learning Is Systematic

Although learner variability in an environment of high expectations can seem to be a formidable planning challenge, a good deal of variability is actually predictable or systematic and, therefore, can be planned for in advance. For example, it is reasonable to expect that young children know and are able to do less than adults. This type of variability, developmental variability, is systematic; thus it can be expected and planned for in advance. In fact, such advance planning is regularly done by creating curricula that vary to meet the needs of different developmental or age levels.

Individuals also vary as they learn and develop skills, knowledge, and expertise. A novice (e.g., an individual learning something new) in any subject or skill area will learn differently than a person who has developed some understanding, skill, or expertise in that area. For instance, a novice musician will differ in what and how he or she learns a new musical piece from how an expert musician will learn the exact same piece (Bloom, 1985; Dreyfus & Dreyfus, 1980; Karmiloff-Smith, 1992). This is another type of systematic variability that can be expected and planned for in advance.

The main point is if educators know where to expect variability in learners, it is possible to create learning experiences that address the wide range of learner variability without having to retrofit curricula and reduce expectations.

AUTISM AND LEARNING

Where does autism fit into this? The label ASD is used to identify individuals whose interests and communication, social, and executive functioning skills differ broadly from those of learners who are typically developing (National Autism Center [NAC], 2009; National Research Council [NRC], 2001; Quill, 1995). Although differences in these areas are characteristic for anyone with an ASD label, it is important to recall that learners with ASDs also vary considerably from each other, just as all learners do (Grigorenko & Sternberg, 1997).

Not so long ago, learners with ASD were educated primarily in self-contained classes or schools, with modified—and often-reduced—expectations (Rose, Meyer, & Hitchcock, 2005). Today, most learners with ASD are educated in general education classrooms and expected to progress in the general education curriculum (U.S. Department of Education, 2011).

Indeed, learners with ASD can and do learn quite well. There are numerous examples of individuals with ASD who became famous for skills, knowledge, and expertise in very specific areas (Heaton, Williams, Cummins, & Happé, 2008). There are many others, not famous at all, who have amazing skill repertoires in particular areas called *splinter skills*, which often developed outside traditional learning environments (Mottron, 2011).

Traditional Learning Environments

Why is there such a discrepancy between what some individuals with ASD learn on their own and what they learn in a traditional learning environment? Take a step back to think about traditional learning environments. Relying heavily on verbal language, printed materials, and paper-and-pencil assessments, traditional learning environments are designed with

- One means of representing information (text, lecture, etc.)

- One means of acting and expressing what learners know (by listening, reading, and writing)

- One means of engaging with learning (one topic that may or may not be interesting to all)

Traditional classrooms are designed to be responsive to the "illusory average student" and assume a baseline degree of competence in communication, social understanding, and self-regulation. Learners with ASD may not have accrued the knowledge and skills in these areas that other learners have developed. Given that the abilities of learners are a function of the intersections of the skills or knowledge they have (internal resources) and the demands in the environment, learners with ASD may be unprepared for a traditional classroom.

Options to Traditional Learning Environments

There are now many options for teaching materials and methods other than those that a traditional classroom offers. Unlike older fixed technologies, such as print, digital technology makes manipulating the learning context for a wide range of learners faster and easier (Rose, Gravel, & Domings, 2010). This is good news for learners who are perceived as having a disability when using traditional curricula or in traditional contexts. Educators can reduce contextual barriers in the learning environment and offer learners with ASD the flexibility and support they need to be successful by applying the principles of UDL.

UNIVERSAL DESIGN FOR LEARNING

The UDL approach is "a set of principles for curriculum development that give all individuals equal opportunities to learn—not a single, one-size-fits-all solution but rather flexible approaches that can be customized and adjusted based on individual learner needs" (CAST, 2012). UDL views learner variability as a strength to be leveraged, not a challenge to be overcome. Instead of focusing on intrinsic deficits or challenges that are perceived to be present in learners, UDL requires instructional designers and educators to be mindful of areas where they can expect learners to vary naturally, allowing them to plan for this variability in advance. The UDL principles help educators design learning experiences that provide opportunities for all learners, including those with ASD, to have access to, participate in, and progress in the general education curriculum by reducing barriers to learning.

The ultimate purpose of UDL is to help all learners develop into *expert learners*, that is, learners who set their own learning goals and monitor their progress toward those goals. Expert learners also understand the resources they need to engage with and persist with learning tasks in the service of the learning goals they set (CAST, 2011). It is important to note that UDL can help many learners with ASD not only learn, but learn at a rate that would enable them to progress through the general education curriculum alongside or even beyond that of their peers. In the past, academic expectations were low for these learners; but when educators use UDL in their classrooms, all learners have increased opportunities to go beyond rote learning. Learners with ASD and their peers can fully engage with content while simultaneously moving toward the same learning goals.

Universal Design for Learning Principles

The UDL framework addresses three neural networks (recognition, strategic, and affective) that are involved in learning and provides educators with guidance about how to plan for expected or systematic variability. The UDL principles focus on learner needs, highlighting how each area of the curriculum should provide flexible options. Hence, the UDL principles require educators to provide

- Multiple means of representation
- Multiple means of action and expression
- Multiple means of engagement

Associated with each principle are a series of guidelines and checkpoints to help educators design instruction to meet the needs of a broad range of learner variability[2] (CAST, 2011; Table 2.1).

Universal Design for Learning and Learners with Autism Spectrum Disorder

As mentioned, the UDL framework provides educators with guidance about where to expect the most variability in learning. It also offers educators suggestions on how to provide options that will accommodate a wide range of learning needs.

---

[2]See the National Center on UDL (2011a, 2011b) for more detailed information on planning lessons and curricula using the UDL guidelines (http://www.udlcenter.org/aboutudl/udlguidelines).

Table 2.1.   The universal design for learning principles

Multiple means of representation
- Perception
- Language, expressions, and symbols
- Comprehension

Multiple means of action and expression
- Physical action
- Expression and communication
- Executive function

Multiple means of engagement
- Recruiting interest
- Sustaining effort and persistence
- Self-regulation

Applying UDL starts with three initial steps:

1. Understanding or defining the instructional goal

2. Evaluating the demands in the current curriculum or approach

3. Addressing learner variability using the UDL guidelines

In classroom situations, educators formally and informally assess the success of instruction and redesign instructional approaches based on outcome evidence to continuously improve instruction through an iterative process.

   In the following two sections, we offer instructional examples contrasting traditional approaches with strategies that address variability in learners with ASD by applying the UDL framework. In particular, we highlight specific, applicable UDL guidelines (represented by numbers in parentheses). These examples offer curriculum designers and educators suggestions for how to use the UDL framework to design instruction that is less disabling and has fewer barriers for learners with ASD and can actually benefit all learners.

EXAMPLE 1: USING APPROPRIATE VOICE VOLUME

No child comes into the world with an understanding of how to regulate his or her voice or to use discretion to match voice volume with a context or situation. These are rules that are learned over time, though often implicitly. In addition, there is a wide range of expectations, even among adults, about what is an appropriate voice volume in any given situation. For example, one teacher or parent may require soft voices or silence whereas another hears collaborative discussion and raucous play as "music to the ears." Appropriate voice volume is a fluid, implicit, contextually dependent concept, and as such it is a concept that needs to be explicitly taught to learners with ASDs.

   Let's compare a traditional approach to the UDL approach to teach learners how to use appropriate voice volume.

Traditional Approach

Traditionally, the concept of what is appropriate voice volume is implicitly taught across communities, in classrooms, but also in libraries, churches, homes, and elsewhere. Learners who do not experience difficulties regulating voice volume internalize rules over time through social interactions with such elders as parents, teachers, and community members. Typically, the following strategies are used to teach the voice volume concept:

- Adults use verbal prompts, for example, "lower your voice" or "use your library voice" or "use a quiet talking voice."

- Verbal language is often paired with nonverbal cues: holding finger to lips or "zipping" the lips.

- Adults assess when learners are out of appropriate range and then verbally and nonverbally remind them to adjust their voices.

- Learners are exposed to varied contexts (e.g., church, hospital, or silent reading versus center time, recess, or outdoor play) in which various voice volumes may be appropriate.

- Learners are expected to compare their behavior with that of others (models) in order to develop discretion for adjusting their voice volume.

Some learners will pick up these strategies without much effort, but many learners with and without disabilities will, in fact, continue to rely on adult cuing rather than developing the ability to independently regulate their voice volume. For example, learners with ASD are often challenged by the demands of the social domain and tend to require a great deal of scaffolding and supports to help them develop needed skills. With a UDL approach, all learners are encouraged and given opportunities to develop independence and expertise in appropriate voice volume as well as other areas.

Universal Design for Learning Approach

Given that all learners are variable, the UDL approach starts by identifying the goal and then looking at the contextual barriers that are inherent in the traditional approach by asking the following questions: What demands does learning this concept make of learners, and are these demands necessary for learning this concept or are they irrelevant? How high are the irrelevant demands in relation to the learners' resources? How does the UDL framework help reveal where learners are likely to vary? What options can be made available in order to address variability, minimize irrelevant demands, and ensure an appropriate level of challenge? After asking these types of questions, the educator is better able to understand how to utilize the UDL approach to teach learners how to use appropriate voice volume. This is accomplished through a three-step process: 1) articulate the instructional goal, 2) evaluate the demands in the curriculum, and 3) address learner variability.

Step 1: Understand or Identify the Instructional Goal   In utilizing a UDL approach, the first step in instructional planning is to clearly identify and understand the goal. In this example, the goal is that learners will be able to use discretion in regulating their voices depending on the context, but the real task is to make an implicit concept (i.e., appropriate voice volume) explicit for the learner.

Step 2: Evaluate the Demands in the Current Curriculum or Approach   Next, analyze the task by evaluating the demands in the traditional approach:

1.   Verbal language must be understood.

2.   Nonverbal language must be understood.

3.   Role models must be noticed and followed.

4.   Appropriate volume that matches the context needs to be produced, remembered, and internalized as a skill that can be applied in various settings.

Figure 2.1 shows a visual support that might be used to help learners practice this skill.

Step 3: Address Learner Variability

Multiple Means of Representation   The UDL framework encourages educators to provide multiple means of representation (Figure 2.2). To do this, educators must consider the way information is presented and whether learners will ultimately understand and be able to use what is presented. Finally, educators need to determine how much access to a lesson's content is necessary versus that which is irrelevant to achieve the goal.

Educators commonly pair verbal language or printed words with visual supports to offer accessible information while helping a wide range of learners develop language. In accordance with this strategy, the UDL guidelines suggest the use of options for language, expressions, and symbols, thereby clarifying vocabulary and promoting understanding across languages (2.4 in Figure 2.2). In this example, this

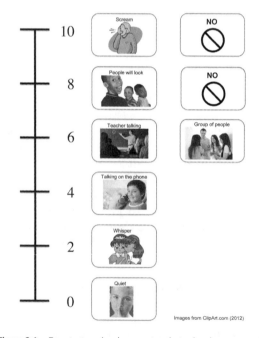

Figure 2.1.   Zero to ten visual support scale to develop appropriate voice volume. (From D. Milewski; adapted by permission.)

I. Provide Multiple Means of Representation

1: Provide options for perception

1.1 Offer ways of customizing the display of information

1.2 Offer alternatives for auditory information

1.3 Offer alternatives for visual information

2: Provide options for language, mathematical expressions, and symbols

2.1 Clarify vocabulary and symbols

2.2 Clarify syntax and structure

2.3 Support decoding of text, mathematical notation, and symbols

2.4 Promote understanding across languages

2.5 Illustrate through multiple media

3: Provide options for comprehension

3.1 Activate or supply background knowledge

3.2 Highlight patterns, critical features, big ideas, and relationships

3.3 Guide information processing, visualization, and manipulation

3.4 Maximize transfer and generalization

Resourceful, knowledgeable learners

Figure 2.2.   Principle 1: Multiple means of representation. ©2011 by CAST. All rights reserved.

abstract concept is made more concrete by creating a visual representation using a chart or graphic organizer, like the one shown in Figure 2.1.

However, simply providing multiple means of representation is not sufficient because doing so provides access only to information, not to deeper understanding. Good learning experiences push beyond access to help learners develop the ability not only to gain information but also to decipher it, apply it to what they already know, and transform it into usable knowledge that can be used in the service of their own learning. The UDL guidelines also advise educators to aid comprehension by providing options for activating or supplying background knowledge (3.1). To this end, educators can help learners develop a deeper, shared understanding of voice volume by modeling examples and nonexamples of various volume levels and helping the learners agree on what each level means. This strategy explicitly provides a model rather than expecting the learner to implicitly understand the need to pay attention to a peer model in an otherwise distracting social environment.

Multiple Means of Action and Expression   The UDL framework encourages educators to provide multiple means of action and expression (Figure 2.3). To do this, educators must provide options in the way learners express their understanding of the concepts being presented. This prevents the means of expression from being a barrier to achieve the goal.

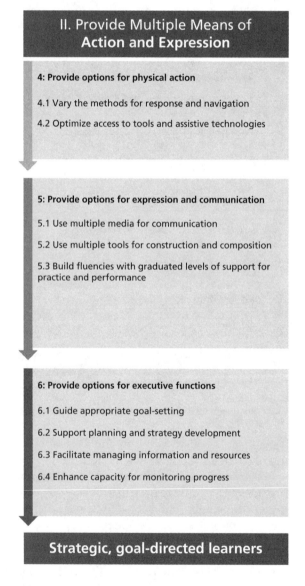

II. Provide Multiple Means of Action and Expression

4: Provide options for physical action

4.1 Vary the methods for response and navigation

4.2 Optimize access to tools and assistive technologies

5: Provide options for expression and communication

5.1 Use multiple media for communication

5.2 Use multiple tools for construction and composition

5.3 Build fluencies with graduated levels of support for practice and performance

6: Provide options for executive functions

6.1 Guide appropriate goal-setting

6.2 Support planning and strategy development

6.3 Facilitate managing information and resources

6.4 Enhance capacity for monitoring progress

Strategic, goal-directed learners

Figure 2.3.   Principle 2: Multiple means of action and expression.
©2011 by CAST. All rights reserved.

Learners express their understanding by pairing the model (above) with options of concrete symbols (e.g., icons, pictures, numbers). Doing this provides them with multiple means of expression and gives them access to learning through something that they personally understand. By connecting a symbol with the concept of each volume, educators highlight critical features, big ideas, and relationships (3.2 in Figure 2.2) between the concrete (i.e., icon, picture, number) and the abstract idea of the appropriate volume. This is done both verbally and nonverbally.

In addition, a chart (as in Figure 2.1) incorporating all the representations above is cocreated by the educator and the learners and posted in the classroom environment. Learners participate in creating the representations in order to promote their understanding of the different levels and to enhance relevance for each of them. To guide appropriate goal setting (6.1), a volume goal is set ahead of time for each activity and a magnet, clothespin, or other pointer shows the appropriate volume to the learners. Over time, such a chart can be faded or left in the environment as a support.

Multiple Means of Engagement   The UDL framework encourages educators to provide multiple means of engagement (Figure 2.4). A vital role for educators is to ensure that all learners are engaged in their work by ensuring learners are "hooked," engagement is persistent, and they can effectively self-regulate their own learning. In this particular example, the educator provides other means of engagement for learners who are not motivated to comply with social norms. Having learners participate in choosing and assigning meaning helps optimize relevance, value, and authenticity (7.2 in Figure 2.4) for each individual. In the volume chart, numbers in the range correspond to various volume levels and are paired with images. For some learners, numbers enhance authenticity; for others, the visual representations do the same. In both cases, they add relevance to the expectations.

Educators refer to the volume chart periodically to point out appropriate and inappropriate examples, thereby helping to sustain effort and persistence (8). The permanence of the chart in the environment serves to heighten the salience of the goal (8.1) and helps to enhance learners' capacities for monitoring their own progress (6.4 in Figure 2.3). Learners are guided to develop the ability to self-assess and reflect (9.3)—both key to developing independent self-regulation skills and expertise.

By adding options for representation, expression, and engagement, the educator is able not only to make the lesson much more accessible to a wider range of learners but also to build expertise and independence in all learners.

Additional Examples   To provide multiple means of representation, educators can employ several strategies:

- Use digital examples offered in blogs or such teacher support web sites as Hands in Autism (http://www.handsinautism.org/pdf/Voice%20Chart.pdf), Geneva Centre for Autism (http://www.elearning.autism.net), and KinderKraziness (http://www.kinderkraziness.blogspot.com)

- Create a customized version of the chart in the example using pictorial representations such as those available from Picture It (http://www.slatersoftware.com/pit.html) or ToonDoo (http://www.toondoo.com)

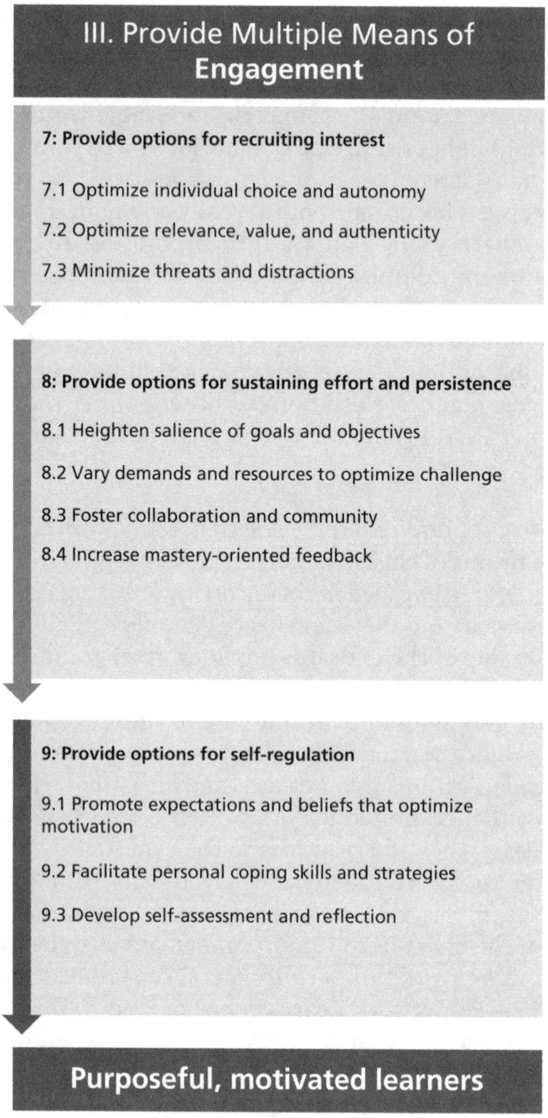

Figure 2.4. Principle 3: Multiple means of engagement. ©2011 by CAST. All rights reserved.

- Provide alternatives for auditory information (1.2) using digital tools and assistive technologies, for example, using a portable voice volume monitor (available from http://www.ibridgenetwork.org) to model and compare various volume levels

- Illustrate through multiple media (2.5) using digital technologies, for example, Softpedia BOT 1.0 (http://www.mac.softpedia.com/get/Utilities/BOT.shtml)

To provide multiple means of action and expression, educators can use these strategies:

- Support planning and strategy development (6.2) and enhance learners' capacity for monitoring their own progress (6.4) using stories to build deeper understanding

- Use story models, for example, prepared social story and success story examples related to modulating voice volume, available online from such publishers as Carol Gray's Center (http://www.thegraycenter.org/social-stories) and Sandbox Learning (http://www.sandbox-learning.com) or from autism resource centers

To provide multiple means of engagement, educators can apply these approaches:

- Facilitate personal coping skills and strategies (9.2) and develop self-assessment and reflection (9.3) using video applications, for example, Camtasia (http://www.techsmith.com/camtasia.html), or using animation applications, for example, Animoto (http://www.animoto.com/education)

- Increase relevance and authenticity (7.2) with Blabberize (http://www.blabberize.com), which allows educators to upload a picture of the student, add an audio recording of the student's voice, and produce an animated photo with a mouth that moves in sync with the student's voice

EXAMPLE 2: DEVELOPING READING COMPREHENSION AND INFERENCE-MAKING STRATEGIES

Reading is "the most critical academic skill a child can learn," according to the President's Commission on Excellence in Special Education (U.S. Department of Education, 2002, p. 60), because weak literacy skills compromise success across the curriculum. According to the report of the National Reading Panel (National Institute of Child Health and Human Development, 2000), reading comprehension, or making meaning from text, is an essential component of reading. It affects a person's ability not only to read for enjoyment but also to learn and obtain information. Reading comprehension is tied to success in school after third grade, when reading to learn becomes the primary mode of delivering information in traditional classrooms (Annie E. Casey Foundation, 2010). Reading comprehension relies upon vocabulary and background knowledge to make connections with the text and to make inferences or predictions. Good comprehension strategies are also strategies used by good listeners, so there is a great deal to be gained by teaching the strategies explicitly. See also Chapter 8 for more on reading comprehension and strategies for students with ASDs.

Some learners, particularly those with ASD, are precocious decoders of text and fluent oral readers, seeming to learn to read without being taught (Grigorenko, Klin, & Volkmar, 2003). This skill set is often coupled with poor reading comprehension, particularly of narrative text (Grigorenko et al., 2002). This combination of strengths and challenges is often referred to as hyperlexia. The ease with which hyperlexic learners acquire reading skills and improve fluency often masks their poor comprehension until they are much older (Gately, 2008).

Reading comprehension in typical children has been correlated with fluency (Pinnell et al., 1995); hyperlexic learners, however, do not make the predictions or inferences required nor do they comprehend text well despite reading fluently. As a result, their difficulties with comprehension may be affected by their inability to make inferences or predictions as a result of a lack of background knowledge in social and emotion understanding (for more information on the connection with social and emotion understanding, also see Steps 1 and 3 below under the heading "UDL Approach").

To explore this connection, CAST conducted a demonstration project in 2011 called Building Comprehension Through Social Understanding (BCSU), which focused on the goal of developing social understanding or theory of mind[3] skills through the reading comprehension strategies mentioned (i.e., making predictions, making connections, inferencing).

In this intervention, CAST's work in UDL-based solutions was extended to improve the reading comprehension and social understanding of learners with ASD. Preliminary results on this implementation of UDL-related strategies for learners with ASD showed that addressing learners' development of theory of mind and imaginative skills as part of literacy instruction can result in improvements in theory of mind and reading skills (Domings, 2012).

To examine how the UDL framework was applied to this study, let us unpack how reading comprehension skills are traditionally taught and compare that approach with the UDL approach designed by researchers at CAST.

Traditional Approach

According to the NRP, reading comprehension is "an active process that requires an intentional and thoughtful interaction between the reader and the text" (2000, p. 13). The traditional approach to teaching reading comprehension (Harvey & Goudvis, 2000) involves instructing readers in specific strategies, including

• Making predictions about what is (or may be) coming next

• Making connections between self and the text

• Making connections between the text and other texts

Some of the traditional methods for helping readers develop these strategies include questioning the reader, having the reader develop and ask questions, and asking the reader to summarize what he or she has read.

Universal Design for Learning Approach

As noted before, after a teaching goal is determined, it is important to begin by looking at the elements that may pose barriers to learning by asking the following questions: What demands does learning this concept make of learners, and are these demands relevant to learning this concept or are they irrelevant? How high are the irrelevant demands in relation to the learners' resources? How does the UDL framework help to reveal where learners are likely to vary? What options can be made available in order to address variability, minimize irrelevant demands, and ensure an appropriate level of challenge? After asking these types of questions, the educator is better able to understand how to utilize the UDL approach to teach his or her learners the skills required to improve their reading comprehension. The BCSU study used the following three-step process: 1) articulate the

---

[3]Theory of mind is part of a larger group of skills referred to as emotion understanding. To have a theory of mind, one must be aware that others have differing beliefs, desires, and knowledge from our own and that these beliefs will affect their thoughts, behavior, and emotions. A person uses this knowledge to understand, explain, and predict the other person's knowledge, behavior, or emotion (Premack & Woodruff, 1978).

instructional goal, 2) evaluate the demands in the curriculum, and 3) address learner variability.

Step 1: Understand or Identify the Goal   The first step in any good instructional planning and teaching is to clearly identify and understand the goal. In the BCSU study mentioned above, CAST researchers determined that the goal was to help learners develop inferencing and prediction skills in order to comprehend text. In order to do so, learners need to have adequate skills for strategic comprehension of text and background knowledge in social understanding (i.e., theory of mind; more detail is provided in Step 3).

Step 2: Evaluate the Demands in the Curriculum or Current Approach
Once the goal was determined, the demands in the traditional approach for teaching reading comprehension were evaluated and found to include six key demands:

1. Text must be decoded.

2. The topic of the text must be comprehensible to the reader. In other words, both the language and concepts need to be understood. This level of comprehension involves several requirements:

    a. The reader must understand the language of instruction.

    b. Vocabulary must be sufficient.

    c. Background knowledge of the topic must be sufficient. Note: Narrative text requires background knowledge in social and emotion understanding to allow the reader to understand the beliefs, desires, and motives of the characters and in order to make inferences or predictions about their thoughts, behaviors, or emotions (this is often referred to as theory of mind understanding).

3. The reader needs to be actively engaged with the text by making and testing predictions, making connections between the reader and the text and between the text and other texts.

4. Information from the text needs to be encoded into memory that can later be recalled.

5. Reading comprehension requires the reader to be able to make predictions (or inferences), which rely on the ability to imagine an outcome based on this background knowledge.

6. Making connections requires the ability to remember and hold one idea in mind while seeing connections or commonalities with the reader's life and with other texts that have been read.

In the case of social and emotion understanding, background knowledge typically develops through social interaction and imaginative play. In most learners, this ability develops through social interaction between 3 and 5 years of age, developing first as a child comes to understand his or her own emotions and then later when he or she comes to understand the emotions of others. A large body of research has focused on the way these skills develop in children who are typically developing and those elements that are correlated with higher scores on theory of mind assessments (e.g., Cutting & Dunn, 2003; Dunn, Brown, & Beardsall, 1991; Harris, 1989; Pons, Harris, & de Rosnay, 2004; Pons, Lawson, Harris, & de De Rosnay, 2003; Wimmer & Perner, 1983).

Variability in theory of mind development has been documented in learners with ASD (Baron-Cohen, Leslie, & Frith, 1985). Factors related to the way autism develops tend to limit the experiences in socioemotional and imaginative play that build these foundational skills and background knowledge. Given that traditional reading curricula assume a baseline of socioemotional and imaginative understanding and skills, reading curricula contain barriers to comprehension for learners who do not have these skills and understanding.

Step 3: Address Learner Variability   The following section describes how the BCSU study addressed the UDL guidelines.

Multiple Means of Representation   Using multiple means of representing information (see Figure 2.2) is one way that educators can address variability in classrooms. The stories used in the BCSU study were created in a digital authoring environment, CAST Book Builder.[4] These stories included alternatives to auditory and visual information (1.2 and 1.3) through the inclusion of multiple media (e.g., audio clips, images). By offering multiple means of representation, BCSU increased external resources, scaffolded the language, and allowed learners to focus on meaning.

The guidelines suggest aiding comprehension by providing options for activating or supplying background knowledge (3.1). This was the major focus of the BCSU study: to explore the teaching of reading comprehension to learners who do not have a high degree of socioemotional understanding. One way to supply the background knowledge the researchers suspected was missing in this population was to create stories that make explicit the way that nonverbal cues are connected to characters' emotions. Stories were authored to specifically target concepts that represent the stages of emotion understanding as they typically develop (from recognition of emotion to theory of mind). Digital coaches on each page highlighted the critical features and relationships (3.2) between the nonverbal cues or events and pointed out which character emotions learners needed to notice when trying to make a prediction or connection. Digital coaches are animated avatars or buttons that allow the learner to access prompts, hints, or models just in time, allowing her to be provided with the right kind of support as needed.

The guidelines suggest options for language, expressions, and symbols, clarifying the vocabulary (2.1) of emotion (e.g., happy, sad). To do this, the BCSU study included "thought bubbles." To make the abstract more concrete, sticky notes were used to make the implicit thoughts of the characters explicit through a visual representation in the form of "thought bubbles." This also helped to guide information processing and manipulation (3.3) to help learners follow and remember the events on the page. The thought bubbles are permanent reminders that help to minimize the unnecessary demand of having to remember what the character is thinking as the learners develop expertise in theory of mind.

---

[4]Freely available on the CAST web site (http://www.bookbuilder.cast.org).

Multiple Means of Action and Expression   Traditional methods for teaching reading comprehension frequently use verbal language both as a means for instruction and as a means for assessment. The guidelines suggest that options for action and expression be provided to meet the range of variability (see Figure 2.3). As learners progress in their understanding, they can be asked to make a prediction or connection and fill in the thought bubbles. Learners can either write words or draw in the thought bubbles as a way to reduce expressive language demands. They can also work with a scribe to reduce unnecessary fine motor demands, all the while being supported as they build fluency (5.3) in the different methods of expression. Making the implicit thoughts of the character explicit helps support planning and strategy development (6.2), a skill that can transfer to other texts and situations.

CAST Book Builder allowed the inclusion of three digital coaches on each page, allowing leveling from an open-ended prompt to a model response. This hierarchical prompt model—going from an open-ended question to a model response—matches learners' development, providing graduated levels of support (5.3) as they progress in their understanding, all the while promoting independence and their ability to monitor their own progress (6.4). It is important to note that digital technology makes it simple to embed these coaches into each page, allowing the learner to practice independently, but an educator or parent can also provide similar support in person.

Multiple Means of Engagement   Providing topic choices and both digital and paper stories, the BCSU project offered multiple means of engagement (see Figure 2.4). Research shows that even providing small choices enhances motivation (Patall, Cooper, & Robinson, 2008). Allowing learners to personalize the reading experience helps them optimize relevance, value, and authenticity (7.2) and helps sustain effort and persistence (8). The addition of role-playing activities and video self-analysis of the role playing not only aids in developing skills in prediction but also enhances the capacity for monitoring one's own progress (6.4 in Figure 2.3) and aid in transfer and generalization (3.4 in Figure 2.2) providing practice in taking on the role of others through pretend play. In addition, the video self-analysis helps learners to develop the ability to self-assess and reflect (9.3)—both skills key to developing independent self-regulation and expertise.

By adding options for representation, expression, and engagement, the BCSU project reduced irrelevant demands and also provided access by enriching learning experiences that helped learners build expertise in this foundational domain.

Additional Examples   To provide multiple means of representation, educators can use several strategies:

- Clarify vocabulary (2.1) in subject matter content, such as science and social studies materials and preteach new vocabulary and concepts

- Illustrate through multiple media (2.5) by

  - Presenting graphic organizers, for example, Education Oasis (http://www.educationoasis.com/curriculum/graphic_organizers.htm)

  - Creating voice avatars (i.e., a vocal character representing a real person) for digital text presentation, for example, Voki (http://www.voki.com)

- Using computer software to teach early reading skills, for example, Starfall (http://www.starfall.com)

- Provide options for perception (1) by offering vocal directions matched with printed and visual or image representations, for example, pictured directions in learning centers

- Reference online applications to clarify syntax and sentence structure (2.2), for example, Grammar Girl (http://www.grammar.quickanddirtytips.com)

- Provide links to support background knowledge (3.1) through digital media available on such content web sites as Teacher Tube (http://www.teachertube.com) and Kids National Geographic (http://www.kids.nationalgeographic.com/kids)

- Highlight critical features (3.2) by including color shading used for emphasis, for example, Visuwords (http://www.visuwords.com) and Interactives: Elements of a Story (http://www.learner.org/interactives/story) to teach narrative structures

To provide multiple means of action and expression, educators can use these strategies:

- Offer multiple tools for construction and composition (5.2), including, for example,

  - Slide show demonstrations using:

    - PowerPoint (Microsoft Office) or Prezi (http://www.prezi.com)

    - Word bubbles, using Wordle (http://www.wordle.net)

- Add use of Writing Fun by Jenny Eather to develop expressive writing skills (http://www.writingfun.com)

- Build fluencies with graduated levels of support (5.3) by providing outlines of subject matter content created from PowerPoint presentations using the outline feature

To provide multiple means of engagement, educators can apply these approaches:

- Provide choices (7.1) of topics for projects

- Provide simple self-monitoring (6.4) checklists in learning centers for learners to self-assess completion and accuracy

- Use consistent attention-getting techniques (7) that use visual as well as auditory cues

- Foster collaboration (8.3) by pairing with peers to share small-group activities

Additional examples can be found on the National Center on UDL (2011b) web site (http://www.udlcenter.org/implementation/examples). Under each principle are checkpoints that provide a series of concrete examples under the "Tell Me More" link and the "Examples and Resources" link.

DEVELOPING EXPERT LEARNERS

The fundamental goal of the UDL framework is to develop *expert learners,* that is, learners who understand the way they learn and can independently use internal and external resources and manage irrelevant demands on their own learning (CAST,

2011). Research in the learning sciences has shown that learners change as they develop expertise (Bloom, 1985; Dreyfus & Dreyfus, 1980). Novices tend to treat and attend to all elements of a situation equally. Their attention may appear to be scattered. They are concrete in their understanding of a topic or domain, and they strictly adhere to rules in making decisions regardless of the context. As learners develop expertise in a subject area, they become better able to regulate their attention to focus only on the critical features. Their understanding becomes holistic and fluid; they employ rules in a flexible, discretionary way that accounts for the context. They are also able to manipulate elements in the abstract in order to achieve their goals.

The UDL guidelines (Version 2.0) help educators design learning experiences that enable all learners to become experts in their own learning (CAST, 2011). The guidelines provide explanations for curriculum options and offer scaffolds for learning by 1) allowing access to content, 2) providing guided practice with the content, and 3) helping learners understand information. By supporting learner variability in comprehending, planning, and self-regulation, educators help all learners become expert learners, that is, learners who know how they learn best, who leverage those strategies, and who do so as independently as possible.

Meeting All Learners' Needs

It is important to remember that as educators, we should always have the highest expectations possible for *all* learners. The UDL guidelines help educators to move beyond just providing access to content, enabling us to instead move toward providing access to quality learning experiences—those that help all learners achieve their full potential. When the curriculum is designed in a way that removes barriers and minimizes irrelevant demands, learners with ASD can and do learn and progress in the general education curriculum. Furthermore, as shown in the foregoing examples, from the simplest behavior modification to an academic goal, learners with ASD can and do develop into expert learners.

The UDL framework offers a way to create a flexible, responsive curriculum that reduces or eliminates barriers to learning. Using a UDL approach, educators proactively offer curriculum options that present information and content in varied ways (multiple means of representation), options in the manner in which learners can express what they know (multiple means of action and expression), and options to engage learners in meaningful, authentic learning (multiple means of engagement).

Finally, UDL allows educators to teach effectively in diverse classrooms and spend more time on instruction, facilitating learning rather than accommodating a one-size-fits-all curriculum. The bottom line is that UDL helps educators meet the needs of learners with ASD. In fact, UDL helps educators address the needs of all learners.

REFERENCES

Annie E. Casey Foundation. (2010). *Early warning! Why reading by the end of third grade matters* [Kids Count special report]. Retrieved January 5, 2012, from http://www.aecf.org

Baron-Cohen, S., Leslie, A.M., & Frith, U. (1985). Does the autistic child have a "theory of mind"? *Cognition, 21*(1), 37–46.

Bloom, B. (1985). *Developing talent in young people.* New York, NY: Ballantine Books.

CAST. (2011). *Universal design for learning guidelines version 2.0.* Wakefield, MA: Author.

CAST. (2012). What is universal design for learning? In author, *CAST: About UDL.* Retrieved November 8, 2012, from http://www.cast.org/udl/index.html

Cutting, A.L., & Dunn, J. (2003). Theory of mind, emotion understanding, language, and family background: Individual differences and interrelations. *Child Development, 70,* 853–865.

Domings, Y. (2012). *Building comprehension through social understanding: A demonstration project* (Manuscript in preparation).

Dreyfus, S.E., & Dreyfus, H.L. (1980). *A five-stage model of the mental activities involved in directed skill acquisition.* Washington, D.C.: Storming Media.

Dunn, J., Brown, J., & Beardsall, L. (1991). Family talk about feeling states and children's later understanding of others' emotions. *Developmental Psychology, 27,* 448–455.

Fischer, K.W., & Bidell, T.R. (2006). Dynamic development of action, thought and emotion. In W. Damon & R.M. Lerner (Eds.), *Theoretical models of human development. Handbook of child psychology.* (6th ed., Vol. 1, pp. 313–399). New York, NY: Wiley.

Gately, S. (2008). Facilitating reading comprehension for students with autism spectrum disorders. *TEACHING Exceptional Children, 40*(3), 40–45.

Grigorenko, E.L., Klin, A., Pauls, D.L., Senft, R., Hooper, C., & Volkmar, F. (2002). A descriptive study of hyperlexia in a clinically referred sample of children with developmental delays. *Journal of Autism and Developmental Disorders, 32*(1), 3–12.

Grigorenko, E.L., Klin, A., & Volkmar, F. (2003). Annotation: Hyperlexia: Disability or superability? *Journal of Child Psychology and Psychiatry and Allied Disciplines, 44*(8), 1079–1091.

Grigorenko, E., & Sternberg, R.J. (Eds.). (1997). *Intelligence, heredity, and environment.* Cambridge, England: Cambridge University Press.

Harris, P.L. (1989). *Children and emotion: The development of psychological understanding.* Cambridge, MA: Basil Blackwell.

Harvey, S., & Goudvis, A. (2000). *Strategies that work: Teaching comprehension for understanding and engagement.* Portland, ME: Stenhouse.

Heaton, P., Williams, K., Cummins, O., & Happé, F. (2008). Autism and pitch processing splinter skills: A group and subgroup analysis in autism. *Autism, 12*(2), 203–219.

Karmiloff-Smith, A. (1992). *Beyond modularity.* Cambridge, MA: MIT Press.

Luria, A.R. (1976). *Cognitive development: Its cultural and social foundations.* Cambridge, MA: Harvard University Press.

Mottron, L. (2011). Changing perceptions: The power of autism. *Nature, 479*(7371), 33–35. Retrieved November 5, 2012, from http://www.nature.com/nature/journal/v479/n7371/abs/479033a.html

National Autism Center (NAC). (2009). *Evidence-based practice and autism in the schools: A guide to providing appropriate interventions to students with autism spectrum disorders.* Randolph, MA: Author.

National Center on UDL. (2011a). Learner variability and UDL. *UDL Series.* Retrieved December 7, 2012, from http://www.udlseries.udlcenter.org/presentations/learner_variability.html?plist=explore

National Center on UDL. (2011b). *UDL examples and resources.* Retrieved May 28, 2011, from http://www.udlcenter.org/implementation/examples

National Education Association. (2006). *The puzzle of autism.* Washington, D.C.: Author.

National Research Council, Committee on Education Interventions for Children with Autism, Division of Behavioral and Social Sciences and Education. (2001). *Educating children with autism.* Washington, D.C.: National Academy Press.

National Institute of Child Health and Human Development. (2000). *Report of the National Reading Panel. Teaching children to read: An evidence-based assessment of the scientific research literature on reading and its implications for reading instruction* (NIH Publication No. 00-4769). Washington, D.C.: U.S. Government Printing Office.

Patall, E.A., Cooper, H., & Robinson, J.C. (2008). The effects of choice on intrinsic motivation and related outcomes: A meta-analysis of research findings. *Psychological Bulletin, 134*(2), 270–300.

Pinnell, G.S., Pikulski, J.J., Wixson, K.K., Campbell, J.R., Gough, P.B., & Beatty, A.S. (1995). *Listening to children read aloud.* Washington, D.C.: Office of Educational Research and Improvement, U.S. Department of Education.

Pons, F., Harris, P.L., & de Rosnay, M. (2004). Emotion comprehension between 3 and

11 years: Developmental periods and hierarchical organization. *European Journal of Developmental Psychology, 1*(2), 127–152.

Pons, F., Lawson, J., Harris, P., & de Rosnay, M. (2003). Individual differences in children's emotion understanding: Effects of age and language. *Scandinavian Journal of Psychology, 44,* 347–353.

Premack, D., & Woodruff, G. (1978). Does the chimpanzee have a theory of mind? *Behavioral Brain Sciences, 1,* 515–526.

Quill, K.A. (1995). *Teaching children with autism: Strategies to enhance communication and socialization.* Albany, NY: Delmar

Rose, D.H., Gravel, J.W., & Domings, Y.M. (2010). *UDL unplugged: The role of technology in UDL.* Retrieved December 5, 2011, from the National Center for UDL at http://www.udlcenter.org/resource_library/articles/udlunplugged

Rose, D.H., Meyer, A., & Hitchcock, C. (2005). *The universally designed classroom: Accessible curriculum and digital technologies.* Cambridge, MA: Harvard Education Press.

Rose, L.T., & Fischer, K.W. (2009). Dynamic systems theory. In R.A. Shweder, T.R. Bidell, A.C. Dailey, & J. Dixon, (Eds.), *The child: An encyclopedic companion.* Chicago, IL: University of Chicago Press.

Siegler, R.S. (1994). Cognitive variability: A key to understanding development. *Current Dimensions in Psychological Science, 3,* 1–5.

U.S. Department of Education, National Center for Education Statistics. (2011). *The digest of education statistics, 2010* (NCES 2011-015), Table 46. Retrieved January 5, 2012, from http://www.nces.ed.gov/fastfacts/display.asp?id=59

U.S. Department of Education, Office of Special Education and Rehabilitative Services. (2002). *A new era: Revitalizing special education for children and their families.* Washington, D.C.: Author.

van Geert, P., & Fischer, K.W. (2009). Dynamic systems and the quest for individual-based models of change and development. In J.P. Spencer, M.S.C. Thomas, & J.L. McClelland (Eds.), *Toward a unified theory of development: Connectionism and dynamic systems theory re-considered* (pp. 313–336). New York, NY: Oxford University Press.

Wimmer, H., & Perner, J. (1983). Beliefs about beliefs: Representation and constraining function of wrong beliefs in young children's understanding of deception. *Cognition, 13,* 103–128.

Classroom Tools

Katharina I. Boser

■ ■

As discussed in Section I, recent decades of education reform and advocacy have focused more on the benefits of technologies for both teacher and student (see http:// www.cosn.org, http://www.iste.org, and the National Technology for Education Report, 2011). For students with autism, schools have generally moved more from an exclusion environment with separate and often clunky, expensive assistive technologies to an environment where fun, engaging tools offering instant assessment of abilities for teachers and feedback for students are part of a national policy for universal design for learning (UDL) for all educational environments. In these chapters, authors explore not only our current best-case scenarios for students adopting technology tools to improve and support a variety of skills, but also attempt to bridge the gaps. The latter two chapters offer innovative ideas and research on ways that virtual reality, robotics and programming, and do-it-yourself approaches can be more easily integrated into the curriculum.

"Classroom-Based Technology Tools," by Christopher R. Bugaj, Melissa A. Hartman, and Mark E. Nichols, brings to light the incredible responsibility public schools have of providing every student with a free appropriate public education (FAPE). The authors address the task of incorporating all students' individual needs, unique characteristics, strengths, and learning styles into a universal learning program. Bugaj, Hartman, and Nichols have the experience of delivering services in a large school district in Northern Virginia in which a network of supports and support teams attempt to address the varied needs of every individual in the system. The network of technology tools employed by their public school system tries to "cast a wide net" in order to meet the needs of as many students as possible. The chapter authors describe the specific tools that schools are using for all students while at the same time illustrating

ways in which more tailored supports are given to individuals with autism spectrum disorder (ASD) who may need additional assistance beyond what is provided universally. Bugaj, Hartman, and Nichols explore this matrix of tools through a description of a student's school day, showing how the student uses these tools to navigate different academic subject areas, interacts socially with teachers and students, and functionally adapts to schedules and routines for greater independence.

In "Using Virtual Reality Technology to Support the Learning of Children on the Autism Spectrum," Sarah Parsons, Nigel Newbutt, and Simon Wallace focus on the use of virtual reality (VR) in training and rehabilitation for people with autism. They describe technology that can simulate a digital 3-D virtual world that is interactive. Strong arguments have been made about the specific benefits of VR for individuals on the autism spectrum, chiefly because it can offer simulations of authentic real-world situations in a carefully controlled and safe environment. For a group of people partially defined by difficulties in socializing, this technology has therefore been argued to offer distinct advantages for social skills training compared to other approaches. Although true educational VR has not yet made it into mainstream use in classrooms, recreational games using 3-D imagery are common. The general ubiquity of technology in classrooms and the popularity of interactive computer games and online virtual worlds (e.g., Second Life) suggest that VR technologies could play a vitally important role in our future classrooms. The chapter authors suggest that VR is an appealing technology for educational use in part because of its openness. Yet its openness and flexibility also create challenges, especially when determining how VR can be effectively designed to support learning. VR systems can be viewed as too difficult to implement and too expensive to be of much educational use beyond niche academic research. However, Parsons, Newbutt, and Wallace nicely argue that the principles from the use and potential of such technologies can be distilled and applied into real-world classrooms through ever-increasing sophistication of available technologies (e.g., through enhanced affordability, flexibility, and capabilities of the new wave of interactive whiteboards and interactive surfaces).

The final chapter in this section, "Using Therapeutic Robots to Teach Students with Autism in the Classroom" by Katharina I. Boser, Corinna E. Lathan, Charlotte Safos, Rita Shewbridge, Carole Samango-Sprouse, and Marek Michalowski, is organized around several areas of autism impairment that have been shown to be successfully moderated by use of robots. These areas include peer-to-peer social engagement, peer-to-robot social engagement, nonverbal language and attention skills (joint attention, eye gaze, and imitation), motor imitation, and basic verbalization and language. Addressed are a number of themes that surround the argument for adoption of robots for the classroom, including UDL, science- and engineering-based education (STEM), project-based learning philosophy (do-it-yourself constructivist learning), and 21st century skills. The chapter authors highlight the way in which robots naturally motivate and drive students with autism to learn and also improve attention support through cueing. The robot could be used to sense conditions under which certain social cues would need to be shared, for example, when a student is standing too close to another student. Robots can be programmed to increase the amount of social interaction to allow students to interact gradually in a relatively controlled environment. This controlled interaction could lessen the social anxiety observed in more typical social situations. Finally, the authors introduce ways in which robots can be integrated into a 21st-century classroom to support students who are digital natives. Robots in classrooms can prepare students for learning in environments that are increasingly digital. Many ASD learners have different expectations for learning in such environments, and robotic sensors and sensing equipment have the potential to provide the necessary support.

In this section, we move from a chapter about current best practices in effective assistive technologies and UDL environments used in a large public school system, to the unknown quantity of how robots could eventually be used in such an environment. Although learning how to program robots is a skill ASD students enjoy, currently, using robots as interactive social and teaching agents in the classroom is still being developed. In Chapter 4, VR tools are presented that are advancing in terms of implementation and ease of adaptability to contemporary classrooms. One goal for upcoming designers is to integrate the best of all these innovative environments into more modern classrooms that might better support students with ASD. This goal may best be accomplished through the collaboration of students on the spectrum with researchers, designers, and teachers.

3

Classroom-Based Technology Tools

Christopher R. Bugaj, Melissa A. Hartman, and Mark E. Nichols

A vast array of low- to high-tech tools may be utilized to reduce and even eliminate educational barriers for students with autism spectrum disorders (ASDs). This chapter describes a sampling of the tools available to support students in accessing the general education curriculum to the greatest extent possible. Examples of how the tools may be utilized with students and integrated into the curriculum are provided via vignettes. It is important to note that the tools and strategies presented in this chapter must be adapted to meet the needs of the individual student. Technology tools should never be globally grouped and categorized around a specific disability. A tool that may appropriately support one student to varying degrees may not adequately support another student with the same disability. Any tools selected for use should be based on student need, the environment(s) for which the tools are required, and the educational tasks for which the student requires support (Zabala, 2005).

TOOLS FOR ROUTINES AND SELF-MANAGEMENT

Routines are integral parts of daily life for students with ASDs and foster successful engagement and increased independence by helping a student manage the social and academic pressures associated with various school environments. Disruptions to normal routines can often trigger confusion and adverse behaviors. It is imperative that teachers of students with ASDs reinforce appropriate routines and transitions to prevent students from developing their own systems, which may not be as adaptive or effective as those developed by the teacher (Mesibov, Shea, & Schopler, 2005). A clearly defined and structured environment is vital in creating positive outcomes.

Technology tools can readily support a student in reaching full academic potential. Sometimes, the least restrictive solutions for engaging students within the curriculum involve common tools found within the home, school, or work environment. For instance, Microsoft Word and Microsoft PowerPoint, two powerful tools that are common in many classrooms, have a variety of premade templates that can quickly be accessed to create learning resources. Both Word and PowerPoint can be used and modified in conjunction with clip art to create personal visual schedules, behavior charts, or even contextual stories depicting appropriate student social interaction. Visual schedules provide clear direction while requiring minimal social exchange by the educator, thus eliminating potential confusion by the student.

The research of Bryan and Gast (2000) supports the benefits of utilizing visual schedules with students with ASDs. Students were able to learn how to follow the schedule and were able to generalize the schedule to different settings successfully. When the visual schedules were removed, productivity and ability to transition decreased. An individualized visual schedule may be prominently posted on the wall, on the student's desk, or in a folder or notebook. The most common visual schedules list activities by times. For example, the day may be divided into 30-minute increments with pictures and/or phrases that can be moved from area to area depending upon the day and the activities. For durability, schedules should be laminated with information that is fixed. Velcro dots may be attached to pictures and/or phrases and affixed to the chart at the appropriate times (Figure 3.1).

Figure 3.1. Linear student schedule. Linear schedules help organize sequentially occurring activities or tasks for a student. This schedule depicts five specific periods throughout the student's day (math, write, science, lunch, read). (The Picture Communication Symbols ©1981–2010 by Mayer-Johnson LLC. All Rights Reserved Worldwide. Used with permission. Boardmaker™ is a trademark of Mayer-Johnson LLC.)

Behavior charts help facilitate independent self-monitoring and discrimination between appropriate and inappropriate behavior. These charts may be self-sustained by the student or managed by an educator. As with visual schedules, the behavior chart should be easily accessible to the student. Affixing the chart or schedule in a consistent location across environments is beneficial to promote self-management. These resources may be printed, laminated, and affixed to the student's desk, placed within the student's personal agenda book, displayed on the classroom wall, or manipulated virtually on an electronic device.

A variety of self-directing supports should be accessible throughout the school day. These may include, but are not limited to, a specific cool-down area or space with sensory materials (e.g., lotions, stress balls, items of specific interest to the student). Colored tape can be used to create a defined personal space on the floor in front of a whiteboard or particular workstation as a visual cue for students to remain seated within the square to help elicit engagement during group activities (Figure 3.2). The targeted skill (of staying seated during group activities) can be reinforced by the tape and visuals attached to the tape on the floor. Alternatively, the teacher can present various visual choices to allow for greater self-direction and independence.

We live in an era where an ever-increasing number of students arrive at school with portable computers in their pockets and backpacks. These handheld mobile devices have revolutionized the way students can access web-based resources,

Figure 3.2. Desktop workspace marker. Desktop workspaces can be isolated by using masking tape.

manage lifestyles, communicate with others, and be entertained through a vast array of multimedia. These tools provide on-demand access and supports for maintaining continuity in student learning across all environments. For students with ASDs, these tools may assist in self-managing behavior, monitoring routines and schedules, and ultimately increasing independence. For example, the device could have a pre-loaded digital story that visually reminds the student how to handle stressful situations when feelings of anger or frustration are predominant. One student may use mobile electronics to quickly pull up a feelings chart with appropriate coping strategies to foster an environment of self-recognition of feelings, whereas another student may use the tool to watch a short video modeling successful self-management techniques when engaged in a particular task or activity. Alternatively, when an environment becomes overly stimulating due to loud noises or disruptions, students may find comfort in using headphones and listening to music in order to focus on the task at hand. Students may utilize mobile technology in varying degrees to help support achievement across the environments in which they interact.

TRANSITION TO SCHOOL

When Mike steps on the bus, he sees the driver pointing to a picture. The picture is one of many that are strung around the driver's neck on a lanyard (Figure 3.3). His finger taps the symbol of a boy sitting on a seat. Mike looks at the driver and says "hello" just as it says to do in his social situation story. The bus driver replies, "Good morning, Michael," and Mike takes his seat. Mike gets out his handheld device and turns it on. He navigates to his personalized story on the device and by swiping his finger, reviews his story. Each page has a picture of Mike engaging in tasks throughout the day. The first picture shows Mike eating breakfast, the second brushing his teeth, the third getting dressed, and the fourth Mike getting on the bus. The next picture depicts Mike arriving at school. Mike has earphones so he can listen to his "morning routine" social situation story but typically chooses to watch the story and read the short text that appears beneath. Sometimes, the constant roar from the bus engine distracts Mike. When this happens, Mike's independent self-management technique involves listening to soft music through his headphones to help him stay focused on the next aspect of his morning routine, arriving at school.

TOOLS FOR STRUCTURING THE CLASSROOM ENVIRONMENT

Students with ASDs require a structured day and a predictable, calm environment in which to navigate the school day effectively (Cumine, Leach, & Stevenson, 1998). Classrooms that serve students with ASDs should be flexible and contain academic, sensory, and group and individual spaces (Vogel, 2008). Students should have their own workstations or offices that are relatively free from distractions, complete with specified areas for necessary materials and visual schedules (Figure 3.4). Teachers may use dividers (portable walls) or bookshelves to provide a specific area for each student. This area may contain bins of activities, both preferred and academic, as well as any materials necessary to complete work. The workspace should be arranged in a natural progression with work to be completed in a folder or bin on the left side of the desk and completed work on the right. Some teachers utilize plastic bins for this purpose; others attach folders to each side of the desk. The materials used will depend upon the individual needs of the student.

Figure 3.3. Communication lanyard. Communication lanyards are a great way to quickly relay or elicit communication regardless of environmental conditions. (The Picture Communication Symbols ©1981–2010 by Mayer-Johnson LLC. All Rights Reserved Worldwide. Used with permission. Boardmaker™ is a trademark of Mayer-Johnson LLC.)

Figure 3.4. Student study carrel. Study carrels are a great low-tech method for creating a customized learning support to reinforce concepts and to meet the needs of each individual student.

In her article "Design for Living and Learning with Autism," Vogel (2008) outlines that classrooms should be safe, predictable, nondistracting, controllable, attuned to students' sensory needs, noninstitutional, flexible, and adaptable. The article provides excellent detail and examples for classroom use that are beyond the scope of this chapter.

Sensory breaks should be listed on the schedule as well as lunch and all other activities the student participates in throughout the day. Utilizing Velcro to post the activities allows teachers or students to change the order and activities as necessary throughout the year. Students can remove the activities upon completion and place them in a "finished" sleeve or container (Figure 3.5). Such software programs as Boardmaker Plus may be used to create the pictures for the schedules. Some students may be more responsive to using digital photos of themselves or others completing tasks, whereas others may just need words or short phrases. Text can be paired with the visuals to reinforce language development and reading skills. Visual schedules should vary depending upon student needs. At the secondary level, students may have a sheet in a notebook containing a simple list of tasks in phrases that can be checked off as the tasks are completed. The key is to have a complete schedule for each day so the student knows exactly what to expect.

The sensory area should contain items collaboratively reviewed by the teacher and any related service providers, such as physical and occupational therapists. Sensory areas may contain a wide variety of apparati and tools, among them swings, mini trampolines, stress balls, exercise balls, weighted vests or lap bands, tents, beanbag chairs, and pillows with differing textures. Students may utilize this area for a "chill out" space where they sit and read or listen to music or take specifically recommended sensory breaks. It is essential that a physical therapist ensure that all classroom staff know how to assist students in utilizing each apparatus correctly and within recommended time limits. Teachers can use visual timers, clocks or timers on the interactive whiteboard, or other digital devices to assist students in moving from one activity to the other.

Figure 3.5.   Nonlinear student schedule. Nonlinear student schedules allow students to select and choose one of the desired activities in a preferred order. (The Picture Communication Symbols ©1981–2010 by Mayer-Johnson LLC. All Rights Reserved Worldwide. Used with permission. Boardmaker™ is a trademark of Mayer-Johnson LLC.)

TOOLS FOR DELIVERING INSTRUCTION

According to the principles of universal design for learning, it is imperative that teachers utilize multiple means for representation when delivering instruction to reach all students regardless of ability (Rose, Meyer, & Hitchcock, 2005). Each student has preferred styles of learning as well as specific strengths and weaknesses when receiving and presenting information. Students with ASDs tend to be visually oriented, thus using interactive whiteboards to present information via video and interactive games and activities is extremely engaging. Interactive whiteboards allow students to participate in tactile and kinesthetic activities. They also provide a way for teachers and students to present videos, including multimedia slideshows such as PowerPoint presentations and Prezis, and digital books to share with the class or individual students. Digital simulations are also very popular. Virtual dissections, math manipulative activities, space exploration, archeological digs, and additional activities are all available on the internet. A simple keyword search will yield more results than teachers can possibly use. Teachers may also utilize cell phones and other handheld devices to present information to students via messaging, podcasts, notepads, voice recordings, and the like (Kolb, 2008).

To eliminate barriers inherent in traditional textbooks and on web sites, text-to-speech software may be utilized on the computer to read web pages, text, and trade books. Such software programs as Read&Write Gold provide students with a variety of accessibility tools, including speech-to-text as well as such editing tools as a spell checker, word predictor, dictionary, word wizard thesaurus, and a sounds alike tool that helps users determine if they have chosen the correct homophones in their writing. In addition, Read&Write Gold provides the following features:

- MP3 converter to convert text into files for later playback on an MP3 player

- Pronunciation tutor, fact-finding tool, and fact-mapping graphic organizer tool

- Voice dictation tool for writing assistance

- Floating toolbar that allows users to access Read&Write Gold from within word-processing or portable document format reader programs (see http://www.bit.ly/aboutrwg)

Free applications that provide similar supports can be found online (e.g., http://www.eduapps.org and http://www.portableapps.com). These applications may be loaded onto a USB drive and easily transported for use on any computer without internet access.

Such interactive digital tablets as the iPad are a portable mode of presenting information to students. Thousands of applications are available on these devices for presenting material in all content areas. These devices can be used as calculators, compasses, art canvases, and more. If you can think of it, there is likely an app for that purpose. It is important to remember when using these devices that many applications have a price tag, and even those that appear to be free may give you a sample of the program but require you to purchase other parts.

Low-tech and no-tech options for presenting material include paper maps, photographs, drawings, graphic organizers, dry erase boards, and books. Regardless of which tools you choose to use, it is important to choose with a specific purpose in mind and to choose the tool that appropriately matches the purpose as well as students' needs.

■ ■

SCIENCE CLASS

Sarah enters the group area of the classroom for the science lesson. The teacher has the goal for the day posted on the interactive whiteboard: to identify three types of volcanic cones. The teacher shows video clips of three different active volcanoes and then asks students to identify the similarities and differences. When it is Sarah's turn to go to the board, she uses the pen to write *smoke* in the similarities column on the whiteboard. The teacher then pulls up a web page with pictures of the different volcanic cones along with their names. For the next activity, Sarah is asked to come up to the board and drag the correct name to the volcanic cone it matches.

■ ■

TOOLS FOR EXPRESSION OF KNOWLEDGE AND PRODUCTIVITY

It is important to recognize that an attribute of the human condition is the need to communicate with others. Successful communication happens in a variety of ways using multiple modalities (Pearce, 1989). Individuals communicate through words, gestures, writing, artistic expression, and more. These means can be organic (speech or gestures) or mechanical (technology) in both analog and digital formats.

The tools 21st century students with ASD have to express themselves are vast and varied. It would be impossible to try to capture every tool students have available to them that could be used to demonstrate their knowledge; however, this infinite array of options can be clustered into categories to help organize the technology into manageable components. In this way, educators can focus on the task to be accomplished and subsequently look at the tool or tools that could be used to facilitate that task.

TOOLS FOR VERBAL EXPRESSION

Difficulties with verbal expression present themselves in a multitude of complex ways, including concerns with the form, structure, and meaning of language, along with the accurate physical production of sounds in connected speech. The tools used to help students communicate can be grouped in two primary categories: augmentative and alternative. Augmentative systems are tools that help people whose primary form of communication is through verbal speech but who demonstrate difficulty with successful communication interactions. This difficulty might include problems with prosody, intelligibility, vocal quality, or language processing or with some other barrier to successful verbal exchanges. Augmentative tools work to facilitate communication by enhancing or supplementing verbal speech. When an individual does not demonstrate the ability to produce verbal speech, an alternative approach to verbal communication is necessary. It is common to refer to both augmentative and alternative communication together using the acronym AAC.

Among other strategies to facilitate communication, AAC technologies, like any other set of tools, span a range from no-tech to very dynamic, intricate digital systems. A pacing board is a set of displayed shapes to help provide and represent a visual, kinesthetic, and tactile model particularly useful for helping students expand their length of utterance and/or change their rate of speech. For instance, when a student makes a one-word verbal request, such as "toy" to indicate he or she wants a particular toy, a communication partner might draw three circles on a piece of paper, point to each circle and say, "I want toy," and then present the circles to the student with the expectation that the student would use the circles as a model for verbal reproduction.

Similar to a pacing board, a sentence starter strip provides a student with a visual representation of what to say in the form of a set of picture symbols followed by an empty cell. Like the cloze procedure for assessments, the expectation of the student is to complete the utterance by verbally filling in the blank. Common sentence starters include "I want…," "I see…," "I am…," and "Where is…" although other phrases are also often used.

Either by pointing or through the exchange of pictures, students could maintain a library of picture symbols to facilitate communication called communication notebooks. These communication systems can be maintained on a single board or within a notebook organized by function. Students locate a picture symbol or sequence of symbols to indicate messages. Velcro is often used to fix the picture symbols in place when making exchanges (Figure 3.6).

Voice output devices generate either a recorded or synthesized message when a cell (like a button) or set of cells is activated. Static voice output devices have a set number of cells that typically cannot be changed. Some devices have levels that allow for a user to access a greater number of messages using the same set of defined cells. For instance, a user might have an array of eight cells each with a different word or phrase set to the first level. Changing the device to Level 2 would allow the student to access an entirely new set of preprogrammed words or phrases.

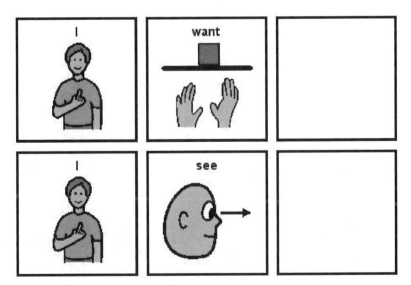

Figure 3.6. Carrier phrases. Communication strips with carrier phrases (created using Mayer-Johnson symbols) can be used to prompt student communication. (The Picture Communication Symbols ©1981–2010 by Mayer-Johnson LLC. All Rights Reserved Worldwide. Used with permission. Boardmaker™ is a trademark of Mayer-Johnson LLC.)

Systems that allow a user to manipulate screens of nearly unlimited choices in vocabulary to make audible selections are considered dynamic voice output devices. These devices often integrate touch technologies to access vocabulary selections. Products range from stand-alone software applications that run on a desktop, laptop, or tablet computer to systems integrated into hardware uniquely designed for the purposes of augmentative or alternative communication.

Communication is a function of life that cannot be segmented into set time frames. Communication occurs all day long, in every setting, with every individual the student encounters (Mirenda, 1997). For this reason, it is necessary for those interacting with a student to work as a cohesive team using similar, seamless strategies. A communication bridge is a tool useful for helping all communication partners understand what has transpired across different settings. A communication bridge can be picture symbols with phrases that a student helps to complete (such as "Today in Art I...") or messages programmed onto a voice output device (Figure 3.7).

Implementation of an entire language system might seem like an overwhelming task when faced with all the possible words and combinations of words that an individual might potentially utilize. Language, however, can be viewed across a spectrum from more commonly used words and phrases to utterances that are less frequently used. These commonly used words are known as core vocabulary, whereas the less frequently used words are known as fringe vocabulary (see Figure 3.8). When developing a communication system, it is paramount that the vocabulary present the user with the ability to create the largest number of phrases. Therefore, vocabulary selected to be placed on a device is often designed to allow a user to readily access such core words as *I, go, want, help, more, here, there,* and *stop.*

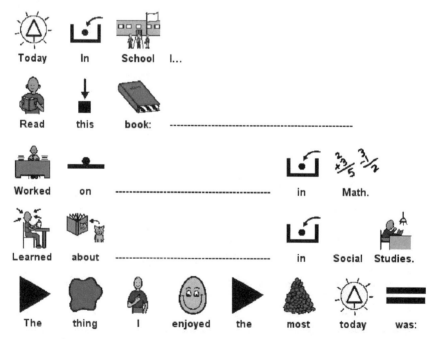

Figure 3.7. Visual rebus/communication bridge. A visual rebus can be used as a communication bridge between home and school and completed by students at the end of each day. (The Picture Communication Symbols ©1981–2010 by Mayer-Johnson LLC. All Rights Reserved Worldwide. Used with permission. Boardmaker™ is a trademark of Mayer-Johnson LLC.)

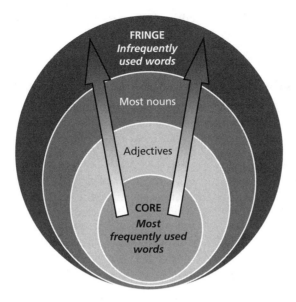

Figure 3.8. Core and fringe vocabulary. Core vocabulary (frequently used words) is the most critical component of a well-organized AAC system. Fringe vocabulary (infrequently used words) is important but use is typically limited to very specific conditions.

When children are learning to speak, they are generally surrounded by models who use verbal communication as their primary form of expression. It stands to reason that when children who are nonverbal are learning to communicate via alternative devices, they should also be surrounded by models who use alternative communication. One strategy to help model communication for students using alternative communication is for the communicative partner to use a voice output device as well. Communication partners will often use the same device, trading it back and forth, to model and foster communication development. This strategy is known as "aided communication" (Sennott, Burkhart, Musselwhite, & Cafiero, 2010).

Although language development follows a typical progression, there is no prerequisite skill set necessary for a student to successfully use an AAC device (Beukelman & Mirenda, 2005; Stuart & Ritthaler, 2008). As a general rule, it is better to assume that a student will demonstrate the ability to learn to be competent rather than to assume that the student will be unable to use a tool to gain a skill. For instance, it would be logical to consider providing an alternative communication device to a student who is nonverbal. During the consideration process, the individual education plan team might look at the skill set of the student to help determine the necessary features and functions the device will require. Typically, the vocabulary placed on multicelled, multileveled devices is organized by categories. One skill the team may be concerned about for a student is difficulty with categorization. It would be incorrect to assume that because a student demonstrates difficulty with categorization, that he would be unable to use a multicelled, multileveled device. Some students with ASDs have shown the ability to memorize the results of sequential cell activation through motor planning. In these instances, the student might not be aware of the visual on the cell or the auditory output that is being produced when the cell is activated, only that when the correct sequence of cells is activated a desired result occurs.

■ ■

EXPRESSIVE COMMUNICATION

Egan is a student with autism who is learning to use a 32-cell TechSpeak with eight levels. Egan is highly motivated by bubbles and bubble-blowing activities. After an activity, he earns a break from his work and chooses to interact with bubbles by pressing Cell 1 on Level 1, Cell 6 on Level 1, Cell 16 on Level 2, and Cell 8 on Level 1, which are each labeled with a picture symbol corresponding with the audio to produce the phrase "I want bubbles please." His teacher blows bubbles, and Egan demonstrates his enjoyment of the activity. Egan does not necessarily receptively understand the pictures' symbols or audio message, only the desired result of bubbles being provided. The communication interaction was a success because Egan understood that pressing Cell 1-1, Cell 6-1, Cell 16-2, and Cell 8-1 equate to his receiving bubbles, whereas pressing a different combination of cells might result in a different outcome or activity.

■ ■

TOOLS FOR WRITTEN EXPRESSION

Learning written expression can be almost as complex as verbal language acquisition. A variety of materials can be used to help a student hold a writing utensil to produce a functional outcome. The size, shape, weight, and other features of a tool, including adjustments to the writing surface itself, can help a student produce legible handwriting.

A common strategy for helping students with the composition of written material is to break down the task into its component parts. The process of producing a composition can be broken down into five integral components. These include planning and prewriting, outlining and drafting, editing and revising, and then producing or publishing.

During the planning and prewriting stages of writing, students are doing research, gathering data, and developing ideas about their chosen topics. Useful tools at this stage include highlighters, erasable highlighters, digital highlighters (e.g., those found within the free toolbar from http://www.diigo.com), student-friendly search engines (e.g., http://www.kidrex.org and http://www.sweetsearch.com), bookmarking sites (e.g., http://www.livebinders.com, http://www.symbaloo.com, and http://www.diigo.com), and referencing/bibliography sites (e.g., http://www.easybib.com).

Presenting any student, with or without ASD, with a blank screen or a blank piece of paper with the expectation to generate a written composition can be intimidating and lead to frustration. Just as it is necessary to structure the physical environment, one must provide structure for how to approach a writing assignment. The visual layout of graphic organizers where there are a finite number of cells present helps to provide guidance and temper expectations. Rather than looking at an empty canvas with the expectation to fill it with text, the student can face a graphic organizer that presents him or her with an achievable, segmented task. When presented with a graphic organizer with five cells, for example, students immediately recognize and understand that content needs to be placed in those five cells. In this way, a graphic organizer for writing assignments parallels the use of a visual schedule for daily activities (Figure 3.9).

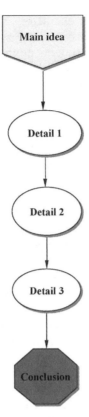

Figure 3.9. Prewriting graphic organizer. Visually organizing a graphic organizer (in this case by shape and color) helps establish and define the necessary steps for completion using familiar concepts.

Many different web sites provide templates with downloadable, printable graphic organizers (e.g., http://www.eduplace.com/graphicorganizer and http://www.freeology.com/graphicorgs). Likewise, there are many different web-based graphic organizers that are interactively dynamic allowing a user to enter text, links to audio and video, and insert images. Examples include http://www.spiderscribe.net, http://www.mindmeister.com, http://www.cacoo.com, and http://www.mindomo.com, but there are also others. Some graphic organizers can be found as apps for mobile devices as well. See Chapter 8 for more.

Report-writing software allows students to engage with a step-by-step, screen-by-screen wizard that guides them through the writing process. Activities using digital graphic organizers can be scaffolded to meet varied student abilities. Some students might be asked to type sentences to produce a five-paragraph essay, for instance, whereas another student might be asked to move the cells around to sequence the preexisting text or images.

Comics provide a visual method that can be scaled to fit the diverse needs of students. Such web sites as http://www.makebeliefscomix.com, http://www.pixton.com, http://www.toondoo.com, and http://www.bitstrips.com allow students the opportunity to generate comics. Educators can use comics as a highly visual way to represent information, and students can use comics to demonstrate what they know within predefined limits. Different levels of expectations can be incorporated into a similar activity through the use of a comic. Some students might create a comic strip from scratch, creating characters, settings, and dialogue. Other students might fill in text bubbles from comic strips that already have panels filled with these artifacts. Still another set of students might sequence the cells of a comic strip to demonstrate understanding of the order of events. Comics can also be paired with social situation stories for students to practice expected responses in a variety of scenarios (Vivian, Hutchins, & Prelock, 2012).

Some students might be able to verbally tell you what they would like to write but demonstrate difficulty when it comes to getting their thoughts out in a text-based format. For these students, making audio recordings is a preferred method of expression. Free sound recording software, such as Audacity (http://www.audacity.sourceforge.net), iPad and tablet recording apps or web-based sound recording sites (e.g., http://www.vocaroo.com or http://www.recordmp3.org) allow a student to record audio to be used later or to be shared with the teacher. If the primary goal of the assignment is not related to spelling, grammar, or language instruction, then perhaps a student might provide only an audio recording to demonstrate his or her knowledge of a specific piece of content. However, if the goal of the assignment is to practice grammar, spelling, or sentence structure, then the recording of audio would be a preliminary step before beginning textual input. Pairing this strategy with a graphic organizer, students record a sentence in each cell. Then, once they finish recording, they go back to listen to each recording, one at a time, typing in the message they recorded. In this way, the students are practicing their auditory comprehension skills, keyboarding skills, and spelling skills all at the same time without having to rely on these skills to complete the task. Students who struggle with spelling, demonstrate frustration, fatigue easily, or need frequent breaks, all benefit from using this strategy.

When a student utilizes a device to complete writing assignments, the student has access to all of the built-in features of the operating system and a word-processing application. Changing font style, font color, font size, background color, and screen resolution; using spelling and grammar checks, macros, and keyboard shortcuts; and making accessibility feature choices—all provide the student with a large array of tools and options to complete written assignments.

For some students, specialized software might be necessary to provide additional features to help improve or lessen the burden of the writing process. Graphic word-processing software that provides pictures paired with words might be necessary to help ensure appropriate spelling and to increase the student's comprehension of reading material. Examples of graphic word-processing software include PixWriter, Intellitools, and the Symbolate feature of Boardmaker Plus software.

Word prediction is another feature that helps to ensure errorless learning of spelling words. Rather than spelling a word incorrectly, seeing a red underline as an indicator of a misspelling, and then going on a hunt to find the appropriate spelling, students who use word prediction software are provided with a list of possible words. Students then select the appropriate word from the list, either by looking at the word or by hearing it read aloud.

Once the first draft is completed, an editing checklist is a useful visual tool that helps a student remember what to check each time he or she reviews a document. A helpful final step would be for the student to listen to the document read aloud by the computer. Listening to a document read aloud allows a student to practice auditory comprehension skills while listening for any potential mistakes, such as leaving out words or using an incorrect word that is correctly spelled in a sentence.

Text-to-speech features might be included in such software packages as Kurzweil 3000 and Read&Write Gold, but there are also free options available such as Natural Reader. Vozme is a free web-based solution allowing a user to type text or copy and paste text to produce an MP3 file. WordTalk is a free add-in for Microsoft Word that provides text-to-speech. Also, the voiceover accessibility feature allows for text to be read aloud on iPads.

There are many opportunities for students to produce written work that has an authentic purpose. Production of a composition that will be read by the teacher only is rarely motivating to a student. Writing something that will be read outside of the classroom and will affect others is not only motivating but may also align with a social interaction goal of a student with ASD. Such activities as leaving comments on blogs, producing one's own blog, microblogging (e.g., leaving a message on a school-based social networking site such http://www.edmodo.com or http://www.schoology.com), and writing movie scripts or reviews for others to read are just some ideas for how students can interact with the world around them through written expression.

When developing lesson plans, educators need to decide if written expression is truly a necessary aspect. Some students might prefer to demonstrate their knowledge by coloring, drawing, sculpting, recording audio, generating a comic, shooting a video, or combining multiple modalities (e.g., through the use of http://www.glogster.com). Each of these modalities of expression might contain text, but unless the text is absolutely necessary as part of what the student needs to learn, students should be allowed to express what they know in the modality that best suits their preferred learning style.

CONCLUSION

The tools presented in this chapter provide just a few examples of technologies educators may use throughout the school day to improve access to education for students with ASDs. Numerous lists of applications and tools are available on the internet. It is easy to become overwhelmed with all the information available today. Yet it is imperative to focus on a student's individual needs, strengths, interests, and preferences within the UDL framework when collaboratively choosing tools to implement. This focus will assist in ensuring that tools are not chosen without purpose. A team effort in determining appropriate tools is key to successful outcomes.

REFERENCES

Beukelman, D.R., & Mirenda, P. (2005). *Augmentative and alternative communication: Supporting children and adults with complex communication needs* (3rd ed.). Baltimore, MD: Paul H. Brookes Publishing Co.

Bryan, L.C., & Gast, D.L. (2000). Teaching on-task and on-schedule behaviors to high functioning children with autism via picture activity schedules. *Journal of Autism and Developmental Disorders, 30,* 553–567.

Cumine, C., Leach, J., & Stevenson, G. (1998). *Asperger syndrome: A practical guide for teachers.* London, England: David Fulton.

Kolb, L. (2008). *Toys to tools: Connecting student cell phones to education.* Eugene, OR: International Society for Technology in Education.

Mesibov, G.B., Shea, V., & Schopler, E. (2005). *The TEACCH approach to autism spectrum disorders.* New York, NY: Kluwer Academic/Plenum.

Mirenda, P. (1997). Supporting individuals with challenging behavior through functional training and AAC: Research review. *Augmentative and Alternative Communication, 13,* 207–225.

Pearce, B. (1989). *Communication and the human condition.* Carbondale, IL: Southern Illinois University Press.

Rose, D.H., Meyer, A., & Hitchcock, C. (2005). *The universally designed classroom: Accessible curriculum and digital technologies.* Cambridge, MA: Harvard Education Press.

Sennot, S., Burkhart, L., Musselwhite, C.R., & Cafiero, J. (2010). *Aided language stimulation: Research to practice.* Research presented at the Assistive Technology Industry Association Conference, Orlando, Florida.

Stuart, S., & Ritthaler, C. (2008). Case studies of intermediate steps between AAC evaluations and implementation. *Perspective on Augmentative and Alternative Communication, 17,* 150–155.

Vivian, L., Hutchins, T.L., & Prelock, P.A. (2012). A family-centered approach for training parents to use comic strip conversations with their child with autism. *Contemporary Issues in Communication Science and Disorders, 39,* 30–42.

Vogel, C.L. (2008, May/June). Classroom design for living and learning with autism. *Autism Asperger's Digest.* Retrieved from http://www.designshare.com/index.php/articles/classroom_autism

Zabala, J. (2005). *Using the SETT framework to level the learning field for students with disabilities.* Retrieved from http://www.joyzabala.com/uploads/Zabala_SETT_Leveling_the_Learning_Field.pdf

Using Virtual Reality Technology to Support the Learning of Children on the Autism Spectrum

▪ ▪

Sarah Parsons, Nigel Newbutt, and Simon Wallace

The original vision of virtual reality (VR), particularly from the media, was that people in the future would somehow be plugged into complex machines that take the person away to an exciting new world. The reality in 21st-century technology is a little different, and the current use of VR technology is often for practical (e.g., training, online tours) or game-playing purposes. People are becoming increasingly reliant on, and familiar with, conducting transactions in virtual environments (VEs), whether that be shopping, communicating, socializing, or teaching and learning. Indeed, we are becoming demanding consumers of a sophisticated and informative virtual experience. In the coming years these transactions can only become more numerous, technologically complex, and diverse, meaning that more opportunities will be identified to use VR technologies to support and enhance the lives of people with autism.

Previous review papers have highlighted the advantages of VR in delivering interventions to people with autism spectrum disorders (ASDs; e.g., Goodwin, 2008; Parsons & Mitchell, 2002; Schmidt & Schmidt, 2008; Trepagnier, 1999). In many ways VEs are well suited to providing educational and therapeutic interventions because they are programmable spaces in which all features (visual and audio) can be carefully selected and controlled, and which can represent any context or place without the cost, complexity, or limitations of relying upon real-world places. Rizzo et al. note that

> A primary strength that VR offers assessment and rehabilitation is in the creation of simulated realistic environments in which performance can be tested and trained in systematic fashion. By designing VEs that not only look like the real world but actually incorporate challenges that require functional behaviors, the ecological validity of assessment and rehabilitation methods could be enhanced. (2006, p. 37)

The idea is that the person with autism can build confidence in developing skills with the knowledge that he or she can safely make mistakes in a VE and doing so will not cause damage or embarrassment (to self or others) (Rizzo & Kim, 2005). The content can often be tailored to the individual requirements of the participant, making it more relevant to the participant's needs or goals. Motivation is vital for learning, and a person with autism may be excited by the opportunity of practicing a skill in a VE as a bridge to taking that skill into a real-world setting. Making the case for using VR is relatively straightforward, but to date, there has been a lack of good research into the effectiveness of VR intervention programs or an assessment of where the potential in using these technologies really lies. This chapter briefly defines what VR technologies are, explores some of the background regarding using VR in the field of autism research, outlines some case studies from research, and explores future research and practice opportunities.

WHAT IS VIRTUAL REALITY TECHNOLOGY?

The term *virtual reality* "refers to a set of computing technologies used to create, and allow users to experience simulated digital or 'virtual' environments (VEs)" (Cobb, 2007, p. 211) that "can be explored and interacted with in real-time" (Cobb & Sharkey, 2007, p. 52) and may be controlled through "special headsets that respond to head movements while a glove responds to hand movements" (Health Resources and Services Administration [HRSA], 2010) but can also be explored and interacted with via standard input devices (e.g., mouse, joystick, arrow keys on the keyboard). Whether designed to be realistic in appearance or an abstract or imaginary world, most VEs are created for users to primarily experience visually; however, VR can be designed to include such other types of sensory feedback as sound, touch, or motion. The implication is that a VE can be run, played, interacted with, and then closed when completed—like a computer game.

A *collaborative virtual environment* (CVE) is a VE that allows more than one person to be present at the same time, and so it is a multiuser environment. The notion of people being able to experience each other is key to this form of environment; Redfern and Naughton (2002, p. 201) describe CVEs as places in which "people can meet and interact with others." Within CVEs, participants are represented as avatars (virtual embodiments that can be humanoid in appearance or can take the form of any object or fantastical character) and experience the environment from their own subjective viewpoint. One of the principal attractions with this form of interaction and communication lies in the 3-D immersion afforded in devising simulations of real-world environments and expressive avatars. From the early 1990s, CVEs have prevailed (Joslin, Di Giacomo, & Magnenat-Thalmann, 2004), albeit in very basic form, to develop into more advanced programs offering immersive, expressive, and emotional avatars seen in many modern online games often referred to as MMOGs, or massively multiplayer online games. It is within these more modern and technically advanced versions of CVEs where users and players have the ability and flexibility to customize their avatars and create social networks between one another.

Virtual worlds (VWs) are a particular form of CVE that tend to be persistent rather than coming to an end when a game or program is closed. Second Life

Table 4.1.   Distinguishing features of virtual reality technologies

Three-dimensional (3-D): A virtual environment is a space in which the user feels that the representation and the objects within it are three-dimensional.

Adaptability: Virtual environments can be adapted for different types of users. This may be achieved by changing the complexity of the virtual surroundings or the methods of interaction.

Real-time responses: The virtual environment and the objects within it respond immediately to the users in order to mimic real-life interactions.

Collaboration: Collaborative virtual environments can allow several users to interact and work together in a virtual world; this may help users develop their social and collaborative skills.

Sensory feedback: Virtual environments provide the user with sensory feedback. This is primarily visual feedback but can also include sound, touch, and even smell. Sensory feedback can help the virtual environment appear more realistic to the user.

Interactivity: Users may interact with the virtual environment either through directly manipulating objects or through experiencing different sensations as they navigate.

Flexibility: Every virtual environment starts off as an empty space, allowing complete flexibility in the design of the space.

Immersion: A virtual environment aims to immerse the user in the virtual world. That is, the user feels directly involved and present in the virtual scenario. This can be achieved either through physical immersion (e.g., wearing a headset) or through the user being absorbed or engrossed in the virtual world.

Source: Parsons et al. (2000).

(developed by Linden Lab, Inc.) is one well-known example of a VW, which DeAngelis (2009) reported on in terms of therapeutic potential for people with ASDs. In the DeAngelis case study, the researchers developed a private island where users with ASDs can interact with each other, with therapist support to guide and encourage responses if and when needed. Few details about the intervention are available, however, and results from the work have not yet been published, so it is difficult to know whether and in what ways this approach could be of specific benefit. Nevertheless, the multiple users, interaction, and customizable avatars of VWs may provide interesting opportunities for children with ASD to socialize, and these aspects are explored further in the case study section below. Table 4.1 outlines the characteristics that distinguish VR from other digital technologies and make them of particular use for educational applications (adapted from Cobb, Neale, Crosier, & Wilson, 2002; see also Cobb, 2007).

WHY VIRTUAL REALITY FOR AUTISM SPECIFICALLY?

The early 1990s saw the first discussions in the academic literature regarding the potential of VR to support learning generally, both within mainstream (general) education (Bricken, 1991) and for children and adults with disabilities or special educational needs (Murphy, 1996). Bricken (1991) suggested that VR has particular features that make it of special value to educators, namely, that it is experiential, allows natural interaction with information, and offers a shared experience. In addition, it allows unique capabilities "in which you can control time, scale and physics," and it can be tailored to individual needs (Bricken, 1991, p. 180; see also Dalgarno & Lee, 2010, for a more recent discussion of the "learning affordances" of VEs). In recognition of this potential, there was a multidisciplinary burgeoning of research interest in this area, with many authors proving enthusiastic about the applications of

VR for supporting access to safe, new, or otherwise inaccessible environments for people with learning, social, cognitive, or physical impairments or difficulties (e.g., Brown, Cobb, & Eastgate, 1995; Cromby, Standen, & Brown, 1996; Trepagnier, 1999). Since then, a review of the applications of VR in the disability field demonstrates the breadth of applications that have been developed and tested; these include using acoustic and haptic environments for people with visual impairments, accurate modeling of sign language to provide training, investigation of responses (e.g., memory, social rules) of patients following stroke, and motor rehabilitation for individuals following spinal injury, to name only a few (see Cobb & Sharkey, 2007, for more details; also Parsons, Rizzo, Rogers, & York, 2009). More recently, the discussion about the potential usefulness of VR in education has been extended to consider its role in training teachers how to support children with different learning needs (Andreasen et al., 2008; Dieker, Hynes, Hughes, & Smith, 2008).

Applications for autism, as well as recognition of the potential of VR for children on the autism spectrum, began to appear in the mid to late 1990s with Dorothy Strickland pioneering the testing of early hardware with two young children with autism (Strickland, 1996, 1998; Strickland, Marcus, Mesibov, & Hogan, 1996). Cheryl Trepagnier (1999) also recognized the potential of VR for people with autism early on, arguing that the ability to reduce distraction and support executive functions and communication within VEs make them particularly noteworthy for cognitive rehabilitation, including social skills training for children with autism. She argued, "Virtual environments, if they are appropriately configured and appealing, could become an effective addition to the intensive social training required by children who have missed the natural acquisition of these skills" (1999, p. 70). Parsons and Mitchell (2002) developed this argument further and suggested that VEs could be particularly helpful educational tools for people on the autism spectrum because they offer the potential to combine the strengths of effective intervention components from both the cognitive and behavioral research traditions. Examples of the combination of both cognitive and behavioral types of effective teaching strategies in VEs might include repetition and practice of the skill across a range of contexts, role play within realistic settings from different perspectives, explanation and interpretation of the social skill(s) being taught, and support in understanding how one's own behavior and communication influences or affects others. The nature of VEs means that these strengths could then be extended through the safe and supportive space of a VE, which allows users to have active control over their participation. The VE enables interaction to take many forms (e.g., users may communicate verbally or through text via their avatars) and does not necessitate face-to-face communication, which many people with autism find uncomfortable; the level and number of nonverbal and verbal features of communication can be directly controlled and manipulated and adapted for individual needs; and behaviors and responses can be practiced and built upon in a context that shares some similarities with the real world, thereby offering greater potential for transfer of skills and understanding to real-world situations (Parsons & Mitchell, 2002). Overall then, there are good reasons for thinking that VR may offer useful, safe, and possibly uniquely beneficial spaces in which to encourage and support learning by and with children with autism. The following section takes a look at the extent to which this potential has been realized so far.

RESEARCH EVIDENCE INTO THE EFFECTIVENESS OF VIRTUAL REALITY FOR SUPPORTING THE LEARNING OF CHILDREN WITH AUTISM

This section illustrates some of the applications that have sought to support the learning of children on the autism spectrum and is not intended to be an exhaustive review of the research in this area. The research being carried out can be helpfully contextualized with reference to Gartner's hype cycle (Gartner, n.d.), which describes the typical phases of development for new technologies over time (see Figure 4.1). The cycle proceeds from the early stages when the technology first becomes available, the "technology trigger," and research tends to focus on "proof-of-concept"; moving next to a hype "peak" on the basis of media coverage and a surge of interest; and then to a "trough of disillusionment," where interest fades if early promise of the technologies fails to be delivered. Thereafter, more mature phases for technology implementation follow through the "slope of enlightenment," where benefits of implementation become clearer and better understood; they then move through to a "plateau of productivity," where a technology is considered to have broad appeal and is adopted into mainstream use.

We suggest that VR applications for autism remain a considerable distance away from the plateau of productivity (i.e., mainstream use; cf. Weiss et al., 2009) and probably sit somewhere between the trough of disillusionment and the slope of enlightenment, represented by "less than 5% of the potential audience has adopted fully" and heading toward "methodologies and best practices developing" (Gartner, n.d.). More generally, VR applications may be heading toward or

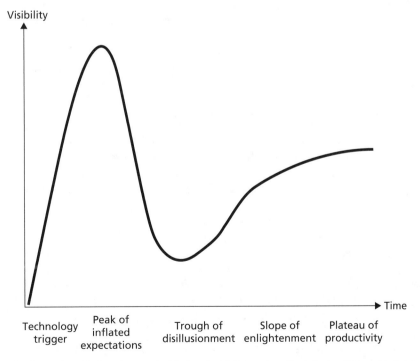

Figure 4.1. Gartner's technology hype cycle. (Gartner [n.d.]. *Research methodologies: Hype cycles.* Retrieved from http://www.gartner.com/technology/research/methodologies/hype-cycle.jsp; adapted by permission.)

sit within more widespread and mainstream use, although notably, Gartner's hype cycle from 2011 positioned VWs within the trough of disillusionment with an estimated 5–10 years before mainstream adoption (Gartner, 2011). Considering the relative position of VR technologies on the cycle is helpful because it is reflected in the research evidence and applications available for scrutiny, and perhaps explains to some extent why the research is still limited so many years after early promise was noted.

Early Applications of Virtual Reality for Autism

Parsons and Cobb (2011) review the evidence of how VR has been applied and evaluated in research focusing on children on the autism spectrum since the 1990s. Early applications of VR technology for children with autism tended to focus on questions of interacting with, responding to, and exploring the environments to see whether children would accept the visual stimuli presented as well as the input and display devices used. For example, Kijima, Shirakawa, Hirose, and Nihei (1994) developed a virtual sandbox in which different children played (including a child with autism) and found that the children were able to use and interact with the system despite minimal instruction about the aim of the task. Strickland (1996, 1998; Strickland et al., 1996) reported case studies of two minimally verbal children with autism using head-mounted displays to experience a VE showing cars moving down a street. Children tracked the movement of the cars by moving their heads in the right direction and verbally labeled objects and the color of objects, although the headset (weighing 8 pounds or 4 kg) was reported to be heavy and the children took some time to accept wearing it. Other early exploratory studies (Brown et al., 1995; Eynon, 1997) showed that people with disabilities, including autism, could focus on scenes presented within VEs and interact meaningfully through the technology. These small-scale studies, usually involving one or two participants, were appropriate for exploring VR technologies in its early stages with hitherto untested groups and provided initial encouragement that applications for autism could be pursued for development.

Social Conventions, Understanding, and Competence

Subsequent projects sought to move beyond questions of basic usability to focus instead on social aspects of VEs, both in terms of social understanding and behaviors and the representation of basic emotions, albeit still on a small scale given the novelty of applying this technology for autism. The AS (Asperger's Syndrome) Interactive project in the United Kingdom developed café and bus VEs for more able children on the autism spectrum based on suggestions from teachers about social contexts that were particularly difficult to teach about in real life (Cobb, Beardon, et al., 2002). Single-user VEs, that is, those allowing only one person to navigate the environment at any time, were developed to support the learning objectives of queuing and finding somewhere to sit. In a single-user environment, a facilitator sits alongside the participant to help him or her interpret the social scene and make decisions about what to do; the VEs are viewed on standard laptops and navigated via a joystick and mouse. Cross-sectional studies comparing the responses of children on the autism spectrum with typically developing children matched for nonverbal IQ, and children with learning disabilities but without autism matched for verbal IQ, showed that children with autism were able to use and interpret the single-user VEs in a similar way to typically developing children (Parsons, Mitchell, & Leonard, 2004), and tended to respond similarly to typically developing children in relation to social conventions within a VE (Parsons, Mitchell, & Leonard, 2005). When asked to explain why they had responded in particular ways, the children with autism were less likely to talk about the social inappropriateness of walking between two people having a conversation compared to typically developing children who commented that they would not do this in real life. Two adolescents on the autism spectrum liked using the VEs and identified other areas of their lives in which they would find them useful (Parsons, Leonard, & Mitchell, 2006). Crucially, Mitchell, Parsons, and Leonard (2007) also showed that four out of six students on the autism spectrum included in a small-scale learning intervention improved their awareness of social conventions and their social reasoning after using the VEs, although their learning was not tested in real-world contexts. This series of studies confirmed the early suggestions of potential with demonstrations of understanding and learning from relatively small-scale comparative studies and a learning intervention.

More recently, Wallace et al. (2010) explored the responses of adolescents with ASD to immersive VR, which physically surrounds the individual. This case involved a "blue room," which shows animations projected onto the walls and ceilings of a screened space and which does not require headsets or goggles for the participant to feel perceptually immersed. Participants experienced street, playground, and school corridor scenes and were asked to rate their feelings of *presence*, a psychological feeling of immersion within the scenes. They reported similar levels of presence as a typically developing group and no negative sensory experiences; as part of the presence measure they also judged the scenes to have a high ecological validity (i.e., represented things or scenes that were lifelike), but the general feedback was that they wanted to be able to interact with the content more.

An important finding from this study by Wallace et al. (2010) was the responses of children with autism compared to those of their typically developing peers when responding to the different social approaches of a child avatar called Danny in a virtual playground. In one scene, Danny was encouraging the participating child to engage in behavior that may get the child into trouble (smoking a cigarette). In the other scene, Danny was acting in a responsible manner (the cigarettes would be handed into the school office). After viewing these scenes, the participating children were asked to rate the two different Dannys using the Social Attractiveness Questionnaire (Nowak & Biocca, 2003). Whereas the typical comparison group rated the badly behaved Danny as significantly less attractive compared to the well-behaved Danny, the children with autism rated the two Dannys almost identically. This finding suggests that immersive VR offers the potential to recreate realistic looking and nonaversive scenes that could form the basis of important social role play; nevertheless, because this study was reported at the proof-of-concept stage of technology development according to Gartner's cycle, this use for VR is likely some way from making it into more widespread and mainstream applications.

The COSPATIAL project (2009–2012) in the United Kingdom, Italy, and Israel sought to implement collaborative technologies that may be more usable and accessible for use in schools than has hitherto been the case. The project developed prototype games using CVEs and Shared Active Surfaces (a table-top multitouch device that allows users to work together on particular tasks) and focused on supporting social conversation and collaboration skills for pairs of children on the autism spectrum in both special and mainstream schools. The project was informed throughout by participatory design methods that closely involved teachers as well as children with and without autism; as well as the theoretical framework of cognitive behavioral therapy, which emphasizes the importance of both thinking and behavior in relation to improving social competence (Bauminger, 2002, 2007a, 2007b). Although yet to report on its formal evaluation of whether children were able to learn effectively using the technologies, the usability studies and pilot studies from the project suggest that children like and can use the games, and that these support communication and cooperation during task completion (Garib-Penna & Parsons, 2011; Millen, Cobb, & Patel, 2010, 2011; Millen, Glover, Hawkins, Patel, & Cobb, 2011; Parsons, Millen, Garib-Penna, & Cobb, 2011).

Facial Expressions, Eye Gaze, and Social Attention

David Moore and colleagues in the United Kingdom (Fabri, Elzouki, & Moore, 2007; Fabri & Moore, 2005; Moore, Cheng, McGrath, & Powell, 2005) explored the understanding and responses of children with autism to basic emotions (e.g., happy, sad, angry, frightened) represented via a humanoid avatar in a simple VE. Although not tested through direct observation, responses from parents to a questionnaire sent with a software demo showed that children with autism understood the different emotions being displayed at a level significantly greater than chance, suggesting that the VEs were a meaningful and understandable way of displaying this information. Perhaps unsurprisingly, given the core difficulties of children with autism in relation to understanding and interpreting the social cues and emotions of people, other groups of researchers have argued that VR could be especially useful for investigating and supporting understanding of facial expressions by children with autism (e.g., Grynszpan et al., 2009; Trepagnier et al., 2005; Trepagnier, Sebrechts, & Peterson, 2002), although results from these studies have not yet been reported. However, Cheng and Ye (2010) reported on the use of a CVE by three children with autism (ages 7–8 years) and found they were motivated by and responded appropriately to the emotional expressions of avatars, again suggesting promise in this area, albeit in the form of a small-scale study.

More recently, Lahiri, Warren, and Sarkar (2011) have reported on the development of their Virtual Interactive Gaze-sensitive Adaptive Response Technology (VIGART) system, which is designed to use eye-tracking technology to monitor gaze behavior and provide dynamic feedback to children on the autism spectrum. In their usability study, the authors found that six adolescents on the autism spectrum accepted the use of the eye tracker, and there was some evidence that the feedback given by the system encouraged an increase in gazing toward the face of the avatar within the VE. This technology is still being developed, and studies comparing responses of children with and without autism would be needed to understand whether, and in what ways, this system could be of use.

Led by Peter Mundy, a similar project, underway at the University of California, Davis in Sacramento, has developed a virtual classroom aimed at supporting the social attention behaviors of high-functioning adolescents on the autism spectrum. In the classroom, virtual peers are designed to fade when giving talks if they are not given enough attention (measured by number of looks) by the user. In an early report (Mundy, 2011) comparing the responses of 18 children (ages 8–16) with high-functioning autism (HFA) with 20 age-matched typically developing children, there was no difference in number of looks to the virtual peer between younger children with HFA and controls, but there was a difference between older children with HFA and controls, with the former group showing significantly fewer looks toward peers than the latter group. Nevertheless, all groups were reported to show significant increases in looking when the virtual peer was faded, suggesting this could be a useful educational tool for encouraging greater social attention of all children generally toward their peers in the classroom. Again, however, this technology remains at the proof-of-concept phase and will require substantial further testing and implementation to determine whether the social attention skills learned within the virtual classroom can ultimately be transferred to a real one.

Mundy's work builds upon the ideas of Rizzo and colleagues, who have developed virtual classrooms over many years for different user-groups. Of particular relevance here is their work with children with attention-deficit/hyperactivity disorder (ADHD; Parsons, Bowerly, Buckwalter, & Rizzo, 2007; Rizzo et al., 2006), which, despite not focusing on children with autism, makes an important contribution to the evidence base given the high comorbidity of ADHD in children diagnosed with ASD (Goldstein & Schwebach, 2004; Simonoff et al., 2008). Their studies have shown that the virtual classroom (experienced through a head-mounted display) can be used to identify and assess attentional difficulties in groups of children with ADHD that yield a good correlation between performance in the VR and standard real-world assessment tests. In addition, there were no negative effects reported by the children with ADHD during their use of the virtual classroom. Thus, much in the same way as the Wallace et al. (2010) study reported earlier, these findings suggest that VEs are not experienced as aversive, can reflect real-world difficulties, and therefore offer the potential for a therapeutic learning environment that can help overcome difficulties in behavior, cognition, or attention.

Extending this idea for young children with autism (ages 5–7 years), another project is seeking to develop VEs to support joint attention behaviors. The ECHOES project in the United Kingdom has developed a 3-D system that is interacted with via a large multitouch LCD display, in which "children interact with intelligent, semiautonomous virtual characters (embodied agents) in socially realistic situations. The agents inhabit a sensory garden ... filled with interactive objects that can become the focus of (joint) attention between them and the child" (Porayska-Pomsta et al., 2012). Like the COSPATIAL project noted earlier, ECHOES has adopted a participatory design process involving practitioners as well as teenagers with ASDs. The formal evaluation of the ECHOES environment is yet to be reported, but early formative evaluations suggest that children find the technology intuitive and engaging and they are able to follow the direction of the gaze and gesture of the virtual character (Alcorn et al., 2011). Once again, there seems to be an encouraging picture of use and engagement emerging from these projects that researchers hope can be translated into usable and accessible technologies for classroom use.

Real-World Safety and Transfer of Skills

Demonstrating the generalizability (transfer) of skills and understanding between virtual and real environments is considered to be the holy grail for much educational research applying VR for children with autism (Parsons, 2007). After all, the hypothesis that the visual similarities between scenarios experienced in VR compared to the real world should make learning generalize more easily is a primary rationale for continuing to pursue this line of research (Parsons & Cobb, 2011; Parsons & Mitchell, 2002); thus, studies that have attempted to answer this question directly are of particular interest. So far, studies have tended to focus on helping children to learn appropriate responses in situations where training in the real world could be more difficult or dangerous; results suggest that at best, transfer of skills is patchy. First, Strickland, McAllister, Coles, and Osborne (2007) developed desktop VEs to teach fire safety skills to young children (3–6-year olds) on the autism spectrum. Tasks within the VE included recognizing smoke, leaving the house swiftly, and waiting outside in an appropriate place. Some children were trained using a PC while at home, and other children were trained on the VE at school. Eleven out of the fourteen children who took part completed the fire safety VE without error, again showing support for the use of VR for learning about new skills and situations, even for very young children. In addition, all children who used the VE at home showed successful transfer of their learning to a real meeting place at their home immediately following use of the VE; children who undertook their VE training at school were also able to answer questions correctly about what they would do in response to a fire (although their behavioral response was not tested directly).

Self, Scudder, Weheba, and Crumrine (2007) also developed a fire safety VR and another for tornado warnings. Eight children with autism (ages 6–12 years) were involved in a study to explore whether skills could be successfully learned and then generalized either via a VR condition or through an alternative "visual treatment" model not involving VR. Self et al. found that children in the VR group tended to learn skills in the VR condition more quickly than did the comparison group; however, although there was evidence that some children could use the VEs appropriately, their responses varied widely and there was limited evidence of unprompted generalization of skills to the real world.

Perhaps most promising so far, though still on a small scale, is a study by Josman, Milika Ben-Chaim, Friedrich, and Weiss (2008), which developed a street-crossing VE to help children with autism learn how to cross the street safely. Six children with autism took part in the study (alongside six typically developing children matched for chronological age). Of these, five were able to learn to use the VE successfully with support within two reasonably short sessions (10–30 minutes), although several participants remained unable to use the VR independently by the end of the study. By contrast, all six of the typically developing children completed all stages of the VE within one 45-minute session, suggesting they were easily able to learn to use the VE (although they were not matched for learning difficulties with the ASD group). Nevertheless, all the children with ASD succeeded in making significant improvements from their starting point in the VE to their final session, showing they were able to learn useful information about street crossing from the VE. Moreover, three out of the six children with autism showed significant improvements from pre- to postintervention in their real-world street-crossing skills, suggesting they could have learned this from the VE.

Concluding Comments on the Evidence Base

Overall, studies applying VR to the field of autism remain small scale and often exploratory in nature, tending to focus on small groups in usability or proof-of-concept studies. This variability reflects the fact that different methods and study designs are appropriate for answering different research questions about technologies at varied stages of development and implementation. It is important to note that Rizzo et al. caution that "prior to any clinical tests, the early application of user-centered design methods is vital for the reasoned development of any VR application" (2006, p. 39). Thus, it would not be appropriate to fund and run a large-scale randomized controlled trial comparing the effectiveness of VR for learning compared to alternative methods and approaches at a stage when our knowledge has been drawn from widely varying studies in terms of participants (age and ability), learning objectives, and scale (e.g., numbers involved, inclusion of comparison or control groups). This may be possible in the future, but only when there has been thorough evaluation of the learning potential and gains made through the application of VR technologies. At present, the current evidence base reinforces the fact that the mainstream uptake and application of these technologies remains, at best, quite a few years away.

There is some evidence of successful learning from VEs among children with different severity of autism symptoms and different age groups, supporting the early optimism of the potential of VR technologies. However, there has not yet been any convincing demonstration on a larger scale that VEs can support transfer of learning from the virtual to the real world, although it should be emphasized that this remains a limitation of many other learning interventions for autism and is not specific to VR (Parsons, Guldberg, et al., 2009, 2011). Moreover, whether or not children transfer their learning from VR to the real world, there is likely to be intrinsic value in the use of VR for supporting learning, and so children's responses to different scenarios and tasks in VR remain of interest in their own right, given the integral part that technologies now play in our everyday lives. Thus, the search for effective learning environments and interventions continues and, on balance, we feel it is appropriate for VR technologies to remain a part of that endeavor. Children seem to be motivated and engaged by the technologies (Mineo, Ziegler, Gill, & Salkin, 2009) and like using them; they can learn new information from them (Mitchell et al., 2007) and also understand them as useful representations of the real world (Parsons et al., 2004). Individuals with autism also seem not to find virtual scenes perceptually aversive (Wallace et al., 2010), suggesting that known sensory sensitivities for some individuals may not impede acceptance of VR technologies. At the very least, we have found no evidence that VR technologies may be harmful to children with autism and at least some evidence that shows it is likely to be of some benefit. Only time will tell whether, and in what ways, VR technologies may make it into mainstream use for supporting learning, social interaction, and communication for children with autism.

CURRENT USE AND DEVELOPMENT OF VIRTUAL ENVIRONMENTS

The potential of VR remains considerable, but the availability and usability of educational applications for use in everyday classrooms is currently limited (Parsons & Cobb, 2011), although recreational games using 3-D imagery are relatively common.

The difference between widely available manufactured 3-D games and VEs for education is that the former are preprogrammed to respond in particular ways and navigation through the games operate according to prespecified pathways, whereas VEs can be navigated in real time and dynamic communication and interactions (i.e., not preprogrammed) can take place. As noted earlier, this openness and flexibility of VR technologies is one of the reasons that makes it appealing for educational use because it can, in theory, be developed to target specific learning needs. This flexibility creates research challenges, however, in terms of how VEs can be designed to support learning effectively; furthermore, there are still many questions that remain to be explored in this area. One of the ways in which researchers have sought to develop useful educational VEs with pedagogical validity and user acceptability is to involve end-users, including teachers and pupils, in their design and development (Millen et al., 2010; Millen, Cobb, et al., 2011; Porayska-Pomsta et al., 2012; Rizzo et al., 2006). Given the lack of established VR use in classrooms, we include below two case studies, each from different projects in which the authors have been involved, to illustrate how users have been included in their design and development.

Case Study 1: Involving the Users in Design Decisions

The Your World project in the United Kingdom was carried out from 2006 to 2008 and adopted an inclusive design approach to VR design involving young people with and without ASDs, as well as parents and other expert stakeholders. The project focused on the use of a blue room, which is "state-of-the-art technology that works by animations being projected onto the walls and ceilings of a screened space, with sophisticated software working to run these screens in synchrony to create a highly immersive and fluid virtual experience" (Wallace et al., 2010, p. 201). The aim of the project was to discuss the ways the blue room could be used specifically in educating children on the autism spectrum, to make recommendations for new virtual environments to be built, and to develop some examples that could then be tested more formally with young people with autism.

The blue room is a large enough space in which users can stand at full height; it is not enclosed at the back, so participants can step in or out very easily (see Figure 4.2). The blue room differs from immersive VR environments that can be experienced through head-mounted devices and/or gloves because, at the time of the project, the screens were not interactive; that is, users could not touch the screens to change or respond to stimuli presented and the scenes were played through from start to finish as users sat or stood within the space. However, the scale of the room coupled with the sophisticated visual displays and powerful sense of movement created through the virtual scenes combined to produce a strong feeling of immersion.

The inclusive design process involved running focus groups to allow different stakeholders (adults and children) to comment on the pros and cons of the blue room as well as make suggestions for specific environments or scenarios that could be developed as part of the project. The groups visited the blue room on different days and were introduced to the project team and the aims of the project; they then spent some time experiencing the technology that showed scenes that had been created for demonstrating the technology to a general audience (e.g., driving along a London street, helicopters flying through a valley, an underwater scene). Following the experience of the scenes, participants were engaged in discussions that asked about their reactions to the blue room,

Figure 4.2. Scenes from the "blue room." (Image on left reprinted by permission from Wallace, S., Parsons, S., Westbury, A., White, K., White, K., & Bailey, A. [2010]. Sense of presence and atypical social judgments in immersive virtual reality: Responses of adolescents with autistic spectrum disorders. *Autism, 14*[3], 199–213. Image on right courtesy of S. Wallace.)

what they thought about the educational potential of the technology, and whether or how they felt it could be designed and developed for the Your World project.

Comments from the Adult Stakeholder Group

The adult group comprised a man with Asperger syndrome, relatives of individuals with autism spectrum diagnoses, and experts in the fields of education, information and communication technologies (ICT), and ASD. Discussion focused on concerns that children on the autism spectrum would have negative reactions to specific sensory stimuli inside the virtual environments and that it would be unsuitable for certain individuals. It was recommended that a stop-button be in the room for the child to press if he or she became upset by certain stimuli. The group suggested that the content of the blue room should be a combination of fantasy environments, to attract and maintain the child's attention, and learning environments that more closely represent or capture real-world scenarios. Some suggested that humanoid avatars may cause some children to respond negatively and that some children would find the technology aversive. It was suggested that possible uses of this technology would be in preparing anxious children for new schools, to desensitize individuals who have specific phobias, and to reduce stress. Road safety was suggested by a number of members as a good potential use for this technology.

Comments from the Students

The student group included five pupils on the autism spectrum and three typically developing pupils (ages 12–15 years) who all attended the same school. Overall, the group felt that the blue room offered a very exciting environment in which they could learn, and they identified many scenarios that could be developed to help them deal with real-world concerns, including fire drills, bullying, phobias, and "stranger danger." They commented that having the screens all around and the sound effects made the scenario feel real for them, though some students felt a little bit dizzy, as if they were on a fairground ride. They suggested that the blue room could help children with sensory and other impairments to see, hear, and experience things they may not otherwise be able to but that it would also be important to maintain realism in the scenes (e.g., not walking through objects). It is of interest, and in contrast to the adult group, that the students were very keen to have human characters represented in the scenes so that they could develop their understanding about the behaviors and intentions of others, particularly around bullying so that they could see how this happens and how negative peer relationships could be avoided or reduced. Suggestions for new environments included conflict resolution and choice making, creating planets and walking on the moon, going shopping, going back in time to experience historical environments, and driving a Formula 1 car.

Development and Application

The Your World project subsequently developed three different scenes based on these recommendations: a street scene to practice safe crossing, a playground scene involving a character with either good or not-so-good intentions, and a school corridor scene that gradually became noisier and busier. Some of the findings are discussed earlier, in the "Social Conventions, Understanding, and Competence" section of this chapter; overall, participants with ASD liked their experiences in the blue room and did not find it aversive, responding similarly to an age-matched typically developing group, contrary to what may have been suggested during the focus groups. Given the understandable cautionary response from the adult stakeholder group and the untested nature of this technology with children with ASDs, it was necessary to proceed carefully with the study. It is notable that whereas the adults were greatly concerned about the responses of the children using the technology, the students themselves were much more positive and were keen to explore it. The students could see how the technology could 1) allow them to explore and have fun and 2) be of use to them; in particular, the students with ASDs knew the areas in which they had social difficulties and specifically made design recommendations in those areas. Similar findings were reported in Parsons et al.'s (2006) case study with two teenagers with ASD who reflected on how the VEs used in that study could be developed in the future to help them with aspects of the real world that they found challenging. This result underscores the importance of involving students with ASDs in the development of technologies because they offer essential insights into potential applicability as well as areas for future development.

Case Study 2: Virtual Worlds in Real-World Classrooms to Support Communication

Newbutt's doctoral research (e.g., Newbutt & Donegan, 2010) examined the benefits VWs can offer users with ASDs and involved a group of U.K. secondary school students (six males and two females, ages 15–16 years) in the design, layout, and format of the VW. The aim of the project was to facilitate communication and collaboration between users and to explore how the group interpreted the VW. Through a structured assessment (Australian Flexible Learning Network, 2006; Konstantinidis, Tsiatsos, & Pomportsis, 2009) of five different VW platforms (Second Life, OpenSim, Active Worlds, OLIVE, and Blue Mars), Second Life appeared to be the most suitable because it included such features as facial expressions, text chat, voice chat, body gestures, and immersive graphics. Second Life also provided a mechanism in which a private island could be set up (for the users of this study only) and could be designed with maximum speed and flexibility. It is important to note, also, that Second Life proved more compatible with computer equipment in schools, requiring a lower specification graphics card and less computer memory.

Once the platform was decided and tested, a final important factor to the infrastructure setup was communication through the school's firewall (a security system that adds a level of protection between computers and the internet that can limit what information may be transmitted). For example, a student using the internet at school would be blocked from various sites deemed inappropriate by the local authority (i.e., school district) as part of its ICT and e-safety policy. Because the VW requires communication to and from its servers in a location outside the school, a request had to be made by school personnel to open various ports in order to allow data back and forth from the VW, with permission eventually granted. The necessity of overcoming this likely common challenge is worth highlighting here for two reasons: 1) Successful implementation of new technologies in real-world settings does not rely only on the research team's "getting it right"; there is significant input required from the settings in which the technology will be used in order to understand the (often unanticipated) real-world constraints that may arise; and 2) child protection and other statutory responsibilities of schools and local authorities have to be taken into account when undertaking such projects because they may have important implications for the availability and compatibility of technology infrastructure.

In developing content for the VW, the project initiated a series of meetings with both the student group and the teachers, and weekly tasks with the students were developed in close communication with the lead ICT teacher at the school to ensure that appropriate educational content was included and was pitched at the right level for the students (challenging enough to be interesting and of value, but not so difficult as to be demotivating). Working with the students meant asking for their feedback on what they would like to see in the VW. Following an iterative design process, the island was ready in terms of design, activities, layout, and testing. Figure 4.3 highlights a corner of the island; the main building is the café, with an information center, log flume ride, and a signpost.

Figure 4.3.   Screenshot of a corner of VIRTAUT (© 2011 N. Newbutt).

The case study took place over a series of sessions for 9 weeks, with each session incorporating planned activities and lasting between 30 minutes and 1 hour. One of the aims of the study was to examine how users with autism represent themselves via an avatar in a VW. It is interesting that most of the students in this case study were largely uninterested in customizing the appearance of their avatars, except for the two female students who were much more conscious of their avatars' appearance and included more detail than did the male participants. Nevertheless, despite an apparent lack of interest in avatar customization, the students with ASD appeared to be engaged in the activities and environments available to them within the VE as evidenced by an observed reduction of stereotypic behaviors in the classroom. During interactions within the VW, students tended to engage in these positive behaviors:

1. *Mirror real-world behaviors.* This behavior seemed to reflect social difficulties in the real world with the autistic students turning their avatar away from their conversational partner so that they did not have to face the partner or make eye contact; note that this is contrary to some of the predictions and rationale made for why VEs would be appealing and less threatening environments for individuals on the autism spectrum (cf. Parsons & Mitchell, 2002).

2. *Increase their communication and conversation with peers compared with within-classroom observation.* This behavior was evidenced by witnessing users who tended not to speak very much within the classroom but had much to say in the VW. In some cases, this provided a chance for teachers to converse with the student for the first time in a detailed and meaningful way, and they were surprised and excited by this opportunity. Other participants reported that the use of a VW provided a helpful mechanism to slow down the communication channels and so provided a chance to think before responding. They also reflected that the VW gave them added confidence and that they "said things they would not normally say in the real world."

3. *Show good collaboration with peers.* This was evident in the behaviors of several pairings of students; they were quickly able (and willing) to collaborate on tasks, for example, by taking notes in the real world while working together in the VW, which involved effective communication throughout.

4. *Identify basic social norms and conform to them.* For example, the students followed pathways; took turns to purchase items from shops; and when "speaking" using text chat and gestures, had reciprocal conversations through the use of these communication mechanisms in the VW.

More generally, all the students were able to navigate, interact with, and understand the functions of the virtual world and were very comfortable, able, and willing to use the text chat as a way to communicate with each other. A few utilized some of the advanced features of communication available to them (e.g., facial expression and gestures), though most did not do this, thereby suggesting that the feature of being able to augment communication with the avatar's facial expressions was less interesting, relevant, or important to them than were other aspects of the communication. Overall, however, the students liked interacting within the VW, and its facilitative effect on communication, especially with teachers, is particularly notable and encouraging. Indeed, the use of the VWs seemed to have an intuitive appeal for the students and the teachers, with clearly observable benefits. This finding aligns strongly with Rizzo and Kim's suggestion that there is an opportunity for VR to become a viable rehabilitation tool that has "widespread intuitive appeal to the public" as well as "academic and professional acceptance" (2005, pp. 136–137).

FUTURE DIRECTIONS

The arguments and optimism for the application of VEs to support learning in children with ASD continues to endure despite there being a rather modest evidence base to date. The powerful intuitive appeal of VEs is apparent, and this will continue to inspire research endeavors and, we hope, willingness by practitioners to implement and explore VE technologies in their classrooms. Indeed, the general ubiquity of technology in classrooms (at least in the United Kingdom), in addition to the popularity of interactive computer games and online VWs, means that there is great scope for VR technologies to play an important role in the future learning experiences of students in schools.

One of the criticisms of the existing VR systems is that they can be too unwieldy and expensive to be of much educational use beyond niche academic research. However, the increasing sophistication of available technologies (e.g., through enhanced capabilities of interactive whiteboards and improvements in desktop computer screens), as well as developments in making interactive surfaces low cost and flexible, means that it should become easier to install interactive technologies in real-world classrooms. However, the challenge is still not just about supplying usable and motivating technologies and software; it is about teachers adopting and accepting technologies and shaping their use by considerable exploration underpinned by sound pedagogic principles (Demetriadis et al., 2003; Hannafin & Savenye, 1993; Mooij & Smeets, 2001). In other words, these types of applications need to be researched in real-world classrooms in order for us to understand how they can best be used to support effective learning; there is a need to concentrate research efforts in this area, with the essential support and involvement of visionary teachers and other practitioners.

When considering the implementation of VEs in the classroom, administrators must from the outset consider the ease of use of the system and any requirements around teacher training. From our experience, teachers can often feel they are underskilled or lack the time to take on what can be seen as a burden of having a new technology in the classroom. Therefore, it may be better for researchers to survey what technologies currently exist in the classroom and how these known or accepted forms of technology could be used or adapted to include virtual teaching environments. As part of the same survey, it would be fruitful to ask teachers what they think could be useful learning applications for VR technology. In addition, when designing new VR technology teaching tools, it will be important to include interfaces and functionality (e.g., drop-down menus; the capacity for uploading files) that are familiar to most people to reduce some of the apprehension of using a new technology. It is also essential to engage with teacher needs and involve various personnel within the school, including the supervisors or principal, as well as teaching assistants, paraprofessionals, and technical staff, so that there is full acceptance of the technology as well as distributed expertise.

When it comes to the person with autism, applied VR research should ideally be aiming for a context where researchers or practitioners are able to assess children's needs and develop personalized VEs accordingly, rather than producing a one-size-fits-all approach to VE design. However, VR technologies may not yet offer sufficient flexibility and ease of use for this goal to be attainable at present, although we hope that such possibilities could be within reach in the near future. One of the real strengths of technology research is the involvement of end-users in the design and development of VR outputs. For example, in the Your World study referred to earlier in the chapter, the children with autism, their parents, and their teachers were at the center of the design process. A separate, unpublished study from Your World saw adolescents with autism interact using Active Worlds (similar to Second Life), two of whom decided to buy site licenses and design their own VWs and share them with others. Many children are skilled and motivated by technology, and so this is a good opportunity for teachers to work with their students on projects that can focus on their students' strengths and to work collaboratively in designing new learning environments. Thus, VR technologies have a real potential for allowing people with autism to take ownership over their spaces and design them to their own needs. It also allows communities to form around people with autism, such as in the case of the Second Life island Brigadoon.

Finally, it is important to emphasize that good research does not always need to include large populations, be quantitatively oriented, or conform to particular research designs that, at least in medicine and related clinical fields, tend to be hierarchically graded as more or less robust irrespective of the quality of research or fidelity of implementation. One of the advantages of the technology field is that a range of research methodologies can be appropriate; for example, in some cases a well-constructed comparative study using survey data may be necessary, whereas in other instances a study may require qualitative feedback on functionality and user perspectives. Nevertheless, it is necessary to highlight the need for a general improvement in the direction and quality of research around VR technology and autism, in particular, through the greater participation and consideration of teachers in the design and application of technologies for learning. We see this participation as essential for developing VE applications through Gartner's slope of enlightenment and into the plateau of productivity, where mainstream use and acceptance is commonplace.

REFERENCES

Alcorn, A., Pain, H., Rajendran, G., Smith, T., Lemon, O., Porayska-Pomsta, K., ... Bernardini, S. (2011, January). Social communication between virtual characters and children with autism. In G. Biswas, S. Bull, J. Kay, & A. Mitrovic (Eds.), *Artificial Intelligence in Education* (pp. 7–14). Berlin, Germany: Springer Berlin Heidelberg.

Andreasen, J.B., Haciomeroglu, E.S., Akyuz, D., Coskun, S., Cristwell, P., & Whitby, P.S. (2008). Teacher training in multiple environments: Microteach versus virtual. *Florida Association of Teacher Education E-Journal, 1*(8), 1–20.

Australian Flexible Learning Network. (2006). *Virtual world checklist.* Retrieved from http://www.virtualworlds.flexiblelearning.net.au/content/section%202.4(checklist).htm

Bauminger, N. (2002). The facilitation of social-emotional understanding and social interaction in high functioning children with autism: Intervention outcomes. *Journal of Autism and Developmental Disorders, 32,* 283–298.

Bauminger, N. (2007a). Group social-multimodal intervention for HFASD. *Journal of Autism and Developmental Disorders, 37,* 1605–1615.

Bauminger, N. (2007b). Individual social-multi-modal intervention for HFASD. *Journal of Autism and Developmental Disorders, 37*, 1593–1604.

Bricken, M. (1991). Virtual reality learning environments: Potentials and challenges. *Computer Graphics, 25*, 178–184.

Brown, D.J., Cobb, S.V.G., & Eastgate, R.M. (1995). Learning in virtual environments (LIVE). In R.A. Earnshaw, J.A. Vince, & H. Jones (Eds.), *Virtual Reality Applications* (pp. 245–252). London, England: Academic Press.

Cheng, Y., & Ye, J. (2010). Exploring the social competence of students with autism spectrum conditions in a collaborative virtual learning environment: The pilot study. *Computers & Education, 54*, 1068–1077.

Cobb, S.V.G. (2007). Virtual environments supporting learning and communication in special needs education. *Topics in Language Disorders, 27*(3), 211–225.

Cobb, S., Beardon, L., Eastgate, R., Glover, T., Kerr, S., Neale, H., ... Wilson, J.R. (2002). Applied virtual environments to support learning of social interaction skills in users with Asperger's syndrome. *Digital Creativity, 13*, 11–22.

Cobb, S.V.G., Neale, H.R., Crosier, J.K., & Wilson, J.R. (2002). Development and evaluation of virtual environments for education. In K. Stanney (Ed.), *Virtual Environment Handbook* (pp. 911–936). Hillsdale, NJ: Erlbaum.

Cobb, S.V.G, & Sharkey, P.M. (2007). A decade of research and development in disability, virtual reality and associated technologies: Review of ICDVRAT, 1996–2006. *International Journal of Virtual Reality, 6*, 51–68.

Cromby, J.J., Standen, P.J., & Brown, D.J. (1996). The potentials of virtual environments in the education and training of people with learning disabilities. *Journal of Intellectual Disability Research, 40*, 489–501.

Dalgarno, B., & Lee, M.J.W. (2010). What are the learning affordances of 3-D virtual environments? *British journal of Educational Technology, 41*(1), 10–32.

DeAngelis, T. (2009). Can Second Life therapy help with autism? *Monitor on Psychology, 40*(8), 40–41. Retrieved from http://www.apa.org/monitor/2009/09/second-life.aspx

Demetriadis, S., Barbas, A., Molohides, A., Palaigeorgiou, G., Psillos, D., Vlahavas, I., ... Pombortsis, A. (2003). "Cultures in negotiation": Teachers' acceptance/resistance attitudes considering the infusion of technology into schools. *Computers & Education, 41*, 19–37.

Dieker, L., Hynes, M., Hughes, C., & Smith, E. (2008). Implications of mixed reality and simulation technologies on special education and teacher preparation. *Focus on Exceptional Children, 40*(6), 1.

Eynon, A. (1997). Computer interaction: An update on the AVATAR program. *Communication*, Summer 1997, 18.

Fabri, M., Elzouki, S.Y.A., & Moore, D. (2007, July). Emotionally expressive avatars for chatting, learning and therapeutic intervention. *Proceedings of the 12th International Conference on Human–Computer Interaction (HCI International), 4552*(3), 275–285.

Fabri, M., & Moore, D.J. (2005, April). The use of emotionally expressive avatars in collaborative virtual environments. L. Hall & S. Woods (Chairs), *Proceedings of Symposium on Empathic Interaction with Synthetic Characters*. Symposium conducted at the Artificial Intelligence and Social Behaviour Convention, 2005 (AISB 2005), University of Hertfordshire, England.

Garib-Penna, S., & Parsons, S. (2011, May). *Collaboration and perspective-taking in collaborative virtual environments by young people with autism spectrum conditions: A pilot study.* Poster presentation and technology demonstration at the International Meeting for Autism Research (IMFAR), San Diego, CA.

Gartner. (n.d.). *Research methodologies: Hype cycles.* Retrieved May 2, 2013 from http://www.gartner.com/technology/research/methodologies/hype-cycle.jsp

Gartner. (2011). *Gartner's 2011 hype cycle special report evaluates the maturity of 1,900 technologies.* Retrieved from http://www.gartner.com/newsroom/id/1763814

Goldstein, S., & Schwebach, A.J. (2004). The comorbidity of pervasive developmental disorder and attention deficit hyperactivity disorder: Results of a retrospective chart review. *Journal of Autism and Developmental Disorders, 34*(3), 329–339.

Goodwin, M.S. (2008). Enhancing and accelerating the pace of autism research and treatment: The promise of developing innovative technology. *Focus on Autism and Other Developmental Disabilities, 23*, 125–128.

Grynszpan, O., Nadel, J., Constant, J., Le Barillier, F., Carbonell, N., Simonin, J., ... Courgeon, M. (2009, June). A new virtual environment paradigm for high functioning autism intended to help attentional disengagement in a social context: Bridging the gap between relevance theory and executive dysfunction. In *Virtual Rehabilitation International Conference, 2009* (pp. 51–58). New York, NY: IEEE.

Hannafin, R.D., & Savenye, W.C. (1993). Technology in the classroom: The teacher's new role and resistance to it. *Educational Technology, 33,* 26–31.

Health Resources and Services Administration (HRSA). (2010). *U.S. Department of Health and Human Services: Health Resources and Services Administration.* Retrieved from http://www.hrsa.gov/ruralhealth/about/telehealth/glossary.html

Joslin, C., Di Giacomo, T., & Magnenat-Thalmann, N. (2004). Collaborative virtual environments: From birth to standardization. *Communications Magazine, IEEE, 42*(4), 28–33.

Josman, N., Milika Ben-Chaim, H., Friedrich, S., & Weiss, P.L. (2008). Effectiveness of virtual reality for teaching street-crossing skills to children and adolescents with autism. *International Journal on Disability and Human Development, 7*(1), 49–56.

Kijima, R., Shirakawa, K., Hirose, M., & Nihei, K. (1994). Virtual sand box: Development of an application of virtual environments for clinical medicine. *Presence: Teleoperators and Virtual Environments, 3,* 45–59.

Konstantinidis, A., Tsiatsos, T., & Pomportsis, A. (2009). Collaborative virtual learning environments: Design and evaluation. *Journal of Multimedia Tools and Applications, 44*(2), 279–304.

Lahiri, U., Warren, Z., & Sarkar, N. (2011). Design of a Gaze-sensitive virtual social interactive system for children with autism. *IEEE Transactions on Neural Systems and Rehabilitation Engineering, 19*(4), 443–452.

Millen, L., Cobb, S.V.G., & Patel, H. (2010, August/September). Participatory design with children with autism: The development of collaborative virtual environments. In P.M. Sharkey & J. Sanchez (Eds.), *Proceedings of the 8th International Conference on Disability, Virtual Reality and Associated Technologies* (pp. 93–102). Viña del Mar/Valparaíso, Chile.

Millen, L., Cobb, S., & Patel, H. (2011). A method for involving children with autism in design. *Proceedings of 10th International Conference on Interaction Design and Children,* June 20–23, 2011 (pp. 185–188). New York, NY: ACM.

Millen, L., Glover, T., Hawkins, T., Patel, H., & Cobb, S. (2011). *Participant representation in use of collaborative virtual environments for conversation with children on the autism spectrum.* Paper presented at the Joint Virtual Reality Conference, September 20–21, 2011, Nottingham, England.

Mineo, B.A., Ziegler, W., Gill, S., & Salkin, D. (2009). Engagement with electronic screen media among students with autism spectrum disorders. *Journal of Autism and Developmental Disorders, 39,* 172–187.

Mitchell, P., Parsons, S., & Leonard, A. (2007). Using virtual environments for teaching social understanding to adolescents with autistic spectrum disorders. *Journal of Autism and Developmental Disorders, 37,* 589–600.

Mooij, T., & Smeets, E. (2001). Modelling and supporting ICT implementation in secondary schools. *Computers and Education, 36,* 265–281.

Moore, D., Cheng, Y., McGrath, P., & Powell, N. (2005). Collaborative virtual environment technology for people with autism. *Focus on Autism and Other Developmental Disabilities, 20,* 231–243.

Mundy, P. (2011). Presentation at the American Psychiatric Association (APA) 2011 Annual Meeting: Symposium 19, No. 4, May 15, 2011. Retrieved from http://www.medscape.com/viewarticle/743343

Murphy, H.J. (1996, June). Virtual reality and persons with disabilities. *Proceedings of the First European Conference on Disability, Virtual Reality, and Associated Technology,* Maidenhead, UK. Retrieved from http://www.icdvrat.rdg.ac.uk/1996/papers/1996_01.pdf

Newbutt, N., & Donegan, M. (2010). A brief review: Assistive technology and autism, a proposal for virtual tools for improved communication and emotional recognition. In C. Crawford, D.A. Willis, R. Carlsen, I. Gibson, K. McFerrin, J. Price, & R.I. Weber (Eds.), *Proceedings of Society for Information Technology & Teacher Education International Conference 2010* (pp. 1998–2003). Chesapeake, VA: AACE.

Nowak, K.L., & Biocca, F. (2003). The effect of the agency and anthropomorphism on users' sense of telepresence, copresence and social presence in virtual environments. *Presence: Teleoperators and Virtual Environments, 12*, 481–494.

Parsons, S. (2007). El uso de entornos virtuales en una terapia de habilidades socials: Resultados actuales y desafíos de futuro [Virtual Environments for social skills intervention: Current findings and future challenges]. In D. García-Villamisar (Ed.), *El autismo en personas adultas. Nuevas perspectivas de futuro* (pp. 47–63). Madrid, Spain: Edit Real Patronato sobre Discapacidad. Ministerio de Trabajo y Asuntos Sociales, Gobierno de España. Depósito legal: M-35365-2007.

Parsons, S., Beardon, L., Neale, H.R., Reynard, G., Eastgate, R., Wilson, J.R., ... Hopkins, E. (2000). Development of social skills amongst adults with Asperger's Syndrome using virtual environments: The AS Interactive project. In Sharkey, P., Cesarani, A., Pugnetti, L., & Rizzo, A. (Eds.), *Proceedings of the 3rd International Conference on Disability, Virtual Reality and Associated Technologies* (pp. 163–170). Reading, United Kingdom: The University of Reading.

Parsons, S., & Cobb, S. (2011). State-of-the-art of virtual reality technologies for children on the autism spectrum. *European Journal of Special Needs Education, 26*(3), 355–366.

Parsons, S., Guldberg, K., MacLeod, A., Jones, G., Prunty, A., & Balfe, T. (2009). *International review of the literature of evidence of best practice provision in the education of persons with autistic spectrum disorders.* National Council for Special Education. http://www.ncse.ie/uploads/1/Autism_Report.pdf

Parsons, S., Guldberg, K., MacLeod, A., Jones, G., Prunty, A., & Balfe, T. (2011). International review of the evidence on best practice in educational provision for children on the autism spectrum. *European Journal of Special Needs Education, 26*(1), 47–63.

Parsons, S., Leonard, A., & Mitchell, P. (2006). Virtual environments for social skills training: Comments from two adolescents with autistic spectrum disorder. *Computers & Education, 47*, 186–206.

Parsons, S., Millen, L., Garib-Penna, S., & Cobb, S. (2011). Participatory design in the development of innovative technologies for children and young people on the autism spectrum: The COSPATIAL project. *Journal of Assistive Technologies, 5*(1), 29–34.

Parsons, S., & Mitchell, P. (2002). The potential of virtual reality in social skills training for people with autistic spectrum disorders. *Journal of Intellectual Disability Research, 46*, 430–443.

Parsons, S., Mitchell, P., & Leonard, A. (2004). The use and understanding of virtual environments by adolescents with autistic spectrum disorders. *Journal of Autism and Developmental Disorders, 34*, 449–466.

Parsons, S., Mitchell, P., & Leonard, A. (2005). Do adolescents with autistic spectrum disorders adhere to social conventions in virtual environments? *Autism, 9*, 95–117.

Parsons, T.D., Bowerly, T., Buckwalter, J.G., & Rizzo, A.A. (2007). A controlled clinical comparison of attention performance in children with ADHD in a virtual reality classroom compared to standard neuropsychological methods. *Child Neuropsychology, 13*, 363–381.

Parsons, T.D., Rizzo, A.A., Rogers, S., & York, P. (2009). Virtual reality in paediatric rehabilitation: A review. *Developmental Neurorehabilitation, 12*, 224–238.

Porayska-Pomsta, K., Frauenberger, C., Pain, H., Rajendran, G., Smith, T., Menzies, R., ... Lemon, O. (2012). Developing technology for autism needs an interdisciplinary approach. *Personal and Ubiquitous Computing, 16*(2), 117–127.

Redfern, S., & Naughton, N. (2002). Collaborative virtual environments to support communication and community in internet-based distance education. *Journal of Information Technology Education, 1*(3), 201–211.

Rizzo, A.A., Bowerly, T., Buckwalter, J.G., Klimchuk, D., Mitura, R., & Parsons, T.D. (2006). A virtual reality scenario for all seasons: The virtual classroom. *CNS Spectrums, 11*(1), 35–44.

Rizzo, A.A., & Kim, G.J. (2005). A SWOT analysis of the field of VR rehabilitation and therapy. *Presence: Teleoperators and Virtual Environments, 14*, 119–146.

Schmidt, C., & Schmidt, M. (2008). Three-dimensional virtual learning environments for mediating social skills acquisition among individuals with autism spectrum disorders. J. Casseell (Chair), *IDC '08: Proceedings of the 7th International Conference on Interaction Design and Children* (pp. 85–88). New York, NY: ACM.

Self, T., Scudder, R.R., Weheba, G., & Crumrine, D. (2007). A virtual approach to teaching safety skills to children with autism spectrum disorder. *Topics in Language Disorders, 27*, 242–253.

Simonoff, E., Pickles, A., Charman, T., Chandler, S., Loucas, T., & Baird, G. (2008). Psychiatric disorders in children with autism spectrum disorders: Prevalence, comorbidity, and associated factors in a population-derived sample. *Journal of the American Academy of Child & Adolescent Psychiatry, 47*(8), 921–929.

Strickland, D. (1996). A virtual reality application with autistic children. *Presence: Teleoperators and Virtual Environments, 5*, 319–329.

Strickland, D. (1998). Virtual reality for the treatment of autism. In G. Riva (Ed.), *Virtual reality in neuro-psycho-physiology* (pp. 81–86). Amsterdam, Netherlands: Ios Press, 1998.

Strickland, D., Marcus, L.M., Mesibov, G.B., & Hogan, K. (1996). Brief report: Two case studies using virtual reality as a learning tool for autistic children. *Journal of Autism and Developmental Disorders, 26*(6), 651–659.

Strickland, D., McAllister, D., Coles, C.D., & Osborne, S. (2007). An evolution of virtual reality training designs for children with autism and fetal alcohol spectrum disorders. *Topics in Language Disorders, 27*, 226–241.

Trepagnier, C.G. (1999). Virtual environments for the investigation and rehabilitation of cognitive and perceptual impairments. *NeuroRehabilitation, 12*, 63–72.

Trepagnier, C.Y., Sebrechts, M.M., Finkelmeyer, A., Coleman, M., Stewart, W., Jr., & Werner-Adler, M. (2005). Virtual environments to address autistic social deficits. *Annual Review of CyberTherapy and Telemedicine, 3*, 101–107.

Trepagnier, C., Sebrechts, M.M., & Peterson, R. (2002). Atypical face gaze in autism. *Cyberpsychology & Behavior, 5*(3), 213–217.

Wallace, S., Parsons, S., Westbury, A., White, K., White, K., & Bailey, A. (2010). Sense of presence and atypical social judgments in immersive virtual reality: Responses of adolescents with autistic spectrum disorders. *Autism, 14*(3), 199–213.

Weiss, P.L., Battocchi, A., Bauminger, N., Cobb, S., Gal, E., Parsons, S., & Zancanaro, M. (2009). *Best practices on technologies for social competence.* Deliverable 1.2 from the COSPATIAL project (Grant Agreement No. 231266).

Using Therapeutic Robots to Teach Students with Autism in the Classroom

Exploring Research and Innovation

▪ ▪

Katharina I. Boser, Corinna E. Lathan, Charlotte Safos,
Rita Shewbridge, Carole Samango-Sprouse, and Marek Michalowski

Over the past 20 years, robots have been introduced as "social agents" for adults and children in a variety of contexts, including adult group homes, day care centers, clinical centers, and some classrooms. Research has shown the potential of robots to be used as companions, mentors, and educators as the students engage and are motivated by the robots (Diehl, Schmitt, Villano, & Crowell, 2012; Robins, Dautenhahn, Te Boekhorst, & Billard, 2005; Robins, Dickerson, Stribling, & Dautenhahn, 2009; Scassellati, 2005, 2007; Stanton, Kahn, Severson, Ruckert, & Gill, 2008). In this chapter we discuss several types of research findings where robots have been shown to have unique outcomes with typically developing children and children with autism spectrum disorder (ASD). New tools are being developed for students with autism, of which sensors and robots show the greatest promise (Goodwin, 2008). Our purpose in writing this chapter is to allow teachers to imagine contexts in which robots might supplement, improve, and enhance their teaching of students with special needs. In particular, we focus on the potential for robots to allow greater independence and differentiation for students with ASD in classrooms that employ the universal design for learning (UDL) approach, a set of principles for developing curriculum that gives all individuals the opportunity to learn (see CAST, http://www.cast.org/udl).

There are several reasons why robots might be of special benefit to teachers working with students who have autism. Robots may assist students with ASD in four specific areas:

1. Cueing and joint attention

2. Social skills learning

3. Language and communication

4. Motor skills learning

In addition to assisting the student with these key areas, robots can be beneficial to the teacher and can be used as an embodied social agent, assisting with communicating ideas, cueing, and providing a model for the student on an ongoing basis. Teachers are often bogged down by the need to collect data while teaching; robots may be of assistance by providing ongoing assessment and evaluating how students are behaving in realistic environments and in real time.

Before venturing into the world of robots, we must first clearly define what we mean by a robot. When defining robots, we can imagine several different kinds of robotic devices: robots for manufacturing, robotic vacuum cleaners, and interactive toys. As referred to in this chapter, robots can loosely be defined as objects that can be remotely controlled or programmed to be fully or semiautonomous and self-controlled through sensors and actuators. Under this definition, any object that is programmable—for example, a small consumer off-the-shelf microcontroller such as an Arduino[1] with attached sensing capabilities (i.e., light, audio, motors)—can be seen as a robot.

Here, we introduce some of the robots that we explore in this chapter. Keepon Pro (Figure 5.1), developed by BeatBots, is a social therapeutic robot that has been used in various studies with children with ASD to facilitate social development and assist with imitation, eye gaze, and joint attention. My Keepon, based on Keepon Pro, is an entertaining dancing robot that includes a built-in microphone and touch sensors.

CosmoBot (Figure 5.2), developed by AnthroTronix, Inc., is a robot for use with children with and without disabilities to promote educational and therapeutic activities. CosmoBot has been tested with children with a range of abilities, including children with autism, Down syndrome, cerebral palsy, muscular dystrophy, apraxia, neurodevelopmental disorders, and language development disorders, as well as children with neurotypical disorders.

NAO, developed by Aldebaran Robotics, is an autonomous, humanoid robot that can be used in a variety of contexts that range from education to entertainment.

Figure 5.1.   My Keepon, developed by BeatBots. (Image courtesy of Beatbots LLC.)

---

[1]Open-source prototyping platform (http://www.arduino.cc).

Figure 5.2. CosmoBot, developed by AnthroTronix. (Image courtesy of AnthroTronix, Inc.)

NAO has been employed by researchers to investigate its use with older adults and in teaching students about science, technology, engineering, and math (STEM) through programming. NAO has also been used in social skills therapy for children with ASD (Diehl, 2013).

Kismet is a robot developed at MIT in the 1990s. Kismet simulates emotion through various facial expressions, vocalizations, and movements. Facial expressions are created through movements of the ears, eyebrows, eyelids, lips, jaw, and head.

KASPAR (Kinesics and Synchronization in Personal Assistant Robotics; Figure 5.3) is a minimally expressive, therapeutic robot developed by Dr. Kerstin Dautenhahn, Professor of Artificial Intelligence, and Coordinator of the Adaptive Systems Group at the University of Hertfordshire's School of Computer Science. KASPAR has been used in research to improve the social interaction and communication skills of autistic children (Dautenhahn & Werry, 2005; Robins et al., 2005; Robins et al., 2009).

Bandit (Figure 5.4) was designed by researchers at the University of Southern California. The child-sized metallic robot has humanlike features: a movable mouth, archable eyebrows, and camera eyes (Feil, Seifer, & Mataric, 2005, 2009).

Figure 5.3. KASPAR, developed at the University of Hertfordshire. (Image courtesy of Adaptive System Research Group, University of Hertfordshire.)

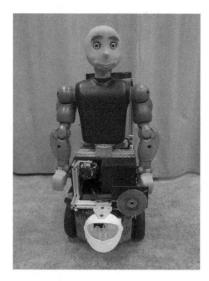

Figure 5.4. Bandit, developed at the University of Southern California. (Image courtesy of David Feil-Seifer.)

Tito and Roball (Figures 5.5 and 5.6) are mobile robots that were developed by researchers at the Université de Sherbrooke in Quebec, Canada. Tito was designed to study how mobile robots could facilitate reciprocal interactions, such as imitation with autistic children. Roball, although not a humanoid robot, is an autonomous robotic ball that has been used in studies to evaluate the influence of autonomous motion on children between 12 and 18 months of age (Michaud & Caron, 2002; Michaud & Theberge-Turnel, 2002; Michaud et al., 2005).

Figure 5.5. Tito, developed at Universite de Sherbrooke in Quebec, Canada. (Image courtesy of François Michaud.)

Figure 5.6. Roball, developed at the Universite de Sherbrooke in Quebec, Canada. (Image courtesy of François Michaud.)

Muu (Figure 5.7) was developed by Michio Okada, of Advanced Telecommunication Research (ATR), an international institute. The robot Muu focuses on social bonding with humans. The character also works as an embodied interface that mediates social bonding that people establish in everyday conversations. Christoph Bartneck extended Muu with the ability to express emotions and named it emotional Muu, or eMuu (Miyamota, Lee, Fujii, & Okada, 2005).

Pleo is an animatronic toy dinosaur that moves autonomously and responds to its environment and users touch; for example, it can be fed and petted. Pleo has been used in a variety of studies ranging from speech prosody to studying individuals' social attachment to artificial pets (Kim, Leysberg, Short, Paul, & Scassallati, 2009; Scassellati, 2005).[2]

It is our goal in this chapter to inspire teachers to work with engineers (and maybe some high-functioning students) to create and program their own robots using relatively accessible and inexpensive technology. We include a section at the end of this chapter with programming and technology resources available for this purpose. We are confident that as you are reading this chapter, some enterprising student has already designed the right robot for use in your classroom.

Figure 5.7. Muu, developed by Michio Okada. (Image courtesy of Michio Okada.)

---

[2]Note that the only commercially available robots from the foregoing list are My Keepon, NAO, and Pleo.

UNIVERSAL DESIGN FOR LEARNING

The UDL approach attempts to remove barriers to learning through applying three principles dealing with forms of representation, expression, and engagement. (Refer to Chapter 2 for more details from the developers of UDL, CAST.) Robots can fulfill each of these areas through their multimedia and sensory functions that can be specifically tailored for each child with ASD and allow independence. Interactive robots produce a response in children with ASD that may surpass what can be achieved through human therapists alone (Kim et al., 2009; Scassellati, Admoni, & Matarić, 2012). Through appropriate development of targeted treatment, the robot creates a means of engagement and learning previously unavailable to educators with this population of children. When we envision robots in the classroom, we often think of such robotics programs as LEGO or VEX, which teach students how to program and engineer moving objects using basic parts. In the classroom with students that have ASD, we will want to consider "social" robots; that is, human and animal-like devices that interact with the user in physical and nonphysical ways to cause an effect or to cue the student regarding his or her behavior.

Only a handful of robots have been tested, mostly in laboratory learning settings to determine the basic affinity children with ASD might have for them relative to interacting with only a human therapist or parent. In the next section we will highlight existing research studies with robots that have shown results in the four primary domains noted earlier: cueing and joint attention, social skills learning, language and communication, and motor skills learning. The research includes findings related to children with neurotypical disorders and ASDs.

Cueing and Joint Attention

In this section we provide some documentation of studies that support the idea of robots eliciting greater participation in the learning process.

Robots Can Naturally Motivate Students with Autism to Learn   In order to learn effectively, students need to be able to pay attention in class and stay on task. Those individuals who work with students with ASD begin with typical attention-eliciting tasks focusing on getting the student to follow eye gaze by finger pointing and turning the student's head and therefore his or her attention to the learning task. Teachers often need to build in rewards for attending and staying on task. Robots can be harnessed to increase these important social interactions because the student with ASD is more likely to watch and be interested in a robot (Dautenhahn & Werry, 2004; Diehl et al., 2012; Scassellati et al., 2012; Werry & Dautenhahn, 1999; Werry, Dautenhahn, Ogden, & Harwin, 2001). The robot itself can become the reward for the behavior a teacher wants to elicit in the student (Costa, Santos, Soares, Ferreira, & Moreira, 2010; Costa et al., 2009). A difficulty for persons with ASD is physiological hyperarousal (e.g., as evidenced by persistent increased galvanic skin response, heart rate, or breath rate; Goodwin et al., 2006).

Findings of impairments to the autonomic system in ASD may shed some light on why interactions with humans can be so difficult for this population, leading to avoidance or even self-stimulatory or self-injurious behaviors (Goodwin et al., 2006; Hirstein, Iverson, & Ramachandran, 2001; Tochi & Kamio, 2003). The problem with this type of reaction is that atypical behaviors result in a lack of interaction with others; thus, children with ASD often do not get the practice with others they require to learn joint attention skills. However, recent studies using robots in a therapeutic capacity have demonstrated the reduction of self-stimulatory, repetitive, or stereotyped behaviors associated with hyperarousal in children with ASD (Duquette, Michaud, & Mercier, 2007). This result is a promising indicator that the robot acts as a calming device, given its predictability, reducing hyperarousal. The Duquette et al. study (2007) also demonstrated the child's preference for the robot in lieu of animated characters or mobile objects and toys, a finding that replicates other research (Breazeal, 2003a; Kidd & Breazeal, 2006). Preference for the robot over animated objects or toys indicates the intrinsic value of the more human-like robot for interaction in this population. In addition, robots can easily pace the degree of interaction and are themselves data-tracking devices (e.g., built-in camera, timing mechanisms). This combination of findings suggests that the robot is a perfect therapeutic device to initiate the early skills necessary as a foundation for more complex ones.

Research of students with autism has shown that they are more likely to attend to a robot than to a teacher and will spend more time with the robot than with other types of toys or animated devices (Dautenhahn & Werry, 2004; Diehl et al., 2012; Robins et al., 2005; Robins et al., 2009). One study that included CosmoBot (Boser et al., 2011) demonstrated that less verbal students seem to enjoy and are drawn to the more machinelike CosmoBot, verbalizing and engaging with the large eyes on the robot. In contrast, animal-like animatronic toys included in the study were less engaging to students on the spectrum even though their typically developing counterparts enjoyed and spoke to them. It seems some of the random natural and less predictable behavior of these toys made them less appealing to students with ASD. No such issues were observed in typically developing children with the same ability level. The fact that students with autism are specifically drawn to machinelike, systematic devices has been pointed out by other researchers working with this population. Simon Baron-Cohen and the team at the Autism Research Centre at the University of Cambridge developed the "Transporters" (see Chapter 9) and found that students with ASD can be taught to recognize and imitate facial emotion using the mediator of a mechanical or computerized object, in this case a train with a face on the front. Baron-Cohen argues that people with ASD prefer systematic knowledge and patterns to the less predictable emotional connection with others. They have a preference for more systematic, rather than empathetic, information processing. Robots may appeal to this systematic preference because they can be designed to mimic or reproduce human qualities and biological movements (Braezael, 2004; el Kaliouby, Picard, & Baron-Cohen, 2006; Pierno, Mari, Lusher, & Castiello, 2008; Pioggia et al., 2008). Keepon Pro is designed with an appearance somewhere between the minimalism of such robots as Roball or Muu and the anthropomorphism of such robots as Kismet or KASPAR. This design is motivated by a belief that the basic traits common to people and animals (e.g., lateral symmetry, two eyes) are important cues to the potential for social agency. At the same time, keeping the appearance simple so that it is aligned with the robot's behavioral capabilities is important for helping people understand and feel comfortable with the robot's behavior. Keepon has been involved in several years of longitudinal studies, with over 400 recorded hours of interaction between Keepon and hundreds of children. Keepon has been observed to serve as a pivot for social interaction between children with ASD and their peers and caregivers; as a mediator for simplified interaction between therapist, teleoperators, and children with ASD; and as a tool for facilitating and recording these social interactive behaviors (Kozima, Michalowski, & Nakagawa, 2008).

Robots Can Act as Social Mediators in Human-to-Human Interaction Engagement between students increases when a robot acts as the intermediary (Kozima et al., 2005; Feil Seifer & Mataric, 2008; Feil-Seifer et al., 2009). This engagement could take place in environments where students are playing together with a robot or where they are encouraged to build or program a robot themselves. Robots can be used to facilitate turn taking, joint attention, and skills sharing in students or used in conditions requiring forced collaboration, that is, at times when some event does not happen unless there is shared collaboration. Forced collaboration also ties into facilitating teamwork, a 21st century skill that can be aided by the use of a robot.

Earlier studies of children with ASD with low verbal skills have demonstrated an increase in social behaviors in the presence of a robot as measured by imitation, touch, proximity, and gaze (Michaud & Caron, 2002, Robins, Dautenhahn, & Dubowski, 2006; Robins, Dickerson, Stribling, & Dautenhahn, 2004). The preference of children on the autism spectrum for, and increased social behavior with, robots arises from their social simplicity, predictability, and responsiveness (Robins et al., 2004). Results from a study showed seven of ten children with ASD demonstrated greater interest in teleoperated robots than in animatronic toys. The majority of these subjects also demonstrated greater imitative behaviors with their peers in the context of the robots. Seven of the ten children with ASD turned or walked away from mechanical animals. A number of different types of social interactions were observed with the two robots (smiles, vocalizations, gestures, gaze). As verbal abilities increased, engagement with the animatronic animals increased (Boser et al., 2011).

Social-Skills Learning

The field of socially assistive robotics (SAR) has risen out of a recognition that there is a need for assistive technologies that support the increasing numbers of persons with lifelong conditions, including diabetes, autism, obesity, and cancer (Feil-Seifer & Matarić, 2005, 2009). The field's efforts are in developing affordable technologies for monitoring, coaching, and motivating from both a cognitive and physical level, addressing the range of needs from prevention to rehabilitation.

Robots Can Help Teach Social Skills and Assist in Social Situations The key innovation in SAR is developing systems capable of assisting users through social, rather than physical, interactions resulting in various behavioral therapy applications. The field focuses on using data from wearable sensors, cameras, or other means of perceiving the user's activity in order to provide the robot with information about the user that allows the machine to appropriately encourage and motivate.

It may seem counterintuitive to assume a robot would be the best social mediator for a child with social impairments; however, there are several arguments to address why robotic devices can serve to bridge the gap between the complex and unpredictable world of human social behavior and the safe, predictable world of simple toys in ASD (Duquette et al., 2007). Persons with ASD have described the difficulty they have with the social world (Grandin, 1995), including the stress and high levels of arousal that social situations incur (Grandin, 1992). The strategies they have adopted involve decreasing stimulation and complexities and learning explicit rules, for example, "to smile when someone smiles at you." Relying on scripts and simplified social rules can be adaptive, described as "a way of decreasing environmental variance so that the social world can be reduced more effectively to a regular, predictable, and systemizable set of scripts" (Baron-Cohen & Belmonte, 2005, p. 116).

Robins et al. (2004) examined turn taking and imitation with robots and children with autism. This study allowed children to improve in simple contexts and then slowly increased the unpredictability of the robot's actions. Robins et al. (2006) found that children with ASD learned to interact with the experimenter or a second person by means of the robot. For example, when the experimenter did not mimic the child correctly using the robot as a puppet, the child sought out the person behind the robot to correct him, thereby initiating social engagement. The approach described here builds on the robot as a coparticipant in the human interactions to allow for the more immediate transfer of behaviors with the robot to occur in natural situations with other humans and also to allow the robot to act more as a mediator than as a substitute for another human. Such transfer of social skills has been observed in research using the diamond touch table to facilitate collaborative games and storytelling between children with autism and their peers (Gal et al., 2009). Gal et al. (2009) used a paradigm of "forced collaboration," where the technology does not produce an effect unless social interaction occurs, seemed to force students into using sharing, turn taking, and interactive skills that transferred to playing without the table as well.

A number of research projects in the field of embodied interaction have developed robots explicitly for interaction with children. For example, Kismet (Breazeal, 2003a) is a pioneering example of a "sociable robot." Kismet engaged people in natural and intuitive face-to-face interaction by exchanging a variety of social cues, such as gaze direction, facial expression, and vocalization. Kismet's elicitation of caretaking behavior from people (including children) enabled a form of socially situated learning with its human caregivers.

Scassellati (2007), who has been building and using social robots for the study of children's social development, observed children with ASD interacting with a robot with an expressive face and found that they showed positive protosocial behaviors (e.g., touching, vocalizing, smiling at the robot) that were generally rare in their everyday life. Michaud and Caron (2002) and Michaud and Theberge-Turnel (2002) have devised a number of mobile and interactive robots, including Roball and Tito, and have observed interactions with children with ASD in order to explore the design space of child–robot interaction for fostering self-esteem. Okada and colleagues (Miyamota et al., 2005) developed a creaturelike robot, Muu, to observe how autistic children spontaneously collaborate with the robot in such shared activities as arranging colored blocks and found increased interest and engagement with this robot as well as shared social activities.

Robots Can Provide Sequenced and Individualized Social Learning

Teachers who work with students on the autism spectrum need to monitor the ongoing abilities of their students, making adjustments to items learned as old items are mastered while also checking for maintenance of already learned materials. There are data management technologies available to correlate specific task data with individual education plan goals and outcomes (see Chapter 12). Several papers have discussed the benefits of using technology that is comfortable to the student (due to its "predictability") that can automatically adjust to meet the student's need (Belmonte et al., 2004; Liu, Conn, Sarkar, & Stone 2007, 2008). Although computer software can also achieve this goal for discrete, academic subjects material (e.g., Vizzle, iPad apps), a robot can gradually adjust its level of social interaction to modify the level of social stimuli provided. By adopting a robot in social interaction learning, we can gradually teach a social skill in step-wise fashion, for example, starting with machinelike behavior and gradually introducing more humanlike behaviors, allowing one sense to be explored at a time. Robots can be programmed to deliver just the right kind of reward after a behavior is exhibited and cue appropriately to elicit the behavior. These rewards and cues need to gradually adapt to the child's learning, something that is at times difficult for a therapist to incorporate during the learning session because the assessment of learning may take time to gather; in contrast, the robot has the potential to immediately and automatically gather this information and use it to provide the appropriate learning stimulus and response.

Robots provide an opportunity for teachers to implement tools that can develop cognition, speech, and perception in a manner that is preferred, familiar, and supportive to the child with ASD. Robots can be a special social partner that initially allows for the needed development of social interaction and play in a medium that promotes engagement that is not observed with humans. Robotics used efficiently allows for the transition of these same skills to human interaction quickly and appropriately (Bird, Leighton, Press, & Heyes, 2007; Cook, Adams, Encarnacao, & Alvarez, 2012). Diehl (2013) from the University of Notre Dame has recently reported promising results using the NAO robot with a group of nineteen 6–13-year-old students with ASD as a "cotherapist" in applied behavioral analysis (ABA) training of social skills. Table 5.1 lists ways in which robots can assist children of different ages and developmental levels to learn basic problem solving and abstract cognitive skills, which are necessary for higher-order social interaction.

Robots Can Assist with Language and Communication Skills   Interactive robotics have been created in various shapes, colors, and forms to foster socially appropriate behaviors and evoke improvement in executive function. This technological platform allows flexibility and creates educational scenarios that may be individually tailored to the child's learning style and specific interests. This adaptability allows teaching in a manner that is both appropriate and uniquely engaging for a child with ASD. In addition, the predictability of the robot, the consistency of the speech patterns, and the simplicity of verbal commands provide a uniformity and obviousness that facilitate learning and generalization in children with ASD (Gillesen, Barakova, Huskens, & Feijs, 2011; see Table 5.2).

Table 5.1. Robot-related skills

	Skill	Definition for robot use	Age considerations for children developing typically	LEGO robot examples
0	No interaction	Child displays no interest in the robot or its actions	NA	NA
1	Cause and effect (causality)	Understanding the relationship between a switch and a resulting effect	<3 years: action is in switch, tried to use disconnected switches >4 years: understood switch made robot move	Use switch to drive robot, knocking over blocks with robot, drawing circles on paper by holding a switch down and turning robot
2	Inhibition (negation)	An action can be negated by its opposite; two opposite effects such as on and not on	4 years: began to understand that switch release stops robot	Releasing switch to stop robot
3	Binary relations (binary logic)	Two opposite effects such as on and not on	5–6 years: understood rocker switch had two opposite effects	2 switches turning robot right or left or go and stop
4	Sequencing (coordination of multiple variable spatial concepts–multiple dimension)	Movement in more than one dimension to meet a functional goal	5 years: could fine-tune a movement by reversing to compensate for overshoot, etc.	Moving roverbot to a specific location in two dimensions
5	Symbolic play	Make believe with real, miniature, or imaginary props	6 years: child ID action in robot not switch, planning of tasks is possible	Interactive play with pretense (i.e., serving at tea party, exchanging toys with friends, pretending to feed animals—all using robot)
6	Problem solving	Problem-solving with a plan, not trial and error, generation of multiple possible solutions	7 years: designed robot and thought about coordinated effects, planning was possible, can understand simple programs and debug	Changing strategies to solve a problem such as avoid an obstacle, changing task to meet the child's own goal, simple programming

Source: Cook, Adams, Encarnacao, and Alvarez (2012).

Motor Learning

Although the core features of ASD are well recognized, the more subtle, yet pervasive, dysfunction of motor abilities is often overlooked or misunderstood. Associated symptomatology includes gross and fine motor deficits with motor dysfunction evident as early as the first year of life, which continues throughout the child's lifetime (Carper, Moses, Tigue, & Courchesne, 2002; Herbert et al., 2002, 2004; Samango-Sprouse, 2007). It is these motor dysfunction and planning deficits that are intriguing and very responsive to interactive robotics as a form of intervention.

Table 5.2.   Language and social skills

Learning objectives and description of robot behavior:

1. Imitation: Robot displays arm movements that have to be imitated by the student.

2. Imitation, joined attention, turn taking: This is the same as #1, except with the added dimension of turn taking.

3. Asking for help: Robot asks for help on a task and student needs to ask if the offered help is useful.

4. Self initiation: Robot states it can do a cool move (e.g., a dance). Student is then provoked to inquire about the move.

5. Problem solving: Robot asks help from the client. Offers solutions and asks if this is the right solution.

6. Asking questions, self-management: Robot engages in a simple dialogue with the student about different topics. Student takes leading role in what to talk about.

7. Sharing, turn taking: Student and robot play a game where blocks have to be colored using a magic wand. Players need to share the wand, using proper turn taking.

8. Evaluation of a movement: Robot wants to learn to wave like the student. Student needs to coach the robot to learn this move.

9. Introducing yourself, introducing the robot: Robot greets student and asks for his or her name. Robot then becomes sad, and student is provoked to inquire what is wrong. Robot states it does not have a name yet and offers to think of a name.

Source: © 2013 IEEE. Reprinted with permission from Gillesen, J.C., Barakova, E.I., Huskens, B.E., & Feijs, L.M. (2011). From training to robot behavior: Towards custom scenarios for robotics in training programs for ASD. *Proceedings of the IEEE International Conference on Rehabilitation Robotics, 20,* 1–7.

Robots Can Assist with Motor Learning and Imitation   Motor movements naturally involve planning and an internal model of the intended external action. Planning is one of the more complicated operations for humans. It is an intricate process and requires the development of a specific, premeditated action, surveillance of the identified action, and alteration of the existing plan if necessary, and then the execution of the action. Numerous studies demonstrate deficiencies in planning and flexibility across a variety of motor and cognitive tasks in children with ASD (Hill, 2004; Ozonoff & Jensen, 1999; Pennington & Ozonoff, 1996). Other studies have focused on impairments in action imitation (Mostofsky et al., 2006; Williams, Whiten, & Singh, 2004). Some studies have found improvements in basic action imitation for children with autism using robots (Pierno et al., 2008; Pioggia et al., 2008). The AuRoRa project (Robins et al., 2004, 2005, 2009) reported that even simple mobile robots provided autistic children with a relatively repetitive and predictable environment that encouraged spontaneous and relaxed interactions (e.g., chasing games). Billard, Robins, Nadel, and Dautenhahn (2007) developed a doll-like anthropomorphic robot, Robota, for mutual imitative play with autistic children; Robins et al. (2004) analyzed two children playing with Robota and observed mutual monitoring and cooperative behavior.

Robots Can Promote Science, Technology, Engineering, and Mathematics
Students with ASD, while often excellent with visual and numeric aspects of STEM areas, do not thrive in the areas of problem solving, verbal or abstract number abilities, and the collaborative aspects necessary for developing technological skills in the 21st century classroom. Although engineering and math can be a draw for students on the spectrum, these students may not be able to complete the mathematics areas that are their strengths because they often cannot complete the math sequence. For example, Temple Grandin often bemoans the fact that she was not allowed to continue through to trigonometry because she could not master the highly verbal and abstract areas of algebra. Students with autism need to be drawn into these areas by focusing

on their areas of strength in math and science and providing support necessary for their planning and verbal, attention, and executive function needs. Robots could provide such support by helping students visualize, enabling interactive engagement in the curriculum, and providing ongoing updates and assessment of skills, thereby allowing repetition necessary for students to engage in the content area.

Combining robotics with computerized instruction that is engaging, compelling, and easily adapted to the individual can meet part of the need for individualized instruction in life skills. Gamelike interactions that effectively address learning goals are appropriate to the cognitive levels of learners, meet learners' needs for materials that look and feel appropriate to their age and self-image (including selection of an avatar), and have considerable potential to improve the effectiveness of life skills preparation. In addition, as computer-based games, they can be used both in the school context and at home, with benefit to generalization of the skills addressed. Computers are intrinsically compelling for young children and can provide a source of motivation for many children who are typically difficult to engage. Increasingly, young children observe adults and older children working on computers, and they want to do so, too. Children get interested because they can make things happen with computers (National Association for the Education of Young Children, 1998) and the interaction with sounds and graphics keeps the children's attention. Children also tend to enjoy the control they have over the computer.

Computer programs such as Google SketchUp have shown to be engaging for high-functioning children on the spectrum (Wright et al., 2011). In addition, for some children on the spectrum, especially those who are nonverbal, SketchUp serves as a way to communicate, allowing them to share their thoughts through crafted images. Some children learn life skills that help them to achieve educational and career goals they might not have even aspired to before SketchUp. Visual programs like SketchUp can provide students with new methods for creating visual content and sharing it with their peers in the classroom. TinkerCAD provides a user-friendly interface that is accessible in a browser to develop 3-D computer-aided design models that can then be printed by a 3-D printer, thereby enabling 3-D design to be brought into the physical world without expensive software or high-technology skill.

Developmentally appropriate software engages children in creative play, mastery learning, problem solving, and conversation. The children control the pacing and the action. They can repeat a process or activity as often as they like and experiment with variations. They can collaborate in making decisions and share their discoveries and creations.

Robotics is one of the latest technological innovations, and a humanoid robot is an ideal learning tool for classes at all levels. Several educational researchers have reviewed various robotics kits, including NAO, VEX, and Lego Mindstorms, among others, for their ability to teach engineering and STEM skills (Beer & Chiel, 1999; Catlin & Blamires, 2010; Gura & King, 2007; Johnson, 2003; Ribeiro, Coutinho, & Costa, 2011). While most recently shown to demonstrate positive results as a therapeutic device for students with autism (Diehl, 2013), the robotics company Aldeberan, developers of the robot NAO, has developed curricula to teach robotics and programming in the general classroom. Robots allow students to connect theory with practice and discover a wide range of robotics-related fields, such as computer science, engineering, and mathematics. Students gain hands-on experience using a robot such as NAO, through which, when used in the lab, they discover such exciting topics as locomotion, grasping, audio and video signal processing, as well as voice recognition (see http://www.valdeberan.com). A software program called Choreographe allows students to program NAO to do what they would like it to do in an easy-to-learn programming environment. By merging sciences like mathematics, physics, and psychology, robots provide cutting-edge innovations that all engineering students need to master. Thus, robotics is the perfect tool for teaching STEM subjects. The NAO robot also allows teachers to integrate teamwork, project management, problem solving, and communication skills in a stimulating setting. NAO offers the flexibility for developing interdisciplinary projects. For students with ASD, the development of team-building and problem-solving skills together with their known propensity for mechanical and logical things makes robotics part of an ideal learning environment.

BRINGING A ROBOT INTO THE CLASSROOM

Today's children have grown up with technology and have been called "Digital Natives" because interaction with technology is key to most activities in which they engage. The question facing educators is simply this: "Does growing up with technology change the way students learn enough to require changes in the methods used by teachers?" Marc Prensky coined the term *digital natives* in his seminal work "Digital Natives, Digital Immigrants," published in 2001. In his article, Prensky assigns this term to a new group of students enrolling in educational establishments that have grown up surrounded by and engrossed with technology; he explains that these Digital Natives require a new language and methodology for learning. Prensky states, "Digital Immigrant instructors, who speak an outdated language (that of the predigital age), are struggling to teach a population that speaks an entirely new language. We need to invent Digital Native methodologies for all subjects, at all levels, using our students to guide us" (2001, p. 5).

Robots used in the classroom can prepare students for learning in environments that are increasingly digital (Sneider & Rosen, 2009). For this kind of digital learning, sensors and sensing equipment can provide the necessary support. Robots can serve as an embodied camera that provides a first-person record of human-to-robot interactions, thereby providing much richer information than can be obtained from a wall-mounted camera. Eye movements, micro facial expressions, and quiet vocalizations can be captured by a robot much more sensitively than by a recorder in the distance. Robots can bridge the divide between digital native and digital immigrants, enabling a common language to engage students in learning.

Using Robots to Guide Learning

We envision a shift in education where technology is integrated within the classroom environment and curriculum, where robots will assist in the inclusive classroom, thereby providing new methodologies for learning. Below we outline three key UDL concepts that can be used to facilitate learning with robots in the classroom: representation, expression, and engagement (CAST, 2011).

1. *Multiple means of representation (the "what" of learning).* Robot technologies can be thought of as a platform, like a computer, that can present content in an interactive way with pacing adjusted to the user. Robots can provide variability in delivering content, reinforcing the "what" of learning by providing learners various ways of acquiring information and knowledge.

2. *Multiple means of expression (the "how" of learning).* The manipulation of existing robotic devices by either deconstruction or construction requires a variety of hands-on skill, from real-time programming to soldering and wiring using varies aspects of cognitive and motor ability. Technologies ranging from pre-created hardware to plug-and-play devices provide learners with alternative methods to demonstrate what they have learned in the classroom. Many of these devices can be integrated into the core curriculum (i.e., math, English, science, and social studies) by providing alternative methods for assessing learning in nontechnical subjects.

3. *Multiple means of engagement (the "why" of learning).* The uncanny ability of robots to engage a child and sustain interest over time is a critical component of the argument for why educators should work with robots. Interest in robotics is growing and cuts across gender and ethnic lines. Furthermore, robotics can be seen as a way to challenge students to learn about subjects in a new and interactive way. Over 250,000 students participated in robotics competition programs in 2012, including over 10,000 students in first through third grade through such programs as FIRST (For Inspiration and Recognition of Science and Technology) and the Robotics Education and Competition Foundation. Robotics can assist in sparking learners' interests, present a challenging learning environment, and motivate students to learn.

In addition to the enhanced interest in learning robotics, there is a new trend in design and making technology accessible. Technologies are seemingly getting smaller and more affordable, enabling families and communities to take part in what was once considered to be a field accessible only to engineers. With the advent of open-source hardware and software, tools to invent and manufacture are readily accessible to parents, therapists, and educators; it is with this shift of openness that we delve into developing do-it-yourself technologies for your classroom.

Benefits of Do-It-Yourself Technology

Core ideas in engineering require the ability to view a problem and come to a proposed design solution. Of significance are the connections of ideas between engineering, science, technology, and mathematics. These "big ideas" (Executive Office of the President, 2010; National Research Council [NRC], 1996) also correlate with the National Science Education Standards, which emphasize the "interdependence of science and technology and suggest that students should understand and acquire the capabilities of engaging in technological design" (NAE, 2010, p. 24).

In particular, the "Abilities of Technological Design" for Grades K–4 involve identifying a problem and proposing a solution, implementing solutions, and then evaluating a product or design and communicating about it. These steps are outlined as follows (National Academy of Engineering, 2010; National Association for the Education of Young Children, 1998):

1. *Identify a simple problem.* Children should develop the ability to explain a problem in their own words and identify a specific task and solution related to the problem.

2. *Propose a solution.* Students should make proposals to build something or get something to work better; they should be able to describe and communicate

their ideas. Students should recognize that designing a solution might have constraints, such as cost, materials, time, space, or safety.

3. *Implement proposed solutions.* Children should develop abilities to work individually and collaboratively and to use suitable tools, techniques, and quantitative measurements when appropriate. Students should demonstrate the ability to balance simple constraints in problem solving.

4. *Evaluate a product or design.* Students should evaluate their own results or solutions to problems, as well as those of other children, by considering how well a product or design met the challenge to solve a problem.

5. *Communicate a problem, design, and solution.* Student abilities should include oral, written, and pictorial communication of the design process and product. Through the NSF National Science Digital Library Program, the Teach Engineering Digital Library was created to provide teachers with the curricular materials to bring engineering into the K–12 classroom (http://www. teachengineering.org).

The engineering design process is "a pedagogical strategy that promotes learning across disciplines ... and introduce[s] young students to relevant and fulfilling STEM content in an integrated fashion through exploration of the built world around them" (Teach Engineering, 2013). Logical problem-solving skills are integral to engineering design, and games are fundamentally suited to teaching problem-solving skills because the player must discover and manipulate the game elements. Emerging out of the goals to teach logical problem-solving skills, to create engaging game content, and to incorporate engineering design came the idea of using robotics as a focal point. Robotics allows students to experience design, innovation, problem solving, and teamwork at the same time they are talking about math, science, and technology. Universities, corporations, government agencies, and nonprofits are all using robotics as a way to build STEM literacy in the next generation (Sneider & Rosen, 2009).

By using open-source hardware and software, these engineering design principles can be put into practice. Educators and students can develop their own do-it-yourself robots for the classroom. Such tools as the Arduino and consumer 3-D printers (MakerBots) enable simple and effective methods to rapidly prototype a design solution. These devices provide a platform for developing basic projects. Once users are able to master the basic skills using these machines, they have the ability to try more complex project ideas. It is not difficult to imagine building robots with these tools in the school environment; projects like the Romibo[3] robot project, for example, suggest the implications of prepackaged do-it-yourself robotics for therapy. Romibo uses open-source hardware and minimalistic design to enable a low-cost, flat-packed, do-it-yourself robot that nonengineers can construct and program (think Ikea for robotics). With the advent of these open and lower-cost technologies, educators will no longer have to envision what kind of robots they would want designed for their classrooms; instead, educators and students will be empowered to create robots that will maximize learning for all students on the spectrum.

---

[3]Romibo is an open-source do-it-yourself robot for therapy (http://www.romibo.org/therapy).

REFERENCES

Baron-Cohen, S., & Belmonte, M.K. (2005). Autism: A window onto the development of the social and the analytic brain. *Annual Review of Neuroscience, 28*, 109–126.

Beer, R., & Chiel, H. (1999). Using autonomous robotics to teach science and engineering. *Communications of the ACM, 42*(6), 85–92.

Belmonte, M.K., Cook, E.H., Jr., Anderson, G.M., Rubenstein, J.L., Greenough, W.T., Bekel-Mitchener, A., ... Tierney, E. (2004). Autism as a disorder of neural information processing: Directions for research and targets of therapy. *Molecular Psychiatry, 9*(7), 646–663.

Billard, A. (2003). Robota: Clever toy and educational tool. *Robotics and Autonomous Systems, 42*, 259–269.

Billard, A., Robins, B., Nadel, J., & Dautenhahn, K. (2007). Building Robota, a mini-humanoid robot for the rehabilitation of children with autism. *Assistive Technology, 19*(1), 37–49.

Bird, G., Leighton, J., Press, C., & Heyes, C. (2007). Intact automatic imitation of human and robot actions in autism spectrum disorders. *Proceedings B of the Royal Society: Biological Sciences, 274*(1628), 3027–3031.

Boser, K., Samango-Sprouse, C., Michalowski, C., Safos, C., Drane, J., Kingery, M., & Lathan, C. (2011). *Using robots to facilitate child–child interaction to promote social-cognitive behaviors.* Poster presented at the International Meeting for Autism Research (IMFAR), Philadelphia, PA.

Breazeal, C. (2003a). Emotion and sociable humanoid robots. *International Journal of Human Computer Interaction, 59*, 119–155.

Breazeal, C. (2003b). Towards sociable robots. *Robotics and Autonomous Systems, 42*(3–4), 167–175.

Breazeal, C.L. (2004). *Designing sociable robots.* Cambridge, MA: MIT Press.

Carper, R.A., Moses, P., Tigue, Z.D., & Courchesne, E. (2002). Cerebral lobes in autism: Early hyperplasia and abnormal age effects. *Neuroimage, 16*(4), 1038–1051.

CAST. (2011). *UDL Guidelines.* Retrieved from http://www.cast.org/library/UDLguidelines

Catlin, D., & Blamires, M. (2010). Principles of educational robotics applications (ERA): A framework for understanding and developing educational robots and their activities. Paper presented at the Constructionism Conference, Paris, France.

Cook, A.M., Adams, K., Encarnacao, P., & Alvarez, L. (2012). The role of assisted manipulation in cognitive development. *Developmental Neurorehabilitation, 15*(2), 146–148.

Costa, S., Resende, J., Soares, F.O., Ferreira, M.J., Santos, C.P., & Moreira, F. (2009). Applications of simple robots to encourage social receptiveness of adolescents with autism. *Conference Proceedings: Annual International Conference of the IEEE Engineering in Medicine and Biology Society. IEEE Engineering in Medicine and Biology Society Conference, 2009* (pp. 5072–5075).

Costa, S., Santos, C., Soares, F., Ferreira, M., & Moreira, F. (2010). Promoting interaction amongst autistic adolescents using robots. *Engineering in Medicine and Biology Society (EMBC), 2010 Annual International Conference of the IEEE* (pp. 3856–3859). doi: 10.1109/IEMBS.2010.5627905.

Dautenhahn, K., & Werry, I. (2004). Towards interactive robots in autism therapy. *Pragmatics & Cognition, 1*, 1–35.

Diehl, J.J. (2013). *Humanoid robots as co-therapists in ABA therapy for children with autism spectrum disorder.* Paper presented at IMFAR International Meeting for Autism Research, San Sebastián, Spain.

Diehl, J.J., Schmitt, L.M., Villano, M., & Crowell, C.R. (2012). The clinical use of robots for individuals with autism spectrum disorders: A critical review. *Research in Autism Spectrum Disorders, 6*(1), 249–262.

Duquette, A., Michaud, F., & Mercier, H. (2007). Exploring the use of a mobile robot as an imitation agent with children with low-functioning autism. *Autonomous Robots, 24*(2), 147–157.

el Kaliouby, R., Picard, R., & Baron-Cohen, S. (2006). Affective computing and autism. *Annals of the New York Academy of Science, 1093*, 228–248.

Executive Office of the President. 2010. *Report to the President: Prepare and inspire: K–12 education in science, technology, engineering, and math (STEM) for America's future.* President's Council of Advisors on Science and Technology, p. 142. http://www.whitehouse.gov/administration/eop/ostp/pcast/docsreports

Feil-Seifer, D., Black, M., Flores, E., Mower, A., St. Claire, E., Lee, C., ... Williams, M. (2009). *Development of socially assistive robots for children with autism spectrum disorders.* Center for Robotics and Embedded Systems, Los Angeles, CA. CRES- 09-001.

Feil-Seifer, D., & Matarić, M.J. (2005, June/July). Defining socially assistive robotics., *Proceedings of the IEEE 9th International Conference on Rehabilitation Robotics* (465–468). Piscataway, NJ: IEEE.

Feil-Seifer, D., & Matarić, M.J. (2008). Toward socially assistive robotics for augmenting interventions for children with autism spectrum disorders. In 11th International Symposium on Experimental Robotics (ISER) Athens, Greece. *Springer Tracts in Advanced Robotics, 54,* 201–210.

Feil-Seifer, D., & Matarić, M.J. (2011, March). Automated detection and classification of positive versus negative robot interactions with children with autism using distance-based features. *Proceedings of the 6th ACM/IEEE International Conference on Human–Robot Interaction* (pp. 323–330). Lausanne, Switzerland. New York, NY: ACM.

Gal, E., Bauminger, N., Goren-Bar, D., Pianesi, F., Stock, O., Zancanaro, M., & Weiss, P.L. (2009). Enhancing social communication of children with high-functioning autism through a co-located interface. *AI & SOCIETY, 24*(1), 75–84.

Gillesen, J.C., Barakova, E.I., Huskens, B.E., & Feijs, L.M. (2011). From training to robot behavior: Towards custom scenarios for robotics in training programs for ASD. *Proceedings of the IEEE International Conference on Rehabilitation Robotics, 20,* 1–7.

Goodwin, M.S. (2008). Enhancing and accelerating the pace of autism research and treatment: The promise of developing innovative technology. *Focus on Autism and Other Developmental Disabilities, 23.*

Goodwin, M., Groden, J., Velicer, W., Lipsitt, L., Grace Baron, M., Hofmann, S., & Groden, G. (2006). Cardiovascular arousal in individuals with autism. *Focus on Autism and Developmental Disabilities, 21*(2), 101–123.

Grandin, T. (1992). An inside out view of autism. In E. Schopler & G.B. Mesibov (Eds.), *High function individuals with autism* (pp. 104–126). New York, NY: Plenum Press.

Grandin, T. (1995). *Thinking in pictures.* New York, NY: Bantam Books.

Gura, M., & King, K.P. (Eds.). (2007). *Classroom robotics: Case stories of 21st century instruction for millennial students.* Charlotte, NC: Information Age Publishing.

Haugland, S.W., & Shade, D.D. (1990). *Developmental evaluations of software for young children.* Albany, NY: Delmar.

Herbert, M.R., Harris, G.J., Adrien, K.T., Ziegler, D.A., Makris, N., Kennedy, D.N., ... Caviness, V.S., Jr. (2002). Abnormal asymmetry in language association cortex in autism. *Annals of Neurology, 52*(5), 588–596.

Herbert, M.R., Ziegler, D.A., Makris, N., Filipek, P.A., Kemper, T.L., Normandin, J.J.,... Caviness, V.S., Jr. (2004). Localization of white matter volume increase in autism and developmental language disorder. *Annals of Neurology, 55,* 530–540.

Hill, E.L. (2004). Executive dysfunction in autism. *Trends in Cognitive Sciences, 8*(1) 26–32.

Hirstein, W., Iverson, P., & Ramachandran, V.S. (2001). Autonomic responses of autistic children to people and objects. *Proceedings B of the Royal Society: Biological Sciences, 268*(1479), 1883–1888.

Johnson, J. (2003).Children, robotics and education. *Artificial Life & Robotics, 7*(1–2), 16–21.

Kidd, C.D., & Breazeal, C.L. (2006). Designing a sociable robot system for weight maintenance, *Proceedings of IEEE Consumer Communications and Networking Conference,* Las Vegas, NV, *1,* 253–257.

Kim, E., Leysberg, D., Short, E., Paul, R., & Scassallati, B. (2009, May). Rich, spontaneous, social engagement with a dinosaur robo (PLEO) [Online abstract]. International Meeting for Autism Research, Chicago. IL.

Kim, E., Paul, R., Shic, F., & Scassellati, B. (2012). Bridging the research gap: Making HRI useful to individuals with autism. *Journal of Human–Robot Interaction 1*(1), 26–54.

Kozima, H., Michalowski, M.P., & Nakagawa, C. (2008). Keepon: A playful robot for research, therapy and entertainment, *International Journal of Social Robotics, 1,* 3–18.

Kozima, H., Nakagawa, C., & Yasuda, Y. (2005). *Interactive robots for communication care: A case study in autism therapy.* IEEE International Workshop on Robots and Human Interactive Communication. Nashville, TN: ROMAN.

Liu, C., Conn, K., Sarkar, N., & Stone, W. (2007, August). *Online affect detection and adaptation in robot assisted rehabilitation for children with autism.* Paper presented at the 16th IEEE International Conference on Robot & Human Interactive Communication, Jeju, Korea.

Liu, C., Conn, K., Sarkar, N., & Stone, W. (2008). Online affect detection and robot behavior adaptation for intervention of children with autism. *IEEE Transactions on Robotics 24*(4), 883–897.

Michaud, F., & Caron, S. (2002). Roball, the rolling robot. *Autonomous Robots, 12*(2), 211–222.

Michaud, F., Laplante, J.-F., Larouche, H., Duquette, A., Caron, S., Létourneau, D., & Masson, P. (2005). Autonomous spherical mobile robot for child-development studies. *IEEE Transactions on Systems, Man, and Cybernetics, Part A, 35*(4), 471–480.

Michaud, F. & Theberge-Turnel, C. (2002). Mobile robotic toys and autism. *Socially Intelligent Agents, Multiagent Systems, Artificial Societies and Simulated Organization, 3*, 125–132.

Miyamoto, E., Lee, M., Fujii, H., & Okada, M. (2005). How can robots facilitate social interaction of children with autism? Possible implications for educational environments. *Proceedings of the Fifth International Workshop on Epigenetic Robotics, July 22–24, Nara, Japan* (pp. 145–146). Lund, Sweden: LUCS.

Mostofsky, S.H., Dubey, P., Jerath, V.K., Jansiewicz, E.M., Goldberg, M.C., & Denckla, M.B. (2006). Developmental dyspraxia is not limited to imitation in children with autism spectrum disorders. *Journal of the International Neuropsychological Society, 12*(3), 314–326.

National Academy of Engineering. (2010). *Standards for K–12 engineering education?* [Report]. http://www.nap.edu/catalog/12990.html

National Association for the Education of Young Children. (1998). *Technology and young children—Ages 3 through 8.* http://www.naeyc.org/about/positions/PSTECH98.asp

National Research Council (NRC). (1996). *National science education standards.* Washington, D.C.: National Academy Press.

Ozonoff, S., & Jensen, J. (1999). Brief report: Specific executive function profiles in three neurodevelopmental disorders. *Journal of Autism and Developmental Disorders, 29*(2), 171–177.

Pennington, B.F., & Ozonoff, S. (1996). Executive functions an developmental psychopathology. *Journal of Child Psychology and Psychiatry, 37*, 51–87.

Pierno, A.C., Mari, M., Lusher, D., & Castiello, U. (2008). Robotic movement elicits visuomotor priming in children with autism. *Neuropsychologia, 46*(2), 448–454.

Pioggia, G., Igliozzi, R., Sica, M.L., Ferro, M., Muratori, F., Ahluwalia, A., ... De Rossi, D. (2008). Exploring emotional and imitational android-based interactions in autistic spectrum disorders. *Journal of CyberTherapy and Rehabilitation, 1*(1), 49–61.

Prensky, M. (2001). *Digital Natives, Digital Immigrants*, On the Horizon. MCB University Press, Vol. 9 No. 5, October.

Ribeiro, C., Coutinho, C., & Costa, M.F. (2011). Educational robotics as a pedagogical tool for approaching problem solving skills in mathematics within elementary education. *Information Systems and Technologies (CISTI), 2011 6th Iberian Conference on ITS.*

Robins, B., Dautenhahn, K., & Dickerson, P. (2009). From isolation to communication: A case study evaluation of robot assisted play for children with autism with a minimally expressive humanoid robot. *Proceedings of the Second International Conference on Advances in Human–Computer Interactions, Cancun, Mexico.* doi:10.1109/ACH.2009.32

Robins, B., Dautenhahn, K., & Dubowski, J. (2006). Does appearance matter in the interaction of children with autism with a humanoid robot? *Interaction Studies: Social Behaviour and Communication in Biological and Artificial Systems, 7*(3), 479–512.

Robins, B., Dautenhahn, K., Te Boekhorst, R., & Billard, A. (2005). Robotic assistants in therapy and education of children with autism: Can a small humanoid robot help encourage social interaction skills? *Universal Access in the Information Society 4*(2), 105–120.

Robins, B., Dickerson, P., Stribling, P., & Dautenhahn, K. (2004). Robot-mediated joint attention in children with autism: A case study in robot–human interaction, *Interaction Studies, 5*, 161–198.

Samango-Sprouse, C.A. (2007). Frontal lobe development in childhood. In B.L. Miller & J.L. Cummings (Eds.), *The human frontal lobe: Functions and disorders* (2nd ed., pp. 576–593). New York, NY: Guilford Press.

Scassellati, B. (2005). How social robots will help us to diagnose, treat, and understand autism. *12th International Symposium of Robotics Research* (ISRR No. 39; 05), 552–563.

Scassellati, B. (2007). How social robots will help us to diagnose, treat, and understand autism. *Robotics Research, 28,* 552–563.

Scassellati, B., Admoni, H., & Matarić, M. (2012). Robots for use in autism research. *Annual Review of Biomedical Engineering, 14,* 275–294.

Sneider, C., & Rosen, L. (2009, June). Towards a vision for integrating engineering into science and mathematics standards. In National Academy of Engineering, *Standards for K–12 engineering education?* [Report]. http://www.nap.edu/catalog/12990.html

Stanton, C.M., Kahn, P.H., Jr., Severson, R.L., Ruckert, J.H., & Gill, B.T. (2008). Robotic animals might aid in the social development of children with autism. *Proceedings of the 3rd ACM/IEEE International Conference on Human–Robot Interaction* (pp. 271–278). New York, NY: ACM.

Teach Engineering. (2013). *Why K–12 engineering?* Retrieved from http://www.teachengineering.org/whyk12engr.php

Tochi, M., & Kamio, Y. (2003). Paradoxical autonomic response to mental tasks in autism. *Journal of Autism and Developmental Disorders. 33*(4), 417-426.

President's Council of Advisors on Science and Technology. (2010). *Prepare and inspire: K–12 education in science, technology, engineering, and math (STEM) for America's future* [Report to the President]. http://www.whitehouse.gov/administration/eop/ostp/pcast/docsreports

Werry, I., & Dautenhahn, K. (1999). Applying mobile robot technology to the rehabilitation of autistic children. In *Proceedings of SIRS99, 7th Symposium on Intelligent Robotic Systems* (pp. 265–272).

Werry, I., Dautenhahn, K., Ogden, B., & Harwin, W. (2001). Can social interaction skills be taught by a social agent? The role of a robotic mediator in autism therapy. In M. Beynon, C.L. Nehaniv, & K. Dautenhahn (Eds.), *Proceedings of the Fourth International Conference on Cognitive Technology: Instruments of Mind* (LNAI 2117; pp. 57–74). Berlin: Springer-Verlag.

Williams, J.H.G., Whiten, A., & Singh, T. (2004). A systematic review of action imitation in autistic disorder. *Journal of Autism and Developmental Disorders, 34*(3), 285–299.

Wright, C., Diener, M.L., Dunn, L., Wright, S.D., Linnell, L., Newbold, K., ... Rafferty, D. (2011). SketchUp™: A technology tool to facilitate intergenerational family relationships for children with autism spectrum disorders (ASD). *Family and Consumer Sciences Research Journal, 40,* 135–149. doi: 10.1111/j.1552-3934.2011.02100.x

Language Tools

Sarah C. Wayland

■ ■

In this section, three chapters describe how to teach language skills to children with autism spectrum disorders (ASDs). They also describe some tools that can be helpful in accommodations. This is an area where the research base targeting students with autism is quite limited. For this reason, chapter authors in this section have taken the approach of describing the challenges associated with language skills in autism and reporting on technological interventions that target those challenges. They describe the different styles of interventions and curricula used by each app so that you can match the communication deficits of an individual child with the appropriate software.

In their chapter, "Language Software for Teaching Semantics, Grammar, and Pragmatics to Students with Autism," Katharine P. Beals and Felicia Hurewitz give an overview of some of the currently available language software specifically designed to remediate missing skills in vocabulary and semantics, grammar, and sentence-level semantics and pragmatics. They compare software programs by describing which skills the software teaches (comprehension or production of vocabulary, syntax, and pragmatics), the method for teaching the skill, type of feedback, and how they track progress. They end their chapter by describing methods for assessing whether the skills are generalizing more broadly.

The next chapter, "Mobile Media Devices: A Paradigm Shift in Assistive Technology for Persons with Autism Spectrum Disorder," by Jessica Gosnell Caron and Howard C. Shane, examines how recent advances in mobile media technologies can facilitate communication for persons with ASDs. They evaluate apps that improve comprehension through the use of visual cues (visual instructional mode, or VIM), enhance expressive communication with visual supports (visual expression mode, or

VEM), or use visuals to schedule and organize (visual organization mode, or VOM). They evaluate apps using a feature description grid with the following categories: purpose (VIM, VEM, VOM), speech output, speech settings, representation (user interface features), display settings, feedback features, rate enhancement (how to control rate of presentation), access (how the user interacts with the device), required motor competencies, support, and miscellaneous other features. They also describe how the software allows the user to customize the above features.

The final chapter, "Technology to Support Literacy in Autism," by Sarah C. Wayland, Katharina I. Boser, and Joan L. Green, describes tools that can help students develop and augment literacy skills. The focus is on six literacy skills: alphabetics, vocabulary, text comprehension, fluency, spelling, and writing. The first part of each section describes research-based approaches to teaching the missing skills, as well as effective accommodations. The second part of each section focuses on technologies and applications that can be used to help with the skill. Although students with autism can also have dyslexia and dysgraphia, there are some cognitive skills (e.g., understanding that words can have more than one meaning or understanding character motivations) that are especially common in students with ASDs. This chapter devotes particular attention to technology that can help remediate these skills.

It is important to understand that language skills are complex and interrelated; for this reason, we advise the reader to consider all three chapters when designing an appropriate intervention.

Language Software for Teaching Semantics, Grammar, and Pragmatics to Students with Autism

■ ■

Katharine P. Beals and Felicia Hurewitz

Communicative impairment is a core component of autism spectrum disorders (ASDs), often persisting throughout the life span (Howlin, Goode, Hutton, & Rutter, 2004). Improvements in language functionality may enhance educational inclusion, expand social networks, improve academic achievement, and ultimately, increase employment and independence. Many studies demonstrate that a variety of language skills respond to remediation if the intervention is intensive, tailored to the baseline level of the individual, based on sound principles of learning and development, and generalizable to new situations (Rogers, 2006). In principle, such structured teaching is modality neutral, deliverable via software as well as via direct interpersonal instruction. This chapter provides an overview of some of the currently available language software that is specifically designed for individuals with autism or similar language impairments.

Advantages of language remediation software include availability and convenience, especially for serving children who may otherwise not receive language services. Most children diagnosed with autism, including the "best outcome" population who eventually lose the diagnosis, continue to have residual language issues (Kelley, Paul, Fein, & Naigles, 2006). Intensive language instruction may not be as available to older children as it is to younger children, and the linguistic needs of the more linguistically capable children may fly under the radar. Opportunities for regular, individualized speech instruction may be limited by parental or school resources, time restrictions, or a desire not to pull a child from regular education or recreational opportunities. Computerized instruction, in contrast, is limited neither by time nor by location, allowing for a consistent methodology across home and school. Furthermore, several studies suggest that children with autism may be as or more motivated during technology-based interventions as they are during interpersonal instruction (Moore & Calvert, 2000; Williams, Wright, Callaghan, & Coughlan, 2002).

In this chapter we summarize some of the currently published linguistic software interventions that have been created specifically to address the needs of children with autism. As we will see, these programs offer a variety of teaching methodologies and target a variety of skills. Although there is emerging evidence that such programs can provide educational benefit (Hurewitz & Beals, 2008; Ramdoss et al., 2011; Whalen et al., 2010; Wilson, Fox, & Pascoe, 2009), none of the software packages described here qualifies as fully "evidence based" when evaluated by rigorous scientific standards (Young, Corea, Kimani, & Mandell, 2010). Our purpose is not to endorse some programs and criticize others but, rather, to describe the curricula and teaching protocols of each of the programs so that teachers of children with ASDs can, in the absence of rigorous scientific guidance, choose judiciously among the programs, matching particular communication deficits to particular intervention styles and curriculum packages.

LEVELS OF LANGUAGE INSTRUCTION

Language is a complex skill set, including procedural, rule-based, and social components, which may overlap in presentation on a general assessment of communicative functioning. Numerous case studies suggest that specific, targeted areas of language acquisition can be taught on an individual basis. Vocabulary (i.e., receptive and productive lexical knowledge) is the most readily instructed area of language and possibly the most responsive to intervention (Bosseler & Massaro, 2003; Hurewitz & Boser, 2010; Whalen et al., 2010). Less obviously remediable are syntax (the ordering and structural relation of words in a sentence), and morphology (the use of prefixes and suffixes to confer grammatical structure and to expand vocabulary). Although a few studies suggest that computerized intervention improves syntax skills (Dressler, 2011; Finn, Futernick, & MacEachern, 2005; Hetzroni & Tannous, 2004; Wilson et al., 2009; Yamamoto & Miya, 1999), these are limited in sample size and assessment of generalization (Young et al., 2010). Perhaps the most recalcitrant aspect of language is linguistic pragmatics, which includes such diverse communicative areas as intonation, gesture, reference (appropriate use of pronouns and deictic phrases such as *this* and *that*), conversational interaction, and indirect speech (or communicative intent). There is very little research addressing the acquisition of pragmatics in typical children, and software programs typically cover only small chunks of pragmatics, such as making appropriate responses to questions or using pronouns in various contexts.

In spite of the dearth of efficacy studies for certain levels of language remediation, we believe that teachers can still optimize a child's progress by matching his or her current level (as per formal assessments of need) to the language skills targeted by particular software programs. One of our goals here, therefore, is to describe which programs target which specific skills. For example, if a child with autism displays age-appropriate vocabulary, lagging instead in syntactic skills or pragmatics, use of a vocabulary acquisition software module cannot be expected to be productive. More generally, when choosing among vocabulary, syntax, or pragmatics modules, existing skills must be carefully assessed. Many language theorists believe that a child has to be ready to learn the particular construction or forms being instructed and that there is a natural order for this acquisition process (Krashen, 1982; Thomke & Boser, 2011). For example, research in typical language acquisition suggests that verbs in English are acquired after nouns, so that the child can "bootstrap" the meaning of the verb to its anchoring noun meanings (Gleitman, Cassidy, Nappa, Papafragou, & Trueswell, 2005). Likewise, adjectives such as *big* or *fluffy* are acquired more readily if they are paired with a noun, for example, *a big cup* makes more conceptual sense than *big* in isolation (Mintz & Gleitman, 2002). Research in second-language acquisition provides supporting evidence for this view, finding that second-language learners are best able to take in new words and forms when their "internal grammar" has reached a particular receptive state (Ellis, 2002). Teachers may want to identify developmental gaps in the child's knowledge as a prime area for instruction.

The software programs reviewed here differ not only in the linguistic topics they cover but also in their tasks, modeling, and feedback strategies. Some focus on comprehension, having students match pictures to words, phrases, or sentences (picture selection or sentence selection); others focus on production, having students actively construct phrases or sentences (fill in blanks or sentence construction). The various comprehension tasks can be subdivided further: Some require students to actively attend to contrasting forms or structures (explicit contrast); others merely expose students to numerous instances of particular forms of structures (implicit exposure). It is important to note that what we are calling *explicit contrast* tasks may occasion only implicit learning of particular forms; for example, in repeatedly mapping pictures involving multiple instances of a given object to nouns with plural endings, the student may learn implicitly that the *s* ending expresses plurality, even if he or she is not explicitly aware of this. Research on second-language acquisition for older learners, which has focused on the question of evidence-based pedagogical techniques for language instruction, continues to debate the interface between implicit and explicit knowledge (Ellis & Larsen-Freeman, 2006). According to one view, explicit contrast may help the learner determine what to attend to in language input (e.g., to search for the *s* ending to determine plurality); however, the capacity to produce this construction may still require practice with the act of production itself (Clahsen & Felser, 2006; Cleland & Pickering, 2006; Ellis, 1994).

In terms of modeling, some programs provide rehearsal opportunities with correct constructions, which may serve as opportunities to transfer explicit knowledge to a performance-based, implicit domain, as per Krashen's idea that when the student produces an utterance (implicit), he or she self-monitors and edits that production for accuracy (Krashen, 1982). In some programs corrective feedback is general (right or wrong), whereas in others it is focused (telling the child specifically which aspect of an answer needs revision).

Given all these dimensions of variability, matching a particular program or module to a particular child's needs might include a consideration of the following:

1. Linguistic topics covered (vocabulary, syntax, pragmatics)

2. Type of task being trained (comprehension vs. production; within comprehension, explicit contrast, or incidental exposure)

3. Type of feedback offered

4. Requirements for reporting on progress and goal monitoring

Software Content and Delivery

Programs reviewed here are found in Tables 6.1 and 6.2. In choosing which to examine, we sought programs that were geared toward English-language instruction for children with ASDs Further, we sought programs that had components that went beyond the one-word stage to instruction in grammar, morphemes, or pragmatics. Finally, we limited ourselves to those programs for which we were able to acquire explicit descriptions and/or demos of the curriculum and pedagogy in action.

Vocabulary and Semantics

Vocabulary is a common area of difficulty for children with autism, who often lack the joint attention skills necessary to acquire word meanings from social environments. Vocabulary skills, both receptive and productive, vary widely across the autistic population, correlating with joint attention skills and also IQ (Tager-Flusberg, Paul, & Lord, 2005). A number of software programs offer a more direct form of vocabulary instruction than is found in the natural social environment, with unlimited opportunities for repeated practice, thus bypassing the learner's weaknesses in joint attention.

Different programs address vocabulary deficits using a variety of strategies. These include Cosmo, Fast ForWord (both Language and Language to Reading) GrammarTrainer, Laureate Learning, Speech with Milo, Sentence Builder, Teach-Town, Timo Stories, and Timo Vocabulary. Most programs train students in comprehension or the identification of word meaning. GrammarTrainer trains production as well, requiring students to actively retrieve the words being taught. All of the above programs vary both in the range of parts of speech they cover and in how sophisticated a vocabulary they teach.

Cosmo, catering to the needs of younger children, covers such basics as concrete adjectives, spatial prepositions, and numbers. Timo Stories focuses on day-to-day vocabulary, taught both in the context of stories and in terms of their semantic and functional classifications. Speech with Milo, an iPad app, shows illustrative animations of over 100 basic action verbs.

TeachTown and Laureate are particularly comprehensive in their coverage of preschool vocabulary, each of them instructing hundreds of basic terms. Teach-Town organizes content by topic, such as animals, colors, and time. Laureate's various basic-level packages (see Table 6.1) cover hundreds of basic nouns, as well as concrete verbs, adjectives, and spatial prepositions.

Timo Vocabulary and Fast ForWord's Robo-Dog teach a more specialized and sophisticated vocabulary that is more appropriate for school-aged learners. Timo Vocabulary organizes basic concepts into 22 categories ranging from animal groups (*pride, school, gaggle*) to weather, with many categories further divided into subcategories. Within the category "animals and habitats," for example, one finds "arctic animals"; within "force and movement," one finds "parts of a bicycle." Fast ForWord's Robo-Dog is similarly specialized, teaching terms from arithmetic, geometry, life science, and earth science.

Other programs—among them Fast ForWord Language, Fast ForWord Language to Reading, HearBuilder, Laureate's Language Links, QuestionQuest, and GrammarTrainer—teach various function words that underpin grammar (see

Table 6.1.   Summary chart of topics covered and delivery method for software programs

Programs	Topics	Training style
Cosmo	Basic vocabulary: —Size terms (*big* vs. *small*) —Shapes —Color terms —Prepositions —Directional terms (*up, down, left*), comparative terms (*more, less, same*) —Number	Comprehension
Fast ForWord's Language and Language to Reading	Vocabulary: —Spatial prepositions —Quantifiers —Temporal adverbs —Function words —Scholastic words Syntax: —Complex sentences —Temporal clause semantics —Negation —Subject–verb–object word order	Comprehension
	Passive sentences	Implicit exposure
GrammarTrainer	Syntax: —Singular vs. plural nouns —Subject–verb–object word order —Comparative vs. superlative adjectives —Articles and deictics —Pronoun case —Possessive noun phrases —Quantifiers —*Wh*-words —Spatial and temporal prepositions —Function words —Complex sentences —Tense —Semantics (simple and compound) —Negated sentences —Temporal clause semantics —Passive sentences —Conditional clause semantics —Modal clause semantics Syntax and pragmatics: —Questions —Pronouns	Production

(*continued*)

Table 6.1.   (*continued*)

Programs	Topics	Training style
HearBuilder's Following Directions	Syntax:	Comprehension
	—Spatial prepositions	
	—Negation	
	—Quantifiers	
	—Temporal adverbs	
	—Function words	
	—Complex sentences	
	—Temporal clause semantics	
	—Relative clauses	
	—Conditional clause semantics	
Laureate's First Words, Exploring Nouns, Exploring Verbs, Adjectives and Opposites, Prepositions	Hundreds of basic nouns (from items around the house to items on a farm), concrete verbs and adjectives, spatial prepositions	Comprehension
Laureate's Language Links	Basic vocabulary and basic tense semantics:	Comprehension
	—Singular vs. plural nouns	
	—Basic verb conjugation	
	—Negation	
	—Possessive noun phrases	
	—Simple tenses	
	Pragmatics:	
	—Pronouns (Language Links and Pronoun Perspective)	
	—Deictics	
	Complex sentences (relative clauses)	Implicit exposure
	Pronoun case (*he, him, his, himself*)	
	Present progressive tense	
	Possessive noun phrases	
Laureate's QuestionQuest	Semantics and pragmatics of questions	Comprehension
	Complex question syntax	Implicit exposure
Laureate's Simple Sentence Structure	Subject-verb-object word order	Comprehension
	Passive sentences	Implicit exposure
LinguiSystems No-Glamour Grammar	Syntax: Basic verb forms: *is* vs. *are*, *do* vs. *does*, *has* vs. *have*	Correct sentence identification
	—Pronoun case (*he vs. him; her vs. hers*)	
	—Negation	
	—Past tense	
	—Simple present tense forms,	
	—Plural and possessive noun phrases	
	—Questions	
Speech for Milo	Verbs only: 100 basic action verbs	Comprehension
Question Builder	Semantics and pragmatics of questions	Comprehension

Table 6.1.   *(continued)*

Programs	Topics	Training style
Sentence Builder	Syntax: —Articles —Deictics —Linking verbs —Modals —Pronoun case	Production
TeachTown	Vocabulary: —Animals —Colors —Calendar —Time —Classroom —Nature —Tools —Transportation terms Parts of speech: —Nouns —Verbs —Adverbs —Adjectives	Comprehension
Timo Stories	Everyday vocabulary	Comprehension
Timo Vocabulary	Scholastic vocabulary (22 categories of words)	Comprehension

Note: Unless otherwise noted, training style involves explicit contrast rather than implicit exposure.

below). Such terms include articles (*a* and *the*), linking verbs (e.g., *be, have*), modals (e.g., *can*), prepositions, negation, quantifiers, temporal adverbs (e.g., *before*), *if* and *then*, and *wh*-words.

Grammar

Grammar is another common linguistic deficit in ASD. As with vocabulary, children with ASD show a wide range of receptive and productive weaknesses in different areas of grammar, again correlating with joint attention skills and IQ, as well as with comorbid conditions like specific language impairment (Tager-Flusberg et al., 2005). These areas range from word endings (morphosyntax) to phrase and sentence structure and the proper use of function words (syntax). As with vocabulary, a number of software programs offer a more direct form of grammar instruction than is found in the ambient social environment, with many more opportunities for repeated practice.

The various software programs cover different subsets of these. The programs vary, as well, in whether they focus on comprehension or production and, in the case of comprehension, whether the comprehension tasks require students to attend to the specific contrasts of the targeted forms (explicit contrast) or merely expose them to repeated instances of these forms (implicit exposure).

Table 6.2. Features of different software programs

Programs	Features	Tasks	Targeted language modality
Cosmo	Oral prompts, data reports, customizable (level of difficulty)	PSM	Speech (comprehension)
Fast ForWord	Oral prompts, animated rewards, data reports	PSM	Speech (comprehension)
GrammarTrainer	Teaching component, text prompts, linguistic feedback, customizable (external reward)	SC	Text (production)
HearBuilder	Oral prompts, animated rewards, data reports	PSM	Speech (comprehension)
Laureate	Placement test, teaching component, oral prompts, text prompts, animated rewards, customizable (criteria for advancement), data reports	PSM	Speech (comprehension)
LinguiSystems No-Glamour Grammar	Text prompts	SS	Text (written conventions)
Speech for Milo	Teaching component		Speech (comprehension)
QuestionBuilder	Customizable	PSM	Text (production)
Sentence Builder	Customizable	FB	Text (production)
TeachTown	Teaching component, oral prompts, animated rewards	PSM	Speech (comprehension)
Timo Stories	Animated rewards, oral prompts, data reports	PSM	Speech and text comprehension
Timo Vocabulary	Oral prompts, data reports	PSM	Speech and text comprehension

Key: PSM: picture selection and manipulation; SC: sentence construction; SS: sentence selection; FB: filling in blanks

Sentence Builder, a production-based (fill in the blanks) program, specifically targets function words (see screenshot in Figure 6.1), in particular, articles, third-person pronouns, and deictics (e.g., *this, these*). Because the program is a work in progress, Sentence Builder's coverage is far from systematic and comprehensive. LinguiSystems No-Glamour Grammar, an error detection–based (sentence selection) program, also focuses on a range of functional elements, including comparative versus superlative adjectives (e.g., *bigger* vs. *biggest*), auxiliary verbs (e.g., *is, have*) and other basic verb forms, negation (e.g., *isn't*), and questions. It, too, is limited in its depth and breadth of coverage, as well as in how systematically it isolates and trains particular syntactic features. In many cases, it presents only a few exercises to train a particular syntactic contrast.

Most of the other programs also focus on comprehension training. Fast For-Word Language's Space Commander module, Fast ForWord Language to Reading's Following Directions module, and HearBuilder's Following Directions module all train students in the comprehension of increasingly complex phrases. In

The		on		the ear.
Then		it		the leaf.
That	bears	or	climbing	the paw.
This		at	falling	the tree.
It		are		the sky.

Select

Figure 6.1. Screen shot of Sentence Builder. (From SentenceBuilder Version 1.4, Copyright © 2011 Mobile Education Store; reprinted by permission.)

HearBuilder, students are tasked with following directions that build gradu-ally from simple noun and adjective-noun constructions to constructions with a variety of prepositional phrases and subordinate clauses. These directions thus range from the simple—*Click on the blue ball*—to the complex—*Click on the large yellow car that is bouncing beside the boat*—to such conditionals as *If a green doll is in the box, put the box on the large truck; if not, put the box on the small truck.*

Fast ForWord's Space Commander and Following Directions give similar directions-following tasks. Although not as complex as the conditional sentences of HearBuilder, these directions are nevertheless reasonably complex, culminating in sentences like *Put the red square between the blue circle and the yellow circle, Touch the red square—no, the white circle, Instead of the green circle touch the yellow circle, After touching the yellow square, touch the blue circle,* and *The girl that is wearing a cape does not have a basket.*

A separate module of Fast ForWord Language, Ele-bot, presents a number of picture selection tasks involving multiple embeddings where the child must sort out which relative clause modifies which noun. For example, the child may be asked to click on *The girl that the boy is watching is standing, The clown that is holding the balloon that is blue is red,* or *The napkin covers the wolf that the basket is holding.* At a more basic level, Ele-bot prompts require implicit identification (through explicit contrast and picture selection) of subjects and objects, both in simple sentences like

The girl is washing the boy versus *The boy is washing the girl*, and in more complex sentences like *It's the girl that the boy is pushing.* Other prompts require implicit discrimination between singular and plural verb forms.

Most comprehensive in grammar coverage are Laureate and GrammarTrainer. Laureate combines explicit contrast tasks (identification of pictures that go with particular structures) and incidental exposure (repeatedly exposing students to a particular structure). Its most basic syntax package, Simple Sentence Structure, begins with basic subject-verb-object order. Here, word-order learning comes from repeated, systematic exposure (incidental exposure) rather than from tasks that require word-order distinctions (explicit contrast). However, the contrasting sentences and corresponding pictures can be distinguished by key words alone, for example, their contrasting subject nouns. The later phases of Simple Sentence Structure do require explicit contrast: The contrasting sentences contain all the same nouns and verbs, and the student must attend to their different word orders in order to click on the correct picture.

Laureate's Language Links packages similarly combine incidental and explicit learning, covering singular, plural, and possessive forms of nouns and pronouns (e.g., *she, they, his*), basic verb tenses (*paint, painted, will paint*), relative clauses (e.g., *The hat that is mine*), and passive sentences (e.g., *The cat is chased by the mouse*). In later modules of Language Links, present progressive (*The mother is holding the baby*), relative clauses, and passive sentences are all taught incidentally, through repeated exposure: At no point does the student need to attend to the details of the syntactic structure in question in order to identify the correct picture.

Laureate's QuestionQuest covers one of the most syntactically complex structures of all: Questions. However, its question prompts are all in the present progressive (e.g., *What is the boy holding*). It therefore does not expose students to the more complex elements of question formation, for example, the insertion of the appropriate form of *do* and the conversion of the main verb to its bare infinitive form (e.g., *The father paint who* becomes *Who did the father paint?*). Its teaching of this present-progressive subset of question syntax, furthermore, is only via incidental exposure; as with the later modules of Language Links, at no point does the student need to attend to the details specific to question syntax (e.g., the overall word order, including the inversion of the auxiliary verb) in order to identify the correct picture. In the case of the above prompt, for example, it is enough simply to identify the words *who, father,* and *painting,* and then click on what the boy in the picture is holding (see screenshot in Figure 6.2).

GrammarTrainer covers many of the same topics as Laureate but focuses on production rather than on comprehension, thus going beyond implicit exposure and explicit contrast to explicit knowledge (as per Krashen, 1982). Moving from simple noun phrases to complex sentences, it covers simple and compound tenses (e.g., *ate, has eaten*), sentence negation (including auxiliary support, as in *didn't walk*), relative clauses (e.g., *the box that the girl is standing on*), passive sentences (e.g., *The boy is being hugged by the girl*), conditional sentences (e.g., *If the girl says "boo" the boy will feel scared*), comparative constructions (e.g., *The lower the sun, the longer the shadow*), a variety of embedded clauses (e.g., *He asked whether the girl would help him tie his shoes*), and question syntax (e.g., *Who is the boy pointing to?*).

Figure 6.2. Screen shot of Laureate QuestionQuest. (From QuestionQuest Level I, Version 2.1.1, Copyright © 2010 Laureate Learning Systems, Inc.; reprinted by permission.)

Sentence-Level Semantics and Pragmatics

Two other common areas of linguistic difficulty in autism are sentence-level comprehension (or sentence-level semantics) and pragmatics, with pragmatics, grounded as it is in social situations, being one of the greatest challenges across the autistic spectrum (Tager-Flusberg et al., 2005). Here, software programs have been created to bypass some of the challenges of generalization from real-life social situations to language acquisition. These software programs teach certain pragmatic and sentence comprehension skills in a more controlled and simplified learning environment. Indeed, all of the above-described programs provide some implicit exposure to sentence-level semantics and pragmatics in that nearly all the prompts are given in full sentences. In addition, a number of these programs provide students with more explicit training in particular types of sentence-level semantics and pragmatics. In most cases, as with vocabulary and syntax, training focuses on comprehension rather than on production.

HearBuilder's Following Directions and the Fast ForWord's Space Commander and Following Directions focus on the comprehension of increasingly complex sentences, including sentences with temporal clauses and, in the case of HearBuilder, conditional clauses as well.

Although Timo Stories focuses most obviously on story comprehension, the stories involve short paragraphs consisting of a few sentences apiece. The comprehension questions and subsequent semantic exercises can often be answered by focusing on the appropriate key word; the student nonetheless receives incidental exposure to different sorts of questions. More explicit training in question comprehension is offered by TeachTown.

The semantics and pragmatics of questions is the key focus of both Sentence Builder's Question Builder module and of Laureate's QuestionQuest. QuestionQuest is particularly comprehensive, requiring the student to discriminate among yes-no questions and the full range of *wh-* questions (explicit contrast). In addition, the student receives incidental exposure to a sort of complex *wh-* question not seen in any of the other programs: multiple *wh-* questions as in *Who is eating what?* and *Who is eating what where?* While the student may use a linguistic comprehension strategy in answering such questions, however, it is also possible to use a purely pictographic strategy, selecting from a matrix of pictured objects the pairs or triples that match the objects that go together in the larger picture to which the question refers.

Laureate's Language Links trains comprehension in several other aspects of sentence-level semantics and pragmatics. With pictures that show—some more clearly than others—actions that are about to be undertaken, actions that are in progress, and actions that have already occurred, it trains students in the semantics of present, past, and future tensed sentences. With pictures that show objects nearer to or farther from the speaking character, it trains students in the use of the deictics *here* versus *there* and *this/these* versus *that/those*. With characters who address one another or, breaking the "fourth wall," address the student directly, Language Links, along with Laureate's specially designated package Pronoun Perspective, trains students in the use of first- versus second- versus third-person pronouns (e.g., *I* vs. *you* vs. *she*). When it comes to first- and second-person possessive pronouns (e.g., *my* vs. *your*) in particular, it should be noted that some of the contrasting pictures convey a simplified sense of what possession means: *my cat* is not necessarily the cat that the speaker is holding; *your cat* is not necessarily the cat that the addressee is holding.

GrammarTrainer trains sentence-level semantics and pragmatics via production as well as comprehension. The latter includes training in the semantically appropriate production of sentences in a variety of tenses and moods: progressive (*is walking*), perfective (*has walked*), imperative (*Help me tie my shoe*), conditional and counterfactual (*If the girl says/had said "Boo," the girl will feel scared*), and modal (*may/might*), as well as in comparative and *tough*-movement constructions (*These rocks are hard for the boy to carry*), temporal clauses (*The girl was swimming while the boy was reading*), and semantically and pragmatically appropriate questions (e.g., *who* vs. *what* vs. *where*). With characters who address one another or the student directly, and with cartoon balloons the student either fills in or reports on, the program also trains users to comprehend and make pragmatically appropriate productive choices among first-, second-, and third-person pronouns (e.g., *I* vs. *you* vs. *she*) and direct versus indirect discourse (*I want you to help me* vs. *The boy said that he wants the girl to help him*). GrammarTrainer's pictures, however, lack the 3-D clarity of Laureate's, and so some students may have difficulty understanding who the characters are supposed to be speaking to and/or referring to, particularly when they are breaking the so-called fourth wall and looking and/or pointing directly at the student software user.

Teaching Methodology

The foregoing programs vary not just in what linguistic topics they cover but also in their teaching methodologies. Some—for example, Fast ForWord, LinguiSystems No-Glamour Grammar, Sentence Builder, and Timo—offer no explicit teaching component at all but launch directly into the exercises and, in the case of LinguiSystems, rely on a speech language therapist to do any necessary preliminary or additional instruction.

Other programs vary in the degree to which they capture the underlying principles as opposed to simply highlighting the correct answer. TeachTown, with its sophisticated, applied behavioral analysis (ABA)–inspired system of gradually introducing and gradually strengthening distracters, initially makes the correct answer the most salient one without further explanation. Laureate shows a few sample prompts and answers, highlighting both the answer and the relevant part of the prompt. GrammarTrainer employs a multiple-choice phase in which all choices model the structures being taught, and from which the student can copy his or her selection word for word. Speech with Milo, which has only a teaching component, uses animation and sample sentences to demonstrate the meanings of verbs.

The programs also vary in the sort of reinforcement they give for correct and incorrect answers. Many—Cosmo, Laureate, Sentence Builder, TeachTown, and Timo—respond to correct answers with oral praise, sometimes reinforced with text-based praise (Laureate) and/or an animation (Fast ForWord, Laureate, TeachTown). Cosmo offers an interactive free play phase once the student completes a module. GrammarTrainer has neither sound nor animation, and its reinforcement is entirely text based, including numerical points and references to an external award chosen by the child or supervisor. A pictographic point system (e.g., stars or other objects accumulating along the edge of the screen) is another component of the positive reinforcement in both HearBuilder and Timo.

As far as corrective feedback goes, a distinction is drawn in second-language acquisition between implicit feedback, such as modeling the right form of speech, and explicit feedback, which may be a metalinguistic description of how to arrive at the right response (Ellis, 2002). Feedback for responses vary across the reviewed software programs. Fast ForWord, HearBuilder, Laureate, LinguiSystems, Teach-Town, and Timo Vocabulary simply repeat the prompt and (either immediately or after a second or third incorrect response) highlight the correct answer. Cosmo, Sentence Builder, and Timo Stories notify the student explicitly that the answer is wrong. If the student still responds incorrectly, Cosmo first provides auditory and visual hints and then grays out and deactivates all but the correct answer. GrammarTrainer provides metalinguistic feedback, highlighting different types of linguistic errors one type at a time, accompanied by a text-based explanation as to what needs to be fixed, moving on to any remaining types of errors only after the student has corrected the one being highlighted (see Figure 6.3).

Prompts and tasks also vary. Some programs use entirely auditory prompts with accompanying pictures (TeachTown and Fast ForWord). LinguiSystems uses only text-based prompts, whereas Laureate's prompts are both auditory and text based (with accompanying pictures), and GrammarTrainer's involve text-based references to particular pictures, its pictures being more schematic and crudely rendered than those in the other programs (Figure 6.3).

As for the corresponding tasks, most of the programs—Cosmo, Fast ForWord, Laureate, and TeachTown, for example—have the student selecting from a choice of pictures, or from among objects within a picture. In the directions-following components of HearBuilder and Fast ForWord, the student may click on a sequence of pictures or pictured objects or move around (drag and drop) one pictured object with respect to another. Such tasks indicate that linguistic training is operating at a level of comprehension, as opposed to production.

The exceptions to this type of picture selection task are LinguiSystems, Sentence Builder, and GrammarTrainer. LinguiSystems has the student select one of two possible sentences, which typically vary minimally in terms of a particular feature

Describe the picture, using the word GIVE.

Some of your words are in the wrong order (1st, 2nd, 3rd,...). Change the order of the words in red.

the boy is giving to the book **the girl**

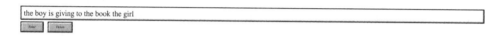

Click or type the words to form the correct response. Then click 'Enter'.

Figure 6.3. Screen shot of GrammarTrainer.

(correct or incorrect pronoun form, correct or incorrect word ending, correct or incorrect insertion of auxiliary). Thus, this selection task essentially involves distinguishing a correct feature from an incorrect feature within minimally contrasting sentences. Of concern is that the student, in the process, is repeatedly attending to grammatical errors and possibly mislearning from them.

Sentence Builder and Question Builder use a "picker wheel" (Figure 6.1). Here, the task essentially involves filling in blanks in a sentence by picking from several choices of nouns, verbs, or function words, as opposed to building up a sentence from scratch.

Constructing a sentence from scratch, adjusting it based on incremental feedback, is the main task assigned by GrammarTrainer. Here, instead of clicking on pictures, selecting whole sentences, or filling in blanks, the student either types letters on the keyboard or clicks on word buttons on the screen to construct phrases and sentences word for word. The word buttons include not just the correct words in their correct forms but all others that students might reasonably select in error, so the particular buttons displayed do not give away the correct answer.

Nearly all the software programs base advancement on student performance. Many advance students to the next module once they have gotten a certain percentage of trials correct—80% is typical. Fast ForWord and Laureate allow their mastery settings to be customized for particular students. Exceptions to automatic advancement based on percentage correct are Cosmo, Sentence Builder, and Timo. Timo does not require a certain percentage initially correct; instead, it requires that the student correct all mistakes before moving on. Cosmo and Sentence Builder do not provide any automatic advancement but leave it up to the therapist. GrammarTrainer operates via a combination of percentage correct and exercise-specific mastery.

What happens when the student continues to struggle with certain exercises? In most programs, so long as the problematic exercises in a given module compose a small fraction of the total, the student can still get the requisite percentage correct and advance to the next level without mastering these exercises. If the student racks up enough incorrect responses, those programs that offer teaching and modeling phases—Laureate, GrammarTrainer, and TeachTown—return the student to the module's teaching phase.

More fundamentally, what determines where a new student is initially placed within the various modules of a program? Only Laureate has its own internal placement tests; Teachtown uses a ranking questionnaire for teachers, and the others rely on therapists or teachers and general guidelines about student age and language level to make the initial determination. Therefore, when choosing software, consideration should be given to the level of expertise of the person who will oversee the use of the software.

Data Reports

Finally, what type of data is collected on individual students as they progress through the programs? In the current versions of GrammarTrainer and Sentence Builder, the only information saved is what lesson the child was last working on. Fast ForWord, HearBuilder, Laureate, TeachTown, and Timo, on the other hand, provide comprehensive data about the level of mastery of specific modules that both are available to therapists and teachers and determine at which point in the program the student should be placed the next time he or she resumes training. The most useful reports to language professionals are found in those software programs whose modules are described linguistically, for example, Cosmo, Hear-Builder, and Laureate.

The Issue of Generalization

The ultimate goal of any language remediation program should be to improve the ability of the child to generalize to natural settings. However, students with ASD find naturalistic settings confusing and overstimulating until they know the unspoken "rules" of the situation. Therefore, most ASD-specific interventions begin with a phase of direct instruction in which skills are explicitly taught and broken into component parts. A second phase of instruction typically would encourage and reinforce generalization. Since lack of generalization is a common problem with some of the rote instructional techniques that are used with children with ASD, it is especially important to support and monitor generalization of skills acquired from software packages.

Besides formal assessments like the Peabody Picture Vocabulary Test and the Comprehensive Assessment of Spoken Language, there are more naturalistic measures of spontaneous productive language, particularly for syntax: The Mean Length of Utterance, which is based on the average number of morphemes in a sample of the child's utterances, and the Index of Productive Syntax, a quantification of grammatical complexity, also derived from utterance samples.

For more informal monitoring, as well as support, therapists and educators can observe and create opportunities for spontaneous speech in classrooms and other settings. For vocabulary in particular, thematic lessons or activities based on recent or earlier trainings, whether everyday words or more specialized academic vocabulary, can create opportunities for ongoing assessment, reinforcement, and retrieval practice. Sentence-level comprehension might be monitored and supported through activities involving multistep directions or listening and reading comprehension questions. For syntax and pragmatics, one should include numerous opportunities for spontaneous, open-ended discourse, for question asking and answering, and for interactive conversation more generally.

CONCLUSION

Software programs offer a promising avenue for delivering supplemental language services to children in schools, home, or the community. Parents and teachers can maximize a child's success by matching his or her particular needs to the particular topics and tasks trained by the various programs and by regularly collecting progress data to ascertain whether the child is benefiting from the chosen program's pedagogical style, content, delivery rate, and schedule of reinforcement. As discussed in this chapter, it is especially important to monitor generalization to natural language usage, the ultimate goal of any language remediation program. However much a child may benefit from one or more of these programs, it is important to bear in mind that none of them should be considered a replacement for a full language curriculum. As researchers, we hope that future research and development will both provide more evidence about the efficacy of the different linguistic software packages and better integrate such packages into a broader language curriculum, one that includes the sort of authentic communicative exchanges that should be the ultimate goal of all language interventions for autism.

REFERENCES

Bosseler, A., & Massaro, D. (2003). Development and evaluation of a computer-animated tutor for vocabulary and language learning in children with autism. *Journal of Autism and Developmental Disorders, 33*, 653–672.

Clahsen, H., & Felser, C. (2006). Grammatical processing in language learners. *Applied Psycholinguistics, 37*, 3–42.

Cleland, A., & Pickering, M. (2006). Do writing and speaking employ the same syntactic representations? *Journal of Memory and Language, 54*, 185–198.

Dressler, J. (2011). *The generalization of text-based computer-aided instruction to verbal speech production by students with autism* (Unpublished master's thesis). Drexel University, Philadelphia, PA.

Ellis, N. (2002). Frequency effects in language processing: A review with implications for theories of implicit and explicit language acquisition. *Studies in Second Language Acquisition, 24*, 143–188.

Ellis, N., & Larsen-Freeman, D. (2006). Language emergence: Implications for applied linguistics [Introduction to special issue]. *Applied Linguistics, 27,* 558–589.

Ellis, R. (1994). A theory of instructed second language acquisition. In N.C. Ellis (Ed.), *Implicit and explicit learning of languages* (pp. 79–114). San Diego, CA: Academic.

Finn, D., Futernick, A., & MacEachern, S. (2005, November). *Efficacy of language intervention software in preschool classrooms.* Paper presented at the annual meeting of the American Speech Language Hearing Association, San Diego, CA.

Gleitman, L., Nappa, R., Cassidy, K., Papafragou, A., & Trueswell, J. (2005). Hard words. *Language Learning & Development, 1*(1), 23–64.

Hetzroni, O.E., & Tannous, J. (2004). Effects of a computer-based intervention program on the communicative functions of children with autism. *Journal of Autism and Developmental Disorders, 34*(2), 95–113.

Howlin, P., Goode, S., Hutton, J., & Rutter, M. (2004). Adult outcomes for children with autism. *Journal of Child Psychology and Psychiatry, 45,* 212–229.

Hurewitz, F., & Beals, K. (2008, May). *GrammarTrainer, a software based language intervention.* Poster presented to The 7th Annual International Meeting for Autism Research, London, England.

Hurewitz, F., & Boser, K. (2010, May). *Advantages of CAI for single word production and grammar production training.* Poster presented to The 9th Annual International Meeting for Autism Research, Philadelphia, PA.

Kelley, E., Paul, J.P., Fein, D., & Naigles, L. (2006). Residual language deficits in optimal outcome children with a history of autism. *Journal of Autism & Developmental Disorders, 36,* 807–828.

Krashen, S. (1982). *Principles and practice in second language acquisition.* Oxford, England: Pergamon.

Mintz, T.H., & Gleitman, L.R. (2002). Adjectives really do modify nouns: The incremental and restricted nature of early adjective acquisition. *Cognition, 84,* 267–293.

Moore, M., & Calvert, S. (2000). Brief report: Vocabulary acquisition for children with autism: Teacher or computer instruction. *Journal of Autism & Developmental Disorders, 30*(4).

Ramdoss, S., Mulloy, A., Lang, R., O'Reilly, M., Sigafoos, G.L., Didden, R., &

El Zein, F. (2011). Use of computer-based interventions to improve literacy skills in students with autism spectrum disorders: A systematic review. *Research in Autism Spectrum Disorders, 5,* 1306–1318.

Rogers, S. (2006). Evidence-based interventions for language development in young children with autism. In T. Charman & W. Stone (Eds.), *Social & communication development in autism spectrum disorders: Early intervention, diagnosis, & intervention* (pp. 143–179). New York, NY: Guilford Press

Tager-Flusberg, H., Paul, R., & Lord, C. (2005). Language and communication in autism. In F. Volkmar, A. Klin, & R. Paul (Eds.), *Handbook of autism and pervasive developmental disorders* (3rd ed., pp. 335–364). Hoboken, NJ: Wiley.

Thomke, B., & Boser, K. (2011). Language construction in an autistic child: Thoughts regarding language acquisition and language therapy: translation, update, and commentary on a 1977 case report. *Cognitive Behavioral Neurology, 24,* 156–167.

Whalen, C., Moss, D., Ilan, A., Vaupel, M., Fielding, P., MacDonald, K., ... Symon, J. (2010). Efficacy of TeachTown: Basics computer-assisted intervention for the intensive comprehensive autism program in Los Angeles Unified School District. *Autism: The International Journal of Research & Practice, 14,* 179–197.

Williams, C., Wright, B., Callaghan, G., & Coughlan, B. (2002). Do children with autism learn to read more readily by computer assisted instruction or traditional book methods? A pilot study. *Autism, 6,* 71–91.

Wilson, M.S., Fox, B.J., & Pascoe, J.P. (2009). *Laureate's language development programs: Theory and research* [Laureate Learning Systems monograph].

Yamamoto, J., & Miya, T. (1999). Acquisition and transfer of sentence construction in autistic students: Analysis by computer-based teaching. *Research in Developmental Disabilities, 20,* 355–377.

Young, J., Corea, C., Kimani, J., & Mandell, D. (2010). *Autism spectrum disorders (ASDs) services: Final report on environmental scan.* Prepared for the Centers for Medicare & Medicaid Services.

Mobile Media Devices

A Paradigm Shift in Communication Technology for Persons with Autism Spectrum Disorder

■ ■

Jessica Gosnell Caron and Howard C. Shane

Recent developments in consumer technology have led to smaller, faster, and lighter assistive technology (AT) devices. However, few provide the same access to multimedia, web, and interactivity offered by mass market, relatively low-cost mobile communication devices. In this chapter we examine how recent advances and trends in consumer mobile media devices can be used to facilitate and enhance communication, improve social participation, and enable greater independence for persons with autism spectrum disorder (ASD). For purposes of this chapter, we define *mobile media devices* as portable, multifunctional technology that allows access to communication and a host of web-based applications (e.g., information, audio, video). Our discussion of the burgeoning mass market technology applications will be organized and conceptualized around Shane and Weiss-Kapp's framework (2007) for the use of visual supports by persons with ASD. According to this schema, symbols and visual supports are used to improve comprehension (VIM, visual instructional mode), expression (VEM, visual expressive mode), and organization (VOM, visual organization mode). Also discussed are communication applications that have been designed specifically for persons with ASD (e.g., iPrompts) as well as general applications that can also, with clinical ingenuity, enhance the communication of this population (e.g., Pogg). We offer specific guidelines for implementation of current technology, discuss potential pitfalls, and consider future directions with respect to AT and ASD. Included in this chapter are a number of tables highlighting many popular applications (apps). It is not the intent of this chapter, however, to provide a compilation of all existing apps that potentially apply to persons on the autism spectrum. Instead, we offer a framework for app selection and clinical usage.

Research and clinical observations have noted the strong attraction to electronic media by persons with ASD (Shane & Albert, 2008). Children with ASD have been shown to learn concepts effectively through use of video-based instruction paired with graphic symbols (Shane et al., 2012). At the same time, there is growing interest in mobile media devices, particularly using the Apple iOS platform, as effective tools to teach such communication-related skills as language acquisition, syntax, and attention. Clinical observations also suggest that many children with ASD not only are able to easily manipulate and interact with this platform with little or no instruction but also become engaged with the technology for considerable periods of time. Because of this opportunity (advantage), the iOS platform is rapidly becoming an integral part of a clinical toolkit for assisting persons with ASD to communicate independently and effectively. In the relatively short time since the introduction of the platform, there has been rapid response by developers who have created a number of applications that support language development, speech and sound production, receptive language, and organizational skills, as well as augmentative communication. In what we consider the first phase of communication app development, the majority of apps that run on mobile media devices mimic communication applications that have been applied clinically on laptop and tablet computers as well as dedicated communication devices. The next wave of app developments can be expected to utilize more of the feature set of mobile media devices, including global positioning system functionality, voice recognition, and between-device interactivity. The expected result will be communication apps containing exciting new features that will enhance and expand overall communication possibilities.

VISUAL INSTRUCTIONAL MODE

The visual mode VIM focuses on the use of visual cues for the purpose of improving comprehension (Shane & Weiss-Kapp, 2007). Comprehension is a foundational skill for acquiring and applying language. As learners become more proficient at understanding the meaning of the visual symbols presented in conjunction with spoken language, they can apply this knowledge in the generation of novel expressive statements (Shane, O'Brien, & Sorce, 2009). Intervention focusing on receptive language skills, at the most basic level, targets comprehension of language and language concepts.

A plethora of apps aim to improve receptive language skills. Table 7.1 includes a representative sampling of apps that have been created specifically to enhance receptive language knowledge. Some of the apps included in Table 7.1 are designed in game format, thereby requiring the child to point out or manipulate an object or picture on the screen (e.g., Preposition Remix and Splingo's Language Universe). Many apps require the child to "talk out" answers (e.g., "If...then...") or describe scenes (e.g., House of Learning: "The boy is in the bed..."); some apps record a response (Gosnell, 2011).

Use of a Device's Photo Library to Support the Visual Instructional Mode

Spoken directives are often problematic for individuals with ASD because of difficulty comprehending spoken language. Changes in behavior (e.g., reduced tantrums and noncompliance) are sometimes observed when spoken language is accompanied by visual representations of these same directives. Shane et al. (2009)

Table 7.1. Apps supporting receptive language development

Fun with Directions HD
Speech with Milo: Sequencing
STS House
Speech with Milo: Verbs
Let's Talk: Following Instructions
Speech with Milo: Prepositions
WH- Questions Island
ABA Receptive ID
One Step Two Step
StoryPals
ABA Receptive Identification by Noun
Splingo's Language Universe
Fun Deck: Following Directions
House of Learning
EasyConcepts
Preposition Remix
WH- Questions App
Magical Concepts

advocated the use of scene or element cues to enhance comprehension and support overall communication. These visual supports can be presented in a low-tech format (e.g., printed photograph, Mayer-Johnson icon) or high-tech format (e.g., text or graphics on an iPad).

Scene cues can be used as visual representations that bypass language processing and comprehension of language structure. These cues can be either dynamic (e.g., full-motion videos) or static (e.g., digital photographs) in nature and capture a prototypical moment in an action scene. In practice, when a spoken directive is given, the learner is presented with the representative scene cue (i.e., a graphic depicting the intent of the spoken message) and expected to imitate the depicted action (Shane & Weiss-Kapp, 2007). Through an organized photo library on mobile media devices, scene cues for drill and tabletop activities—for example, targeting prepositions and verbs, as in "The boy pushes the car," as seen in Figure 7. 1— and activities for extension to the natural environment (e.g., a photograph of a boy getting his coat to support the verbal prompt "Go get your coat") can readily be provided.

Scene cue presented on the iPod Touch

Element cue presented on the iPod Touch

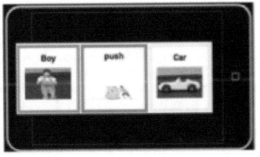

Figure 7.1. Visual examples of a scene cue and element cue presented from the photo library on an iPod Touch.

Similar to scene cues within an organized photo library, element cue supports can also be uploaded onto mobile media devices. This built-in feature is commonly untapped, yet it can easily be utilized to support a broad range of activities. Element cues can be combined to create visually based messages; thus, as provided in the example of Figure 7.1, the elements for agent (boy), action (push), and object (car) are represented from a photo library on an iPod Touch. The goal of language instruction at this level is generative sentence creation, whereby the learner understands the meaning of individual symbols and the syntactic rules governing their combinations, allowing the learner to both follow and generate novel directives (Shane & Weiss-Kapp, 2008).

VISUAL EXPRESSION MODE

The visual mode VEM focuses on the use of visual supports to supplement and enhance expressive communication. Individuals with ASD often have difficulties using speech functionally (Prizant & Wetherby, 2005), making visual supports an important augmentative tool to supplement spoken output. In the VEM, such visual symbols as line drawings, photographs, and entire visual scenes can be used to express myriad thoughts or ideas. The symbols may supplement spoken language or stand alone. Most mobile applications geared toward individuals with autism have been created to support the use of visuals for expressive communication. Most present symbols in a traditional gridlike display; for example, in Proloquo2go, the representation of this app can vary and include line drawings, text, or photographs. Other apps are more scene based (e.g., AutisMate), offering an entire visual scene to communicate a message. The VEM entails many communication operations, including requests, comments, transitions, directives, questions, and social pragmatics (Shane et al., 2009). Apps have been created to target and support specific pragmatic functions (e.g., My Choice Board, an exclusive request app), or they are created to be all-encompassing with programming built in to support a variety of functions (e.g., TouchChat, which has commenting, questioning, and sharing of information already organized and built within the app). It is important to note that the VEM is not unique to individuals with ASD. Table 7.2 identifies many commonly used augmentative communication applications, which have been designed to address communication needs arising from a wide range of causes. As of this writing, at least 100 communication applications are available for download from the App Store, and there is little doubt that the number will continue to grow. Web sites, blogs, and Google documents are a common source of compiled lists of augmentative communication apps (e.g., http://www.spectronicsinoz.com/article/iphoneipad-Apps-for-aac); these sources can often be used as a first step toward acquiring information about available apps (Gosnell, Costello, & Shane 2011). In addition, a chart that details features believed to represent critical and fundamental clinical considerations for a broad profile of people with complex communication needs can be found at http://www.childrenshospital.org/acp (Gosnell et al., 2011).

VISUAL ORGANIZATION MODE

The visual organization mode VOM includes use of visuals to sequentially organize a task, activity, or schedule. Daily schedules and other time-oriented displays

Table 7.2. Commonly used augmentative communication applications available for download in the iTunes Store

AutisMate
Proloquo2go
Answers Yes/No HD
MyTalkTools Mobile
Expressive
Assistive Chat
GoTalk Now
TapSpeak Choice
Alexicom AAC
TapSpeak Sequence
LAMP Words for Life
Grace
SpeechHero
TouchChat-AAC
TalkTablet US
Predictable
Avaz
SoundingBoard

(e.g., timers, countdowns displays, first-then displays) are common examples of the VOM. The VOM is an effective tool for helping individuals with ASD handle transitions encountered throughout a typical day and better react to unexpected changes in routine, thereby minimizing anxiety and reducing disruptive behaviors. Communicating information about organization and transition supports the learner's ability to recognize what is going to happen next, confidently begin a new activity, lay out the steps of that activity, and move smoothly between tasks (Shane & Weiss-Kapp, 2007). A number of apps have been created to support one or all of the aforementioned objectives. For example, iPrompts includes a visual timer and schedule, Time Timer include a visual countdown timer for a specified activity, and Steps includes a visual schedule, task sequencer, and countdown and token reinforcement boards. Table 7.3 includes apps commonly recommended to support activity engagement, transitions, and prepare for what might be next.

In addition to apps created specifically as VOM, the built-in photo library of a mobile device allows quick access to static images of timers, visual schedules, and photographs of "reward" choices. Figure 7.2 show examples of an organized photo library, a visual schedule for "after school," and reward choices.

CREATIVELY UTILIZING MASS MARKET APPS

The search for appropriate apps should not be limited to dedicated applications (i.e., apps created with the focus of supporting persons with ASD) because in doing so, many well-designed apps that offer motivating and fun learning opportunities would be overlooked. Siri, Calendar, Clock, and other internal features within the iDevices are options that can service and supplement an individual with minimal to no adaptation or creativity. Yet, in addition to using these built-in features

Table 7.3. Visual organization apps available for download

Time Timer
Time Tracker
iPrompts
Steps
iReward
iEarned That
Picture Prompt Timer
With Routinely
Visual Schedule Planner
First-Then Board
Visual Routine
ChoiceWorks
Pictello
PhotoMind
Turn Taker
Video Scheduler
iCommunicate

Organized library	Visual schedule	Photos for "reward" choices

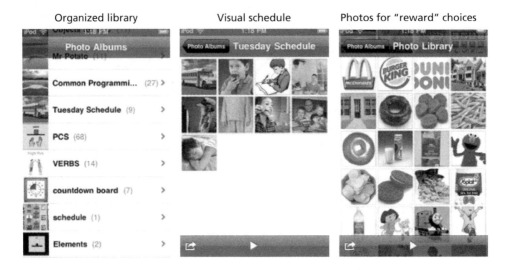

Figure 7.2. An organized photo library, a visual schedule, and photos for "reward" choices stored in the photo library of the iDevice.

or apps created for a speech-related purpose, inventive clinicians are encouraged to reach beyond the intended purpose of an app through adaptation in order to support their clinical interventions (Gosnell, 2011). Apps that are created for other purposes can, when adapted, lend themselves to specific clinical purposes and motivate patients to engage in activities they might otherwise not be willing to participate in. For example, the "Case Example Utilizing Pogg Creatively to Support Communication Goals" sidebar describes how one student, Justin, uses the app Pogg to achieve several intervention goals, including increased knowledge of verbs and imitation of action verb concepts (e.g., *clap, yawn, jump*).

CASE EXAMPLE UTILIZING THE APPLICATION POGG CREATIVELY TO SUPPORT COMMUNICATION GOALS

Justin, a 9-year-old boy with autism spectrum disorder, currently vocalizes minimally and uses a Springboard Lite as his electronic communication device. Justin communicates primarily for requesting, using single-noun graphics. His intervention targeted expanding pragmatic intents, including directing, labeling (especially actions), and action imitation (e.g., clap, jump).

   Outcomes when using traditional AAC intervention techniques (e.g., video modeling on the computer, topic displays in his device for common intervention activities, [i.e., bubbles]) are:

- Noncompliance
- Hand-over-hand interactions
- Inattention
- Prompting to participate
- Working for reinforcements and breaks after three trials

Outcomes when using creatively adapted apps (e.g., Pogg) are:

- Engaged with the iPad, demonstrating increased attention to task
- Produced two-word utterance in correct syntactical form (e.g., [agent + action], [Pogg + jump]) on his Springboard Lite (using a topic display; see the Pogg image for an example of a topic display)
- Imitating actions produced by Pogg (e.g., clap, jump)
- Working for breaks after 10 trials
- Minimal prompting

(Images of Pogg App for iPhone and iPad, Version 1.4.1, Copyright © 2012 Ricky Vuckovic; reprinted by permission.)

   Like Pogg, many apps can be transformed from an original intent to entertain into a useful therapy tool. For example, Doodle Buddy, a free application created for painting, scribbling, and drawing, can be adapted to meet several expressive, receptive, and organizational intervention goals (see Figure 7.3). Although this app was not designed for speech intervention, it lends itself naturally to uses beyond its original intent in order to support a variety of expressive and receptive goals and activities (Gosnell, 2011).

Mode	Visuals within Doodle Buddy that correspond with expressive uses	Case examples
Expressive		Tim supplemented his speech output by writing on this whiteboard app.
Receptive	Visuals within Doodle Buddy that correspond to receptive uses	Case examples James demonstrated prepositional knowledge by circling the dog IN the tree. In this case an imported scene (photograph) was used. The "coolness" factor of manipulating concepts through technology motivated him to engage, whereas previous strategies had been rejected.
Organization	Visuals within Doodle Buddy that correspond with organizational uses	Case examples Erica followed her visual schedule when it was imported into the whiteboard, allowing her to "cross off" each task when it was completed.

Figure 7.3.   Adaptation of Doodle Buddy enabled a number of therapeutic goals to be achieved.

Table 7.4 lists several additional apps that were not created to explicitly target receptive or expressive communication goals but lend themselves to be effective materials for therapy. Potential goals addressed may include but are not limited to following directions (e.g., My Playhome, Cupcakes), increasing vocabulary (e.g., Opposites, Pogg), or sequencing (e.g., More Pizza). Looking at applications, a skilled clinician can see inherent therapeutic value in an app that is marketed for children's entertainment. For example, the My Playhome application is created for children to pretend play with a virtual dollhouse. The dollhouse offers different rooms with interactive components (e.g., a sink that will pour water if you turn it on, a toilet that flushes, a fridge that opens). Instead of using the application for independent pretend play, a clinician can use the application to work on following directives (e.g., "Put the boy in the crib, turn on the water, and then put a plate in the sink.") and increasing vocabulary (e.g., "The boy is bouncing, what is another word for bouncing? Jumping? Let's make the boy jump!"). For additional ideas and app lists, visit Therapy App 411 (http://www.therapyapp411.com), Geek SLP (http://www.geekslp.com), or Speech-Language Pathology Sharing (http://www.slpsharing.com). These blogs and web sites provide lists of apps and examples of ways to use an app

Table 7.4. Applications adapted for expressive and receptive language

Expressive apps
- The Mouth: Talking Doodles
- Starfall
- Mickey Mouse Clubhouse Road Rally
- Talking Carl
- Crazy Face
- BalloonAnimals
- Create My Own Flashcards
- Doodle Buddy
- Book Creator for iPad
- Talking Baby Hippo
- iPuppet—Voice Activated Dummy
- Pogg

Receptive language apps
- Faces iMake
- My PlayHome
- Create a Car
- Pogg
- Draw a House
- Cupcake Corner
- Toca Hair Salon
- Toca Tea Party
- Lego Build Your Brain
- More Pizza!
- Silly Story Maker
- Magnetic Draw

Note: These applications can be used in many different ways (speech production, pacing, voice feedback, sequencing, age-appropriate concepts, following directions, etc.) and have been classified here based on common uses of these apps.

beyond its designated intent to support a variety of expressive and receptive goals and activities (Gosnell, 2011).

FEATURE MATCHING

The popularity, availability, and flexibility of mobile media devices are altering the traditional clinician–consumer relationship within the AT field. There has been a democratization of AT, where consumers and professionals alike are learning about new developments at the same time. As a result, there seems to be a shift away from the trained clinician as the driving force behind selection of AT and intervention strategies to a more consumer-driven model. In some instances, families are choosing to "self-treat"; in others, an educator or technology department is selecting iPads and choosing apps for communication as well as other purposes. This tendency is causing some practitioners to fit the client into the available device and apps as opposed to fitting the AT to the client (AAA-RERC, 2011; Gosnell et al., 2011); given this trend, caution is warranted when choosing any application intended to improve human performance.

We contend that a comprehensive assessment remains an important part of technology selection. In other words, there remains the need for a foundation upon which a device and app or any other tool or strategy is based.[1] The popularity of mobile media devices, coupled with the impressive speed with which apps that parallel desirable features of dedicated speech-generating devices are being produced, has resulted in many practitioners forgoing, or at least temporarily suspending, well-established clinical assessment strategies (Gosnell et al., 2011). When selecting the device and apps without assessments, there is the risk of making decisions without sufficient experience or clinical judgment and knowledge. The pitfalls include lacking sufficient awareness of the individual's language abilities or needs, lacking knowledge of other AT communication device options, and lacking knowledge of the differentiating features of apps. Surely the greatest harm resulting from reckless clinical decisions based on such insufficiency is the time wasted by the learner using an inappropriate communication technology. From our perspective, as a way to ensure appropriateness of apps, two primary questions should always be asked: "Was the device platform and accompanying app selected through a thorough clinical feature matching process?" and "Are we fitting the device and communication app to the person, or are we fitting the person's needs systematically to the device's features?" (Gosnell et al., 2011).

Example of the Feature-Matching Process

The rapid and continuing development of new apps and mobile media device features makes it impossible to conduct a comprehensive review of communication apps or device features. Rather, here we offer an example of a clinical framework for comparing and selecting apps. Figure 7.4 lists features known to represent critical and fundamental considerations for a broad profile of people with ASD and complex communication needs. Along the horizontal axis, the chart contains desired features broken down into 11 main categories and then an additional "customization"

---

[1] The idea of the practitioner making technology decisions based on matching clinical needs with available technological options is not a new one (Shane & Costello, 1994), but it is an idea that seems to have been forgotten in all the hype surrounding mobile devices.

Apps	Purpose of use — Expressive	Receptive	Organizational	Output — Digitized	Synthesized	Male	Female	Child	Multiple languages	No voice output	Speech settings — Voice recognition	Voice recording	Temporary volume	Pause speech	Speak after letter	Speak after word	Speak after punctuation	Speak upon selection	Speech to symbol dictate	Cust. of S.S. — Pronunciation	Adjust speech rate	Customize speak after	Representation — PCS	Symbolstix	Photographs	Clipart	Minspeak	Text
Proloquo2go	X	X			X	X	X	X								X		X		X	X	X		X	X			X
Grace	X	X								X															X	X		
Assistive Chat	X				X	X	X									X		X			X	X						X
Sounding Board	X	X		X		X	X					X						X							X	X		
Speak It!	X				X	X	X		X									X		X	X							X

Note: For formatting purposes, only a portion of the chart is represented in this table. The whole chart (including all the features and definitions of the features) can be downloaded at Children's Hospital Boston's web site (http://www.childrenshospital.org/acp). The chart will change over time as apps are updated.

Key: Cust of S.S., customization of speech setting.

Figure 7.4. Selection features with example of app comparisons. (From Gosnell, J. [2011]. Feature matching communication applications. Boston, MA: Children's Hospital. Retrieved from http://childrenshospital.org/clinicalservices/Site2016/Documents/PDFofFeatureChart.pdf; adapted by permission.)

column for when customization options affect components of the features; for example, being able to import your own photographs is a customization component of the "representation" category (Gosnell et al., 2011).

The most desirable app features useful for persons with ASD are broken down into the following 11 categories:

- *Purpose of use*: Whether the app was created for the purpose of expressive communication, receptive communication, and/or organization

- *Output:* The type of speech (or no speech) produced when using the communication application (e.g., digitized or synthesized)

- *Speech settings and customization of speech settings:* The volume, pitch, rate, and options for when the device speaks out loud (e.g., speak after a word vs. speak upon selection)

- *Representation and customization of representation:* The different icons and symbols within the app (e.g., Symbolstix, photographs, PCS) and the ability to import your own photographs and add more than one icon to a button

- *Display and customization of display settings:* Different layouts (e.g., choice boards vs. scene based) and dynamic versus static options; options for changing sizes of symbols, font, color, borders, and so on

- *Feedback features and customization of feedback features:* Options that may be turned on or off to add additional input when an icon is presented (e.g., highlight, zoom, or enlargement of an icon; auditory review) or when an icon is selected (e.g., tactile or vibration feedback)

- *Rate enhancement and customization of rate enhancement:* A technique or strategy used to speed up output and increase efficiency (e.g., encoding and prediction strategies), customizable by turning strategies on or off and modifying to unique needs (e.g., predict common phrases vs. words)

- *Access and customization of access:* How the user will interact with the device (e.g., direct selection, pointer), customizable through support to assist with access (e.g., dwell)

- *Required motor competencies:* Motor movements that have to be used in order to interact with the app (e.g., swipe and/or pinch)

- *Support:* The different ways in which users and those who support the users can learn about the app and how the support team resolves technical issues

- *Miscellaneous and customization of miscellaneous:* Features that support a variety of functions commonly requested by users of Complex Communication Needs (CCN; e.g., e-mail, texting)

It is important to note that not all the foregoing features currently exist in apps (highlighting the importance of matching a person's needs to the right tools rather than try to fit a person to a specific platform or app). It is also important that in its master location (at http://www.childrenshospital.org/acp), this chart is dynamic, changing with apps and features as new clinical solutions become available through innovations that further develop and change technology. Communication applications are placed along the vertical axis, enabling the user to add as many apps as he or she would like to compare. For the portion of the chart shown in Figure 7.4, we have selected a few popular communication applications (e.g., Proloquo2go, Grace, Assistive Chat) and fit them into the schema of the table for purposes of comparison.

Clinical Application of the Chart

Not all 100 or more communication applications need to be compared with the chart at once. After the clinician identifies key features for the individual, the key features themselves, in addition to the professional's general knowledge of the current communication applications, will start ruling out apps (e.g., if the individual cannot spell or read, text-to-speech apps should be ruled out among expressive communication options and thus not be placed in the chart comparison). Once the key features are narrowed down to the "must haves" and mismatched apps are ruled out, the chart can then be filled out, thus narrowing down the field of apps to a handful to trial with the patient.

A case study, Mike, is used to illustrate application of the assessment process summarized in Table 7.5 and use of the app feature matching process charted in Figure 7.4. The information gathered during the assessment is identified and applied to key app features (the key features are a narrowed selection from a large feature list and are the features considered to be of "highest priority"). The key features are then broken down and compared to a select number of apps, ruling out apps until a final app is chosen (Figure 7.5).

Table 7.5. Key needs and features based on assessment outcomes for Mike, a 13-year-old boy with autism spectrum disorder

	Information gathered during assessment	Key features based on information gathered during the assessment
Representation	• Able to use text, photographs, and Mayer-Johnson icons	• Text, is reading and writing
Display settings	• Able to navigate dynamic displays • Consistently preferred opening apps with a keyboard as opposed to navigating arrays for whole words	• Dynamic display, yet preferred keyboarding displays (QWERTY)
Efficiency strategies	• Able to use word prediction • Able to navigate to recently used lists • Preferred prestored text-based icons	• App needs word prediction and prestored message capabilities
Purpose of use	• Sharing information • Requesting • Answering and asking Questions • Commenting	• Expressive tools • Voice output (digitized or synthesized) • Boards with the ability to expand beyond just choice making

	Synthesized	Speak after selection	Adjust speech rate	Text	Keyboard-QWERTY	Adjust text size	Word prediction	Abbreviation expansion	Logical letter	Ability to store phases	"Recent used" list	Adjust dwell	Rule-out factors
iMean				X	X						X	X	No voice output
ShapeWriter				X	X	X	X				X		No voice output
TalkAssist	X	X		X	X						X		No efficiency strategies
SayIt	X	X		X	X						X		No efficiency strategies
SpeakIt!	X	X	X	X	X	X					X	X	A good low cost alternative, but was willing to pay more for efficiency strategies
Proloquo2go	X	X	X	X	X			X			X	X	Comparing word predictions – Mike said Assistive Chat "found his word better"
EasySpeak	X	X	X	X	X			X			X		Ruled out due to voices (attempts)
Assistive Chat	X	X	X	X	X			X			X		

Figure 7.5. Mike's key features compared to eight different communication apps.

Assessment findings (summarized in Table 7.5) for Mike include the need to use text in a QWERTY keyboard (vs. an ABC or frequency-of-use layout). In addition, Mike demonstrated the ability to use the dynamic features of a device (e.g., navigation), yet had a strong preference for a QWERTY keyboard with message window. Therefore, despite his ability to rapidly navigate to submenus and efficiently transition from pages, Mike preferred using the keyboard rather than utilizing symbols in a grid-based, menu-driven setup. Regarding efficiency, Mike was using direct selection with word prediction, prestored messages (text based), and recently used lists. Lastly, the purpose of the app was for expressive communication and social participation; therefore voice output with synthesized male speech was needed.

Eight applications were selected (including Speak It!, Prloquo2go, Assistive Chat), placed along the vertical or y axis, and compared to the app features that were found to be critical (e.g., expressive tool, use of text, rate enhancement) and listed along the horizontal x axis. The chart was filled out by placing an x in the column if the app contained the feature. The apps containing the most x marks would be the apps to trial with Mike. In Mike's case, many apps were ruled out because they lack voice output or the app did not have efficiency strategies (the last column of Figure 7.5 explains why the app was ruled out). Figure 7.5 reveals that both Proloquo2go and Easy Speak each have features that match those of the final app choice, Assistive Chat. Yet in trialing the apps in the assessment with Mike, due to quality of voice (British accents) and price ($200 vs. $30 in comparing Proloquo2go to Assistive Chat when Mike was not using symbols or dynamic arrays), Assistive Chat was chosen as the app that best fit Mike's communication needs.

The speed with which apps for mobile media devices have become available has caused many clinicians, educators, and potential consumers of AAC to search these apps for a quick fix. Although this platform and certain apps may indeed be a good match to the strengths and needs of some individuals, it is important that the needs of each individual be considered case by case using a through and clinically based feature-matching approach. To this end, the use of Figure 7.4 (initially by narrowing down key features for comparison and then matching the user's needs to the app's specifications) will assist clinicians in continuing to utilize best practice by applying a featuring-matching approach to apps, once the device platform is deemed most appropriate (Gosnell et al., 2011).

CONCLUSION

Research has shown that many individuals with ASD rely on visual processing as a dominant information-processing mode and because of that strength they usually possess a heightened interest in visual materials (Shane et al., 2012). As highly visual media, the iOS device platform and similar mobile media devices are technology that can bridge the gap in the life of persons with ASD, offering a means of communicating, engaging, participating, playing, and interacting in expansive and unique ways they did not have access to before. In this new era of educating and engaging tech-savvy children and parents, we as providers must continue to learn and challenge ourselves to develop more engaging and generationally relevant assessment and intervention strategies. To this end, mobile media devices can be loaded with free and affordable apps that may be used to support individuals with ASD. Apps and the mobile media platform can be utilized by clinicians within therapy and diagnostic sessions. In addition, through informed clinical judgment, clinicians can implement the mobile platform as an individual's voice output device, scheduler, or learning tool.

Throughout this exciting time of technological revolution, there remains a need for evidence-based research surrounding the efficacy of these tools and new clinical decision-making processes. Balanced with this, we predict and hope, the momentum of the lighter, faster, more affordable, "cool" mainstream technology will continue to develop in both hardware options and accessibility (e.g., joystick access) and apps (e.g., speech-to-symbol dictate).

REFERENCES

AAC-RERC. (2011, March). *Mobile devices and communication apps*. Retrieved from http://www.aac-rerc.psu.edu/index.php/pages/show/id/46

Gosnell, J. (2011). Apps: An emerging tool for SLPs : A plethora of apps can be used to develop expressive, receptive, and other language skills. *The ASHA Leader.* http://www.asha.org/publications/leader/2011/111011/apps–an-emerging-tool-for-slps.htm

Gosnell, J., Costello. J., & Shane, H. (2011). Using a clinical approach to answer "What communication apps should we use?" *Augmentative and Alternative Communication, 20*, 87–96.

Prizant, B.M., & Wetherby, A.M. (2005). Critical considerations in enhancing communication abilities for persons with autism spectrum disorders. In F.R. Volkmar, R. Paul, A. Klin, & D.J. Cohen (Eds.), *Handbook of autism and pervasive developmental disorders* (3rd ed., Vol. 2, pp. 925–945). Hoboken, NJ: Wiley.

Shane, H.C., & Albert, P.D. (2008). Electronic screen media for persons with autism spectrum disorders: Results of a survey. *Journal of Autism and Developmental Disorders, 38*, 1499–1508.

Shane, H., & Costello, J. (1994, November). *Augmentative communication assessment and the feature matching process*. Mini-seminar presented at the Annual Convention of the American Speech-Language-Hearing Association, New Orleans, LA.

Shane, H., Laubscher, E.H., Schlosser, R.W., Flynn, S., Sorce, J.F., & Abramson, J. (2012).

Applying technology to visually support language and communication individuals with autism spectrum disorders. *Journal of Autism and Developmental Disorders, 42*(6), 1228–1235.

Shane, H.C., O'Brien, M., & Sorce, J. (2009). Use of a visual graphic language system to support communication for persons on the autism spectrum. *Augmentative and Alternative Communication, 18,* 130–136.

Shane, H.C., & Weiss-Kapp, S. (2007). *Visual language in autism.* San Diego, CA: Plural.

Technology to Support Literacy in Autism

∎ ∎

Sarah C. Wayland, Katharina I. Boser, and Joan L. Green

The ability to read and write is fundamental to full participation in society, yet individuals with autism spectrum disorder (ASD) are not always taught these important skills. This is in part because other skills have been considered higher priority, including appropriate social interaction, behavior, and verbal communication. In addition, professionals used to believe that the ability to speak was a prerequisite to learning how to read and write (Vukelich, Christie, & Enz, 2002). The fact that many people with autism struggle to speak because of difficulty with motor skills (Gernsbacher, Sauer, Geye, Schweigert, & Hill Goldsmith, 2007) was not understood until more recently. Previously, many professionals believed that people with autism who could not speak did not have the capacity for language. Without language, it seemed useless to try to teach reading.

Luckily, current consensus is that those with autism are perfectly capable of learning to read, and that they can effectively communicate by writing (and especially typing). Indeed, communication via the written word can allow children who were previously unable to express their thoughts to communicate effectively with others (see Millar, Light, & Schlosser, 2006, for a review of how alternative modes of communication allow nonverbal children learn how to speak). More and more, individuals on the autism spectrum are compensating for and overcoming their literacy challenges with the help of appropriately selected and implemented technologies.

The sections of this chapter are organized around six literacy skills: alphabetics (including phonics and phonemic knowledge), vocabulary, text comprehension, fluency, spelling, and written composition. In keeping with the universal design for learning (UDL) framework, the first three areas are *input skills* (reading skills) and the last three are *output skills* (writing skills in the case of spelling and written composition, oral reading and writing in the case of fluency). Fluency can apply to both reading skill and writing skills. See Figure 8.1 for a mind map that shows how

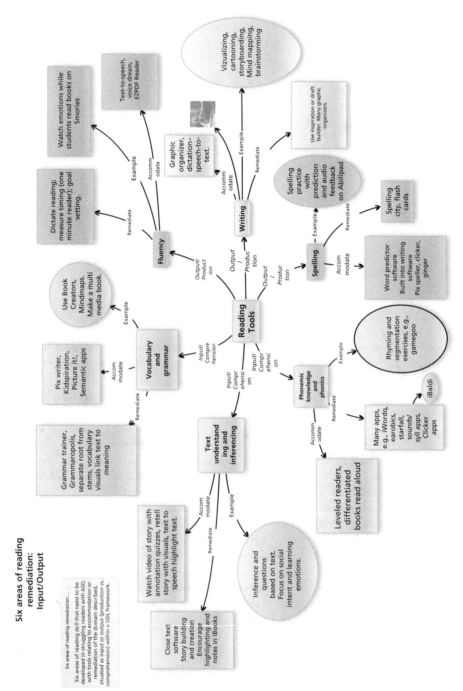

Figure 8.1. A mind map depicting literacy skills discussed in the chapter and organized by UDL principles of *input* (phonics and phonemic knowledge, text understanding, vocabulary/grammar) and *output* (fluency, spelling, writing).

the literacy skills are categorized. The first part of each section describes research regarding how to improve students' ability to understand and communicate using the written word—both by teaching the missing skills and by providing effective accommodations. The second part of each section focuses on specific technologies and applications that can be adopted to help with the skill. It is important to enlist the assistance of a speech-language pathologist trained to work with people on the autism spectrum; these clinicians can select appropriate technologies and design an effective program to support the individual person's needs.

Many of the technologies described here can be used to teach more than one skill so we explicitly refer the reader to other sections when a technology serves more than one purpose. For example, we have a section on text-to-speech (TTS) technologies that can be useful in reading intervention programs, but which can also be integrated into word processors and writing organizers to improve writing. Figure 8.1 indicates a few of the types of accommodations and remediating applications discussed in each of the six sections.

EFFECTIVE READING INSTRUCTION

The *Report of the National Reading Panel* (National Institute of Child Health and Human Development [NICHD], 2000) describes three main areas of instruction that respond well to intervention: alphabetics (including phonemic awareness and phonics), fluency, and comprehension (including vocabulary and text comprehension). Below, we describe each of these areas, in particular, the skills they involve and effective remediation strategies.

Alphabetics

In learning to read English, awareness of how the letters of the alphabet relate to the sounds of the language is a key skill. This involves being aware of the sounds that make up spoken words (phonemics) as well as how those sounds relate to letters (phonics).

Phonemic Awareness Instruction   Phonemic awareness is the ability to hear, identify, and manipulate the sounds that make up spoken words. In written language, these sounds are represented by letters (e.g., the word *bat* is made up of the sounds /b/, /æ/, and /t/) or combinations of letters (e.g., the word *shock* is made up of the sounds /ʃ/, /a/, and /k/). It is important to remember, though, that phonemes are the sounds of language, and letters do not have a one-to-one correspondence with letters (think about how you say the *o* in *collate* and *college* and *color*). Understanding how these sounds can be manipulated to change the meaning of the word (e.g., *bat* does not mean the same thing as *pat* or *back*) helps children learn to spell, and it also helps them to be more effective readers.

Phonemic awareness can be developed through a number of activities, including asking children to discriminate phonemes (Is that a *p* or a *d*?), categorize (Is *cat* more like *cut* or *hut*?), blend phonemes to form words (I have a /b/ sound, an /l/ sound, and an /o/sound. What what happens when we put them all together?), segment words (What sounds make up the word *cat*?), delete or add phonemes to form new words (What new word do you get when you add an *s* to the beginning of the word *treat*?), and substitute phonemes to make new words (If you substitute a /k/ sound for the *b* in *bat,* what word do you get?).

Children are usually taught phonemic awareness in English by having them learn the correspondence between phonemes and letters of the alphabet; instruction is most effective when it does this by focusing on only one or two of the activities listed above at a time (NICHD, 2000).

Children on the autism spectrum can be slower to develop these skills than other children; they overgeneralize the rules (Marcus et al., 1992), and they are slower to learn the exceptions to the rules (M. Dixon, personal communication, 2013). When children overgeneralize, words are pronounced oddly; for example, the word *monopoly* might be pronounced as /mo/ /no/ /po/ /li/ instead of /mə/ /nɑ/ /pə/ /li/.

Phonics Instruction One of the primary tasks in learning to read involves decoding the systematic relationships between letters and phonemes. Phonics instruction helps readers learn how the letters of written language map to the sounds of spoken language. When taught systematically, explicit phonics instruction significantly improves word recognition and paves the way for better reading comprehension.

There are many approaches to teaching phonics; these methods are most effective when the instructor has explicit information about how to systematically teach letter–sound relationships in a logical sequence. One such approach teaches people to convert letters or letter combinations into sounds and to blend the sounds to form recognizable words (e.g., /k/, /æ/, and /t/ → *cat*). This approach, called *synthetic phonics,* teaches the student how the sounds work in isolation and then how to integrate the sounds to form words.

The counterpart to synthetic phonics is *analytic phonics,* in which the reader learns to analyze the letter–sound relationships in words they already know. Analytic phonics teaches the reader to pronounce sounds in context while teaching the reader how to segregate the word into its constituent parts (e.g., *cat* → /k/, /æ/, and /t/). *Onset-rime phonics* instruction is similar to analytic phonics in that it teaches readers to break one-syllable words into an onset (which includes the letters before the first vowel, e.g., *c* in the word *cat*) and a rime (the remaining part of the word, e.g., *at* in the word *cat*). Once readers can do this, they can learn how to pronounce the onset as separate from the rime, combining the two as they become more proficient.

Phonics through spelling teaches readers to segment words into phonemes (like analytic phonics) and to make words by writing letters for the phonemes they want to represent (like synthetic phonics).

There is one other approach to consider, one in which readers are taught to think about how words relate to each other. In *analogy-based phonics* instruction, readers learn to think about how words they do not know are made up from parts of other words they do know. For example, if you do not know the word *antidisestablishmentarianism,* you can still pronounce it by breaking it into parts that you do know: *anti-dis-establish-ment-arian-ism.* These methods for teaching alphabetics can help readers learn how to relate the sounds of English to the printed word. Each approach has been shown to be effective (Lyon et al., 2001; NICHD, 2000), especially if the instructor also provides ample opportunities for emerging readers to apply what they are learning in the context of reading words, sentences, and stories. With sufficient practice and exposure, readers learn to recognize words automatically and no longer need to sound them out. With this increased ease in recognition, they become more fluent readers.

Technology to Support Alphabetics   There are many computer software programs and mobile apps that use a drill and practice approach to improve early literacy skills using a phonetics approach as well as a sight word approach (see Table 8.1 for some examples). Most offer tasks at a variety of levels, use engaging graphics that can be customized, provide immediate feedback regarding the accuracy of the response, and document performance. Many programs also automatically advance to harder tasks as levels are mastered. The phonics and phonemic awareness products listed in Table 8.2 teach early literacy skills with multisensory engagement using high-quality graphics. Users can tap on pictures and text to hear sounds and words and receive instant feedback to promote learning and comprehension. Programs listed in the table offer assistance with such important skills as recognizing sounds and patterns, sequencing and blending sounds, learning the alphabet, writing letters, rhyming, and learning new words. There are also applications (apps) for mobile tablets that contain letter-tracing activities. (See the section on handwriting for more of these.) The products are very effective learning tools, rewarding the individual for accurate motor movement as he or she simultaneously hears the sounds of the letters.

Fluency

Fluency is the ability to read a text accurately and effortlessly. When reading aloud, fluent readers can make their reading sound like spontaneously generated natural speech; it is both expressive and meaningful. This is possible because fluent readers are able to hold previously recognized words in memory while continuing to read and also because they understand each word as it is read. This skill allows them to link the words together to create meaningful phrases before they speak them. Readers who have not yet developed fluency read slowly, word by word. They struggle to integrate the words into meaningful phrases because their cognitive resources

Table 8.1.   Highly engaging literacy activities

Between the Lions: Free online interactive web site based on PBS award-winning television show.

http://www.pbskids.org/lions

Explode the Code: Online subscription; online, data-driven phonics instruction. Break through the code with online, data-driven phonics instruction.

http://www.explodethecode.com

MimioSprout and MimioReading: Online subscription program. MimioSprout early reading individualized instruction and MimioReading individualized instruction are part of an award-winning, interactive, online reading program that meets the National Reading Panel guidelines for instruction in phonemic awareness, phonics, fluency, vocabulary, and reading comprehension. Printed stories and detailed individualized automated performance reports accompany the program.

http://www.mimio.com/headsprout/index.html

Earobics/Gamegoo: Activities for all areas of reading (comprehension too), but best-known great tools for alphabetics: sound blending, phonemic awareness games, segmentation. Highly engaging games that involve sound and music. CDs for computer, or web-based integration.

Free games on Gamegoo.

http://www.earobics.com and http://www.earobics.com/gamegoo

HearBuilder Phonological Awareness: Requires CD. HearBuilder is a series of educational software programs designed to help students improve their listening and memory skills.

Develops phonological awareness, sequencing, following directions, and auditory memory.

http://www.hearbuilder.com

Table 8.2.   Phonics and phonemic awareness

ABC PocketPhonics: Teaches letter sounds (phonics) app for mobile iOS. Aimed at preschool kids and older children with disabilities, PocketPhonics uses animated graphics, sound, and touch. Also teaches how to write letters and how to blend letter sounds together to make words.

http://www.appsinmypocket.com

Sound Literacy: Sound Literacy is an instructional tool and resource for teaching phonemic awareness, phonological processing, the alphabetic principle, and word study focusing on morphology. Encourages teachers and students to work together in an intensive word study program. With an abundance of "sound knowledge," Sound Literacy provides a platform for teaching students to hear, see, and analyze words.

http://www.blog.soundliteracy.com

Bob Books: Bob Books introduce new letter sounds, using consistency, repetition, and stories. Letters are sounded out as users touch them. Students touch and drag letters to position after hearing story. Varying levels.

http://www.learningtouch.com/products

Interactive Alphabet: Interactive Alphabet turns every letter into an interactive toy. Original artwork, animations, music, and sound effects. Flashcards engage children in sound–letter learning, encourage fine motor skills, and promote thinking and problem-solving skills.

http://www.piikeastreet.com

Starfall ABCs: Starfall.com opened in September 2002 as a free public service to teach children to read with phonics. Uses a systematic phonics approach in conjunction with phonemic awareness practice. Includes leveled books, short videos about letter sounds and phonemes, templates for writing and playing with letters and words.

http://www.starfall.com

iSpyPhonics: Allows user to add pictures highly relevant to the individual when learning sounds and letters.

http://www.miasapps.com

are used up trying to sound out each word. Reading fluently is possible only when decoding the words has become so automatic that doing so does not tax the reader's cognitive resources. Fluency frees readers to focus their attention on the meaning of the text, allowing them to make connections to and between the ideas in the text.

Reading aloud is the best way to develop fluency. This gives students the opportunity to practice fluid decoding and to automate the decoding of letters into words. In addition to asking students to read aloud, either individually or as a group, instructors can model fluent reading by reading aloud to their students so the students can hear others speaking the words aloud. Fluency can be developed using technology by having students record their own voices and playing the recording back to them, a feature a number of customizable book creators have in common. Recommended technologies for practicing fluency include book creators, digital and read-aloud applications, and the software presented at the end of the following section.

Supporting Fluency with Interactive Books, Digital Books, and Print Awareness   The research literature has established that reading traditional books aloud to all children from an early age is critical in order to set the stage for literary success (Lyon et al., 2001; NICHD, 2000). Shared book readings, encouraging listening, and peer-to-peer communication via text all help to develop the skills that are the building blocks for early literacy. Interactive books on a computer, e-books read aloud by an e-Reader, and tablets with TTS and interactive capabilities can be very engaging for individuals with ASDs (see Table 8.3).

Customized Digital Stories   Teachers, clinicians, and parents can facilitate interest by creating talking books using pictures from a child's environment, the sound of a parent's voice, and pictured daily routines from the child's life. By allowing students to record their stories digitally, these books can help develop fluency. Many of these apps can also be used to create social stories (Gray, 1995). The importance and value of social stories in teaching students with autism cannot be underestimated. Support for teaching skills through social stories has been highlighted by a number of researchers and educators (Chan & O'Reilly, 2008; Gray, 1995; Hagiwara & Myles, 1999). Video modeling tools can improve fluency through social engagement, thereby helping students with autism to develop an understanding of social intent and behavior. See chapter 10 for more on this technique.

StoryBuilder (http://www.mobile-educationstore.com) is typical of an interactive digital story tool. This app works to build story structure and comprehension, but it also requires the user (e.g., therapist, teacher, student) to speak. Individuals respond to questions about a picture, and StoryBuilder records their verbal responses. The answers are then put together and can be played back as a coherent story that can be listened to,

Table 8.3.   Creating digital stories

Pictello: Pictello is a simple way to create talking photo albums and talking books on an iOS system (iPad, iPhone, and iPod Touch). Anyone can make a story including important events or the latest holiday pictures to share with family who live far away.

http://www.assistiveware.com

Make an interactive story on your computer: Upload image, text, and audio to site to create an e-book on your computer that is viewable on a variety of devices. Use CAST Book Builder to create books and interactive quizzes.

http://www.epubbud.com

http://www.bookbuilder.cast.org

Stories2Learn (S2L): S2L offers the ability to create personalized stories using photos, text, and audio messages. Preloaded stories can be used to promote an individual's literacy, provide leisure activities, and foster social skills. It can be used to teach social skills related to reciprocal play, nonverbal communication, playground and school rules, turn taking, and the like. The user is able to create audio and dialogue that correspond to the photos.

http://www.look2learn.com

iBook Creator: The simple way to create your iBooks, adding color, images, text, and sound. Add hyperlinks to images. Read them in iBooks, send them to your friends, or submit them to the iBookstore. Ideal for children's picture books, photo books, art books, cook books, manuals, textbooks, and the list goes on.

https://itunes.apple.com/us/app/book-creator-for-ipad/id442378070?mt=8

Calibre: E-book management for your computer. Convert files into e-books, convert one type of e-book into another. Update your tablet or reader with newest news, books.

http://www.calibre-ebook.com

Creative Book Builder (CBB): Creative Book Builder enables everyone to create, edit, and publish e-books in a few minutes on the go. All published e-books can be read by any e-pub reader, including iBooks. Most flexible e-pub creator. Import text, photo, music, video, EPUB from Dropbox, Google Drive, and FTP Server. Edit image (red-eye removal, filters, etc.). Add internal links to different chapters. Embed PDF, doc, xls, ppt, pages, keynote, and numbers files. Add table, multiple-choice questions. Import terms from Quizlet or other book-import PDF as images. Search chapters within the book.

http://www.getcreativebookbuilder.blogspot.com

StoryPatch: Story Patch comes with over 800 illustrations as well as customizable characters. Characters fit into each page by changing facial expressions, body position, and skin and hair color. Easy-to-use controls for making illustrations and importing photos from the iPad's photo library to use as backdrops in a story. Share a PDF version with friends. Story themes help children by asking them a series of questions, then based on their responses building a story for the child to illustrate.

http://www.storypatch.com

ı, or e-mailed as a sound file. A more difficult level requires inferencing skills (see
.t Comprehension" below). Book creator and book builder applications (available
the tablet and PC) can also be adapted to serve many different functions. Digital
read-aloud stories also allow for a number of different fluency skills to be developed.

Vocabulary Instruction

Having an adequate vocabulary means that a child knows the words needed to communicate effectively, whether speaking and listening (oral vocabulary) or reading
and writing (reading vocabulary). Readers must know what most of the words mean
before they can understand what they are reading. Having a large oral vocabulary
helps typically developing beginning readers make sense of the words they see in
print. As they sound out the words, they match those sounds to the sounds of words
they already know; this is how they learn to associate the meaning of the word with
its written form. Thus, as readers who are typically developing learn more spoken
words, their written word vocabulary also increases (Iland, 2011).

Unfortunately, many children on the autism spectrum have a condition known
as hyperlexia. Hyperlexia is characterized by "an intense focus or preoccupation with
numbers and letters, the early and spontaneous ability to read words, and a significant
gap between word-level decoding and comprehension" (Iland, 2011, p. 21). Readers with
hyperlexia are fluent, often at a very young age, due to their excellent phonemic awareness and good ability with phonics. This fluency is deceptive, however, because though
persons with hyperlexia have strong word recognition skills, their ability to understand
what they are reading is quite poor (Grigorenko, Klin, & Volkmar, 2003; Randi, Newman, & Grigorenko, 2010). They are thus less able to add new words to their vocabulary
through reading. Not all persons with ASD are hyperlexic, but 65% them do have poor
comprehension (Nation, Clarke, Wright, & Williams, 2006; Nation & Norbury, 2005).

Remediation of Vocabulary Deficits It is important to note that the strategies and skills recommended by the National Reading Panel (NICHD, 2000) were
based on research with readers who are typically developing, not readers with
autism. Indeed, Chiang and Lin (2007) did a meta-analysis of the literature on
improving reading comprehension and found that of 754 peer-reviewed articles
identified as relevant, only 11 included at least one participant with ASD. This chapter describes more targeted strategies to help readers with ASD who are hyperlexic
understand the meaning of what they have read (Iland, 2011).

Because children with autism may have limited oral language exposure due
to limited socialization and/or restricted and repetitive interests, they often have a
vocabulary that is focused on areas of interest, without the breadth typical of most
young language learners (Iland, 2011). This means that one of the strategies recommended by the National Reading Panel (NICHD, 2000), indirect learning, will not
likely be an effective method for increasing vocabulary in learners with hyperlexia. Students on the autism spectrum are much more likely to benefit from direct
instruction, where they are explicitly taught both individual word meanings and
word-learning strategies prior to exposure to the material in the passage to be read.
In addition, before even beginning to teach reading, the teacher must take care
to explicitly relate what is taught to the material presented in the passage. This
prereading procedure is important because the autistic reader has difficulty making use of relevant knowledge when interpreting ambiguous language in a written
passage (Wahlberg & Magliano, 2004).

A number of specific vocabulary skills must be taught to students on the autism spectrum (from Iland, 2011):

1. Knowing that words can have more than one meaning (e.g., *bank* or *pound*) and deciding which meaning is relevant to the context in which the word appears

2. Recognizing which connotation of a word is appropriate (e.g., *modern* meaning "belonging to recent times," which is the literal definition, or "new," "up-to-date," or "experimental")

3. Understanding double meanings (jokes, irony, sarcasm)

4. Understanding figurative and nonliteral meanings (idioms, metaphors, indirect requests)

5. Labeling emotions (Bosseler & Massaro, 2003; Chan & O'Reilly, 2008; Happé, 1994; Losh & Capps, 2003)

6. Categorizing objects in terms of concepts (Cartwright, 2006)

7. Using context to understand unknown words and infer meaning (O'Connor & Klein, 2004)

8. Activating the correct meanings of words in memory (Randi et al., 2010)

Teaching Word Meanings with Technology   Bosseler and Massaro (2003) presented printed vocabulary words simultaneously with a 3-D talking head, "Baldi," that demonstrated proper mouth movements during speech, as well as emotion and intention. During the course of the experiment, the researchers gradually eliminated the printed vocabulary words and Baldi's speech so that students were able to listen only to the spoken words. Reading vocabulary improved both with the computer and in more natural reading environments. Students also improved in emotion recognition (learning adjectives of emotion). The technology underlying Baldi has been integrated into the reading components of the Timo stories (available on http://www.amazon.com).

Other methodologies abound. Another great technique is to use "head shot" videos of other children who use appropriate emotion and inflection while reading (the web site Smories [http://www.smories.com] is a great example for explicitly teaching both emotion recognition as well as word intonation/inflection appropriate to the meaning of the written word). Word meaning can also be taught using interactive books that contain prompts and activities focusing on word meanings. The interactive books and book-building apps discussed in the "Fluency" section above can be used to work on meaning as well as fluency, particularly when the customizable features are used to highlight or contrast meanings of words through sound and images. Applications for tablets that work on such aspects of meaning as synonyms or metaphors, for example, are presented here but can also be found in the curricula of many of the packaged software programs mentioned after the "Text Comprehension" section, below. Integrated packages will work on all levels and aspects of reading.

Also, visual mind maps that develop conceptual understanding can be used to work on individual word meaning understanding by connecting one word's meaning with others (see Table 8.4). For example, Inspiration software includes a word guide that allows users to highlight a word and find definitions, spelling, and synonyms while writing or reading. We include mind maps in the next section as well.

Table 8.4. Single-word vocabulary

The Opposites: This is a great leveled game that helps kids practice matching opposites. As the siblings yell words at each other (almost Electric Company style), you have to match the opposites that float up in word bubbles and bounce around the top of the page. You have to match as many opposites as you can before the bubbles reach the floor and game is over. A built-in dictionary for all the game's words. The game includes increasingly difficult levels as students master the earlier levels.

http://www.mindshapes.com/Products

Same Meaning (plus other games by NRCC): Toss word stones into the wishing well to earn gold coins and jewels by choosing the best synonym. Luna or Leo, master the magic of words and correctly identify the synonym that best completes the puzzle sentence. Earn a gold coin when you drag the correct word stone into the wishing well. See also Opposite Ocean, Grammar Dragon, and Same Sounds apps by Gameslab and NRCC.

http://www.gameslab.radford.edu/iLearn/apps.html

Barron's Reading Comp: Fill-in-the-blank exercises in an arcade game style based on reading a passage. Available for iPod and iPad and also on Android and Windows Phone.

https://itunes.apple.com/us/app/painless-reading-comprehension/id521373101?mt=8

English Idioms: What is the meaning behind English idioms, and where do they come from? Join Professor Potts to discover the secret history of more than 160 beautifully illustrated English idioms, from *Achilles heel* to *wrong side of bed*. Idiom guide available on Android by Flash by Night.

http://www.robotmedia.net/#products

http://www.flashbynight.com

Reading Comprehension: Reading skills for developing nonfiction understanding using word and sentence completion and other engaging games for science and social studies reading. Includes data collection for teachers. See also figurative language "kidioms" with word drop, sound effects, and interactive learning activities by Ventura Educational Systems.

http://www.venturaes.com/ipadapps/kidioms2.html

There are many ways technology can be used to present digital stories that promote interest for individuals with literacy challenges and increase vocabulary (Table 8.5). Digital stories encourage interactive exploration of text and are available online, on CDs, and on mobile devices. Features may include multilevel games, a variety of page-turning modes, bookmarking capabilities, picture–word association, professional narration, and options to customize highlighting and reading aloud. Digital books are also very helpful for improving fluency, vocabulary, and alphabetics.

Text Comprehension

Of all the skills used in reading, text comprehension is the most dynamic and complex. Good readers must be able to think intentionally about what they are reading so that they can construct meaning by relating what they read to what they know. Reading is thus a purposeful and active process for learning, finding information, or entertainment (Lyon et al., 2001; NICHD, 2000). Readers want to understand what they are reading and put this understanding to use. The National Reading Panel identified eight specific cognitive strategies that can help struggling readers accomplish this goal. Although some of these strategies are not well suited to readers with ASD, the three strategies listed below may be helpful:

1. Graphic and semantic organizers, including story maps, that allow readers to graphically represent the meanings and relationships described in the text (De la Paz, 2001; Dye, 2000)

Table 8.5. Electronic and interactive children's book readers

Adapted books/read aloud

BookShare: A subscription-based online service—currently free for students with documented print disabilities—provides thousands of accessible searchable books, textbooks, and articles. Some apps for read aloud (Android interactive).

http://www.bookshare.org

Accessible books: Easy readers and picture books. They also offer switch-accessible book versions using Intellitools, Clicker, or Boardmaker Plus formats.

http://www.accessiblebookcollection.org

Bookbox: Digitally narrated text with simple animation and streaming text across the bottom.

http://www.bookbox.com

One More Story: Beautifully illustrated books read by real narrators, often including sounds and music in the background. Includes highlighted text and the ability to click on and hear back individual words.

http://www.onemorestory.com

Browser books: Over 600 interactive books sorted by level and character. Digital downloads as well as mobile apps.

http://www.staff.prairiesouth.ca/~cassidy.kathy/browserbooks/index.htm

See also http://www.tarheelreader.org and e-readers listed on http://www.udltechtoolkit.wikispaces.com

Kids' books read aloud (for mobile reading)

iStoryTime: A library of narrated children's books for iDevices. http://www.istorytimeapp.com

MeeGenius: Digital books with integrated reading support, including text-to-speech, graphics, and highlighted text.

http://www.meegenius.com

OceanHouse: Digital books with integrated reading support (e.g., Dr. Seuss and Berenstein Bears books).

http://www.oceanhousemedia.com

AppleTreeBooks: Digital books with integrated reading support, including text-to-speech, graphics, and highlighted text. Recording of text also available.

http://www.appletreebooks.com

TumbleBooks: Online talking picture books, apps to read and interact with books on mobile devices.

http://www.tumblebooks.com

RAZ Books: An online library of interactive leveled books and quizzes for each book.

http://www.raz-kids.com

Learning Ally: Offers thousands of audiobooks that can be played back on computers and mobile devices.

http://www.learningally.org

Literactive: Free online interactive beginner books.

http://www.literactive.com

Start-to-Finish Library and Core Content: An accessible book collection developed for older elementary and early adolescent students reading below grade level. Two readability levels in three media formats: paperback, audio and computer. A comprehension quiz is available after each chapter.

http://www.donjohnston.com

Storyline Online: Free online video streaming of stories read aloud by actors as readers follow along with text.

http://www.storylineonline.net

Tar Heel Reader: Free online, each book is switch accessible and speech enabled. Create a browser tab on a tablet.

http://www.tarheelreader.org

Thinking Reader: This program uses unabridged core literature with instruction on seven proven reading comprehension strategies, including summarizing, clarifying, visualizing, reflecting.

http://www.tomsnyder.com

News-2-You: A weekly internet-based picture newspaper that features current events and other articles of interest. Also available as an app.

http://www.news-2-you.com

2. Explicit analysis of the story structure, which helps the reader answer *who* (characters), *what, when* (timelines), *where,* and *why* question about the plot (Whalon, Otaiba, & Delano, 2009)

3. Using multiple strategies flexibly and in response to the specific needs and interests of the reader (Castellani & Jeffs, 2001)

Emily Iland (2011) believes that the following National Reading Panel recommendations will not be effective for students with autism unless they are explicitly taught how to apply them, instead of having the classroom teacher simply "demonstrate, model, or guide the [learners] in their acquisition or use" (NICHD, 2000, pp. 4–5).

1. Comprehension monitoring, in which readers learn to be aware of their understanding (or lack thereof) and use strategies for addressing problems as they arise

2. Question answering, in which the reader answers questions given by the teacher

3. Question generation, in which the reader generates questions ahead of time, or while reading, that are then answered as he or she reads the passage (Whalon & Hanline, 2008)

4. Summarization, in which the reader identifies the main ideas and integrates them into a coherent whole (Whalon et al., 2009)

Iland (2011) also recommends explicit instruction in the following areas to improve comprehension by readers with autism:

1. Notice and relate the title to the text in the passage (Wahlberg & Magliano, 2004).

2. Preteach basic factual concepts before presenting the written passage by asking readers to read a primer passage, 300 words or fewer, that contains basic facts that correctly and unambiguously convey the main ideas presented in the story (Wahlberg & Magliano, 2004).

3. Ask students to read a series of thematically related passages prior to reading the target passage so they can get used to the language and concepts to be presented.

4. Drawing pictures, or writing about each passage after reading it to help cement the new concepts (Colasent & Griffith, 1998).

5. Provide explicit instruction regarding the meanings of idioms (Nation & Norbury, 2005; Norbury, 2004).

6. Provide explicit instruction regarding the meanings of pronouns by asking students to list whom each pronoun refers to (O'Connor & Klein, 2004).

It is important to note that the act of connecting words and sentences to create a global understanding requires the ability to shift attention from the word to the sentence level as well as memory capacity. Both these abilities are in short supply for children with autism, who also struggle to construct an organizational structure or schema to facilitate their memory (Williams, Goldstein, & Minshew, 2006). Oakhill and her colleagues (Oakhill, Cain, & Bryant, 2003; Yuill & Oakhill, 1991) have found that skills such as text integration, metacognitive monitoring, inference making, and working memory all contribute to variability in reading comprehension ability.

None of these strategies addresses more general linguistic strategies necessary for good reading comprehension like teaching inferencing skills, which are necessary for understanding character motivations and trying to determine what the passage author wants the reader to know (Quill, 2000). (See Chapters 6 and 7 to learn more about teaching these critical skills.)

Technologies for Improving Text Comprehension and Grammar   Several apps have reading comprehension activities in which text is read or played out loud, followed by multiple-choice questions that test understanding of the text. Table 8.6 lists a variety of instructional methodologies that can help improve flexibility of thinking, access to character motivation and emotion, and understanding of multiple meanings.

Graphic Organizers and Other Visual Supports for Improving Text Comprehension   There is a large body of research that shows that visual learners learn best when using diagrams and pictures that graphically represent concepts or ideas. The computer is an easy and effective way of delivering a high-quality, large quantity of such visual media (Kearns & Shane, 2008; Shane & Albert, 2008; Shane & Weiss-Kapp, 2007). Using visual icons, scenes, and organizational tools (or webs) can improve vocabulary and comprehension, particularly when paired with sound output (Dye, 2000; Shane, 2006; West, 1997; Wong, 1991).

Graphic organizers and mind maps typically use lines, circles, and boxes to organize information. They are helpful for brainstorming, expressing ideas, improving memory, learning new concepts, understanding how things are related, organizing written narrative, and solving problems (see Brookbank et al., 1999, for vocabulary and comprehension; Gallic-Jackson, 1997; Kim, Vaughn, Wanzek, & Wei, 2004; Meyer, 1995; and Robinson, 1997, for writing). Table 8.7 provides a list of the most commonly used apps and software for generating mind maps available on mobile platforms as well as the computer. The best software allows integration of word prediction and TTS while using the visual map format. Inspiration and Kidspiration on the computer currently allow the student to convert easily from visual map to linear text; however, the corresponding app has fewer features and does not convert to an outline text format. However, these features are always being updated. iThoughts (iOS only), NeuNotes, SimpleMind, Idea sketch, and Mindjet have basic functions for mapping ideas and visual hierarchies. The latter two are available on Android as well. Most can be exported to XMind software for the PC. Popplet is a popular app for students that allows photos to be integrated as well as drawings. Magical Pad is a unique app for the iPad that allows notetaking and mind mapping in one location.

Computer Software that Incorporates Visual Icons to Encourage Early Reading Skills in One Package   The software described in Table 8.8 comprises tools that allow the teacher to use best practices in teaching reading and literacy to students with autism who require discrete, visually-salient information, rewards for positive responses, and immediate feedback, as well as regular built-in breaks for the student and data collection for demonstration of mastery. Among the best software are those that integrate the learning with the individualized education program

Table 8.6. Technologies for improving text comprehension and grammar

Sentence Builder and Question Builder: Sentence Builder assists with building grammatically correct sentences by selecting words on a dial to correspond with a picture. Question Builder is designed to help children learn to answer abstract questions and create responses based on inference. Use of audio clips promotes improved auditory processing for children with special needs and autism spectrum disorders or sensory processing disorders.

http://www.mobile-educationstore.com

Grammar Trainer: Text-based grammar trainer for students with autism. See Chapter 6 for detailed description and http://www.thegrammartrainer.com for more.

http://www.autism-language-therapies.com

Comprehension apps: Speech with Milo, Sequencing, Minimod (fact or opinion, reading for details), Same Meaning Magic, Opposites Ocean, Same Sound Spellbound, and Question Builder. See top 12 reading apps on Reading Rockets. These provide practice with specific comprehension skills, including sequencing, differentiating between fact and opinion, developing word awareness (through antonyms, synonyms, and homophones). See also Mind mapping apps in Table 8.7 http://www.readingrockets.org/teaching/reading101/comprehension/literacyapps_comprehension

Fun with Directions: The fun animation and interactive components make this app appealing to children. At the easy level, users follow one simple direction, such as "Close the gate." The intermediate level increases the complexity by including colors or an additional descriptive element involving such words as *bottom, middle, top, close, erase, open,* and *push* or *touch*. At the advanced level, the length of the direction is the longest and most complex, adding the concepts left/right, size, more adjectives, and/or a second step. After the child follows through on the direction, a screen with a microphone appears. The child is asked to repeat and record the direction by pressing the record button.

http://www.appsforspeechtherapy.blogspot.com/2011/12/apps-for-auditory-comprehension.html

http://www.hamaguchiapps.com

First Phrases: First Phrases focuses on simple grammatical structures presented in command form, for example, "Pour the juice." When the child taps anywhere on the screen (Easy Level), or the pictorial word representations, the narrator verbalizes each part of speech as it is tapped, such as "pour" and "the trash" in the two-part verb + the object setting, or "pour," "the," and "juice" in the three-part verb + the + object choice. Challenge option and option to focus on verb are also available.

http://www.hamaguchiapps.com

Picture the Sentence: In this app, the child listens to a sentence and then selects the picture that goes with the sentence. The app presents the task in two steps. First, the sentence is narrated while a blank screen flashes pictures representing each part of speech. Then the screen automatically advances to show five pictures. The child needs to select the picture that best represents the sentence heard and drag it to the empty frame above. Different levels of play are based on length of sentence and complexity.

http://www.hamaguchiapps.com

Rainbow Sentences, Conversation Builder Teen, and TenseBuilder: Rainbow Sentences teaches the *who, what, where, when,* and *why* of sentence structure. Conversation Builder Teen is a virtual conversation simulator designed just for teens. TenseBuilder is designed to help elementary-age children learn the correct use of tense.

http://www.mobile-educationstore.com

PlayTales: An app designed by SLP Eric Sailers (Artikpiks), PlayTales allows teachers to create their own stories and set up customizable text comprehension quizzes including images from the camera or from the library. Best feature is that teachers can set up their own quizzes for their own books. Full text-to-speech available or self-recording of each story.

http://www.ericsailers.com

(IEP) goals and collect specific performance data on each goal and task (http://www.govizzle.com). This software is also highly customizable, with the integration of multimedia, pictures, video, and audio to enhance learning and also allow personalized learning for each student. Many of the tools for teaching communication via visual means have been available for a long time (e.g., Mayer-Johnson's Boardmaker,

Table 8.7.   Mind mapping apps for text comprehension

iThoughts: ThoughtsHD will import and export mind maps to and from many of the most popular desktop mind-map applications such as MyThoughts, Freemind, Freeplane, XMind, Novamind, MindManager, MindView, ConceptDraw MINDMAP, MindGenius, and iMindmap.

http://www.ithoughts.co.uk

Mindomo: Mind mapping app that lets you create multiple layouts (circular, concept, org chart); add icons, colors, styles, and map themes; embed images (photos) on map topics; visualize notes, links, or tasks on topics; full map history; undo and redo functions. Available on PC and android as well.

http://www.mindomo.com/

Popplet: A free app that allows users to build visual supports for schedules, outlines, and charts. Individuals can add pictures, change colors, add text, and draw images.

http://www.popplet.com

SimpleMind: A mind-mapping tool for iPad, iPhone, or iPod Touch. For brainstorming, idea collection, and thought structuring. See version for Android.

http://www.simpleapps.eu/simplemind

bubbl.us Mindomo & Webspiration: A free basic online program for brainstorming visual thinking of thoughts and ideas. Link boxes and arrows with text and images and collaboration tool.

http://www.bubbl.us.com

http://www.mindomo.com

http://www.mywebspiration.com

Inspiration/Kidspiration: Inspiration was developed for students in grades 6–12 to facilitate visual mapping, outlining, writing, and making presentations. Kidspiration (for grades K–5) combines pictures, text, and audio to develop comprehension, organize ideas, and write stories. Activities are curriculum-aligned. Inspiration iPad app has the same graphical features as the software but does not currently allow a switch to hierarchical written view.

http://www.inspiration.com

http://www.kidspiration.com

Clicker [Cricksoft], and Intellitools), but their integration with an easy-to-use computer platform has improved greatly. Several software companies allow online sharing of curricula and premade materials that the user can download (e.g., Intellitools, Abilipad, and Vizzle). Downloaded lessons from Vizzle (by Monarch Technologies) can then be modified and personalized to meet individual students' needs (http://www.govizzle.com).

Accommodating Reading Comprehension Deficits: Providing Access to All Forms of the Written Word Through TTS   Software with TTS capabilities can read aloud text on a computer screen or tablet or mobile phone. The support provided with this type of software reduces physical effort and assists with organization so that writers are able to focus more on content. Both mainstream word processors and specialized assistive writing technology products offer a wide variety of helpful tools. Using mobile technology makes using this software this much simpler because several apps and operating systems now integrate speech-to-text (STT) and TTS in their programs. Google software found on Android systems and tablets is particularly accessible. Google books, *New York Times*, and other apps have a simple integrated read-aloud function that accesses the Android TTS software. Apple has a TTS option that can be adjusted for selected text when reading e-mails or text in an Apple-produced app (e.g., in iBooks). Apple devices running iOS 6 or later, and Macs running OSX offer TTS functionality such as "speak selection" and "highlighting." In addition, there are several TTS apps that can be added

Table 8.8. Integrated visual platforms for learning how to understand text

Clicker & WriteOnline: Clicker is a reading and writing tool that offers a range of multisensory curricula and accessibility supports for individuals with autism spectrum disorder (ASD). The top portion of the screen is a word processor that is easy to read, can use pictures, and uses with text-to-speech. Clicker Grids are on the bottom half of the screen and provide point-and-click access to whole words, phrases, and pictures that can be used as word banks, sentence starters, and e-books using images, sound, and video. WriteOnline is an online word-processing program that assists with writing using picture symbols and text. Clicker recently came out with iPad apps that run about $20 each. They are called Clicker Docs and Clicker Sentences and allow much of what you could do on the computer from the mobile device.

http://www.cricksoft.com

Custom Boards: An iPad app that uses Smarty Symbols to enable users to create visually based custom boards, schedules, and activities to enhance communication and learning.

http://www.smartyears.com

Visual Boards and Scenes with Text: Visual schedules, story planners, choice board, and scene speak, with sound, image, and text created specifically for ASD students. Some are also available for Android.

http://www.goodkarmaapplications.com

AutismMate: Scenes, visual scheduler, visual stories, sentence builder, video modeling—each piece interacts with the other so that a sentence script will popup, for example, while the user is in the kitchen scene. Available for iPad updated to include feature to integrate multimedia features. Large content library and fully customizable.

http://www.autismate.com/features

Intellitools: IntelliTools classroom suite provides direct instruction with a flexible visually based tool to improve reading, writing, and math skills. Uses picture icons and text with voice-read-aloud feature built in. Many customizable templates and accompanying resources are available.

http://www.intellitools.com

Vizzle: Vizzle is a subscription-based platform created for individuals with ASD. The visually based learning program includes thousands of lessons and can be edited with photos, videos, audio, or media from an included media library. Educators can create such materials as interactive books (including hotspots with quizzes), games, boards, schedules, and timers. Purchase of the software allows access to a very large set of multimedia resources for reading and improving comprehension from an online shared database, accessible by teachers internationally.

http://www.govizzle.com

to the Apple devices that allow reading from portable document format (PDF) or websites. A current favorite is an app called "Voice Dream." Finally, several PDF reading apps (see http://www.adobe.com) will allow you to read the text from any PDF file, and productivity apps like Quick Office will read text out loud as it is typed. EZPDF reader is a favorite on the Android platform.

Among features to look for in any TTS application are those indicated below. See also MacArthur et al. (2001; also MacArthur, 1990, 2000).

- The ability to control auditory features and visual presentation

- The ability to save the documents as audio files that can be downloaded to hand-held devices

- Options that may be customized depending on the software (e.g., voice, rate of speech, highlighting, screen display)

- Text that can be read back a letter, word, line, sentence, or paragraph at a time

- Words that can be magnified as they are read aloud

- The ability to work with e-mail, web sites, and Microsoft Word and PDF documents

More sophisticated products with TTS can also electronically highlight sections of text in different colors, take notes by typing or by voice, prepare outlines, create flashcards and other study materials, use word prediction, read only highlighted sections, and skip to the bookmarked section of text.

Just a few years ago, there was a dependence on use of scanners and optical character recognition (OCR). The latter enabled a user to scan printed material into a computer or handheld unit. The software then converted the image to text, so a text-reading program could read the written material to the user. Now, however, PDF converters on PCs, smartphones, and tablets that have built-in cameras and the ability to easily convert an image to a PDF, make it nearly instantaneous to immediately read aloud text, thus bypassing the previous process of scanning followed by OCR processing.

Android and iOS come with built-in voices, as do most Microsoft operating systems. New voices and TTS software can be purchased inexpensively that work on nearly every system. Voice output for PDF reading applications for iOS and Android are discussed in Table 8.9. Software packages that offer integrated reading and writing support are described in Table 8.12.

Table 8.9. Text-to-speech reading tools for mobile devices and PCs, browsers, and word processors

iBooks: An e-book reader for iDevices compatible with DRM-free EPUB and PDF files and Apple's e-books. Offers different font sizes, highlighting, bookmarking, note-taking ability, search functions, and dictionary. The iPad has a voiceover feature that can read aloud the contents on the screen, is designed for the vision impaired, and requires a different set of manual gestures to interact with the touch screen. The "Speak Selection" feature works even with PDF documents in iBooks.

http://www.iTunes.com

Blio, NOOK for kids, Google Play: Free e-book readers for computers and tablets. Includes original graphics of picture books and great voice reading; also great voices. Blio was designed by Kurzweil. Voices cost. NOOK for kids also reads books, but only certain ones that have been designed to read, but Google Play books will read aloud any book that is formatted for digital character recognition.

http://www.blioreader.com

http://www.barnesandnoble.com/u/nook-kids-for-ipad/379003590

https://play.google.com/store/books?hl=en

Adobe Digital Editions: Free downloadable software to allow you to read e-books on your computer. JAWS software allows you to read books on Windows machine, and Apple voiceover is integrated to read books aloud on Mac.

http://www.adobe.com

Calibre: Free software to organize your e-book library on your computer and also allows conversion from one type of e-book to another for readability on different devices (e.g., PDF, mobi, epub, etc.). Some devices and apps such as iBooks for iOS will only read books that are formatted in epub, others will only read mobi books, and so forth.

http://www.calibre-ebook.com

Click, Speak: A free Firefox extension that reads the internet and highlights phrases and sentences as it reads.

http://www.clickspeak.clcworld.net

VoiceOver: Free text-to-speech (TTS) on a Mac. Produced primarily for individuals with visual deficits. When in use, gestures change on the iPad.

http://www.apple.com/accessibility/voiceover

TextAloud: For PCs, reads aloud from e-mail, web pages, and written documents. Offers word highlighting, masking of items not to be read, saving audio file to MP3 player, among other features.

http://www.nextup.com

(continued)

Table 8.9. *(continued)*

Web Reader HD for iOS: TTS page reader for iOS mobile.

http://www.banzailabs.com/voice.html

NeoPaul and NeoKate for iOS: A free app in which the user types text and hears the text spoken aloud. Phrases and sentences can be saved.

http://www.neospeech.com

Voice Dream for iOS: One of the most versatile TTS readers, allowing copied text, built-in web browsing, and PDF reading.

http://www.voicedream.com

Infovox for iOS: Infovox iVox provides clear and pleasant voices in 26 languages to Mac OS X for blind and vision-impaired users, for individuals who need audible feedback or reading support, for language learning, or for people who prefer listening to their computer. New in Infovox iVox 3.1 are four genuine English children's voices.

http://www.assistiveware.com

Vbookz (iOS): vBookz is an e-book reader (and PDF) that reads any PDF for you. It displays books, has speech ability interface features, and highlights text.

http://www.vbookz.com

Predictable: An iOS app in which users type a message using a customized phrase bank and word prediction engine, and then the program speaks the message using a variety of voices.

http://www.tboxapps.com

Abilipad (iOS): An intuitive and user-friendly interface allows you to take notes, import photos, and design customized keyboards. An integrated filing system allows you to create folders to manage your notepads and keyboards. Word prediction, TTS, multiple keyboards, and multimedia input allow this app to be a very powerful reading teacher and writing tool. Sharing available.

http://www.appytherapy.com

Speakit! (iOS): Users type text and the app reads it aloud. Messages can be saved and sent as a sound file.

http://www.future-apps.net

SVOX (Android): Covers the most languages of any engine (40+). Also has a few different voices for English. Enough variance to keep the voices nonrobotic. iHear Network is deeply integrated with SVOX. See Nuance for other options for voices. Available for Android and embedded in Nuance products.

http://www.nuance.com/products/SVOX/index.htm

Ivona Voices (Android/PC): Ivona Voices has some of the best-sounding voices, and all free. The many variations in how certain phrases are said makes reading longer articles more digestible and less robotic than in other apps. Has advanced speech caching to address delays and deliver a very fluid experience with all engines.

http://www.ivona.com/us

iSpeech for Android: iSpeech TTS and Speech Recognition (ASR) SDK for Android lets users speech-enable any Android app quickly and easily with iSpeech Cloud. The SDK has a small footprint and supports 27 TTS and ASR languages and 15 for free-form dictation voice recognition.

https://www.ispeech.org/developers/android

EZPDF Reader: Multimedia PDF viewer, annotator, and form filler with calculations. This app is available for iOS and Android as well as PC, and it is very flexible with numerous features.

http://www.unidocs.com

LiveScribe Echo and Sky WiFi Pens: LiveScribe Echo and Sky WiFi pens record everything users hear and write. Users can listen to the recorded audio by tapping directly on written words, pictures, or any type of mark that anchors the recording to a particular spot. The Sky WiFi pen automatically syncs notes and audio to your personal Evernote account whenever you have access to WiFi. The pen is especially helpful for individuals who have difficulty taking notes and writing, as well as for individuals with auditory comprehension deficits. A teacher can easily record speech to go with a lesson to elucidate a point of comprehension for the student.

http://www.livescribe.com

EFFECTIVE WRITING INSTRUCTION

For all the problems persons with ASD have with comprehension, many of them also struggle to write effectively. Indeed, in the original description of Asperger syndrome, Hans Asperger noted challenges with handwriting (Frith, 1991). As with reading, writing is a tremendously complicated task involving many different sub-skills. Here, we focus on spelling, handwriting, and composition (Berninger, 2008).

Spelling

Spelling is the act of "converting phonemes (sounds) to corresponding graphemes (letters or letter units)" (Selikowitz, 1998, p. 73). As discussed earlier in the section on alphabetics, some students can find it difficult to relate the written form of a word to its spoken form. These students can sometimes be heard saying the word aloud while writing, as if to cue themselves regarding the phonological structure of the word (National Center for Learning Disabilities [NCLD], 2006). It is interesting to note that students who struggle with alphabetics when reading can have even more dramatic challenges with spelling. This is in part because readers can use context to help disambiguate text that is difficult to read (Sterling et al., 1998; Treiman, 1997), whereas spelling does not afford the use of context in the same way.

As described earlier, these students need explicit instruction about how to translate the spoken word into the written word. As they improve, not only will they be able to read their own work, but they will also be able to produce text more quickly, taxing their working memory less (Richards, 2002).

Barring successful remediation, these students benefit from a variety of accommodations (NCLD, 2006; see also examples in Table 8.10). A complete list is available at the LDOnline web site (http://www.ldonline.org). Among the accommodations listed for poor spellers, several seem well-suited for a technological solution:

Table 8.10.   Reading and writing tools using graphics to support spelling and meaning

Communicate: Symwriter: A talking word processor with symbols.

http://www.mayerjohnson.com

PictureIt PixWriter: Automatic picture–word matching for creating picture-assisted reading. PixWriter is a picture-rich environment for reading and writing. It includes over 10,500 literacy support symbols, and digital images can be added. Pictures are paired with words to support word recognition and reading comprehension. The voice, rate, and pronunciation can be customized. Documents can be saved, and alternative modes of access, such as single-switch scanning and adapted keyboards, can be used.

http://www.slatersoftware.com

Vocabulary Spelling City: Free interactive online program, with options to pay for additional features. There is a series of printable or free online games using a customizable spelling-word list. Individuals can enter spelling or vocabulary words, and the program turns this list into a variety of games and quizzes.

http://www.spellingcity.com

Bluster (McGraw-Hill): Free app for iPad that has leveled vocabulary and activities for improving spelling and word comprehension. Includes synonym matching, rhyming words, adjectives, suffixes, homophones, and prefixes.

https://itunes.apple.com/us/app/bluster%21/id416160693?mt=8

- Write out a list some of the key words before beginning so that the student will not get stuck trying to think of how to spell a word.

- Encourage the use of a spell checker.

- Use word prediction software that fills in the word based on what you have typed so far.

Handwriting

The fine and gross motor skills involved in writing are frequently impaired in children with ASDs (Ghaziuddin & Butler, 1998; Jansiewicz et al., 2006). Furthermore, these children sometimes have trouble sensing where their limbs are in space (Molloy, Dietrich, & Bhattacharya, 2003; Weimer, Schatz, Lincoln, Ballantyne, & Trauner, 2001). Such problems lead to challenges in generating the motions necessary for writing fluidly with a pen or pencil. Children with impairments in proprioception and fine and gross motor skills can have a tight, awkward pencil grip and quickly get tired when asked to write.

Children with ASDs also have trouble coordinating their body movements in response to what they see (i.e., visual-motor integration; see Hellinckx, Roeyers, & Van Waelvelde, 2013). That is, they struggle to generate the correct motor response when asked to copy letters or shapes. Visual-motor integration correlates with handwriting quality in children who are typically developing (Kaiser, Albaret, & Doudin, 2009) and children with handwriting difficulties (Volman, van Schendel, & Jongmans, 2006), such that children with good eye–hand coordination have better handwriting. Conversely, children with poor visual-motor integration have handwriting that is difficult to read. Recent research with children with Asperger syndrome confirms that difficulty with proprioception impairs handwriting in the ASD population as well (Fuentes et al., 2009).

Many of the strategies for helping children with handwriting are not technological in nature. You can find a complete list of effective strategies at the LDOnline web site (http://www.ldonline.org), as well as some resources in Table 8.11. Low-tech options include using alternative pens and pencils, pencil grips, slant boards, and special writing paper. If these strategies are not successful, it may be time to consider assistive technology to help with written expression and the physical act of putting words onto paper (NCLD, 2006).

Accommodations for Handwriting   Several accommodations using assistive technology are available to help with handwriting:

- Practice writing letters and numbers with big arm movements and also with smaller hand or finger motions. The iPad has several apps that can help with this.

- Allow students to use a word processor on a computer as early as second grade.

- Provide tape recorders to supplement note taking and to prepare for writing assignments.

- Use voice-activated software. (See final section of the chapter "Speech-to-Text [STT] and Text-to-Speech [TTS].")

See http://www.onionmountaintech.com and http://www.theraproducts.com for additional ideas.

Table 8.11. Tools for developing handwriting

iWriteWords: iWriteWords teaches the student handwriting while he or she plays an entertaining game. Using a finger, the student follows a small character to the end of the letter.

http://www.giggle-lab.com/iwritewords/

Cursive Practice (for iOS and Android): This application by Brainstop is for practicing English cursive handwriting. Users can practice writing words in uppercase and lowercase letters. Within a given section, font size remains the same, but each section has a different size. The font size is adjusted by length of content.

https://itunes.apple.com/us/app/cursive-practice/id492625990?mt=8

Zaner-Bloser Handwriting in Print or Cursive (iOS): Children practice writing letters and numbers to help a pencil-character get to school.

http://www.highlights.com/apps/zaner-bloser-handwriting-eng-c

Touch and Write (for iOS): Practice writing with shaving cream, ketchup, and other fun textures.

http://www.fizzbrain.com

Handwriting for Kids (web site): Download PDF worksheets into the Notability app or Notes from Nuance app for kids to write on.

http://www.handwritingforkids.com

Various apps for practicing cursive writing: A wide selection of cursive apps for Android from developers like Brainstop, Android Gems, and Abcedaire can be found at Appszoom.com.

http://www.appszoom.com/android_applications/cursive

Dexteria: Dexteria provides a set of therapeutic hand exercises that improve fine motor skills and handwriting readiness in children and adults. The exercises take advantage of the multitouch interface to help build strength, control, and dexterity.

http://www.dexteria.net

Composition

Children with autism have disorders of written expression at a higher rate than do children who are typically developing (Mayes & Calhoun, 2007), and though some of this is due to expressive language challenges, some of it is also due to challenges with executive functioning. These students have trouble organizing their thoughts and keeping track of the thoughts they already wrote down; there is a large gap between what they write and the understanding they demonstrate when talking.

In addition, students with autism also struggle with theory of mind (Baron-Cohen, 2000), which makes it difficult for them to know how much detail to provide and how to understand characters' motivations and emotions (Happé, 1994). A common complaint from these students' teachers is that they do not provide adequate supporting evidence and struggle to determine how much information to include for a reader unfamiliar with the topic (M. Dixon, personal communication, 2013). Instruction for individuals with autism should teach them how to appropriately elaborate their thoughts when writing (Myles et al., 2003; Randi et al., 2010) Research with students using computers when writing has shown benefits in the ability to reflect and learn "process" by writing on the computer (Collins, 1988, 1991).

Chapters 6 and 7 provide lots of ideas for helping persons with ASDs deal with expressive language disorders, so here we focus instead on strategies that will help students with challenges in executive functioning and theory of mind.

Accommodations for Composition Among several strategies available to help persons with ASDs with written expression are the following approaches:

- Find alternative means of assessing knowledge, such as oral reports or visual projects (Castellani, 2000; NCLD, 2006).

- Use STT transcription software so that the student can talk while the computer transcribes what he or she is saying (Castellani, 2000; Castellani & Jeffs, 2001; Myles et al., 2003).

- Allow students to use a computer for written tasks. This has a big advantage in that text can easily be added, deleted, and moved and computer learning allows more self-regulation and situated learning to model process (Castellani & Jeffs, 2001; Collins, 1986, 1988, 1991; Graham & Gillespie, 2011).

Remediation of Composition Skills   When writing skills require remediation, parents, educators, and clinicians can use a variety of approaches to help students express themselves and improve written communication. Table 8.12 provides some of the integrated reading and writing software that can assist with both reading comprehension and writing output. These software packages include important

Table 8.12.   Integrated reading and writing support: Packaged software

---

Co:Writer 6, Solo Literacy, Draftbuilder, Write:OutLoud, Read:OutLoud 6: Co:Writer 6 works with many word-processing and online applications, including e-mail. As words are typed, it interprets spelling and grammar mistakes and offers word suggestions. Solo includes a text reader, graphic organizer, talking word processor, and word prediction in a comprehensive suite of accommodations. DraftBuilder breaks down the writing process into three manageable steps: 1) brainstorming, 2) note taking, and 3) writing the first draft. Includes word predictions, dictionaries, speech-to-text, talking spell-checker, bibliographer, and PC- and Mac-friendly word highlighting as it reads. Write:OutLoud is a talking word-processing program for computers that uses purposeful revision and editing tools to help with writing. Read:OutLoud 6 includes many student-friendly features (e.g., modeling, scaffolding, and practice of reading strategies to comprehend text). Includes an accessible web browser that is compatible with Mac and Windows. It highlights word by word and has Bookshare access.

http://www.donjohnston.com

Kurzweil 3000: A comprehensive software program for reading, writing, and learning for struggling writers. Reads aloud text and provides support for writing and studying, with active learning, studying and test-taking strategies.

http://www.kurzweiledu.com

Premier Literacy: Computer software for a PC that includes a suite of such assistive reading and writing tools as Scan and Read Pro, a talking word processor, work prediction, text-to-audio, the ultimate talking dictionary, and a talking calculator.

http://www.readingmadeeasy.com

Read&Write Gold: Computer software for PCs that includes a customizable toolbar with such supports for literacy as text-to-speech, word prediction, web highlighting, and study tools.

http://www.texthelp.com

WordQ/SpeakQ: WordQ/SpeakQ is a fully integrated text-to-speech, word prediction, and voice recognition with SpeakQ add-on. The SpeakQ add-on is no longer available for systems running MacOS.

http://www.goqsoftware.com

WYNN Scan and Read Literacy Software: This program uses four-color-coded rotating toolbars to support reading, writing, and studying.

http://www.freedomscientific.com

Ginger Software (spelling): Ginger Software offers text-to-speech as well as support for severe spelling and grammatical mistakes on the computer. It analyzes sentences as a complete unit. Only available for PC and as an app.

http://www.gingersoftware.com

---

features such as read aloud, integrated organizers, dictation, word prediction, and dictionaries (MacArthur, 2000):

- Begin writing assignments creatively by drawing, arranging ideas visually (e.g., using a graphic organizer), or speaking into a tape recorder or STT transcription system (Graham, 2010; Graham & Gillespie, 2011; Castellani & Jeffs, 2001; Myles et al., 2003; NCLD, 2006).

- Create a step-by-step plan that breaks writing assignments into small tasks (Graham & Gillespie, 2011; NCLD, 2006).

- Provide explicit instruction about proper sentence and paragraph structure (Myles et al., 2003; Wong, 1991).

- Teach students how to write drafts and proofread so that they can learn to generate content first and then focus on mechanics. This instructional focus requires explicitly teaching students how to edit their writing (Graham & Gillespie, 2011; Myles et al., 2003; Wong, 1991).

- Explicitly teach students how to summarize what they read. Summarization gives students practice using concise, clear writing to convey the main ideas in a text (De la Paz, 2001; Graham & Gillespie, 2011; Wong, 1991).

- Explicitly teach students to write more complex and sophisticated sentences by combining them. Encourage them to apply these skills as they write or revise (Graham & Gillespie, 2011; Wong, 1991).

- Teach students how to elaborate when writing (Myles et al., 2003).

- Engage students in activities prior to writing that help them produce and organize their ideas (Castellani & Jeffs, 2001; De la Paz, 2001; Graham & Gillespie, 2011).

Speech-to-Text (STT) and Text-to-Speech (TTS)   An important technology for accommodating and improving reading and writing, TTS is often integrated into effective writing systems, such as Ginger Software or Kurzweil and even such sophisticated tablet applications as Abilipad, because it is important for writers to be able to listen to what they have written. Such auditory feedback is particularly useful when coupled with a word predictor inside the word-processing software (one with specific dictionaries and learns with the user is best). (See our earlier discussion of word/voice output for improving reading comprehension and Table 8.9 as well as Table 8.12 with integrated software from the previous section.)

The ability to speak and store ideas or translate your thoughts immediately into written words can be crucial for struggling writers as well. This ability is especially useful when the ideas also need to be organized. There are more and more devices and programs that type the words the user speaks. In recent years, this technology has become increasingly mainstream and is now easier to use than before. Windows 7 (and beyond) has a powerful STT generator (and TTS) that has been developed for many years. The current Mac OS (Mountain Lion) has TTS as well as Dictation (STT) that works with most applications on the Mac. The "speak selection" feature makes reading only certain passages or books easier for the student with a reading rather than visual impairment. MacDictation can be purchased for STT on the Mac. Voice recognition capabilities are now included in such online search engines as http://www.google.com, Android and Apple smartphones, and sophisticated word-processing programs. SpeakQ (http://www.goqsoftware.com) is one such voice recognition add-on that works with word-processing software. There are also mobile apps and software such as Dragon Dictate at http://www.nuance.com.

Using visual aids can help writers highlight important themes in written narratives prior to reading; they can also provide context. Also helpful are e-book readers. (E-book readers at CAST are covered in Chapters 1, 2, and 3. Please refer specifically to these chapters for more explicit examples of using these technologies for improving reading for meaning as well as writing output. See web pages at http://www.cast.org and http://www.UDLcenter.org as well as affiliated centers such as http://www.ectacenter.org/topics/atech/udl.asp for more on this topic.)

Monarch Technologies, whose visual learning platform was originally developed by Dr. Howard Shane (Kearns & Shane, 2007; Shane, 2006; Shane & Albert, 2008; Shane & Weiss-Kapp, 2007; also a coauthor of Chapter 7, this volume), has been working with Elena Grigorenko to explore evidence for the efficacy of their computerized multimedia reading program. Although their research is still under way, it is worth checking in with the advances they are making in developing Vizzle, a visual and integrated multimedia platform for use with students with ASD (http://www.monarchteachtech.com).

In the reading world, http://www.readingrockets.org is a resource for research as well as applications and connects with such known reading research centers as those at Vanderbilt University and Yale University's Haskins Lab, which both have teacher outreach centers for reading instruction.

Finally, an up-and-coming reading technology is the integrated e-book reader. Some studies have demonstrated the benefit of video annotation to student reading comprehension progress (McCall & Craig, 2009). Bridge Multimedia and Technical Education Research Centers (TERC), both nonprofit centers with a strong focus on creating accessible learning materials for different learners, are developing e-book readers that are more flexibly integrated with multimedia. These innovative e-books will include video annotation and sign language, along with voice output and input. This technology is one that could really benefit students with autism. (For more on this topic, see research projects at Bridge Multimedia http://www.bridgemultimedia.com and http://www.TERC.org.)

SUMMARY

In short, reading and writing are complex tasks involving many subskills. Knowledge of alphabetics, reading fluency, and comprehension skills are all required of good readers, and good writers must know how to spell, compose, and write. Although certainly not a comprehensive list, the strategies described in this chapter can help students with autism acquire the skills necessary for literacy in the 21st century.

REFERENCES

Baron-Cohen, S. (2000). Theory of mind and autism: A fifteen year review. In S. Baron-Cohen, H. Tager-Flusberg, & D.J. Cohen (Eds.), *Understanding other minds: Perspectives from developmental cognitive neuroscience* (2nd ed., pp. 3–20). New York, NY: Oxford University Press.

Berninger, V.W. (2008). Defining and differentiating dysgraphia, dyslexia, and language learning disability within a working memory model. In M. Moody & E.R. Silliman (Eds.), *Brain, behavior, and learning in language and reading disorders* (pp. 103–134). New York, NY: Guilford Press.

Bosseler, A., & Massaro, D. (2003). Development and evaluation of a computer-animated tutor for vocabulary and language learning in children with autism. *Journal of Autism and Developmental Disabilities, 33,* 653–672.

Brookbank, D. Grover, S., Kulberg, K., & Strawser, C. (1999). *Improving student achievement through organization of student learning.* Masters' Action Research Project, Saint Xavier University and IRI/Skylight.

Cartwright, K.B. (2006). Fostering flexibility and comprehension in elementary students. *The Reading Teacher, 59,* 628–634.

Castellani, J.D. (2000). Universal accessibility and the design of digital educational materials. *Virginia Society for Technology in Education, 14,* 4–7.

Castellani, J., & Jeffs, T. (2001). Emerging reading and writing strategies using technology. *Teaching Exceptional Children, 33*(5), 60–67.

Chan, J.M., & O'Reilly, M.F. (2008). A social stories intervention package for students with autism in inclusive classroom settings. *Journal of Applied Behavior Analysis, 41,* 405–409.

Chiang, H., & Lin, Y. (2007). Reading comprehension instruction for students with autism spectrum disorders: A review of the literature. *Focus on Autism and Other Developmental Disabilities, 22,* 259–267.

Colasent, R., & Griffith, P.L. (1998). Autism and literacy: Looking into the classroom with rabbit stories. *Reading Teacher, 51,* 414–420.

Collins, A. (1986). Teaching reading and writing with personal computers. In J. Orasanu (Ed.), *A decade of reading research: Implications for practice.* (pp. 171–184). Hillsdale, NJ: Erlbaum.

Collins, A. (1988). The computer as a tool for learning through reflection. In H. Mandl, & A. Lesgold (Eds.), *Learning issues for intelligent tutoring systems* (pp. 1–18). New York, NY: Springer.

Collins, A. (1991). Cognitive apprenticeship and instructional technology. In L. Idol & B.F. Jones (Eds.), *Educational values and cognitive instruction: Implications for reform* (Chap. 4, pp. 121–136). North Central Regional Educational Laboratory.

De la Paz, S. (2001). Teaching writing to students with attention deficit disorders and specific language impairment. *The Journal of Educational Research, 95*(1), 37–47.

Dye, G. (2000). Graphic organizers to the rescue: Helping students link and remember information. *Teaching Exceptional Children, 32*(3), 72–76.

Frith, U. (1991). Translation and annotation of "autistic psychopathy" in childhood by H. Asperger. In *Autism and Asperger syndrome* (pp. 37–92). Cambridge, England: Cambridge University Press.

Fuentes, C., Mostofsky, S., & Bastian, A. (2009) Children with autism show specific handwriting impairments. *Neurology, 73*(19), 1532–1537.

Gallic-Jackson, S. A. (1997). *Improving narrative writing skills, composition skills, and related attitudes among second grade students by integrating word processing, graphic organizers and art into a process approach to writing.* Masters' Practicum Project, Nova Southeastern University Practicum Papers.

Gernsbacher, M.A., Sauer, E.A., Geye, H.M., Schweigert, E.K., & Hill Goldsmith, H. (2007). Infant and toddler oral and manual motor skills predict later speech fluency in autism. *Journal of Child Psychology and Psychiatry, 49*(1), 43–50.

Ghaziuddin, M., & Butler, F. (1998). Clumsiness in autism and Asperger syndrome: A further report. *Journal of Intellectual Disability Research, 42,* 43–48.

Graham, S. (2010). Teaching writing. In P. Hogan (Ed.), *Cambridge encyclopedia of language sciences* (pp. 848–851). Cambridge, England: Cambridge University Press.

Graham, S., & Gillespie, A. (2011). Evidence-based practices for teaching writing. *New Horizons for Learning,* retrieved from http://www.education.jhu.edu/PD/newhorizons/Better/articles/Winter2011.html

Gray, C. (1995). Teaching children with autism to read social situations. In K. Quill (Ed.), *Teach children with autism: Strategies to enhance communication and socialization* (pp. 219–240). New York, NY: Tompson Learning.

Green, J.L. (2011). *The ultimate guide to assistive technology in special education: Resources for education, intervention and rehabilitation.* Waco, TX: Prufrock Press Inc.

Grigorenko, E.L., Klin, A., & Volkmar, F. (2003). Annotation: Hyperlexia: Disability or superability? *Journal of Child Psychology and Psychiatry, 44*(8), 1079–1091.

Hagiwara, T., & Myles, B.S. (1999). A multimedia social story intervention: Teaching skills to children with Autism. *Focus on Autism and Other Developmental Disabilities* 14(2), 82–85.

Happé, F. (1994). An advanced test of theory of mind: Understanding of story characters' thoughts and feelings by able autistic, mentally handicapped, and normal children and adults. *Journal of Autism and Developmental Disorders, 24*, 129–154.

Harris, K., Graham, S., & Mason, L. (2003). Self-regulated strategy development in the classroom: Part of a balanced approach to writing instruction for students with disabilities. *Focus on Exceptional Children, 35*(7), 2–16.

Hellinckx, T., Roeyers, H., & Van Waelvelde, H. (2013). Predictors of handwriting in children with autism spectrum disorder. *Research in Autism Spectrum Disorders, 7*, 176–186.

Iland, E. (2011). *Drawing a blank: Improving comprehension for readers on the autism spectrum.* Shawnee Mission, KS: Autism Asperger's.

Jansiewicz, E.M., Goldberg, M.C., Newschaffer, C.J., Denckla, M.B., Landa, R., & Mostofsky, S.H. (2006). Motor signs distinguish children with high functioning autism and Asperger's syndrome from controls. *Journal of Autism and Developmental Disorders, 36*, 613–621.

Kaiser, M.L., Albaret, J.M., & Doudin, P.A. (2009). Relationship between visual-motor integration, eye–hand coordination, and quality of writing. *Journal of Occupational Therapy, Schools & Early Intervention, 2*(2), 87–95.

Kearns, K., & Shane, H. (2008). *The Monarch School for Autism Outcomes Management System.* A short course presented at the annual convention of the American Speech-Language Hearing Association (ASHLA), Chicago, IL.

Kim, A., Vaughn, S., Wanzek, J., & Wei, S. (2004). Graphic organizers and their effects on the reading comprehension of students with LD: A synthesis of research. *Journal of Learning Disabilities. 37*(2), 105–118.

Losh, M., & Capps, L. (2003). Narrative ability in high-functioning children with autism or Asperger's syndrome. *Journal of Autism and Developmental Disorders, 33*, 239–251.

Lyon, G.R., Fletcher, J.M., Shaywitz, S.E., Shaywitz, B.A., Torgesen, J.K., Wood, F.B.,...Olson, R. (2001). Rethinking learning disabilities. In *Rethinking special education for a new century* (pp. 259–287). Progressive Policy Institute & Thomas B. Fordham Foundation.

MacArthur, C. (1997). Using technology to enhance the writing processes of students with Learning disabilities. In K. Higgins & R. Boone (Eds.), *Technology for students with learning disabilities: Educational applications.* Austin, TX: PRO-ED.

MacArthur, C. (1990). Overcoming barriers to writing: Computer support for basic writing skills. *Reading & Writing Quarterly: Overcoming Learning Difficulties, 15*(2), 169–192.

MacArthur, C. (2000) New tools for writing: Assistive technology for students with writing difficulties. *Topics in Language Disorders, 20*(4), 85–100.

MacArthur, C., Ferretti, R., Okolo C., and Cavalier, A. (2001). Technology applications for students with literacy problems: A critical review [Special Issue: Instructional Interventions for Students with Learning Disabilities]. *The Elementary School Journal, 101*(3), 273–301.

Marcus, G., Pinker, S., Ullman, M., Hollander, M., Rosen, T., Xu, F., & Clahsen, H. (1992). Overregularization in language acquisition. *Monographs of the Society for Research in Child Development, 57*, 1–178.

Mayes, S.D., & Calhoun, S.L. (2007). Learning, attention, writing, and processing speed in typical children and children with ADHD, autism, anxiety, depression, and oppositional-defiant disorder. *Child Neuropsychology, 13*(6), 469–493.

McCall, W.G., & Craig, C. (2009). Same-language subtitling (SLS): Using subtitled music video for reading growth. In G. Siemens & C. Fulford (Eds.), *Proceedings of World Conference on Educational Multimedia, Hypermedia and Telecommunications 2009* (pp. 3983–3992). Chesapeake, VA: AACE. Retrieved from http://www.editlib.org/p/32055

Meyer, D.J. (1995). *The effects of graphic organizers on the creative writing of third grade students.* Masters' Project, Kean College of New Jersey.

Millar, D.C., Light, J.C., & Schlosser, R.W. (2006). The impact of augmentative and alternative communication intervention on the speech production of individuals with developmental disabilities: A research review. *Journal of Speech, Language, and Hearing Research, 49*, 248–264.

Molloy, C.A., Dietrich, K.N., & Bhattacharya, A. (2003). Postural stability in children with autism spectrum disorder. *Journal of Autism and Developmental Disorders, 33,* 643–652.

Myles, B.S., Huggins, A., Rome-Lake, M., Hagiwara, T., Barnhill, G.P., & Griswold, D.E. (2003). Written language profile of children and youth with Asperger syndrome: From research to practice. *Education and Training in Developmental Disabilities, 38*(4), 362–369.

Nation, K., Clarke, P., Wright, B., & Williams, C. (2006). Patterns of reading ability in children with autism spectrum disorder, *Journal of Autism and Developmental Disorders, 36,* 911–919.

Nation, K., & Norbury, C.F. (2005). Why reading comprehension fails: Insights from developmental disorders. *Topics in Language Disorders, 25,* 21–32.

National Center for Learning Disabilities (NCLD). (2006). *What is dysgraphia?* Retrieved from http://www.ncld.org/types-learning-disabilities/dysgraphia/what-is-dysgraphia

National Institute of Child Health and Human Development (NICHD). (2000). *Report of the National Reading Panel: Teaching children to read: An evidence-based assessment of the scientific research literature on reading and its implications for reading instruction: Reports of the subgroups* (NIH Publication No. 00-4754). Washington, D.C.: U.S. Government Printing Office. Retrieved from http://www.nichd.nih.gov/publications/pubs/nrp/Documents/report.pdf

Norbury, C.F. (2004). Factors supporting idiom comprehension in children with communication disorders. *Journal of Speech, Language, and Hearing Research, 47*(5), 1179–1194.

Oakhill, J.V., Cain, K., & Bryant, P.E. (2003). The dissocation of word reading and text comprehension: Evidence from component skills. *Language and Cognitive Processes, 18,* 443–468.

O'Connor, I.M., & Klein, P.D. (2004). Exploration of strategies for facilitating the reading comprehension of high-functioning students with autism spectrum disorders. *Journal of Autism and Developmental Disabilities, 34*(2), 115–127.

Quill, K.A. (2000). *Do-watch-listen-say: Social and communication intervention for children with autism.* Baltimore, MD: Paul H. Brookes Publishing Co.

Randi, J., Newman, T., & Grigorenko, E.L. (2010). Teaching children with autism to read for meaning: Challenges and possibilities. *Journal of Autism and Developmental Disabilities, 40*(7), 890–902.

Richards, R.G. (2002). *Strategies for the reluctant writer.* Retrieved from http://www.ldonline.org/article/6215

Robinson, D.H. (1997) Graphic organizers as aids to text learning. *Reading Research and Instruction, 37*(2), 85–105.

Selikowitz, M. (1998). *Dyslexia and other learning difficulties* (2nd ed.). Oxford, England: Oxford University Press.

Shane, H.C. (2006). Using visual scene displays to improve communication and communication instruction in persons with autism spectrum disorders. *Augmentative and Alternative Communication, 15,* 8–12.

Shane, H.C., & Albert, P.D. (2008). Electronic screen media for persons with autism spectrum disorders: Results of a survey. *Journal of Autism and Developmental Disorders, 38*(8) 1499–1508.

Shane, H.C., & Weiss-Kapp, S. (2007). *Visual language in autism.* San Diego, CA: Plural.

Sterling, C., Farmer, M., Riddick, B., & Matthews, C. (1998). Adult dyslexic writing. *Dyslexia, 4*(1), 1–15.

Treiman, R. (1997). Spelling in normal children and dyslexics. In B.A. Blachman (Ed.), *Foundations of reading acquisition and dyslexia: Implications for early intervention* (Chap. 9). Mahwah, NJ: Erlbaum.

Volman, M.J.M., van Schendel, B.M., & Jongmans, M.J. (2006). Handwriting difficulties in primary school children: A search for underlying mechanisms. *American Journal of Occupational Therapy, 60*(4), 451–460.

Vukelich, C., Christie, J., & Enz, B. (2002). *Helping young children learn language and literacy.* Boston, MA: Allyn & Bacon.

Wahlberg, T.J., & Magliano, J.P. (2004). The ability of high-functioning individuals with autism to comprehend written discourse. *Discourse Processes, 38*(1), 119–144.

Weimer, A.K., Schatz, A.M., Lincoln, A., Ballantyne, A.O., & Trauner, D.A. (2001). "Motor" impairment in Asperger syndrome: Evidence for a deficit in proprioception. *Journal of Developmental and Behavioral Pediatrics, 22,* 92–101.

West, T. (1997). *In the mind's eye.* New York, NY: Prometheus Books.

Whalon, K., & Hanline, M.F. (2008). Effects of a reciprocal questioning intervention on the question generation and responding of children with autism spectrum disorder.

Education and Training in Developmental Disabilities, 432, 367–387.

Whalon, K., Otaiba, S., & Delano, M. (2009). Evidence-based reading instruction for individuals with autism spectrum disorders. *Focus on Autism and Other Developmental Disabilities, 24,* 3–16.

Williams, D.L., Goldstein, G., & Minshew, N.J. (2006). The profile of memory function in children with autism. *Neuropsychology, 20,* 21–29.

Wong, B.Y.L. (1991). Teaching adolescents with learning disabilities and low achievers to plan, write, and revise compare-and-contrast essays. *Learning Disabilities Research and Practice, 6*(2), 117–127.

Wong, B.Y.L. (1999). Interactive teaching: An effective way to teach revision skills to adolescents with learning disabilities. *Learning Disabilities Research and Practice, 12*(1), 2–15.

Yuill, N.M., & Oakhill, J.V. (1991). *Children's problems in text comprehension: An experimental investigation.* Cambridge, England: Cambridge University Press.

Social Skills and Emotion-Regulation Management Tools

Matthew S. Goodwin

■ ■

Many children with autism spectrum disorders (ASD) have core difficulties recognizing and responding to facial expressions and vocal intonation, including understanding the contexts in which they are embedded and their functional meaning. These and related issues also often complicate peer interaction and emotion regulation in children with ASD. In this section, two chapters describe a number of emerging technologies to teach social skills and promote peer interactions, and one chapter describes the development and use of a technology-infused curriculum to facilitate emotion regulation in children with ASD.

In the first chapter, "Using New Technology to Teach Emotion Recognition to Children with Autism Spectrum Disorders," Simon Baron-Cohen, Ofer Golan, and Emma Ashwin review social-emotional difficulties in ASD, followed by a number of existing and evolving computer-based and film-based systems developed specifically for children with ASD to teach emotion recognition. They also discuss how the structured, interactive, and systematic nature of these technologies is particularly suited to the learning styles of persons with ASD and thus suggest that these systems are likely to prove more effective and generalizable than traditional teaching tools commonly in use for this purpose.

In the second chapter, "Incorporating Technology into Peer Social Group Programs," Andrea Tartaro and Corina Ratz discuss social-communication characteristics of children with ASD that can complicate peer social relatedness and interactions. They also review social group interventions commonly employed with this population, including a number of emerging platforms that incorporate technologies related to video modeling, robots, collaborative virtual environments, computer-mediated communication, tabletop displays, and video games. Their chapter ends with a discussion of the affordances technology-mediated approaches provide and practical recommendations for their use in traditional social group programs.

The final chapter in this section, "Technologies to Support Interventions for Social-Emotional Intelligence, Self-Awareness, Personal Style, and Self-Regulation," by Dorothy Lucci, Minna Levine, Kelley Challen-Wittmer, and Donald Scott McLeod focuses on issues relating to self-awareness, stress management, and self-regulation that contribute to social-emotional difficulties in children with ASD. After a thoughtful review of these issues, the authors present a social-emotional curriculum they developed specifically for persons with ASD that infuses a number of innovative physiological and digital self-report technologies. Their chapter ends with an anecdotal, yet detailed, evaluation of their curriculum's utility in applied settings, followed by suggestions for future clinical and research approaches that promote awareness of self and others and better management of stress that may significantly improve emotional understanding and functioning in children with ASD.

Taken together, the chapters in this section highlight social, communication, and emotional difficulties in children with ASD that may fruitfully be overcome using a wide range of existing and emerging technologies to supplement or, in some instances, replace more traditional intervention approaches that target these domains.

Using New Technology to Teach Emotion Recognition to Children with Autism Spectrum Disorders

■ ■

Simon Baron-Cohen, Ofer Golan, and Emma Ashwin

Children and adults with autism spectrum disorder (ASD) have difficulties with *cognitive empathy*, that is, understanding and recognizing what other people might think or feel. This is sometimes referred to as difficulties with theory of mind or degrees of "mindblindness" (Baron-Cohen, 1995). In this chapter we address the question of whether one aspect of empathy (emotion recognition) can be taught using new technologies and why such platforms as computer-based or film-based media might be particularly autism-friendly methods for such teaching. We begin with a definition of empathy. The chapter next reviews the empathy difficulties in autism, the systemizing strengths in autism, and the role of technology in autism

This chapter is reprinted with modification from Baron-Cohen, S., Golan, O., & Ashwin, E. (2009). Can emotion recognition be taught to children with autism spectrum conditions? *Proceedings of the Royal Society, Series B* [Special issue], *364*, 3567–3574. All the authors were affiliated with the Autism Research Centre at University of Cambridge during the study. This work was conducted in association with the NIHR CLAHRC for Cambridgeshire and Peterborough NHS Foundation Trust. Parts of this paper appeared in the *Journal of Autism and Developmental Disorders* (Golan et al., 2010) and in the *Proceedings of the Royal Society of London* (Baron-Cohen et al., 2010). We are grateful to Yael Granader, Suzy McClintock, Kate Day, and Victoria Leggett for help with data collection, and to Gina Owen and Kimberly Peabody and Ben Weiner for useful discussions. Ofer Golan now holds a position at the Department of Psychology, Faculty of Social Sciences, Bar-Ilan University in Israel. We are grateful to Culture Online and the Department for Culture, Media and Sport (DCMS) for funding, and to Catalyst Ltd and Culture Online (particularly Claire Harcup, Paul Bason, Khairoun Abji, and Professor Jon Drori) for their production of *The Transporters*. We are also indebted to the families who participated in the intervention. *The Transporters* series was nominated for a BAFTA in the Children's Awards category, November 2007. In the United Kingdom, 40,000 copies of *The Transporters* DVD were distributed for free in 2007 to families with a child on the autistic spectrum. The DVD is now available for sale via Changing Media Development Ltd, of which Simon Baron-Cohen, Jon Drori, and Claire Harcup are directors. Profits from sales go to autism research and development of new autism educational products.

education. We then summarize an experiment that evaluates a new technology designed to teach this element of empathy to young children with autism. Teaching cognitive empathy to children with ASD is important if they are to achieve greater skills in their social relationships and thus lead to the benefits of greater social inclusion.

WHAT IS EMPATHY?

We define empathy as the ability to attribute mental states to others and to respond with an appropriate emotion to the other person's mental states (Baron-Cohen & Wheelwright, 2004). This definition of empathy suggests that the two main fractions of empathy are a cognitive component (the recognition of another person's mental state) and an affective component (the emotional reaction to another person's mental state). The cognitive component is sometimes also called theory of mind (Dennett, 1989).

Mental states include thoughts and emotions. Thoughts are traditionally fractionated into beliefs, desires, intentions, goals, and perceptions (Baron-Cohen, 1995; Dennett, 1989). Emotions are traditionally fractionated into six basic emotions (happy, sad, angry, afraid, disgusted, and surprised; Ekman, 1999), as well as numerous complex emotions that are acquired at different points in childhood (Baron-Cohen, Golan, Wheewright, Granadar, & Hill, 2010). Complex emotions involve attributing a cognitive state as well as an emotion and are more context and culture dependent than basic emotions (Griffiths, 1997). The basic emotions are held to be so because they are universally recognized and expressed in the same way. It may be that more emotions are universally recognized and expressed than these six, but have been overlooked, possibly because of how expensive, time-consuming, and difficult cross-cultural research is. Indeed, research into complex emotions (usually toward developing taxonomies) has been mostly language and culture specific (Ortony, Clore, & Foss, 1987; Storm & Storm, 1987). Our own work described the development of the emotional lexicon in the English language (Baron-Cohen et al., 2010), suggesting there are at least 412 distinct emotions and related mental states (each with its own descriptor that is not just a synonym for another emotion) that are recognizable by independent judges within the United Kingdom (Baron-Cohen, Golan, Wheelwright, & Hill, 2004).

Having defined empathy into at least two major fractions, we turn to the question of the teachability of empathy. Some individuals in the population may be delayed in the development of empathy for different reasons. These include people with ASD who for neurological—and ultimately genetic—reasons have difficulties in putting themselves into someone else's shoes and knowing how to respond to another's feelings, in real-time. Since such deficits may have a significant impact on their social functioning, this raises the challenge of whether aspects of empathy can be facilitated or taught to individuals with ASD. We summarize some evidence that the first component of empathy, cognitive empathy, can indeed be taught. This task is made easier through the design of educational resources (including computer-based methods) that tap into systematic areas of interest, characteristic of ASD, that are therefore intrinsically motivating. Although we do not rule out that the second component of empathy, affective empathy, can be taught, there is little research in this area to date.

People with ASD have social-communication difficulties alongside circumscribed interests (obsessions) and a strong preference for sameness and repetition (American Psychiatric Association, 1994). Underlying these characteristics are difficulties understanding the emotional and mental states of others (Baron-Cohen, 1995). Individuals with ASD have difficulties recognizing emotions from facial expressions, vocal intonation, and body language separately (Baron-Cohen, Wheelwright, Hill, Raste, & Plumb, 2001; Golan, Baron-Cohen, & Hill, 2006; Hobson, 1986a, 1986b; Yirmiya, Sigman, Kasari, & Mundy, 1992) and in context (Golan, Baron-Cohen, & Golan, 2008; Klin, Jones, Schultz, Volkmar, & Cohen, 2002). Although some individuals with ASD recognize basic emotional expressions (Baron-Cohen, Spitz, & Cross, 1993; Grossman, Klin, Carter, & Volkmar, 2000), difficulties in identifying more complex emotions persist into adulthood (Baron-Cohen, Wheelwright, & Jolliffe, 1997; Golan et al., 2006).

EMPATHY DIFFICULTIES IN AUTISM SPECTRUM DISORDER

The emotion recognition difficulties are in part the result of altered face processing (Dawson et al., 2004; Klin et al., 2002), which in itself may be due to a failure to interpret the mentalistic information conveyed by the eyes (Baron-Cohen, 1995). Others' facial expressions may also be less intrinsically rewarding. Children with ASD show reduced attention to faces and to eyes in particular (Swettenham et al., 1998). The result of this reduced experience with faces is that children with ASD thus fail to become "face experts" (Dawson, Webb, & McPartland, 2005). For example, whereas the typically developing brain shows an electrophysiological response to upright faces called the N170 wave form, the autistic brain shows a reduced N170 (Grice et al., 2005).

SYSTEMIZING STRENGTHS IN AUTISM SPECTRUM DISORDER

In contrast to their difficulties in emotion recognition, individuals with ASD have intact or even enhanced abilities in "systemizing" (Baron-Cohen, 2002, 2006). Systemizing is the drive to analyze or build systems, allowing one to predict the behavior of the system and control it. Systems may be mechanical (e.g., vehicles), abstract (e.g., number patterns), natural (e.g., the tide), or collectible (e.g., a library classification index). The so-called obsessions or narrow interests of those with ASD cluster in the domain of systems (Baron-Cohen & Wheelwright, 1999). These include vehicles, spinning objects, and computers, all of which are attractive to individuals with ASD. At the heart of systemizing is the ability to detect patterns or rules of the form "If a, then b." The systemizing theory of autism relates this affinity to their systematic and predictable nature. In the study summarized below, we illustrate how these special interests can be harnessed when teaching children with ASD, using computer-based or multimedia formats, to keep the children intrinsically motivated.

The systemizing theory of autism has been supported by different studies: Children with ASD have been found to outperform matched controls on tests of intuitive physics (Baron-Cohen, Wheelwright, Spong, Scahill, & Lawson, 2001), and adults with ASD were at least intact on such tests (Lawson, Baron-Cohen, & Wheelwright, 2004), as well as on other tests that involve excellent attention to detail (Mottron, Dawson, Soulieres, Hubert, & Burack, 2006), a prerequisite for good systemizing (Baron-Cohen, 2008; Jolliffe & Baron-Cohen, 1997; O'Riordan, Plaisted, Driver, & Baron-Cohen, 2001; Shah & Frith, 1983). In addition, individuals with ASD score above average on the Systemizing Quotient (SQ), a self-report (or parent-report) measure of how strong one's interests are in systems (Auyeung et al., 2009; Baron-Cohen, Richler, Bisarya, Gurunathan, & Wheelwright, 2003; Wakabayashi et al., 2007; Wheelwright et al., 2006).

TEACHING EMPATHY SYSTEMATICALLY

If children with ASD possess intact or enhanced systemizing skills, it may be possible for them to use such skills to facilitate their empathy, particularly in the cognitive component of emotion recognition. Indeed, various intervention programs could be viewed as tapping systematic skills and interests in order to teach empathy and social skills. Here we review a few published examples.

LEGO Therapy (Owens, Granadar, Humphrey, & Baron-Cohen, 2008) is an example that encourages young children with ASD to build LEGO models in groups of three, thereby gaining opportunities for social interaction. Children participating in LEGO Therapy appear to be intrinsically motivated by LEGO presumably because it involves constructional systems that can be assembled in predictable and repeating sequences.

Another interesting example comes from the field of robotics. Since children with ASD presumably find the systematic motion and structure of robots more predictable and therefore less confusing than humans, and since robots can be designed to have simplified facial features and increase the children's attention to these features (Dautenhahn & Werry, 2004; Michaud & Théberge-Turmel, 2002), robots could be used as another way of teaching empathy to children with ASD (see Chapter 5). Indeed, through child–robot interaction, various social and communication skills of children with ASD, such as joint attention, turn taking, sharing, and greeting, have been shown to improve (Robins, Dautenhahn, Boekhorst, & Billard, 2005). Since robots are highly lawful mechanical and/or electronic systems, their use in teaching social skills in ASD is another clear example of harnessing systemizing to make empathy more autism friendly.

Computer programs provide another good example of the use of systematic preferences when teaching empathy. The computerized environment is predictable, consistent, and free of social demands. Users can work at their own pace and level of understanding, and lessons can be repeated over and over again until mastery is achieved. In addition, interest and motivation can be maintained through different and individually selected computerized rewards (Golan, LaCava, & Baron-Cohen, 2007; Moore, McGrath, & Thorpe, 2000). For these reasons, dozens of computer programs and web sites have been created to teach various skills to children with ASD. Regrettably, however, most have not been scientifically evaluated, leaving parents or persons on the autistic spectrum unable to judge if these are of any significant benefit. Some of the computerized programs teaching empathy-related skills that have been evaluated include Bölte et al.'s FEFFA, teaching emotion recognition from still pictures of facial expressions and strips of the eye region (Bölte et al., 2002); Sliver and Oaks's Emotion Trainer, teaching emotion recognition of basic emotions from facial expressions (Silver & Oakes, 2001); Tanaka et al.'s Let's Face It, teaching emotion and identity recognition from facial expressions (Tanaka et al., 2010); and

Beaumont and Sofronoff's Junior Detective program, which combines computer-based training with group training in order to teach social skills to children with ASD (Beaumont & Sofronoff, 2008).

Mind Reading DVD

Our own attempt at harnessing systematic skills to teach empathy to individuals with ASD via the computer is the *Mind Reading* DVD, a piece of educational software (Baron-Cohen et al., 2004; http://www.jkp.com/mindreading). See Figure 9.1.

This program was designed to be an interactive, systematic guide to emotions. It was developed to help people with ASD learn to recognize both basic and complex emotions and mental states from video clips of facial expressions and audio recordings of vocal expressions. It covers 412 distinct emotions and mental states, organized developmentally and classified taxonomically to be attractive to a mind that learns through systemizing. The principle behind this was that individuals with ASD may not learn to recognize emotional expressions in real time during live social situations because emotions are fleeting and do not repeat in an exact fashion, which may reduce the number of opportunities to systematically learn from repetition. Putting emotions into a computer-based learning environment enables emotions to be played and replayed over and over again in an identical fashion, such that the learner can have control over their speed and the number of exposures needed for the learner to analyze and memorize the features of each emotion.

Figure 9.1. A screenshot from the emotions library of the *Mind Reading* DVD.

Furthermore, since emotions vary depending on who is expressing them, in the real world it can be difficult to see what defines each specific emotion. *Mind Reading* helps its users overcome this problem by having each of the 412 emotions portrayed by six different actors (male and female, old and young, different ethnicities) to facilitate learning to recognize emotions independently of the identity of the person expressing that emotion. In addition, in the real world, emotions can appear inconsistent (some people smile when they are happy, other people smile when they are pretending to be happy, and yet others are happy when they are not smiling at all), so *Mind Reading* imposes some laws onto emotions by assigning a clear label to each emotional expression, including masked or insincere emotional expressions (e.g., emotions in the "sneaky" category). Finally, emotions in the real world can be hard to classify, so *Mind Reading* offers the user a predesigned classification system to assist in finding patterns among inherently unpatterned emotional information.

Using *Mind Reading* over a 10-week intervention (2 hours' usage per week), individuals with ASD improved in their ability to recognize a range of complex emotions and mental states (Golan & Baron-Cohen, 2006). Follow-up questionnaires were filled in by 18 participants with ASD 1 year after completion of the intervention period. Participants who used *Mind Reading* reported improved ability to form friendships and relationships and increased awareness of the importance of emotions and emotional expressions in everyday life, improved understanding of emotions and their corresponding expressions, and an enhanced ability to function socially (Golan & Baron-Cohen, 2007). These findings have been replicated with children in the United States, supporting the cross-cultural validity of this intervention (LaCava, Golan, Baron-Cohen, & Myles, 2007; LaCava, Rankin, Mahlios, Cook, & Simpson, 2010). These are encouraging results because they suggest that at least one cognitive component of empathy can be taught, and that it may have a long-term effect that facilitates social functioning. It is not known if such improvement would be seen if the intervention were shorter in duration, or if the users were not just persons with ASD but had additional learning difficulties (e.g., below-average IQ). Finally, it could reasonably be objected that learning to recognize emotions in the simplified context of a computer screen, devoid of the "noise" of a real social situation like a school playground or a birthday party or an argument, is likely to be simplified and therefore easier to achieve. This objection is important because it raises the question of whether such learning from artificial contexts generalizes to more natural settings. Guarding against the risk of artificiality, *Mind Reading* used real faces rather than cartoon or schematic faces. However, future work using the *Mind Reading* DVD could assess the benefits of a longer intervention than just 10 weeks. The DVD could also be used with more interactive teaching methods, such as social skills groups, or as part of dramatic role play. Other limitations of the *Mind Reading* DVD are that the videos use actors rather than real-life recordings and that the background of each video is a white screen (thus lacking real-world context). Although these design features have their advantages, it may be that future technologies could expand on this earlier design.

Difficulties with generalization from taught material to everyday life have been found in computer-based intervention programs (Bölte et al., 2002; Silver & Oaks, 2001) and social skills–training courses (Barry et al., 2003; Bauminger, 2002). The limited effectiveness of these interventions could be related to a lack of intrinsic motivation, given that they utilize explicit rather than implicit teaching methods. In the study reviewed next, we attempted to rely on intrinsic motivation of children with ASD through the use of animated vehicles.

The Transporters DVD (Animation Series)

This study (reported in detail in Golan et al., 2010) evaluates the effectiveness of an animation series created to motivate young children with ASD to learn about emotions and facial expressions by embedding them in a world of mechanical vehicles. Again, this series is based on the premise that the reason children with ASD love to watch films about vehicles (according to parental report) may be because such children are strong systemizers (Baron-Cohen, 2006, 2008). That is, they are drawn to predictable, rule-based systems, whether these are repeating mathematical patterns, repeating electrical patterns (e.g., light switches), or repeating patterns in films. Kanner's first descriptions of ASD drew attention to their "need for sameness" and their "resistance to change" (Kanner, 1943). At the core of ASD may be an ability to deal effortlessly with systems because they do not change and they produce the same outcome every time; by the same token, there is a disabling difficulty to deal with the social world because it is always changing unpredictably and because the outcome is seldom the same every time.

According to the hypersystemizing theory (Baron-Cohen, 2006), vehicles whose motion is determined only by physical rules (e.g., vehicles that can only go back and forth along linear tracks) would be much preferred by children with ASD over vehicles like planes or cars, whose motion could be highly variable, moving at the whim of the human driver operating them. In vision neuroscience, this theory relates to the distinction between physical-causal or mechanical motion (Michotte, 1963) versus animate or biological motion (Castelli, Happé, Frith, & Frith, 2000; Premack, 1990). The former requires intuitive physics (Saxe, Carey, & Kanwisher, 2004; Wellman & Inagaki, 1997), whereas the latter requires intuitive psychology, in particular the ability to detect others' goals, desires, and intentions (Baron-Cohen, 1995).

We therefore created a children's animation series, *The Transporters* (http://www.thetransporters.com), based around eight characters who are all vehicles that move according to rule-based motion (Figure 9.2).

Onto these vehicles we grafted real-life faces of actors showing emotions. We tested whether creating an autism-friendly context of predictable mechanical

Figure 9.2. Characters from *The Transporters* DVD.

motion could render facial expressions of emotion more learnable and thus increase motivation to learn them. The different toy vehicles (two trams, two cable cars, a chain ferry, a coach, a funicular railway, and a tractor) had motion that was constrained in a linear manner (all the vehicles moved on tracks or cables).

The Transporters is a high-quality 3-D children's animation series and consists of 15 five-minute episodes, each of which focuses on a key emotion or mental state. The 15 key emotions depicted on the vehicles are *happy, sad, angry, afraid, disgusted, surprised, excited, tired, unfriendly, kind, sorry, proud, jealous, joking,* and *ashamed*. The emotions selected include the six basic emotions (Ekman, 1999), emotions that are more complex but still developmentally appropriate (e.g., *jealous, proud, ashamed*), and emotions and mental states that are important for everyday social functioning (e.g., *kind, unfriendly, tired, joking*). These emotions were chosen because children who are typically developing recognize and understand these emotions when they are between 2 and 7 years of age (Bretherton & Beeghly, 1982; Ridgeway, Waters, & Kuczaj, 1985).

In the study by Golan et al. (2010), three groups were assessed twice: at Time 1 and then 4 weeks after at Time 2. In each assessment, participants were tested at four levels of generalization, one testing participants' emotional vocabulary, and the other three testing their ability to match a socioemotional situation to the appropriate facial expression. At Level 1, Emotional Vocabulary, participants were asked to define 16 emotion words and give examples of situations that evoked them. These were the aforementioned 15 key emotions from the series, in addition to *worried*. At Level 2, Situation–Facial Expression Matching, matching of situation and expression was tested using three tasks, each consisting of 16 items (1 for each emotion). Each item included a photo depicting a scene with a short description.

The three tasks represented three levels of generalization: 1) *Familiar close generalization:* Participants had to match familiar situations taken from the intervention series to facial expressions of familiar characters from the series. 2) *Unfamiliar close generalization:* Participants had to match novel situations with novel expressions from *The Transporters* characters. These expressions were *not* shown by these characters in the intervention series. 3) *Distant generalization:* To test generalization to facial expressions that are not attached to vehicles, participants had to match novel situations with novel expressions using a selection of human non-*Transporters* faces taken from the *Mind Reading* software (Baron-Cohen et al., 2004). Examples of items from Levels 1 and 3 are shown in Figure 9.3.

Three groups took part in the study: an ASD intervention group, an ASD control group, and a typically developing control group. Participants in the two clinical groups were randomly assigned and took part according to the following test conditions: 1) *ASD intervention group:* The parents of 20 participants were given the intervention series and DVD guide to use with their child at home. Children were asked to watch at least three episodes per day over a period of 4 weeks. 2) *ASD control group:* During the 4-week interval, 19 participants did not participate in any intervention except for their standard school curriculum. 3) *Typical control group:* For this group, 18 participants were recruited. Using the British Picture Vocabulary Scale (BPVS), researchers matched the three groups for sex, age, and verbal ability (Dunn, Whetton, & Burley, 1997).

At Time 1, there were significant differences between groups on the emotional vocabulary task and on the three Situation-Expression Matching tasks.

(a)   4. Charlie is going to get the pieces for the new special clock.

(b)   6. The neighbor's dog has bitten people before. He is barking at Louise.

Figure 9.3. Examples of questions from two of the three emotion recognition task levels. (a) Level 1 task: Match familiar scenes from the series with familiar faces. (b) Level 3 task: Match novel scenes and faces using real human faces. (From Baron-Cohen, S., Golan, O., & Ashwin, E. [2009]. Can emotion recognition be taught to children with autism spectrum conditions? *Proceedings of the Royal Society, Series B* [Special issue], 364, 3567–3574.)

These differences were due to the significantly higher scores of the typical controls on all tasks compared to the two clinical groups, which did not differ from each other. Analysis of results after Time 2 testing revealed significant Time × Group interactions, with the ASD intervention group showing statistically significant improvement across all task levels between Time 1 and Time 2. Furthermore, this improvement was comparable to levels of performance found in the typical control group. In contrast, the ASD and typical control groups showed no statistically significant improvement on any of the tasks between test sessions. These effects are illustrated in Figure 9.4.

The study we have reviewed (reported in detail in Golan et al., 2010) investigated the effectiveness of individual use of *The Transporters* animated series (with parental support) over a 4-week period. The results show that use of the DVD led children with ASD to improve significantly in their emotion comprehension and recognition skills on tasks including the emotions presented by *The Transporters*:

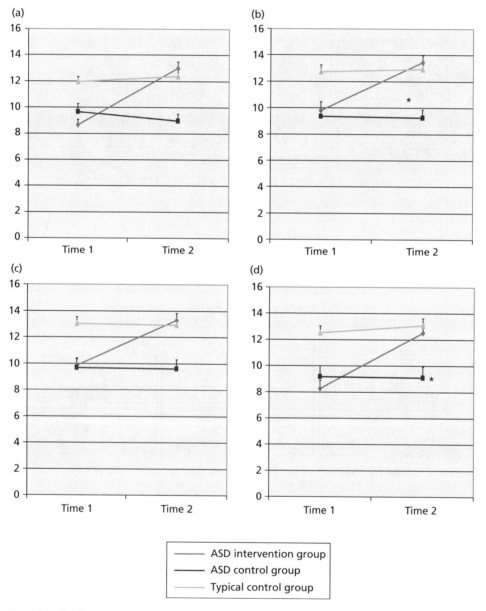

Figure 9.4. Graphs to show mean scores (with standard error bars) for each group on the four tasks. (a) Situation-Expression Matching task—Level 1. (b) Situation-Expression Matching task—Level 2. (c) Situation-Expression Matching task—Level 3. (d) Emotional Vocabulary task. * $p < 0.001$.

from the same level of ability seen with the ASD control group at Time 1, to a level that was indistinguishable from the typically developing group at Time 2.

The improvement of the intervention group was not limited to tasks that required close generalization; these participants were also able to generalize their knowledge to perform at the level of typical controls on the distant generalization task, which required emotion recognition from naturalistic clips of human characters that were not attached to vehicles. *The Transporters* may have facilitated generalization because the series was designed using intrinsically motivating media, such that the children enjoyed watching the vehicles while learning about emotions from real faces grafted onto them (incidental rather than explicit learning). *The Transporters* used characters and an environment that appeal to a preference for order, systems, and predictability that is characteristic of ASD. Anecdotal evidence from the parents of the intervention group suggests that their children became more willing to discuss emotions and became more interested in facial expressions. Parents also noticed a change in their children's behavior and in their ability to interact with others. Such anecdotal changes need formal evaluation.

We expect that the integration of *The Transporters* with other educational or therapeutic methods for children with ASD may improve its effect even further. We conclude that the use of systemizing as an intrinsically motivating method for learning about empathy allows affective information, which would otherwise be confusing, to become more intelligible and appealing to the autistic mind.

CONCLUSIONS

If *The Transporters* is having such a positive effect on the learnability of emotional expressions by children with ASD, might there be other ways to harness the same preference for systemizing in the teaching of emotions to these children? Clearly, vehicles are not the only kind of systems that children with ASD enjoy; others include robots (Dautenhahn & Werry, 2004) or rules (Hadwin, Baron-Cohen, Howlin, & Hill, 1996). We see such interventions as part of an adaptation of the mainstream environment to be more suited to people with ASD, and such environmental adaptations need not be restricted to the teaching of emotions. We conclude that a little empathy on the part of designers of educational resources may therefore facilitate the development of empathy in children with ASD.

REFERENCES

American Psychiatric Association (APA). (1994). *Diagnostic and statistical manual of mental disorders, Fourth Edition (DSM-IV)*. Washington, D.C.: Author.

Auyeung, B., Wheelwright, S., Allison, C., Atkinson, M., Samaranwickrema, N., & Baron-Cohen, S. (2009). The Children's Empathy Quotient (EQ-C) and Systemizing Quotient (SQ-C): Sex differences in typical development and in autism spectrum conditions. *Journal of Autism and Developmental Disorders*, 39(11), 385–395.

Baron-Cohen, S. (1995). *Mindblindness: An essay on autism and theory of mind*. Boston, MA: MIT Press/Bradford Books.

Baron-Cohen, S. (2002). The extreme male brain theory of autism. *Trends in Cognitive Science*, 6(6), 248–254.

Baron-Cohen, S. (2006). The hyper-systemizing, assortative mating theory of autism. *Progress in Neuro-Psychopharmacology & Biological Psychiatry*, 30(5), 865–872.

Baron-Cohen, S. (2008). Autism, hypersystemizing, and truth. *Quarterly Journal of Experimental Psychology*, 61(1), 64–75.

Baron-Cohen, S., Golan, O., & Ashwin, E. (2009). Can emotion recognition be taught to children with autism spectrum conditions? *Proceedings of the Royal Society, Series B* [Special issue], *364*, 3567–3574.

Baron-Cohen, S., Golan, O., Wheelwright, S., Granadar, Y., & Hill, J. (2010). Emotion word comprehension from 4–16 years old: A developmental study. *Frontiers in Evolutionary Neuroscience, 2*, 109.

Baron-Cohen, S., Golan, O., Wheelwright, S., & Hill, J.J. (2004). Mind reading: The interactive guide to emotions. London, England: Jessica Kingsley. http://www.jkp.com/mindreading

Baron-Cohen, S., Richler, J., Bisarya, D., Gurunathan, N., & Wheelwright, S. (2003). The Systemising Quotient (SQ): An investigation of adults with Asperger syndrome or high functioning autism and normal sex differences. *Philosophical Transactions of the Royal Society, Series B* [Special issue], *358*, 361–374.

Baron-Cohen, S., Spitz, A., & Cross, P. (1993). Can children with autism recognize surprise? *Cognition and Emotion, 7*, 507–516.

Baron-Cohen, S., & Wheelwright, S. (1999). Obsessions in children with autism or Asperger syndrome: A content analysis in terms of core domains of cognition. *British Journal of Psychiatry, 175*, 484–490.

Baron-Cohen, S., & Wheelwright, S. (2004). The Empathy Quotient (EQ). An investigation of adults with Asperger syndrome or high functioning autism, and normal sex differences. *Journal of Autism and Developmental Disorders, 34*, 163–175.

Baron-Cohen, S., Wheelwright, S., Hill, J., Raste, Y., & Plumb, I. (2001). The "Reading the Mind in the Eyes" Test, Revised Version: A study with normal adults, and adults with Asperger syndrome or high-functioning autism. *Journal of Child Psychology and Psychiatry, 42*(2), 241–251.

Baron-Cohen, S., Wheelwright, S., & Jolliffe, T. (1997). Is there a "language of the eyes"? Evidence from normal adults and adults with autism or Asperger syndrome. *Visual Cognition, 4*, 311–331.

Baron-Cohen, S., Wheelwright, S., Spong, A., Scahill, V.L., & Lawson, J. (2001). Are intuitive physics and intuitive psychology independent? A test with children with Asperger syndrome. *Journal of Developmental and Learning Disorders, 5*, 47–78.

Barry, T.D., Klinger, L.G., Lee, J.M., Palardy, N., Gilmore, T., & Bodin, S.D. (2003). Examining the effectiveness of an outpatient clinic-based social skills group for high-functioning children with autism. *Journal of Autism and Developmental Disorders, 33*(6), 685–701.

Bauminger, N. (2002). The facilitation of social-emotional understanding and social interaction in high-functioning children with autism: Intervention outcomes. *Journal of Autism and Developmental Disorders, 32*(4), 283–298.

Beaumont, R., & Sofronoff, K. (2008). A multi-component social skills intervention for children with Asperger syndrome: The Junior Detective Training Program. *Journal of Child Psychology & Psychiatry, 49*(7), 743–753.

Bölte, S., Feineis-Matthews, S., Leber, S., Dierks, T., Hubl, D., & Poustka, F. (2002). The development and evaluation of a computer-based program to test and to teach the recognition of facial affect. *International Journal of Circumpolar Health, 61*(Suppl. 2), 61–68.

Bretherton, I., & Beeghly, M. (1982). Talking about internal states: The acquisition of an explicit theory of mind. *Developmental Psychology, 18*(6), 906–921.

Castelli, F., Happé, F., Frith, U., & Frith, C. (2000). Movement and mind: A functional imaging study of perception and interpretation of complex intentional movement patterns. *Neuroimage, 12*(3), 314–325.

Dautenhahn, K., & Werry, I. (2004). Towards interactive robots in autism therapy. *Pragmatics & Cognition, 12*(1), 1–35.

Dawson, G., Toth, K., Abbott, R., Osterling, J., Munson, J., Estes, A., & Liaw, J. (2004). Early social attention impairments in autism: Social orienting, joint attention, and attention to distress. *Developmental Psychology, 40*(2), 271–283.

Dawson, G., Webb, S.J., & McPartland, J. (2005). Understanding the nature of face processing impairment in autism: Insights from behavioral and electrophysiological studies. *Developmental Neuropsychology, 27*(3), 403–424.

Dennett, D. (1989). *The intentional stance.* Cambridge, MA: MIT Press.

Dunn, L.M., Whetton, C., & Burley, J. (1997). *The British Picture Vocabulary Scale, Second Edition.* Windsor, England: NFER-Nelson.

Ekman, P. (1999). Basic emotions. In T. Dalgleish, & M. Power (Eds.), *Handbook of cognition and emotion* (pp. 45–60). Sussex, England: Wiley.

Golan, O., Ashwin, E., Granader, Y., McClintock, S., Day, K., Leggett, V., & Baron-Cohen, S. (2010). Enhancing emotion recognition in children with autism spectrum conditions: An intervention using animated vehicles with real emotional faces. *Journal of Autism and Developmental Disorders, 40*(3), 269–279.

Golan, O., & Baron-Cohen, S. (2006). Systemizing empathy: Teaching adults with Asperger syndrome or high-functioning autism to recognize complex emotions using interactive multimedia. *Development and Psychopathology, 18*(2), 591–617.

Golan, O., & Baron-Cohen, S. (2007). Teaching adults with autism spectrum conditions to recognize emotions: Systematic training for empathizing difficulties. In E. McGregor, N. Nunez, K. Cebula, & J.C. Gomez (Eds.), *Autism: An integrated view* (pp. 236–259). Oxford, England: Blackwell.

Golan, O., Baron-Cohen, S., & Golan, Y. (2008). The "Reading the Mind in Films" Task [Child version]: Complex emotion and mental state recognition in children with and without autism spectrum conditions. *Journal of Autism and Developmental Disorders, 3*(8), 1534–1541.

Golan, O., Baron-Cohen, S., & Hill, J.J. (2006). The Cambridge Mindreading (CAM) Face-Voice Battery: Testing complex emotion recognition in adults with and without Asperger syndrome. *Journal of Autism and Developmental Disorders, 36*(2), 169–183.

Golan, O., LaCava, P.G., & Baron-Cohen, S. (2007). Assistive technology as an aid in reducing social impairments in autism spectrum conditions. In R.L. Gabriels & D.E. Hill (Eds.), *Growing up with autism: Working with school-age children and adolescents* (pp. 124–142). New York, NY: Guilford Press.

Grice, S.J., Halit, H., Farroni, T., Baron-Cohen, S., Bolton, P., & Johnson, M.H. (2005). Neural correlates of eye-gaze detection in young children with autism. *Cortex, 41*(3), 342–353.

Griffiths, P. (1997). *What emotions really are: The problem of psychological categories.* Chicago: University of Chicago Press.

Grossman, J.B., Klin, A., Carter, A.S., & Volkmar, F.R. (2000). Verbal bias in recognition of facial emotions in children with Asperger syndrome. *Journal of Child Psychology and Psychiatry and Allied Disciplines, 41*, 369–739.

Hadwin, J., Baron-Cohen, S., Howlin, P., & Hill, K. (1996). Can we teach children with autism to understand emotions, belief, or pretence? *Development and Psychopathology, 8*, 345–365.

Hobson, R.P. (1986a). The autistic child's appraisal of expressions of emotion. *Journal of Child Psychology and Psychiatry, 27*, 321–342.

Hobson, R.P. (1986b). The autistic child's appraisal of expressions of emotion: A further study. *Journal of Child Psychology and Psychiatry, 27*, 671–680.

Jolliffe, T., & Baron-Cohen, S. (1997). Are people with autism or Asperger's syndrome faster than normal on the Embedded Figures Task? *Journal of Child Psychology and Psychiatry, 38*, 527–534.

Kanner, L. (1943). Autistic disturbances of affective contact. *Nervous Child, 2*, 217–250.

Klin, A., Jones, W., Schultz, R., Volkmar, F., & Cohen, D. (2002). Visual fixation patterns during viewing of naturalistic social situations as predictors of social competence in individuals with autism. *Archives of General Psychiatry, 59*(9), 809–816.

LaCava, P.G., Golan, O., Baron-Cohen, S., & Myles, B.S. (2007). Using assistive technology to teach emotion recognition to students with Asperger syndrome: A pilot study. *Remedial and Special Education, 28*(3), 174–181.

LaCava, P.G., Rankin, A., Mahlios, E., Cook, K., & Simpson, R.L. (2010). A single case design evaluation of a software and tutor intervention addressing emotion recognition and social interaction in four boys with ASD. *Autism, 14*(3), 161–178.

Lawson, J., Baron-Cohen, S., & Wheelwright, S. (2004). Empathising and systemising in adults with and without Asperger syndrome. *Journal of Autism and Developmental Disorders, 34*(3), 301–310.

Michaud, F., & Théberge-Turmel, C. (2002). Mobile robotic toys and autism. In K. Dautenhahn, A. Bond, L. Cañamero, & B. Edmonds (Eds.), *Socially intelligent agents—Creating relationships with computers and robots* (pp. 125–132). Dordrecht, The Netherlands: Kluwer Academic.

Michotte, A. (1963). *The perception of causality.* Andover, MA: Methuen.

Moore, D., McGrath, P., & Thorpe, J. (2000). Computer-aided learning for people with autism—A framework for research and development. *Innovations in Education and Training International, 37*, 218–228.

Mottron, L., Dawson, M., Soulieres, I., Hubert, B., & Burack, J. (2006). Enhancedp perceptual functioning in autism: An update, and eight principles of autistic perception. *Journal of Autism and Developmental Disorders*, 1–17.

O'Riordan, M.A., Plaisted, K.C., Driver, J., & Baron-Cohen, S. (2001). Superior visual search in autism. *Journal of Experimental Psychology, Human Perception and Performance, 27*(3), 719–730.

Ortony, A., Clore, G., & Foss, M. (1987). The referential structure of the affective lexicon. *Cognitive Science, 11,* 341–364.

Owens, G., Granader, Y., Humphrey, A., & Baron-Cohen, S. (2008). LEGO therapy and the social use of language programme: An evaluation of two social skills interventions for children with high functioning autism and Asperger syndrome. *Journal of Autism and Developmental Disorders, 38*(10), 1944–1957.

Premack, D. (1990). The Infants theory of self-propelled objects. *Cognition, 36*(1), 1–16.

Ridgeway, D., Waters, E., & Kuczaj, S.A. (1985). Acquisition of emotion descriptive language: Receptive and productive vocabulary norms for ages 18 months to 6 years. *Developmental Psychology, 21,* 901–908.

Robins, B., Dautenhahn, K., Boekhorst, R., & Billard, A. (2005). Robotic assistants in therapy and education of children with autism: Can a small humanoid robot help encourage social interaction skills? *Universal Access in the Information Society, 4*(2), 105–120.

Saxe, R., Carey, S., & Kanwisher, N. (2004). Understanding other minds: Linking developmental psychology and functional neuroimaging. *Annual Review of Psychology, 55,* 87–124.

Shah, A., & Frith, U. (1983). An islet of ability in autistic children: A research note. *Journal of Child Psychology and Psychiatry, 24*(4), 613–620.

Silver, M., & Oakes, P. (2001). Evaluation of a new computer intervention to teach people with autism or Asperger syndrome to recognize and predict emotions in others. *Autism, 5,* 299–316.

Storm, C., & Storm, T. (1987). A taxonomic study of the vocabulary of emotions. *Journal of Personality and Social Psychology, 53*(4), 805–816.

Swettenham, J., Baron-Cohen, S., Charman, T., Cox, A., Baird, G., Drew, A., ... Wheelwright, S. (1998). The frequency and distribution of spontaneous attention shifts between social and nonsocial stimuli in autistic, typically developing, and nonautistic developmentally delayed infants. *Journal of Child Psychology and Psychiatry and Allied Disciplines, 39*(5), 747–753.

Tanaka, J.W., Wolf, J.M., Klaiman, C., Koenig, K., Cockburn, J., Herlihy, L., ... Shultz, R.T. (2010). Using computerized games to teach face recognition skills to children with autism spectrum disorder: The Let's Face It! program. *Journal of Child Psychology & Psychiatry, 51*(8), 944–952.

Wakabayashi, A., Baron-Cohen, S., Uchiyama, T., Yoshida, Y., Kuroda, M., & Wheelwright, S. (2007). Empathizing and systemizing in adults with and without autism spectrum conditions: Cross-cultural stability. *Journal of Autism and Developmental Disorders, 37*(10), 1823–1832.

Wellman, H., & Inagaki, K. (Eds.). (1997). *The emergence of core domains of thought: Children's reasoning about physical, psychological, and biological phenomena.* San Francisco, CA: Jossey-Bass.

Wheelwright, S., Baron-Cohen, S., Goldenfeld, N., Delaney, J., Fine, D., Smith, R., ... Wakabayashi, A. (2006). Predicting Autism Spectrum Quotient (AQ) from the Systemizing Quotient–Revised (SQ-R) and Empathy Quotient (EQ). *Brain Research, 1079*(1), 47–56.

Yirmiya, N., Sigman, M., Kasari, C., & Mundy, P. (1992). Empathy and cognition in high functioning children with autism. *Child Development, 63,* 150–160.

Incorporating Technology into Peer Social Group Programs

■ ■

Andrea Tartaro and Corina Ratz

Peer social groups offer many benefits for addressing the difficulties children with autism spectrum disorders (ASDs) have interacting with peers. Group work is cost effective; many children can participate in treatment simultaneously, thus lowering therapeutic expenses (Kroeger, Schultz, & Newsom, 2007). In addition, social groups are usually designed to include children around the same age and language ability, so participants have others with whom to practice skills (Kroeger et al., 2007). However, although studies have demonstrated some improvements on targeted skills, like play skills, other skills, like conversation skills, show limited improvement (Barry et al., 2003). It is also unclear how well acquired skills generalize to new settings (Barry et al., 2003; Castorina & Negri, 2011; White, Koenig, & Scahill, 2010). McConnell (2002) recommends using new and varied activities to address some of these problems. In this chapter, we argue that technology used in a social group setting can help overcome the challenges and provide new opportunities for learning and practicing social skills with peers.

In what follows, we first provide background on how ASDs affect peer interactions. We then describe different approaches to social group interventions and review evaluations of these approaches. Next, we review research that examines technologies used in a social group context, including authors' evaluations of their programs. Finally, we provide some practical recommendations for using technology in social group programs.

The authors would like to acknowledge Autism Speaks, Sara Block, Justine Cassell, Jennifer Lira, Valeria Nanclares-Nogués, the Pediatric Developmental Center at Advocate Illinois Masonic Medical Center, Kristina Rodriguez, and Carol Rolland.

AUTISM SPECTRUM DISORDERS AND PEER SOCIAL INTERACTION

The triad of characteristics of autism—impaired communication, impaired quality of social interaction, and patterns of restricted and repetitive behaviors—can have profound effects on the frequency (Orsmond, Krauss, & Seltzer, 2004), context (Orsmond et al., 2004), and quality (Travis & Sigman, 1998) of peer social interactions. Orsmond et al. (2004) found that for adolescents and adults with autism, the more severe their characteristic impairments, the fewer friendships with same-age peers they report. Further, individuals with autism more often participate in organized group activities (e.g., religious or group recreational activities) but not less structured social situations (Orsmond et al., 2004). Even considering those situations where social interaction is more likely to occur, such as on the playground, individuals with autism tend to play on their own, watch other children from a distance, or engage in "challenging behaviors" (McConnell, 2002). Most children diagnosed with ASD have difficulty in understanding and using the rules of social behaviors, such as turn taking and sharing (Kelly, Garnett, Attwood, & Peterson, 2008). Challenges are also caused by individuals with autism displaying intense preoccupations and narrow interests (Sasson, Turner-Brown, Holtzclaw, Lam, & Bodfish, 2008), engaging in ritualized behaviors (Boyd, McDonough, & Bodfish, 2012), or hyper- or hyposensitivity to information that comes through the senses (Simmons & Miller, 2008).

When children and adolescents with autism do participate in social situations, their interactions are often awkward and unsuccessful (Tyson & Cruess, 2012) or have a "learned" quality, as opposed to a natural one. However, quality social interaction is necessary for learning and a highly valued trait in today's society, from college admission interviews, to job opportunities, to sustaining friendships and support networks. Thus, developing these skills is critical.

SOCIAL GROUP INTERVENTIONS

Social group interventions are used with individuals with autism of all ages, including children, adolescents, and adults, to develop social interaction skills (Ruble, Willis, & Crabtree, 2008). Some important therapeutic factors associated with a group setting involve interpersonal learning as well as the development of socializing techniques (Yalom, 1989). The kinds of social skills targeted vary from group to group and can include such conversation skills as initiating and maintaining conversations, such emotional skills as recognizing and responding to others' emotions or dealing with mistakes, such complex social interactions as compromising or dealing with bullies, and such life skills as interviewing for a job or talking to a landlord. However, though social group interventions might be a common intervention approach, they vary widely in format, activities and goals (Ruble et al., 2008).

One common approach is to follow a structured training program that focuses on specific social behaviors. These programs—among them Social Skills Training for Children and Adolescents with Asperger Syndrome and Social-Communication Problems (Baker, 2003), Learning to Get Along (Jackson, Jackson, Bennett, Bynum, & Faryna, 1991), Skillstreaming (McGinnis & Goldstein, 1984, 1990), and SCORE Skills Strategy (Webb, Miller, Pierce, Strawser, & Jones, 2004)—include didactic instruction on and/or discussion about skills and opportunities to practice skills in role play and unstructured activities. For instance, Baker's social skills program, described in his book *Social Skills Training for Children and Adolescents with Asperger*

Syndrome and Social-Communication Problems (2003), outlines 70 skill lessons, such as "taking turns (two-question rule)" or "staying on topic." Baker provides a format called Structured Learning composed of four components: 1) didactic instruction describing specific skill steps, 2) modeling of the skill, 3) role play and feedback using scenarios that elicit the skill, and 4) practice in and outside the group setting. For example, the Baker's two-question rule provides the following skill steps:

1. *When others greet you, greet them back.*

   a. *If they say "Hello," then say "Hello" back to them.*

2. *Two-question rule: When others ask you a question and you answer it, you can ask a similar question right back. Example: "How was your weekend?" "Good. I went to the movies. How was your weekend?" (Baker, 2003, p. 92)*

One example of a role-play scenario from this lesson: "Pick a topic about which people have different preferences (movies, TV shows, food, school subject, etc.). Prompt students to take turns sharing their preferences about each topic" (Baker, 2003, p. 93). Children and parents are then provided with a worksheet to help them practice the skill outside the group.

Groups also often use such activities as games or crafts to provide structure (Faherty, 2000). For example, Legoff (2004) found that LEGO toys are effective as the central activity of the group. Participants in his LEGO Club had to work together to create constructions. One child played the role of the engineer, who gave instructions to the other child, the builder, for building the structures.

To facilitate age-appropriate interaction during both unstructured activities and skills instruction, groups often include children around the same age and language ability. Groups can also include children who are typically developing and can thus model appropriate social behaviors and provide more opportunities to practice newly acquired skills with a patient peer (Wang & Spillane, 2009). Kamps et al. (2002) found that training peers is an important aspect of this practice; significantly more social interactions occur when peers are trained. Peers can also work alongside therapists using behavior strategies to address individualized plans of specific behavior targets for each child (Koenig et al., 2010). However, findings regarding groups that include children who are typically developing are not consistent. For example, in a study conducted by Castorina and Negri (2011), sibling involvement in a social group did not improve the efficacy of the program over a group that did not have peer involvement.

Finally, a different model from the didactic instruction described above is sometimes used, such as in a program designed for adults with ASD, the Aspirations program (Hillier, Fish, Cloppert, & Beversdorf, 2007). Aspirations is a group member–directed program that uses more of a counseling support group model. Members bring in situations they have encountered in their daily lives and discuss them as a group.

The programs described above typically occur in a clinical setting where long sessions are possible, but sessions are often infrequent (i.e., monthly, weekly or twice weekly). In contrast, in a school setting, social programs are often brief but more frequent (Barry et al., 2003). For example, Licciardello, Harchik, and Luiselli (2008) evaluated a classroom-based intervention where classroom assistants were trained to provide evidence-supported procedures, preteaching, prompting, praise, and reward to increase students' social initiations and responses during play situations with their typically developing peers. The authors report that the "intervention required only a few minutes each day," (Licciardello et al., 2008, p. 33) and the classroom assistants reported delivering the intervention was not difficult. Compared to baseline, students' social initiations and responses increased during free play (Licciardello et al., 2008).

As some of the foregoing examples illustrate, social groups have demonstrated success in recent studies. In a metareview examining various approaches to improving social behaviors, Reichow and Volkmar (2010) conclude that although many intervention methods have been successful, a social skills group approach is the only practice that reaches the criterion for "established evidence-based practice (EBP)" (p. 161). Reichow, Volkmar, and Cicchetti (2008) define established EBP as a treatment "shown to be effective across multiple methodologically sound studies conducted by at least two independent research groups. Practices meeting this requirement have demonstrated enough evidence for confidence in the treatment's efficacy" (2008, p. 1315). Cappadocia and Weiss (2011) conducted a metareview of research on social skills training groups specifically and found "preliminary evidence for the efficacy of group-based social skills intervention" (p. 70). They note, however, that few studies used comparison groups or randomized control trial designs and that studies with larger sample sizes are needed (Cappadocia & Weiss, 2011).

Nevertheless, there are limitations to social groups. For example, Barry et al. (2003) evaluated a clinical social group for children with ASD (ages 6–9), which focused on greeting, conversation, and play skills. Although evaluation found some improvements in greeting and play skills, the results on conversation skills were less successful (Barry et al., 2003). Moreover, social group evaluations have a common problem in that skills developed in the groups often are not reflected in measures meant to capture generalization outside the group setting (e.g., Barry et al., 2003; Castorina & Negri, 2011; White et al., 2010). However, generalization measures usually involve parent or teacher rating scales that may not be sensitive to short-term and specific behavior changes (Castorina & Negri, 2011). In addition, studies often assess the skills very shortly after the intervention. From experience as a therapist, one of the authors of this chapter, Corina Ratz, has noticed that improvements in the area of social skills become clearer over time as situations demand use of the skills.

WHAT CAN TECHNOLOGY ADD?

Technology has the potential to address some limitations of social groups by adding an additional "essential ingredient" (Krasny, Williams, Provencal, & Ozonoff, 2003, p. 111). In their review of social skills groups, Krasny et al. outline several of these essential ingredients in the form of "central principles" and "implementation examples" (2003, p. 111). The use of technology can fulfill a number of Krasny et al.'s ingredients, including 1) "provide multiple and varied learning opportunities," such as different teaching modalities (e.g., video) or strategies (e.g., different learning theories); 2) use "socially relevant activities" that could create a context that generalizes easier; 3) "simplify complex behaviors into specific skills"; and 4) arrange "program in a sequential and progressive manner" (2003, p. 111). In addition, Baker (2003) prescribes 5) repetitive practice of skills; technology is tireless and may be available outside of the therapeutic setting. Although some researchers raise concerns that technology can be socially isolating and addictive (Robins, 2007), 6) carefully incorporating technology can also capitalize on a strength or special interest of some individuals with autism. Finally, technology can also support the facilitators of social groups in that 7) some tasks that would normally be the group facilitator's responsibility, such as making sure children are following the rules of a game they are playing, can be automated by the system. Thus, group facilitators can focus on skill instruction and higher level group dynamics.

Developing and evaluating technology to support persons with autism is a burgeoning area of research. Researchers who have evaluated use of technology in a group setting have addressed a variety of tools, including video modeling, robots, collaborative virtual environments, computer-mediated communication, tabletop displays, and video games. For each of these technologies, we describe research projects examining the technology and discuss how each enhances social group curricula based on the potential contributions described above.

Video Modeling

Video modeling is an intervention technique in which children develop new skills by watching a video of the skill being performed by a model (a parent, sibling, peer, therapist, etc.) and then mimicking the video (Bellini & Akullian, 2007). Video self-modeling can also be used; in this approach, the child creates and reviews video recordings of himself or herself performing the desired skill correctly (Bellini & Akullian, 2007). Video modeling can be used to model a variety of skills, from brushing one's teeth to complex social interactions, and has been used in both group and individual therapy sessions (for a review, see Bellini & Akullian, 2007). Video modeling fits well into the structured program many social groups follow; for example, in Baker's Structure Learning program (2003), video modeling can be used during Step 2, the modeling of skill steps after didactic instruction. In fact, Kroeger et al. (2007) compared two social groups for children with autism, one with a didactic component using video modeling and one without a didactic component. In their analysis of pre- and postsession free-play, they found that children in both groups used more "prosocial behaviors" (p. 814) during the posttest, but the group that received didactic instruction with video modeling improved more (Kroeger et al., 2007).

Research on video modeling describes many positive outcomes. Reichow and Volkmar's (2010) review of social skills interventions (mentioned above) concluded that video modeling is a "promising" EBP.[1] In an earlier metareview, Wang and Spillane (2009) also concluded that video modeling meets the criteria for EBP. Nikopoulos and Nikopoulou-Smyrni (2008) conducted a review of video modeling for social skills intervention and suggest that it is a useful addition to peer-mediated strategies. Similarly, Ogilvie (2011) recommends a combination of video modeling and

---

[1]Similar to "established" EBP, described earlier, "promising" EBP describes a treatment "also shown to be effective across multiple studies. However, as a whole, the evidence for the practice is limited by weak methodological rigor, few replications, or an inadequate number of independent researchers demonstrating the effects" (Reichow et al., 2008, p. 1315).

peer mentoring, during which children can practice social behaviors and receive feedback on their performance.

How video modeling is used in a social group setting differs across studies, and researchers have developed a number of variations. Simpson, Langone, and Ayres (2004) describe a project where they used video models to demonstrate three target behaviors—sharing, greetings, and following directions—to four students, ages 5–6, with autism. They recorded two similar-age, typically developing peers performing the behaviors and created four video examples of each behavior. They embedded the videos in a computer-based instruction program that first defined each skill and then played the examples. Using a multiple-baseline design, they evaluated the system during small-group activities that included all four students and a teacher. The teacher provided opportunities for the children to use the skills, and coders identified instances of the target behaviors. All students increased their instances of the target behavior after the system was introduced (Simpson et al., 2004). Sansoti and Powell-Smith (2008) created a similar system that first presented a social story (Gray & Garand, 1993) describing the skill steps for a targeted communication skill and then played a video of a similar age, typically developing peer executing the skill. Three boys with ASD (ages 6–10) participated in an evaluation of the system. The researchers used a multiple-baseline design where unstructured activities, such as recess, were coded for the target behaviors. The results of the study indicate that using the system increased children's use of the target behaviors (Sansoti & Powell-Smith, 2008). Parsons (2006) reports on a program called Survivor Bunch, where individuals with autism (ages 14–22) recorded videos of themselves engaging in role plays with each other. Creating the videos provides opportunities for them to practice social interactions, observe the interactions, and give and receive feedback with their peers. Parsons (2006) found improvements in social skills that parents reported generalized to the home environment.

In a related project currently underway, we are conducting a design-based research study (Sandoval & Bell, 2004) to develop a system, Video Model Maker (VMM), where children with ASD (ages 8–12) create their own video models. The goal of VMM is for children to develop conversational skills by planning, implementing, and revising their own video model for skills described in Baker's (2003) social skills curriculum, such as maintaining a conversation. Children work in pairs to write a script and create their video, and the video is shared with the rest of the group during a didactic lesson on the skill. The motivation for VMM is based on constructionist design principles (Harel & Papert, 1991), where children learn a concept through building artifacts. This adds an additional instructional strategy to a traditional social skills program.

Corbett et al. (2011) used video modeling in a "theater as therapy" program for children with ASD (ages 6–17). Eight children with ASD participated as part of a cast for a musical. Each child was matched with a typically developing peer (who also had a role in the musical) with whom he or she worked throughout the rehearsals. In addition to this support, the peers also made video models of the role the child with autism was playing. The videos were available both in the theater and at the child's home, and the children were encouraged to watch and practice their part daily. Pre- and posttests suggested improvements in perspective taking (theory of mind) and memory for faces, but not in affect recognition. Parental reports showed no significant change. In addition, the authors tested biological indicators of stress (oxytocin and cortisol). There was no significant change in oxytocin or cortisol pre- and post-intervention. However, there was a significant change in cortisol measured during rehearsals (both within one rehearsal and across rehearsals), which may indicate that anxiety decreased because the children had become more comfortable with the environment (Corbett et al., 2011).

The above studies suggest video modeling, which is often paired with a didactic component, is successful as a social intervention and when used in a group context. Video modeling and other video-related projects make a number of contributions to a social group:

1. Video modeling offers a new modality that is both visual and auditory and, in the case of VMM, a different instructional strategy (constructionism).

2. The video models often break down complex social skills into individual behaviors that children can practice and later use in a more complicated context. For example, the individuals who participated in the project by Parsons (2006) were able to look back at an interaction that actually occurred and discuss the individual behaviors that made up that interaction.

3. Videos are easily played repeatedly and can be made available to children to use in their homes. Thus, the actors in the study by Corbett et al. (2011) were able to watch their peer modeling their part in the play daily, whereas in real life a peer would not normally be available daily and might grow tired of repeatedly performing the same part.

Robots

There is increasing research on the use of robots with individuals with autism, though little of it is conducted in group settings. One major concept for investigation is using robots as social mediators. In this idea, the robot works as a "scaffold" to help children move "from solitary play to social and cooperative play" (Ferrari, Robins, & Dautenhahn, 2009, p. 110). Children who avoid social interaction enjoy interacting with the robot, perhaps because it is predictable whereas their peers are not (Ferrari et al., 2009). Ferrari et al. (2009) propose a scenario where a child begins playing with the robot alone, and the robot helps the child feel comfortable in his or her environment. Then another person can join the interaction, and the robot can be the mediator between the two people. Eventually the robot's role in the interaction is faded so that it becomes an interaction between the two people. The authors are particularly interested in using the robots to help children develop play skills they can then use with other children. Although the study authors do not specifically evaluate their robot in a social group setting, the goals of the project align well with the goals of using technology in a social group, such as progressive or faded instruction.

Barakova and Lourens (2010) are involved in developing and implementing new robots that interpret and express emotions through body movement. Their goal is to create robots that can be used with children, particularly those with ASD, to develop social and emotional skills. These robots could either engage in or mediate social interactions. The authors describe their progress toward creating a humanoid robot that can sense and interpret a human's emotional body expression and then respond appropriately with its own body movements. They also describe a cooperative game with a nonhumanoid robot that uses a number of different movements to represent different emotions. Children stand on a large disk and must work together to tilt the disk. Different positions of the disk tell the robot to perform certain movements. The children have to negotiate what they want the robot to express and must coordinate how to move the disk together.

Another approach, recommended by Wainer, Ferrari, Dautenhahn, and Robins (2010), proposes the use of a class on robotics as a social group. In other words, children with autism can work on collaboration skills while learning about and building robots. The authors evaluated seven children (ages 8–14), who participated in a group that worked with programmable LEGO robots. At each session, children received a 15-minute lesson and then worked in groups of two or three on the robots. The authors found that collaborative behaviors, such as the amount of time the children spent talking about the robots or the amount of time they spent "close while sharing gaze," (Wainer et al., 2010, p. 450) improved over the course of the intervention and were correlated with those classes the children most enjoyed. They also concluded that collaborative behaviors generalized to another domain (drawing robots on group-shared paper).

In summary, robots can make several contributions to a social group setting:

1. Robots use a strength or particular interest of some children with autism to address difficulties with social interaction. For example, in Ferrari et al. (2009) robots initially engage children in social interaction that eventually becomes interaction with other people. Learning about and building robots was a motivating activity, and the more the children enjoyed the activity, the more collaborative behaviors they used (Wainer et al., 2010).

2. Robots can provide faded instruction (i.e., sequential and progressive instruction). In Ferrari et al. (2009), the robots act as a scaffold by providing a predictable interaction partner that leads children to less predictable social interactions with people.

3. The process of building and programming LEGO robots in Wainer et al. (2010) can be a socially relevant activity that may generalize to other group construction or computer tasks.

Collaborative Virtual Worlds and Agents

Several projects have looked at using virtual worlds and agents with individuals with autism to teach speech, language, and literacy skills (Cole et al., 2003; Massaro & Bosseler, 2006; Wise et al., 2007), as well as help them develop social skills (Kerr, Neale & Cobb, 2002; Parsons & Cobb, 2011). However, these systems are often designed to be used by a single user and not in a group program (though some potentially could be used for groups). The COSPATIAL project (Zancanaro et al., 2010) looks at how to create collaborative technologies using virtual reality and tabletop displays (the latter will be described below). In one of their systems, Block Party, the collaboration is virtual; users meet as avatars in a virtual world and need to work out how to complete a joint task within that virtual world. The system draws on cognitive-behavioral techniques, including solving social problems, rehearsing behaviors, and explicitly explaining such concepts as emotion recognition and understanding.

In another project, Authorable Virtual Peers, we developed a social group curriculum with a virtual agent as a key component of the program (Tartaro, 2011). An authorable virtual peer (AVP) is a life-size, animated, virtual child that interacts with children using speech and gestures. Users can speak face-to-face with the virtual peer, but they can also create new social behaviors (i.e., new things for the virtual peer to say) and control the virtual peer, in the manner of a puppet, while it interacts with another person. Similar to the Video Model Maker project described above, the AVP Social Group adds these different virtual peer interactions into the Structured Learning framework described by Baker (2003). We developed a 9-week social skills program using lessons from Baker (2003). Each session consisted of a didactic skill lesson, modeling of skill steps, AVP interactions for some participants (all participants worked with the AVP, but not every week), dyadic role-play scenarios based on the week's lesson, and a group activity such as cooking or puzzle making. During the AVP interactions, children first created new interactions for the virtual peer based on the week's lesson and then, working with a partner in the group, controlled the virtual peer for that child and interacted with that child's virtual peer. We found that "whether or not they used the AVP" and "time" (how far along in the intervention) were both significant predictors of children's appropriate use of reciprocity during the role-play scenarios, suggesting reciprocity was better after the children used the AVP and improved over the course of the intervention (Tartaro, 2011).

Virtual worlds and agents thus provide several contributions to social groups:

1. They can provide a new teaching strategy or apply a strategy in a new way. Similar to VMM, AVPs are based on the constructionist principle of learning through building artifacts. COSPATIAL's Block Party applies cognitive-behavioral therapy to virtual interactions.

2. They can simplify complex behaviors. The AVP breaks social skills, such as compromising, into steps that children can build into the AVP themselves. A virtual world can simplify a social context, like a coffee shop, so users can focus on the task they are practicing.

3. In virtual worlds, you can perform the same task with precisely the same situation repeatedly. Similarly, virtual agents can repeat a social interaction the same way many times.

Computer-Mediated Communication

In computer-mediated communication (CMC), partners communicate with each other through their own computer, for example, in an online chat room. The virtual world Block Party, described above, is a type of CMC with a virtual reality component. KidTalk (Cheng, 2002) is an example of an online, text-based, therapy program where children take on roles in a scenario, such as a birthday party, and follow a script that describes a scene and what the characters' roles are in that scene. A group of children work through the script together as a therapist controls the advancement of the scenes. The therapist can also provide online feedback directly in the system's graphical interface. Cheng (2002) reports on the iterative development of the system. In these projects, the implementation of a group differs slightly from real-world implementation; however, virtual reality projects have the potential to reach individuals who would otherwise not get to participate in a social group, for instance, because of geography.

Whereas KidTalk was designed to be a therapeutic system for children with autism, other CMC group interactions form more informally. Individuals with autism often seek out communication with others through blogs or online communities, where there is more predictability and less reliance on nonverbal information than encountered in face-to-face interactions (Burke, Kraut, & Williams, 2010). Burke et al. (2010) conducted a study that interviewed and observed individuals with autism to understand what social experiences they are looking for, how well CMC such as instant messaging, text messaging, and online communities fulfill those needs, and if there are opportunities to improve users' experiences with CMC. They found that individuals with autism find CMC useful for initiating conversations but have difficulty maintaining relationships. Participants reported that it is difficult to find the same users after a first conversation, they do not know how much information is safe to share online, and they have difficulty understanding the nuances of online culture (Burke et al., 2010). Burke et al. propose some ideas for addressing these difficulties: designing social skills training that addresses situations one might encounter during CMC, providing information about an interaction partner that helps users determine if they can trust the partner, and creating visualizations that allow users to track their own online behaviors (Burke et al., 2010).

In sum, there are a number of contributions CMC makes to social group intervention:

1. For interactions, online text, or virtual reality, CMC provides new modalities that not only provide individuals with a different mode of communication but may also make joining a social group possible for individuals previously unable to join a traditional therapeutic social group.

2. Breaking down the complexity of face-to-face interactions, CMC enables individuals to focus on one channel of communication.

3. Finally, CMC is a socially relevant activity, given that interactions over social networking sites, instant messaging, text messaging, and blog posts are increasingly common among all people, with and without disabilities.

Tabletop Displays

Tabletop displays are large, tablelike, interactive screens that can support multiple user interactions simultaneously. Recent research projects have capitalized on this feature to develop collaborative and cooperative skills. For example, Zancanaro et al. (2010) describe a system for a tabletop display called Join-In, which is part of the COSPATIAL project described above. One of the tasks in the system is to work with a partner to move a graphical representation of a basket to catch virtual falling apples. Piper et al. (2006) implemented a system called SIDES, a four-player, tabletop game where children have to work together to solve a problem. Each child is given a limited set of arrow pieces and, using those pieces, must build a path for a frog to move from a starting lily pad to an ending lily pad. The group can earn points if the path intersects with various insects around the board. When the players complete a path, all four must vote for the path to be tested. One of the design features evaluated by Piper, O'Brien, Morris, and Winograd (2006) was to compare a system with explicit game rules enforced by the system, a system with the game rules enforced by the group facilitator, and a system with no rule enforcement. The researchers describe two benefits of the computer-enforced rules. First, the computer-enforced rules are "particularly useful for these adolescents who find comfort in predictable rules and environmental conditions" (Piper et al., 2006, p. 8). Furthermore, the computer-enforced rules give therapists the opportunity to focus on developing cooperation skills rather than refereeing the game. These benefits, they conclude, "make tabletop technologies more compelling for this user population than traditional board games" (p. 9).

Gal et al. (2009) conducted an evaluation of a system for a tabletop display called StoryTable that also had features of enforced cooperation. StoryTable is a system for children to create stories in pairs. They first select a background scenario and then can add characters and other objects to the scene. They then take turns recording story segments that are ordered at the bottom of the screen. Cooperation is enforced during two tasks: selecting the background and playing back the story. Children must perform a "joint touch" for these actions. Six children with ASD (ages 8–10), used the system during eight sessions over 3 weeks. Prior to using the systems in pairs, they received instruction related to collaboration skills, including sharing activities, providing help and encouragement, and learning to persuade and negotiate. The authors analyzed two pre- and posttasks: The first was a low-tech version of the StoryTable system made out of poster board and a tape recorder; the second was use of various pieces (e.g., tunnels and ramps) to construct a maze for a marble to go through. They observed the largest pre- and posttest changes during the marble task, including increases in initiating interaction with peers, collaboration, and shared play. They also found that children engaged in fewer autistic behaviors when using the StoryTable system versus the low-tech version.

Among contributions tabletop displays can make to social group programs are these:

1. They can remove some of the procedural responsibilities, such as enforcing the rules, from the group leaders by automating those responsibilities. This benefit allows group leaders to focus on higher-level aspects of the interaction.

2. They can simplify complex behaviors, specifically collaboration, into smaller tasks. For example, StoryTable isolates one part of creating a story, choosing the scenario, into a discrete task that the children must complete together with "joint touch" (Gal et al., 2009).

Video Games

A small amount of research uses existing computer or video games as an activity in a social group setting. Here, the focus has typically been using technology not as an instructional tool or interaction partner but, instead, as a shared activity during which opportunities to use various social and conversational skills arise. For example, children often need to take turns interacting with a system, they might negotiate what game to play, or they could initiate a conversation about what other games they like to play. An early study by Gaylord-Ross, Haring, Breen, and Pitts-Conway (1984) describes an experiment where a handheld video game (Pacman) is one of three objects around which persons with ASD learned to engage in social interaction with others. They chose this object as an age-appropriate example of a leisure activity. Two individuals with autism (ages 17 and 20) participated in the experiment. The participants were first taught to play the video game using a task analysis: When engaging with the object, they were given positive verbal feedback when they followed the steps in the task analysis in the right order. When they made an error, they were prompted on the next step. After the participants knew how to play the game, they were taught to initiate, maintain, and end a social interaction with a peer about the game. The same task analysis technique was used. The authors found not only that the participants could learn how to engage in a social interaction with a peer about the object but also that their ability to do so generalized to other people.

In a more recent study, Blum-Dimaya, Reeve, Reeve, and Hoch (2010) examine if individuals with autism can be taught to play the video game Guitar Hero II using a combination of activity schedules and video modeling. Again, Guitar Hero II was specifically chosen because it is an age-appropriate activity they can do with peers. Four children with autism (ages 9–12), participated in the study. The results indicated that the children could learn to play Guitar Hero II at an age-appropriate level and manner, and this ability translated to new songs. Although this study does not look at social outcomes, the finding that children with autism can learn to play in an age-appropriate way suggests video games like Guitar Hero II could be a valuable social activity for children with ASD and typically developing children to do together.

Video games can thus make a number of contributions in a social group context:

1. They are a socially relevant activity.

2. They are available to use outside of the therapeutic setting.

3. Many children have their own gaming devices, so using video games in a social group context is natural while also drawing on a special interest and, in some cases, talent with computers.

4. Like the games on the tabletop devices above, some games involve procedural tasks like turn taking and rule following, giving group facilitators the opportunity to focus on more complex aspects of social interaction.

RECOMMENDATIONS FOR CURRENT SOCIAL GROUPS

The research projects described above suggest that technologies can further contribute to the value of social skills groups. For instance, didactic instruction using video modeling can increase the success of a group (Kroeger et al., 2007), therapists report that tabletop technologies can support their role as group facilitators (Piper et al., 2006), and video games can provide a topic with shared interest for social interactions with peers who are typically developing (Gaylord-Ross et al., 1984). Although many of the projects described in this chapter are research in various stages of development, there are some opportunities for current social groups to incorporate technology, as identified here:

1. *Video modeling.* Video cameras can now be obtained relatively inexpensively. The technique by Parsons (2006), described above, where children record their own role plays and play them back for feedback and discussion, can be a good place to start using technology in a social group.

2. *Video and computer games as a social activity.* Video or computer games can be used in place of or in addition to the board games that are commonly used in groups to facilitate social interaction. Many children will encounter this social opportunity outside the social group as well. In fact, many children even have their own games and systems; they can bring in their own games to play with the social group.

3. *Online communities or CMC.* Group leaders can form an online community for group members to use between sessions. This strategy might work particularly well in groups that follow a group-therapy format similar to that used by Hillier et al. (2007), described above. Participants have the opportunity to work through real-life problems between group sessions. In groups with older participants, group facilitators can encourage members to start blogs and read and comment on each other's blogs.

CONCLUSION

In this chapter we argued that peer social groups, a treatment approach that has had some success in helping children with ASD with the difficulties they have interacting with peers, can benefit from the use of technology during group sessions. Although social skills groups have been shown to be an EBP (Cappadocia & Weiss, 2009; Reichow & Volkmar, 2010), they also have limitations. In particular, many of the skills learned in social skills groups do not appear to generalize to other contexts. Technologies may be able to address some of the limitations because they 1) provide a different instructional mode or strategy; 2) leverage a talent or special interest some children with autism have; 3) are socially relevant, so generalization may be easier; 4) break down complex social interactions into basic skills; 5) progress through learning skills in a step-by-step manner; 6) can free up group facilitators from procedural tasks to support children on higher level skills; and 7) allow for tireless repetition. Some technologies that have demonstrated these strengths in a research context include video modeling, robots, virtual worlds and agents, computer-mediated communication, tabletop displays, and video games. While many of these technologies are in various stages of research development, there are some opportunities to use technologies in current social groups, including video modeling, CMC, and video games.

REFERENCES

Baker, J.E. (2003). *Social skills training for children and adolescents with Asperger Syndrome and social-communication problems.* Shawnee Mission, KS: Autism Asperger.

Barakova, E.L., & Lourens, T. (2010). Expressing and interpreting emotional movements in social games with robots. *Personal and Ubiquitous Computing, 14,* 457–467.

Barry, T.D., Klinger, L.G., Lee, J.M., Palardy, N., Gilmore, T., & Bodin, S.D. (2003). Examining the effectiveness of an outpatient clinic-based social skills group for high-functioning children with autism. *Journal of Autism and Developmental Disorders, 33*(6), 685–701.

Bellini, S., & Akullian, J. (2007). A meta-analysis of video modeling and video self-modeling interventions for children and adolescents with autism spectrum disorders. *Council for Exceptional Children, 73*(3), 264–287.

Blum-Dimaya, A., Reeve, S.A., Reeve, K.F., & Hoch, H. (2010). Teaching children with autism to play a video game using activity schedules and game-embedded simultaneous video modeling. *Education and Treatment of Children, 33*(3), 351–371.

Boyd, B.A., McDonough, S.G., & Bodfish, J.W. (2012). Evidence-based behavioral interventions for repetitive behaviors in autism. *Journal of Autism and Developmental Disorders, (42)*, 1236–1248.

Burke, M., Kraut, R., & Williams, D. (2010). *Social use of computer-mediated communication by adults on the autism spectrum.* Paper presented at the Computer Supported Collaborative Work, Savannah, GA.

Cappadocia, M.C., & Weiss, J.A. (2011). Review of social skills training groups for youth with Asperger syndrome and high functioning autism. *Research in Autism Spectrum Disorders, 5*, 70–78.

Castorina, L.L., & Negri, L.M. (2011). The inclusion of siblings in social skills training groups for boys with Asperger syndrome. *Journal of Autism and Developmental Disorders, 41*, 73–81.

Cheng, L. (2002). *KidTalk: Online therapy for Asperger's syndrome.* Redmond, WA: Microsoft.

Cole, R., van Vuuren, S., Pellom, B., Hacioglu, K., Ma, J., Movellan, J., & Yan, J. (2003). Perceptive animated interfaces: First steps toward a new paradigm for human computer interaction. *IEEE: Multimodal Human Computer Interface* [Special issue], 1391–1405.

Corbett, B.A., Gunther, J.R., Comins, D., Price, J., Ryan, N., Simon, D., & Rios, T. (2011). Theater as therapy for children with autism spectrum disorder. *Journal of Autism and Developmental Disorders, 41*, 505–511.

Faherty, C. (2000). *Asperger's... What does it mean to me?* Arlington, TX: Future Horizons.

Ferrari, E., Robins, B., & Dautenhahn, K. (2009). *Therapeutic and educational objectives in robot assisted play for children with autism.* Paper presented at the 18th IEEE International Symposium on Robot and Human Interactive Communication, Toyama, Japan.

Gal, E., Bauminger, N., Goren-Bar, D., Pianesi, F., Stock, O., Zancanaro, M., & Weiss, P.L.T. (2009). Enhancing social communication of children with high-functioning autism through a co-located interface. *AI & Society, 24*, 75–84.

Gaylord-Ross, R.J., Haring, T.G., Breen, C., & Pitts-Conway, V. (1984). The training and generalization of social interaction skills with autistic youth. *Journal of Applied Behavior Analysis, 17*, 229–247.

Gray, C., & Garand, J.D. (1993). Social Stories: Improving responses of students with autism with accurate social information. *Focus on Autistic Behavior, 8*(1), 1–10.

Harel, I., & Papert, S. (1991). Situating constructionism. In I. Harel & S. Papert (Eds.), *Constructionism* (pp. 1–11). Norwood, NJ: Ablex.

Hillier, A., Fish, T., Cloppert, P., & Beversdorf, D.Q. (2007). Outcomes of a social and vocational skills support group for adolescents and young adults on the autism spectrum. *Focus on Autism and Other Developmental Disabilities, 22*(2), 107–115.

Jackson, D.A., Jackson, N.F., Bennett, M.L., Bynum, B.M., & Faryna, E. (1991). *Learning to get along: Social effectiveness training for people with developmental disabilities.* Champaign, IL: Research Press.

Kamps, D., Royer, J., Dugan, E., Kravits, T., Gonzalez-Lopez, A., Garcia, J., ... Kane, L.G. (2002). Peer training to facilitate social interaction for elementary students with autism and their peers. *Council for Exceptional Children, 68*(2), 173–187.

Kelly, A.B., Garnett, M.S., Attwood, T., & Peterson, C. (2008). Autism spectrum symptomatology in children: The impact of family and peer relationships. *Journal of Abnormal Child Psychology, 36*, 1069–1081.

Kerr, S.J., Neale, H.R., & Cobb, S.V.G. (2002, July 8–10). *Virtual environments for social skills training: The importance of scaffolding in practice.* Paper presented at the Assets, Edinburgh, Scotland.

Koenig, K., Williams White, S., Pachler, M., Lau, M., Lewis, M., Klin, A., & Scahill, L. (2010). Promoting social skill development in children with pervasive developmental disorders: A feasibility and efficacy study. *Journal of Autism and Developmental Disorders, 40*(10), 1209–1218.

Krasny, L., Williams, B.J., Provencal, S., & Ozonoff, S. (2003). Social skills interventions for the autism spectrum: Essential ingredients and a model curriculum. *Child and Adolescent Psychiatric Clinics, 12,* 107–122.

Kroeger, K.A., Schultz, J.R., & Newsom, C. (2007). A comparison of two group-delivered social skills programs for young children with autism. *Journal of Autism and Developmental Disorders, 37,* 808–817.

LeGoff, D.B. (2004). Use of LEGO© as a therapeutic medium for improving social competence. *Journal of Autism and Developmental Disorders, 34*(5), 557–571.

Licciardello, C.C., Harchik, A.E., & Luiselli, J.K. (2008). Social skills intervention for children with autism during interactive play at a public elementary school. *Education and Treatment of Children, 31*(1), 27–37.

Massaro, D.W., & Bosseler, A. (2006). Read my lips: The importance of face in a computer-animated tutor for vocabulary learning by children with autism. *Autism: The International Journal of Research and Practice, 10,* 495–510.

McConnell, S.R. (2002). Interventions to facilitate social interaction for young children with autism: Review of available research and recommendations for educational intervention and future research. *Journal of Autism and Developmental Disorders, 32*(5), 351–372.

McGinnis, E., & Goldstein, A.P. (1984). *Skillstreaming the elementary school child.* Champaign, IL: Research Press.

McGinnis, E., & Goldstein, A.P. (1990). *Skillstreaming in early childhood.* Champaign, IL: Research Press.

Nikopoulos, C.K., & Nikopoulou-Smyrni, P. (2008). Teaching complex social skills to children with autism: Advances of video modeling. *Journal of Early and Intensive Behavior Intervention, 5*(2), 30–43.

Ogilvie, C.R. (2011). Step by step: Social skills instruction for students with autism spectrum disorder using video models and peer mentors. *Teaching Exceptional Children, 43*(6), 20–26.

Orsmond, G.I., Krauss, M.W., & Seltzer, M.M. (2004). Peer relationships and social and recreational activities among adolescents and adults with autism. *Journal of Autism and Developmental Disorders, 34*(3), 245–256.

Parsons, L.D. (2006). Using video to teach social skills to secondary students with autism. *Teaching Exceptional Children, 39*(2), 32–38.

Parsons, S., & Cobb, S. (2011). State-of-the-art of virtual reality technologies for children on the autism spectrum. *European Journal of Special Needs Education, 26*(3), 355–366.

Piper, A.M., O'Brien, E., Morris, M.R., & Winograd, T. (2006). *SIDES: A cooperative tabletop computer game for social skills development.* Paper presented at the Conference on Computer-Supported Cooperative Work CSCW, Banff, Alberta, Canada.

Reichow, B., & Volkmar, F.R. (2010). Social skills interventions for individuals with autism: Evaluation for evidence-based practices within a Best Evidence Synthesis framework. *Journal of Autism and Developmental Disorders, 40,* 149–166.

Reichow, B., Volkmar, F.R., & Cicchetti, D.V. (2008). Development of the evaluative method for evaluating and determining evidence-based practices in autism. *Journal of Autism and Developmental Disorders, 38,* 1311–1319.

Robins, B. (2007). *Mediators versus isolators—The effect of robots on children with autism and other user-groups.* Paper presented at the 16th IEEE International Conference on Robot and Human Interactive Communication, Jeju, Korea.

Ruble, L., Willis, H., & Crabtree, V.M. (2008). Social skills group therapy for autism spectrum disorders. *Clinical Case Studies, 7*(4), 287–300.

Sandoval, W.A., & Bell, P. (2004). Design-based research methods for studying learning in context: Introduction. *Educational Psychologist, 39*(4), 199–201.

Sansoti, F.J., & Powell-Smith, K.A. (2008). Using computer-presented Social Stories and video models to increase the social communication skills of children with high-functioning autism spectrum disorders. *Journal of Positive Behavior Interventions, 10*(3), 162–178.

Sasson, N.J., Turner-Brown, L.M., Holtzclaw, T.N., Lam, K.S.L., & Bodfish, J.W. (2008). Children with autism demonstrate circumscribed attention during passive viewing of complex social and nonsocial picture arrays. *Autism Research, 1*(1), 31–42.

Simmons, K., & Miller, L.J. (2008). Sensational stars with autism. *The Exceptional Parent, 38*(4), 14–20.

Simpson, A., Langone, J., & Ayres, K.M. (2004). Embedded video and computer based instruction to improve social skills for students with autism. *Education and Training in Developmental Disabilities, 39*(3), 240–252.

Tartaro, A. (2011). *Authorable virtual peers: Technology as an intervention for difficulties with peer social interaction in autism spectrum and related disorders* (Doctoral dissertation). Northwestern University, Evanston, IL.

Travis, L.L., & Sigman, M. (1998). Social deficits and interpersonal relationships in autism. *Mental Retardation and Developmental Disabilities Research Reviews, 4*(2), 65–72.

Tyson, K.E., & Cruess, D.G. (2012). Differentiating high-functioning autism and social phobia. *Journal of Autism and Developmental Disorders, 42,* 1477–1490.

Wainer, J., Ferrari, E., Dautenhahn, K., & Robins, B. (2010). The effectiveness of using a robotics class to foster collaboration among groups of children with autism in an exploratory study. *Personal and Ubiquitous Computing, 14,* 445–455.

Wang, P., & Spillane, A. (2009). Evidence-based social skills interventions for children with autism: A meta-analysis. *Education and Training in Developmental Disabilities, 44*(3), 318–342.

Webb, B.J., Miller, S.P., Pierce, T.B., Strawser, S., & Jones, W.P. (2004). Effects of social skill instruction for high-functioning adolescents with autism spectrum disorders. *Focus on Autism and Other Developmental Disabilities, 19*(1), 53–62.

White, S.W., Koenig, K., & Scahill, L. (2010). Group social skills instruction for adolescents with high-functioning autism spectrum disorders. *Focus on Autism and Other Developmental Disabilities, 25*(4), 209–219.

Wise, B., Cole, R., van Vuuren, S., Schwartz, S., Snyder, L., Ngampatipatpong, N., & Pellom, B. (2007). Learning to read with a virtual tutor: Foundations to literacy. In C. Kinzer & L. Verhoeven (Eds.), *Interactive literacy education: Facilitating literacy learning environments through technology* (pp. 31–45). Mahwah, NJ: Erlbaum.

Yalom, V.G. (1989). *Concise guide to group therapy.* Washington, D.C.: American Psychiatric Press.

Zancanaro, M., Weiss, T., Gal, E., Bauminger, N., Parsons, S., & Cobb, S. (2010). *Teaching social competence: In search of design patterns.* Paper presented at the International Conference on Interaction Design and Children, Barcelona, Spain.

Technologies to Support Interventions for Social-Emotional Intelligence, Self-Awareness, Personal Style, and Self-Regulation

▪ ▪

Dorothy Lucci, Minna Levine, Kelley Challen-Wittmer, and Donald Scott McLeod

Over the years, educational goals for individuals diagnosed with an autism spectrum disorder (ASD) have focused on skill development. Broad review articles on evidence-based practice have evaluated behavioral intervention approaches that facilitate management of the three primary areas of difficulties in autism: communication, social interaction, and repetitive behaviors (American Psychiatric Association, 1994). A growing body of work is emerging that is more holistic and focuses on the quality of life of individuals on the spectrum—the individual's subjective impression of his or her social-emotional, psychological, and physical functioning. Rather than solely addressing training of particular skills or management of particular behaviors, this literature and the interventions designed from this perspective address a broader domain: the intertwined issues of social-emotional intelligence (SEI), self-awareness, personal style, self-regulation, and stress management (Groden, Kantor, Woodard, & Lipsitt, 2011). This chapter provides a framework for this broader approach to interventions for social, emotional, and psychological function. It presents examples of interventions consistent with this approach, with details about the Massachusetts General Hospital Aspire program's multifaceted curriculum for educating teens diagnosed with ASD that targets the broader issue of self-awareness: *Science of Me.* This curriculum is an example of how educational content related to these constructs can be enhanced by and integrated through innovative uses of new technologies.

We begin the chapter by providing the framework for this approach, including a review of its three key underlying constructs: 1) SEI, 2) self-awareness and

---

The work using SymTrend software described in this chapter was done independently of SymTrend, Inc.

processing differences, and 3) self-regulation and stress management. We then provide an overview of programs targeting some of or all these constructs. A detailed description of the *Science of Me* curriculum is provided to enhance the reader's understanding of how components addressing these three constructs can be linked together. Finally, we present outcomes analyses and discuss opportunities for future discovery.

BACKGROUND

Adult quality of life is often measured by personal contentment in areas such as meaningful social relationships, career gratification, and financial security. Child quality of life measures are similar to adult measures. They include meaningful social relationships, academic success, and enjoyment in recreational activities. Personal traits such as optimism and resilience enhance quality of life. These personal traits are bolstered by strong self-awareness, self-regulation, and social awareness. A growing body of research supports the premise that physical and mental health is rooted in the ability to manage one's stress. The ability to manage stress has a tremendous impact on quality of life outcomes (Dickerson & Kemeny, 2004).

The number of individuals being diagnosed with an ASD continues to rise. The rate currently is 1 out of 88 (Centers for Disease Control, 2012). Given this increase in numbers, effective intervention is urgently needed to improve the overall quality of life for these individuals.

At the core of SEI are the principles of attachment and attunement. Attachment develops between the caregiver and infant early in infancy. This bond ultimately becomes the regulator of arousal and in essence is the dyadic regulator of emotion (Sroufe, 1996). Attunement is defined as the purposeful attention of one person to the internal world of another person (Siegel, 2007). Attunement harnesses the neural circuitry that enables two people to "feel felt" by each other, and attuned relationships promote resiliency and longevity (Siegel, 2007). By purposefully addressing and developing attunement, the brain may grow in ways that encourage improved self-regulation. The brain itself is modified by this process of neural integration. This change enables improved flexibility and self understanding (Fornagy & Target, 2002; Siegel, 2007). SEI is the cornerstone that leads to a life that includes greater empathy and compassion for oneself and others and an improved quality of life.

Social-Emotional Intelligence

The first underlying construct, SEI, is broadly defined as a skill set that includes self-management (i.e., recognizing emotions in self and others), self-awareness (i.e., understanding of one's strengths and challenges), social awareness (i.e., compassion for self and other), responsible decision making, and relationship skills (e.g., handling conflicts constructively and ethically; CASEL, 2012). Research has increasingly shown that the SEI skill set plays a more important role in school and life success than do cognitive abilities or other specific skills or talents (Durlak, Weissberg, Dymnicki, Taylor, & Schellinger, 2011; Goleman, 1995, 2006; Greenberg et al., 2003; Spencer & Spencer, 1993; Zins, Weissberg, Wang, & Walberg, 2004). Individuals with autism are thought to have deficits in SEI and are more likely to struggle with empathy (Baron-Cohen, 2002). Individuals with Asperger syndrome (AS) are more likely to show evidence of alexithymia, that is, the difficulty with appraising and expressing emotions verbally, difficulties distinguishing emotional states from bodily states, and difficulties using feelings to appropriately guide behavior. Berthoz and Hill (2005) found that individuals with ASD were able to report on their own emotional processes (the degree of arousal or upset) but lacked insight into emotional experiences, having trouble identifying the emotions, verbalizing about them, and analyzing their origin and meaning.

In addition to difficulties in SEI, individuals with an ASD often have difficulty with emotional understanding (Baron-Cohen, 1995; Fein, Lucci, Braverman, & Waterhouse, 1992; Happé, 1994), emotion regulation (Myles & Southwick, 1999), and attunement to others (e.g., theory of mind, perspective-taking; Frith, 2001; Happé, 1994). Psychiatric comorbidity is common among individuals with high-functioning autism (HFA) and AS: Leyfer et al. (2006) reported that 72% of their mixed sample of 109 children and adolescents with "relatively high-functioning autism" had at least one *DSM-IV* Axis I diagnosis in addition to autism. Anxiety was the most common diagnosis, with specific phobias reported in 44% of participants in one study (Leyfer et al., 2006) and 38% in another (de Bruin, Ferdinand, Meester, de Nijs, & Verheij, 2007). The presence of psychiatric comorbidities among this population is important because emotional competence has an impact on behavior and social skills. Individuals diagnosed with AS have higher rates of unemployment than do their neurotypical peers, despite having average-to-superior cognitive capacity; this is true in large part because psychosocial deficits often overshadow their high cognitive abilities (Higgins, Koch, Boughfman, & Vierstra, 2008). Many psychosocial interventions for depression and anxiety require as a precondition for treatment success that certain metapsychological capabilities are present, including awareness of feelings and an awareness of how those feelings affect the person who has them as well as family members and friends (Gaus, 2007).

The emotional and psychosocial limitations of this population are often related to heightened levels of stress and a lack of awareness of the causes and physiological signs of their stress (Baron, Groden, Groden, & Lipsitt, 2006; Goodwin et al., 2006; King, Hamilton, & Ollendick, 1994), as discussed in a later section.

Self-Awareness and Processing Differences

Individuals diagnosed with ASD often have challenges in the broad area of self-awareness and often show unique information-processing differences that affect their executive functioning and limit their success in managing their lives, maintaining a job, and navigating the social world. Clinicians designing interventions need to be aware of and accommodate these differences.

Self-Awareness Difficulties with self-awareness are reported in the literature. As cited earlier, the work of Berthoz and Hill (2005) reported problems with identification of emotions and verbalizing about them. Jackson, Skirrow, and Hare found that individuals with AS, compared to neurotypical controls, either had a diminished capacity for self-awareness and self-reflection as measured by a Self-Understanding Interview or required "more deliberate self-reflection, self-evaluation and education in an objective, logical, and semantic understanding of me" (2012, p. 704).

Processing Differences   Individuals diagnosed with ASD are often described as perceiving the world differently than neurotypical persons. The literature commonly focuses on the cognitive challenges of persons with ASD: deficient abstract thinking and reasoning (Meyer & Minshew, 2002), diminished central coherence (Frith, 2003), and impaired cognitive flexibility (Attwood, 2008). Other researchers, however, highlight strengths individuals with ASD often have in such areas as visual processing, attention to details, pattern recognition, and rote learning (Samson, Mottron, Soulières, & Zeffiro, 2012). For example, Soulières, Dawson, Gernsbacher, and Mottron demonstrate that individuals on the spectrum excel on the Raven's Progressive Matrices test, a marker for "fluid intelligence, which in turn encompasses reasoning and novel problem-solving abilities" (2011, p. 1). Snyder and Mitchell (1999) describe persons diagnosed with ASD as perceiving the world as a slide show of an object, with privileged access to lower levels of raw information (e.g., more basic). In our clinical experience, the main processing difference is that individuals with ASD often need support to be refocused from the raw details onto the bigger gestalt picture to make sense of the world. With guidance, they are able to "see" the gestalt and make better sense of what is happening around them.

Sensory Differences   Another processing difference that is relatively common among individuals with ASD is in the area of sensory reactivity. Occupational therapists have described a condition called sensory defensiveness, which they hypothesize is an overactivation of the autonomic protective response (Wilbarger & Wilbarger, 1991); individuals who have this condition may be overly sensitive to extremes in any of the sensory systems, such as loud noises or strong smells. Some individuals with ASD are described as "sensory seekers," that is, individuals whose behavior suggests a craving for a bombardment of sensory stimulation, such as those who are constantly moving, fidgeting, bumping into things. These over- and undersensitivities are thought to derail psychosocial interactions, activities of daily living, and cognitive and academic performance.

Other differences in processing and interpreting sensations and information that can affect both social and cognitive success are not well documented among the population with ASD but are recognized anecdotally. Many checklists and algorithms for determining learning, processing, and personality differences have been published, among them the Myers-Briggs Type Indicator (Myers, McCaulley, Quenk, & Hammer, 1998), the 4MAT Learning System (McCarthy, 1990), and Howard Gardner's theory of multiple intelligences (Gardner, 2011). The 4MAT system describes how people learn, how they perceive (sensing and feeling vs. thinking and analyzing), and how they process or interpret events and information (*watchers,* who reflect and filter through their experiences first, vs. *doers,* who act on information immediately and reflect only after trying first). Hurley, Losh, Parlier, Reznick, and Piven (2007) developed the Broad Autism Phenotype Questionnaire, which enables defining personality types of parents of children with autism. Parents of children with autism had significantly higher scores on all three subscales: aloof personality, rigid personality, and pragmatic language.

Self-Regulation and Stress Management

One's level of arousal is the physiological and psychological state of being awake or responsive to stimulation. Although many authors have hypothesized a link between arousal and behavior in people with autism, there is little research supporting an involvement of arousal in the profile of cognitive, behavioral, or emotional problems in individuals with autism (Goodwin et al., 2006). An important paper in this area that demonstrated support for this notion (Hirstein, Iversen, & Ramachandran, 2001) found differences in autonomic responses of children with autism at baseline, engaged in everyday activities, in response to their mothers, and during engagement in self-stimulatory behavior. According to arousal modulation theories of autism cited in Goodwin et al., "Both anxious and agitated responses characteristic of over-arousal and passivity and lethargy characteristic of under-arousal can interfere with this population's ability to attend to, process, and interact with the environment and can result in the failure to learn normative behaviors and skills from other people" (2006, p. 100). This arousal response is part of the *stress response*, which comprises "three periods of interaction between a stressor [any stimulus or circumstance that compromises an individual's physical or psychological well-being] and the individual's response: 1) before the stressful event occurs, 2) during the stressor, and 3) after the stressor, when the individual may experience some of the residual effects of the event" (2006, p. 100). All the features of the cognitive and executive functioning and emotional and psychosocial profiles of individuals with ASD mentioned above may be secondary effects of problems with management of arousal and stressful stimuli and/or may make these individuals more vulnerable to stressful stimuli and less able to cope.

Changes in many systems in the body and brain regions involved in emotion and memory occur in response to positive and negative stressors in the internal and external environment. These physiological changes are controlled in large part by the autonomic nervous system, including its sympathetic and parasympathetic branches. The two branches of the system work in opposite directions to keep the person in equilibrium. Some of these internal changes are externally visible and/or measurable. Research related to the impact of stress on individuals with autism uses these indicators both to evaluate stress and to design interventions that target these responses.

Goodwin et al. (2006), cited above, found that individuals with autism showed significant cardiovascular responses—for example, heart rate (HR) elevation—to stressors less often than do their neurotypical peers. This may have been secondary to their having a higher basal HR and reduced variance in responsivity. This higher basal HR may have been an indication that the autistic participants were overly aroused by the testing situation or that they may have been in a general state of what they call "autonomic defensiveness." The authors questioned whether HR was an optimal indicator or whether heart rate variability (HRV) would allow a finer analysis. The participants in these early studies were not individuals with AS or pervasive developmental disorder–not otherwise specified (PDD-NOS). It is unclear if the autonomic responsivity is different among individuals at different ends of the spectrum.

Skin conductance level (SCL), also known as galvanic skin response is a method of measuring the electrical conductance of the skin, which varies with its moisture level, sweat. Sweat glands are controlled by the sympathetic nervous system, so SCL is used as an indication of psychological or physiological arousal. Stress management products using skin conductance are commercially available, but there is little scientific research into their effectiveness, particularly with children with disabilities.

The Institute of HeartMath has conducted extensive research on the importance of emotion regulation and the physiology of optimal learning and performance (Bradley, McCraty, Atkinson, & Tomasino, 2010; McCraty, 2005). Both HR and HRV provide information on regulation between the sympathetic and parasympathetic branches of the autonomic nervous systems (ANS; Porges, 1992). Considered a psychophysiological marker of emotion regulation and shifting attention, HRV is also an indicator of physiological resilience, behavioral flexibility, and an individual's capacity to adapt effectively to stress and environmental demands (Appelhans & Luecken, 2006; Beauchaine, 2001; Lloyd, Brett, & Wesnes, 2010). Products developed by the institute that incorporate this framework are described in detail below.

CURRICULUM AND TECHNOLOGY FOR SOCIAL-EMOTIONAL INTELLIGENCE, SELF-AWARENESS, AND SELF-REGULATION

Individuals with ASD often have tremendous interest and abilities in visually represented information. Many individuals diagnosed with ASD are drawn to and excel at video games and computer graphic, visual, and computational applications. Multiple authors (Bölte, Golan, Goodwin, & Zwaigenbaum, 2010; Higgins & Boone, 1996; Moore, 1998; Silver & Oakes, 2001) indicate that many technological devices are promising teaching tools for individuals diagnosed with an ASD. Intervention designers should accommodate and capitalize on the cognitive learning style of individuals with ASD as visual learners and technology aficionados. Including science, data, and technology in the curriculum makes the abstract world of inner thoughts, feelings, and SEI more accessible and puts personal data external to the individual; a concrete data point to interpret and control, while helping the individual toward self-awareness (McLeod & Lucci, 2009). By approaching inner thoughts and SEI scientifically, the curriculum provides an effective way for individuals diagnosed with an ASD to further their understanding of themselves (and others) as social, emotional, and cognitive beings. Such a curriculum would have a number of core features:

- Real life experiences and natural consequences

- Concrete, direct, and ongoing feedback that relies on visual representations of the data about the inner worlds, feelings, and physiology of persons with ASD

- Technology support for teaching, guidance, self-monitoring, and self-regulation

An approach and curriculum that incorporates the frameworks described in the introduction with the above core features was developed at Aspire (http://www.mghAspire.org), a program of the Lurie Family Center for Autism at Massachusetts General Hospital. Aspire uses *Science of Me* in a variety of therapeutically based programs, as well as part of consultation to schools and professional development, to support the growth of individuals diagnosed with ASD or other social-cognitive challenges. The *Science of Me* curriculum integrates skill content from many different published resources as well as unique content to create an all-encompassing SEI curriculum.

Table 11.1 lists critical cognitive-social skill areas and a sampling of sources and interventions described in the literature that address them. The Aspire program

Table 11.1. Curriculum content: Skill areas and intervention sources

Social-emotional intelligence	Self-awareness and personal style: Strengths and challenges	Self-regulation and stress management
	Curriculum content: Specific skill areas	
• Recognition of emotions • Relationships • Empathy • Handling interpersonal interactions • Teamwork • Conflict and negotiation	Who you are in terms of: • Cognitive flexibility • Executive functioning • Personality style • Sensory: engine speed, reactivity, modulation • Learning style	• Stress as a part of life • Brain–body connection: brain and autonomic nervous systems • Triggers • Define what stress looks like, feels like • Coping strategies and techniques: mindfulness, progressive muscle relaxation, deep breathing, visualization • Exercise, sleep, nutrition
	Sample of interventions	

• Social Thinking
• HeartMath emWave Desktop, Inside Story, Test Edge
• Science of Me
• SymTrend
	• Style definition: Myers-Briggs Type Indicator, Gregorc Style Delineator,
	• Multiple Intelligences, 4MAT System
	• Social Thinking
	• Sensory awareness:
	  Zones of Regulation
	  The Alert Program
	• Unstuck and On Target!
	• Science of Me
	• SymTrend
		• Sensory regulation: Zones of Regulation, The Alert Program, Henry OT Sensory, Integration Tools
		• Mindfulness
		• HeartMath emWave Desktop
		  Inside Story
		  Test Edge
		• Science of Me
		• SymTrend

draws from many of these interventions, tying them together with technology and a data-driven, visual, unified approach. The next section of this chapter reviews these skill areas and interventions, as well as the technologies that facilitate their accessibility to people with ASD.

Social-Emotional Intelligence Curricula

A comprehensive literature review that involved 317 studies and a total of 324,303 child and adolescent participants found that adult-instructed, social and emotional learning curricula were among the most successful interventions offered to school-age youth. Benefits included enhanced self-awareness, self-management, social awareness, and positive attitudes, as well as fewer conduct problems, less emotional distress, and better grades and achievement scores (Payton et al., 2008). Cooper (2007) argued that for students diagnosed with special needs, this result is even more pronounced. For without diversity of instruction and flexibility in the types of service delivery to students with special needs, such students will be increasingly marginalized.

One of the most popular curricula for SEI for children and teens with ASD is *Social Thinking* by Michelle Garcia Winner (2000, 2005, 2007). Winner has published many books related to social-cognition as well as step-by-step methods for teaching social-cognitive and communicative skills. She focuses on social cognition, rather than social skills, encouraging students and their caregivers to learn her social thinking vocabulary as part of developing perspective-taking and understanding how perspectives of others is the foundation of interpersonal relationships with others. Her curriculum helps students view their own behavior relative to what are socially expected and unexpected behaviors in different situations. There are exercises to analyze one's behavior as indicative of thinking of "just me" or "thinking of you."

Researchers and clinicians at the University of California, Los Angeles, have developed an evidenced-based social skills training program called PEERS (Program for the Education and Enrichment of Relational Skills). It is a 12- to 16-week program for teens and young adults that addresses friendship development through social communication, social cognition, social awareness, social motivation, cooperation, and peer interactions (Laugeson, Frankel, Gantman, Dillon, & Mogil, 2012). The program includes didactic lessons, role-playing demonstrations, and behavioral rehearsal exercises. PEERS also contains a concurrent parent group that teaches similar content and provides guidance for generalization of learning for the teens. Participants enrolled in this program have to want to participate and be motivated to change and must agree to engage in the exercises.

Supporting Social-Emotional Intelligence with Technology Whereas many of the SEI curriculum concepts of many programs are related, the Aspire program sought to complement the *Science of Me* didactic lessons about SEI with technology and visual representations to fit the learning style of the mixed population it serves: persons with ASD, HFA, and nonverbal learning disorder (NVLD). It adopted the SymTrend software on Palm PDAs and then the Apple iPod Touch and HeartMath's stress management curriculum and the emWave software technology to track an individual's understanding of specific concepts and vocabulary taught and to review the data as visual representations with them individually and in groups. These tools facilitate a rich learning experience for individuals with ASD, their peers, and the adults working with them (see Chapter 12).

The SymTrend software facilitates multifaceted behavioral observation, coaching, team communication, and user-friendly graphical data for use by professionals and individuals diagnosed with ASD. In the Aspire summer program, the software was utilized with teens to improve skill development and understanding by analyzing data, discussing results and other's varying perspectives, while charting progress over time. Individuals and staff simultaneously recorded activities, behaviors, program events, and group interactions multiple times each day on their mobile devices, each from his or her own perspective. Teens and staff then reviewed the visual representation of both assessments plotted on the same page together for comparison and discuss the personal data in an objective manner. In this way, the individuals did not view the feedback, even if negative, as upsetting or emotionally triggering.

Aspire primarily uses the simultaneous self and other reporting as a clinical teaching tool for self-regulation, including health awareness, social awareness, stress management, and executive functioning. SymTrend has a feature for self-authoring of both the data collection screens and the graphical representations, which affords the opportunity to 1) load the *Science of Me* curriculum content, including elements related to the *Social Thinking, Alert,* and HeartMath's *Inside Story* lessons on the mobile device; and 2) choose the graphic display option that the teens can interpret with greatest ease.

SymTrend data consisted of a variety of questions that the teens answered about themselves and a staff person answered about the teen (see Figure 11. 1). Occasionally two teens rated each other. The questions ranged from basic health information (e.g., "Did you sleep through the night?") to specific information (e.g., "Check any stressors you experienced or thought about during the previous activity"). Checklists about interventions used were also included (e.g., "Check any relaxation strategies you used during the previous activity"), as were fill-ins about hindrances (e.g., "During the last activity I was stuck on..."). The latter generated a variety of responses (looping thought, having my own way, etc.). During

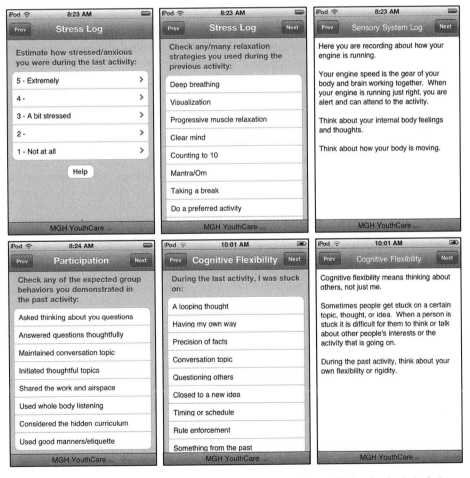

Figure 11.1. Screens for entering data into SymTrend software on iPod Touch during the day in Aspire's summer program.

moments of stress, frustration, or cognitive inflexibility during the day, teens were reminded of what they were learning. They were encouraged to implement positive thinking self-talk, to think socially, and to use relaxation techniques and other strategies. They checked the strategy they used on their device. Up to six different relational comparisons in a graph form were reviewed each week. For example, in didactic sessions, teens were taught how "stuckness" (cognitive inflexibility) and "group participation" (how a teen was perceived during an activity by others) related to each other. From then on, teens and staff rated the teen's inflexibility and participation each day, interpreting results and sharing perspectives with each other during group sessions. (See Figure 11.2 for a sample of three such comparison charts.)

Notice that the top line in Figure 11.2 displays a happy/sad scale and the second line displays an anxious/relaxed scale. Staff or Teacher Recording is represented as an open circle (o), and the Student Recording is represented as a blackened circle (•). Note that in the first two "feelings" graphs, there is relative agreement and similarity of the curvature of the line. This indicates that the adult and the teen were in close agreement about whether the teen was happy or sad and anxious or relaxed. During the group-counseling session, these ratings were discussed from the perspective of self-awareness of others' views of observable behavior. Of paramount importance in this discussion was teaching the individuals that how they look and behave externally gives other people a window into their internal state of mind. These discussions provided direct lessons on the concept of theory of mind and on "feeling felt" by another.

Dual data collection by teens and staff was a research design feature deliberately chosen and carefully orchestrated. *Social Thinking* and other curricula include didactics and role play to teach about multiple perspectives and how one's behavior affects interrelationships. Aspire's design of the Sym-Trend application directs attention to the effects of perspectives, feelings, and

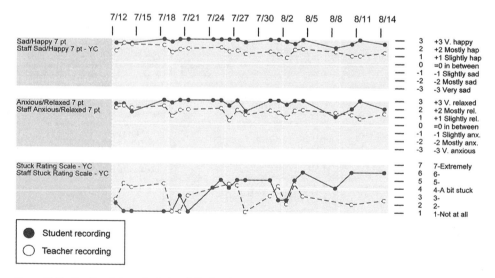

Figure 11.2. SymTrend chart displaying daily data for one teen on three rating scales, as entered by the teen and a staff observer.

thoughts in a visual and technological way. Aspire also utilizes video analysis coupled with the technological data. Whereas *Social Thinking* has such paper visuals as Social Behavior Maps to look at the relationship between behaviors and consequences, SymTrend charts displaying both may be more compelling. The teens saw how their behavior has an effect on them and others and saw the direct relationship between behaviors and triggers, such as how the amount of exercise and/or sleep they get may have an impact on their participation or attention during the day, how their individual participation affects the overall group performance, or how their reaction to a stressful trigger can either help them regroup or explode further (Lucci & McLeod, 2008; Lucci, McLeod, & Challen-Wittmer, 2010; McLeod & Lucci, 2008; McLeod, Lucci & Challen-Wittmer, 2010). The discussions about the charts afford the opportunity to ask such questions as "When you said or did..., I felt.... Was that your intent?" Another example: "Hmm, I noticed you are consistently rating yourself as sad, but others don't seem to detect it." The results suggest broader application of this approach could prove useful in helping individuals with theory of mind deficits and emotional perception or awareness difficulties improve their understanding of how they are perceived by others. Further, this approach encouraged sharing of events and reactions that many individuals with ASD would not spontaneously share. For example, a participant once rated himself as sadder than usual. When queried about this change in emotion, he shared that his dog had recently died (a fact not spontaneously mentioned previous to our reviewing the data).

Additional SEI components of *Science of Me* were included to teach teens how attention, memory, learning, problem solving and decision making, motivation, and social functioning are intricately involved with emotions. Emotions interplay with learning in a profound way; emotional responses create a cascade of physiological responses that influence the mind, body, and brain (Damasio, Grabowski, Frank, Galaburda, & Damasio, 1994). Emotion regulation is an underpinning of intellectual development, academic attainment, and generalization and application of learned knowledge into a variety of settings and situations (Ledoux, 2002).

There is extensive research on the importance of emotion regulation in learning, and the Institute of HeartMath has contributed to this body of work. Their research demonstrated a positive impact of their emWave technology and educational techniques on school performance (Bradley et al., 2010,; McCraty, 2005). These techniques have been used with children diagnosed with special needs (e.g., attention-deficit/hyperactivity disorder [ADHD], anxiety disorder, learning disability, autism).

Four specific HeartMath educational techniques were taught to the teens in the Aspire programs to facilitate their SEI, in particular emotion regulation. Specific vocabulary and strategies from HeartMath's *The Inside Story* and *Test-Edge* (e.g., Clear Mind, Looping Thought, Freeze Frame) were added to SymTrend screen content. Teens were taught Neutral, Quick Coherence, Heart Lock-In, and Freeze Frame. Neutral and Quick Coherence are emotion refocusing tools. The third and fourth techniques are emotion restructuring techniques. All are designed to help the teens to think about a positive emotional experience and/or feeling to assist in shifting their physiology. Learning of these cognitive techniques and others was enhanced by the emWave Desktop, a system for emotion self-regulation, to be described later in this chapter.

Self-Awareness and Processing Differences: Strengths and Challenges

Three elements of self-awareness and processing differences that are challenges for individuals with ASD are the focus of this review of curricula and technologies: learning and processing style, body and sensory awareness, and cognitive flexibility.

Learning Style   The cognitive and perceptual differences of individuals with ASD, as described earlier in this chapter, often lead to frustrating interactions in inclusive classrooms and the world at large. Teachers, peers, and employers who are not familiar with how an individual with ASD thinks and learns are often unable to adjust their part of instruction or a conversation to accommodate the learning and social style of the individual. The Aspire program helps teens learn about their processing differences and modes of response. In this program, teens complete versions of self-typing instruments and learn about their personal styles. Myers-Briggs Type Indicator (Myers et al., 1998), Howard Gardner theory of multiple intelligences (Gardner, 2011), and the 4MAT Learning System (McCarthy, 1990) are examples of typing methodologies. Others are available and used with the *Science of Me* curriculum. Participants learn about their type and that of others and learn how to manage an interaction with someone of a different type (Armstrong, 2009, 2010; Levine, 1993).

Self-Awareness   The *Science of Me* curriculum includes units about one's sensory reactivity, modulation, and general arousal level. These units incorporate features of the Alert program (Williams & Shellenberger, 1994) and Zones of Regulation (Kuypers, 2011). As mentioned earlier, many individuals with ASD have differences in sensory reactivity, whether as expressed as sensory defensiveness or sensory seeking. These curricula emphasize teaching individuals about their level of arousal, the effect of arousal on their ability to engage and participate in other activities, and how to get themselves to a point where their arousal is optimal. The curriculum uses different analogies to teach about optimizing arousal: an engine with three speed levels (high, low, and "just right") or traffic signals (red, yellow, blue, which means "rest," and green zone, which means "ready-to-go").

A related area of self-awareness is knowing where you are in personal space relative to others and how your behavior affects them. Role playing and video analysis is used by many social skills training programs to facilitate self-awareness of personal space relative to others. Elements of the *Social Thinking* curriculum focus on building an individual's self-awareness vis-à-vis the environment and the perspectives of others. In addition, individuals are taught to think about "whole body listening," that is, about brain and body, in the group, and other social concepts.

Cognitive Flexibility   Cognitive flexibility is a core concept of the *Unstuck and On Target!* curriculum (Cannon et al., 2011) as well as the *Science of Me* curriculum. The *Unstuck and On Target!* curriculum includes instruction about situations that trigger inflexibility and its adaptive role. It also includes "flexibility scripts" to help guide the individual to avoid triggers, to get unstuck, to compromise, to determine whether the situation at hand is a big or a little deal, and to consider what choices are available. The *Science of Me* curriculum includes instruction related to internal and external triggers, reframing, and positive self-talk scripts, among others. A variety of technologies can be used to implement scripts on mobile devices.

The Aspire mobile application incorporates flexibility monitoring, a feature described in the last section of this chapter.

Supporting Self-Awareness with Technology   Screens that capture perception of engine speed and participation in groups as well as other areas were added to SymTrend self-monitoring screens. The Aspire application included a checklist about group participation and was completed after some groups included the *Social Thinking* concept of "being present in the group with brain and body." One teen was a "pacer" (i.e., and individual who walked back and forth in a straight-line repetitive pattern); the staff observer rated the teen as "not in the group," whereas the teen rated himself as "in." During a group chart review, the observer explained her rating by saying that pacing is an example of "body not in the group." A teen in the group disagreed, saying, "You call yourselves psychologists! He's autistic, of course he paces." The charts evoke such teachable moments, where the staff can support self-awareness but also indicate which behaviors are expected by neurotypical peers. This general format was used with many other charts with varying themes to improve the teens' understanding of themselves, their peers, and neurotypical individuals.

The Aspire mobile application included a sensory section that was used multiple times a day to both record a teen's engine speed and to suggest strategies for changing the speed. Guidance screens that defined the term and how to evaluate one's state appeared for each recording. The application also included a section about inflexibility. The third line in Figure 11.2 displays a "Stuck Rating Scale"; both the teen and the staff observer applications included a rating of the teen's cognitive flexibility during group activities. A discrepancy between the staff person's entries about the teen and the teen's data about himself was evident. The teen, when engaging with staff and peers, had a tendency to repetitively tell the same religious jokes. Upon questioning and discussion, he only marginally ("a bit stuck") interpreted this as being stuck or cognitively inflexible. The direct teaching involved sharing with the teen and the group that when a person perseverates on telling the same joke repeatedly, it is no longer funny in other people's minds. The staff provided basic information about joke telling within the cultural and societal norms. As this discussion unfolded, the teen's peers agreed with the general description of joke telling and the staff rating. The staff's initial theory was that the teen did not understand the concept of flexibility as it pertained to joke telling and did not realize the effect his behavior had on others. The graph shows that after the initial discussions in July, the teen indicated that he understood the concept of stuckness as it applied to his joke telling. After reviewing the data and watching videos of these situations, the teen understood how he was aggravating his peers. However, note in the graph that after July 30, the ratings shift: He indicated that he was almost "extremely stuck" (Level 7), whereas staff indicated that he was "a bit stuck" (Level 4). He reported to the group that he was learning to inhibit his repetitive telling of jokes. However, he described himself as internally stuck on the concept of not being stuck. This was why he rated himself at Level 7. It is interesting to us that outwardly he appeared to others as having mastered the concept of stuckness because his behavior had dramatically shifted to minimal repetitive joke telling. This revelation was a profound moment for staff, who realized that they were incorrectly interpreting his outward behavior. Without the graphic representational data, they would not have been able to explore his deeper learning to help him with this insight. This example serves as a model to demonstrate the use of SymTrend programs and to describe the process of instruction. It highlights the ebb and flow of the teen's learning and the ultimate unfolding of his self-awareness. Without the technology and the visual representation, it would have been extremely difficult to have such a rich and powerful discussion with him and the other group members. The staff did not try to change teens' self-ratings in these discussions: The goal was not to achieve two identical graphs but to inform teens how others may perceive them and then allow them to decide to change their behavior if they choose.

Self-Regulation and Stress Management

As in the other two arenas, interventions are available to foster self-regulation and stress management with and without technology. The Aspire program incorporates such common nontechnical interventions as mindfulness and sensory regulation and very innovative biofeedback approaches. Teens are encouraged to consider some of the nontechnical concepts when working with the biofeedback and self-monitoring gear.

Mindfulness Research on the neurophysiology of mindfulness in adults conducted through the Mindfulness-Based Stress Reduction (MBSR) programs, first developed in 1979 by Jon Kabat-Zinn, have found dramatic results from the adults' participation in 8-week programs (Kabat-Zinn, 1982). Mindfulness practice can improve attention, emotion regulation, flexibility in thinking, and emotional health, such as reduction in symptoms of anxiety and depression (Allen, Chambers, & Knight, 2006; Grossman, Nieman, Schmidt, & Walach, 2004; Kabat-Zinn, 1990; Segal, Williams, & Teasdale, 2002). Given these positive results with adults, researchers have begun to explore these techniques with children and teens. Researchers have replicated the findings of improved attention, emotion regulation, social competence, and overall well-being with children and teens (Meiklejohn et al., 2012), but some of the studies have not included randomized control trials.

Many school districts are implementing broad SEL programs such as: PATHS, Reach Out to Schools: Social Competency, Responsive Classroom, and I Can Problem Solve in grades K–12 with promising results (CASEL, 2003). Such mindfulness curricula as *Mind Up, Learning2 BREATHE, Mindful Schools, Building Resilience from the Inside Out—Grades K–12,* and *BE Peace* are also showing positive results. Linda Lantieri and colleagues, leading authors and thinkers in this area, are conducting empirical research within the New York City schools on the curriculum *Building Resilience from the Inside Out—Grades K–12* (Lantieri & Goleman, 2008; Lantieri & Patti, 1996).

The cognitive and emotional areas for which MBSR is effective in individuals without ASD are areas of deficits in individuals diagnosed with AS. Individuals with ASD are described as often being in a heightened state of fight or flight. In his book *Buddha's Brain: The Practical Neuroscience of Happiness, Love and Wisdom,* Rick Hanson (2009) asserts that the practice of breathing can dampen the activation of the fight-or-flight response and the parasympathetic nervous system. This suggests that individuals diagnosed with ASD may benefit from participating in mindfulness or other deep-breathing approaches. Preliminary data from a modified MBSR program demonstrated a decrease in anxiety, depression, and rumination symptoms and an increase in positive affect in adults diagnosed with high-functioning ASD (Spek, van Ham, & Nykliček, 2012). Work with neurotypical adults found changes in the gray matter concentration of other brain areas after 8 weeks of MBSR: in the left hippocampus, the posterior cingulate cortex, the temporo-parietal junction, and the cerebellum (Hölzel et al., 2011); this work has not been replicated with children with developing brains or with individuals with ASD, but what has been published shows promise. Singh and colleagues (2011) conducted a multiple-baseline design across three subjects diagnosed with AS and aggression. They participated in an 18–24-week period of instruction during which their incidents of aggressions dropped; at a 4-year follow-up, with continued practice, all three students had zero incidents of physical aggression. Mitchell (2009), an adult diagnosed with AS, described how the practice of mindfulness helped him with his emotion regulation and social and executive functioning.

Given these positive findings with AS participants, lessons taken from the mindfulness literature—for example, focusing on one's breathing, mindful listening, mindful walking, mindful eating, and mindful thinking—were included in the *Science of Me* curriculum. All these exercises conducted with instructions to teens to use "purposeful attention to the task" (e.g., breathing, eating, walking), with a nonjudgmental attitude. Some of these practices were embedded throughout the day during transition times, moments of stress, and while engaging in classroom or group activities. Mindfulness vocabulary was included on the SymTrend screens about strategies used, including phrases such as *clear mind* (mindful thinking) and *deep breathing*.

Sensory-Based Self-Regulation   Williams and Shellenberger (1994) present activities for discovering the effect of one's internal and external environment on each of the senses, such as delineating where one's engine speed is before and after doing things. They present tools and activities for adjusting one's speed. The books *Zone of Regulation* (Kuypers, 2011) and *Sensory Integration Tools for Teens* (Henry, Wheeler, & Sava, 2004) present activities for modulation of arousal as well.

Biofeedback devices have been used for many years in clinical and medical settings to help individuals manage stress. The use of biofeedback for stress management involves recording such physiological activity as HR, brainwaves, breathing, muscle activity, and/or skin temperature or dampness and providing some sort of graphical or auditory picture of that activity as it is recorded. Users view the information or listen to the pitch or volume of sound and engage in such tasks as reciting positive or negative statements or imagining peaceful places and watching the change in the physiological response. In time, the users learn which thoughts or images help change the physiological response in the desired direction and call on those thoughts when under stressful situations in their lives.

Biofeedback programs, therefore, have two critical elements: recording and displaying technology and the curriculum that goes with it to get users to 1) learn about their physiological responses, that is, what they feel like in the clinical setting and what they feel like during stressful events in life; 2) think about stressful triggers in their life, namely, those events and situations that are associated with the physiological symptoms occurring; and 3) guide them to the thoughts and/or images that will successfully calm them down.

Stress Management Devices   In this section we first describe some of the commercially available technologies, research conducted with the technology, and the curriculum that is available for use to teach stress reduction techniques. We then describe the Institute of HeartMath emWave technology that Aspire chose to use in its programs, explain why Aspire chose it, and elaborate on how it has been used in the Aspire program.

Wild Divine (http://www.wilddivine.com) created the Relaxing Rhythms and Journey to the Wild Divine. These stress management programs utilize the Iom finger sensors (three sensors on one hand) that measures SCL and HR. These programs use a video game format to help users learn about emotions, thoughts, and breathing. Journey to the Wild Divine has been used in research with children with ADHD, but there is no curriculum or teacher's guide. Amon and Campbell (2008) used Journey to the Wild Divine as a tool to teach breathing techniques and relaxation techniques to reduce disruptive behavior with children diagnosed with ADHD and found promising results.

Somatic Vision (http://www.somaticvision.com) created a variety of stress reduction video games that use HR and HRV. To operate each of these video games, one needs the ear or finger sensor from Wild Divine or HeartMath. They all integrate coaching and performance tracking as well as specific stress reduction techniques (e.g., breathing).

Created by Thought Technology (http://www.thoughttechnology.com), GSR is a small, portable handheld galvanic skin response monitoring device that emits varying sounds related to stress level. The GSR Temp2X is also a portable handheld biofeedback device that includes a temperature sensor and remote electrodes that attach to the hands or feet. It includes an earphone, CD, and instruction manual on "hand-warming" techniques that influence stress levels. Hand-warming techniques are such self-talk phrases as "I am feeling relaxed. My muscles are loose and warm. I can feel the blood running into my hands. My hands are feeling heavy and warm." There is no curriculum or teacher's guide.

Helicor created StressEraser (http://www.stresseraser.com), a portable handheld device that measures HRV and displays cardiovascular changes graphically. One's index finger rests in an opening on the handheld StressEraser. The finger sensor measures the real-time beat-to-beat HR pulsation. The StressEraser portrays a visual pulse rate wave. It uses triangles to represent the peak of the wave (fastest point of the HR). The goal is to move from a jagged wave to a smoother wave pattern so that a person can modify his or her breathing rhythm to an optimal breathing rhythm. There is no curriculum or teacher's guide with Helicor's StressEraser.

Q sensor is the newest version of a commercially available wireless ANS sensor from Affectiva (http://www.Affectiva.com). It is the commercial version of the iCalm ANS sensor developed at the MIT Media Lab (http://www.media.mit.edu) and by Matthew S. Goodwin (one of the editors of this volume). The iCalm has over 10,000 hours of ANS data in vivo from more than 100 infants, children, and adults with and without an ASD diagnosis. The Q sensor is worn on the wrist or ankle and records electrodermal activity, temperature, and motor movements in real time. Its cost is substantially greater when compared with the aforementioned devices. Research at universities as well as commercial enterprises is currently underway. At universities it is being used with individuals diagnosed with a variety of conditions

(ASD, anxiety, depression, among others). Aspire hopes to include this technology to enhance data collection to include additional objective data in conjunction with SymTrend self and other data. (Figure 11.3 shows an example of a sensor. At the time of this publication, Affectiva was no longer manufacturing the Q Sensor. It is our understanding that the MIT Media lab may have further information.)

As previously mentioned, the Institute of HeartMath (http://www.Heart-math.org) has, over many years, been conducting research into stress management, psychophysiology, HR, and HRV. This research has taken place in hospitals, universities, educational settings, and the military. The HeartMath's emWave Desktop System is a stress management system that utilizes an ear or finger sensor. The sensor collects real-time, beat-to-beat HR and HRV. The emWave Desktop portrays the HR and HRV. It also displays a bar graph indicating heart coherence (a smoother HRV). In addition to the emWave Desktop, there is a portable version called the emWave2. The emWave2 displays cardiovascular changes visually in real time via LED lights or tones. The sensor detects pulse in real time, and the breathing pacer synchronizes to the heart rhythms utilizing LED lights and/or audible tones.

emWave allows the user to understand how thoughts and emotions affect the heart and the ANS. When stressed, frustrated, or angered, a person has a heart rhythm with an irregular, jagged, and more incoherent wave pattern. When a person is in a more positive emotional state, the heart rhythm pattern changes to a smoother, more coherent wavelike pattern. Figure 11.4 shows a coherent heart rhythm and an incoherent heart rhythm pattern.

Figure 11.3. Wrist band sensor.

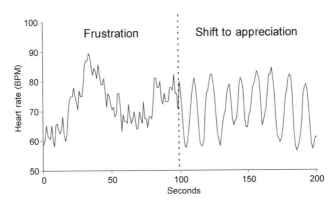

Figure 11.4. Shift to coherence. An individual using a HeartMath emotion-refocusing technique, initially experiencing frustration shifts (at the dotted line) to appreciation; the heart rhythm shifts accordingly. (Copyright © 2013 Institute of HeartMath; reprinted by permission.)

Aspire chose HeartMath's emWave Desktop System as its technological stress management system for a variety of reasons. First, HeartMath has curricula to go with their devices that have been well-researched with children with and without special needs. *The Inside Story* and *Test-Edge* are two such curricula that were compatible with our *Science of Me* curriculum, so aspects of these were implemented as part of the curriculum. Each of these includes "heart-focused techniques" addressing self-awareness, self-management, and self-regulation. *The Inside Story* (HeartMath, 2006) is a broad curriculum teaching concepts related to the heart–brain connection, whereas *Test-Edge* (HeartMath, 2002) covers similar content but primarily focuses on test-taking anxiety. *Test-Edge* was used more heavily in consultation because it related more directly to the issues that pertain to academic performance. The "heart-focused techniques" center on "heart focus, heart breathing, and heart feeling" and are intended to enhance the development of positive emotional thinking, improved emotion self-regulation, emotion refocusing, and emotion restructuring.

The HeartMath techniques of Heart-Focused Breathing, Neutral, and Quick Coherence involved shifting one's attention to the area around the heart and breathing easily and naturally or slowly. While practicing this technique, the individuals were instructed to elicit a positive emotion by thinking of a happy time. Learning these techniques was enhanced by the emWave Desktop. The teens viewed the computer and received visual graphic representational data on their coherence level (HRV) in real time as a thought or feeling pattern changed. As the teens mastered the graphic mode, they progressed to the video game format, where they have predetermined amounts of time (3–5 minutes) to achieve heart coherence. Figure 11.5 shows a specific student's emWave chart. On the computer, HRV was constantly changing in real time based on the individual's heart focus, heart breathing, and heart feeling (in the language of HeartMath). This allowed the teens to see

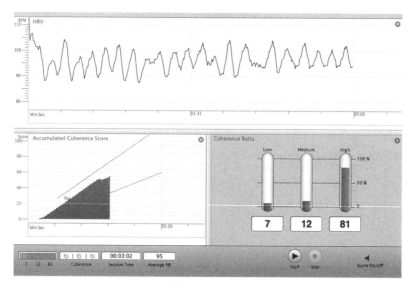

Figure 11.5.   emWave Desktop graphic display of a teen's actual session, showing 81% coherence ratio within 3 minutes.

the effects of their thinking, feeling, and breathing. The visual representation of HR and HRV enhanced the teens' ability to visualize their internal states and to improve understanding of how their thoughts, feelings, and behaviors were connected. Notice the upper portion of Figure 11.5, which shows the HRV wave. The lower left-hand corner shows the "zone graph," whereas the lower right shows the percentage of time spent in coherence. The zone graph represents the amount of time in the heart rhythm coherence zone. Coupled with the emWave Session Form (Figure 11.6), using this chart allowed the teens to compare the effect of the activity on the resulting emWave Desktop, display stress levels before and after the session, and what the staff thought about their stress levels. Also, the emWave Desktop allowed for printing a variety of types of charts that could help the teens and teacher or staff assess, monitor, and track performance.

OUTCOME ANALYSES AND OPPORTUNITIES FOR FUTURE DISCOVERY

In this final section, the *Science of Me* curriculum is presented in more detail and is expanded to include specific examples of application and analysis. This section presents a combination of individual and aggregated data that were collected at school programs and at the Explorations Program using the *Science of Me* curriculum. The integrated use of technology and the visual representational graphs enhanced self-regulation, self-awareness, and SEI. Individual forms and results demonstrated enhanced learning. A promising feature is that each school can modify its usage to best match its particular needs and structure. Preliminary personal and aggregated data from schools and in the therapeutic program indicates that the *Science of Me* curriculum in conjunction with HeartMath tools and Symtrend can be powerful tools for self-discovery and personal change for individuals diagnosed with social-cognitive challenges.

	emWave Session Form		
	Date and time	Date and time	Date and time
Location			
Minutes	10 15 20	10 15 20	10 15 20
Antecedent			
1–5 scale before			
Student			
Teacher			
Describe activity: emWave game? Other game?			
Other relaxation tools			
1–5 scale after			
Student			
Teacher			
Final staff notes			
Turnaround time (minutes)			
Questionnaire completed	Y N	Y N	Y N

Figure 11.6. Aspire created emWave session form for the teen and teacher to track pre- and poststress level and context and class.

Summary: *Science of Me* Curriculum

The *Science of Me* curriculum was implemented in middle schools (grades 6–8) and high schools (grades 9–12) in the Boston area in special education classes and as part of the general education course selection. Social Thinking: Theory and Practice was cotaught by a speech-language pathologist and an English teacher and Managing Stress was taught by a wellness and health teacher and a special educator. Each class was offered for one semester for one credit each. All general and special education students were able to enroll. The program comprised a track of classes offered over 3–4 years, which build on the previous year's content and individual student learning. At the end of each school year, each student created a personal binder that includes specific information about the student in relation to the three cognitive social areas mentioned earlier as well as the science behind them.

Science of Me was offered through the special education department and took place one to two periods each week for approximately 45 minutes. Instruction took place in small groups (four–eight students) over the course of a full academic year (10 months). Each class involved direct adult instruction with active and passive student learning. Instructional modalities included lecture, discussion, reading of scientific articles, worksheets, videos, self-assessment checklists, and scientific experiments. Lessons were supplemented with the use of HeartMath's emWave Desktop System and the SymTrend curriculum. Throughout the day, teachers and assistant teachers would prompt students to engage in a variety of wellness and stress management techniques (e.g., mindfulness, deep breathing, Quick Coherence, and visualization). When using the emWave Desktop System from Heart-Math, practice took place under a variety of conditions, among them engaging in a heart-focusing technique, listening to music, reading a book, and doing homework (see Figure 11.6).

Many of the students were so engaged in this curriculum that teachers created additional worksheets, videos, and games and located web sources for future inclusion in the curriculum. Examples of topics include the brain, the role of dopamine and serotonin in our daily lives, and how oxytocin and cortisol influence health. During every special education instructional period, whether an exclusively dedicated *Science of Me* instructional period or not, the students engaged in a variety of stress management techniques from the HeartMath program's curriculum (e.g., Quick Coherence Technique).

Outcomes

The *Science of Me* curriculum described in this chapter was under development and refinement for several years throughout Aspire programs. Aspire offers a "typical" summer experience called Explorations; using this curriculum targeted the needs, learning styles, and strengths of the participants. They have increased their knowledge of themselves and their understanding of their neurotypical peers and SEI while demonstrating a change in outward behavior. Given the brief period of data collection during an intensive 6-week summer program, formal experimental testing was not possible. Anecdotal evidence for the program's success comes from quotes from families and from schools that have subsidized the tuition for children to attend the program as part of their individualized education plans.

Postprogram analysis of SymTrend-entered data supported the development effort. One such analysis investigated the awareness of signs of stress and the types of stress management techniques and strategies chosen by a group of teens to deal with the stress (Lucci, McLeod, & Challen-Wittmer, 2010; McLeod, Lucci, & Challen-Wittmer, 2010). Teens reported that eye–head discomfort more frequently accompanied arguments with peers than discomfort of the stomach or jaw or neck and more frequently than after arguments with adults (see Table 11.2). Although the teens were taught several stress management strategies, they initiated use of them during stress with differing regularity. Ten different stress management strategies were taught. Out of all the different stress management strategies suggested, only clear mind (46% of the recordings with stress), deep breathing (41%), and visualization (36%) were consistently used by the teens. Teens used such strategies as mantras, progressive muscle relaxation, or counting to 10 fewer than 10% of the time. An interesting finding was that given the short duration of the summer program, these results mirrored the relative amount of time devoted to each strategy in the teaching protocol.

Use of these strategies varied with the stress the students experienced. A correlation matrix of this data is shown in Table 11.3. There was a significant positive correlation (at the .01 and .05 level) between use of each of the strategies and each of the following stressors: unexpected change, unmet expectation, and perseverative thinking. There was a negative correlation between use of each of these strategies and the stressor of feeling "forced to do an activity." The negative correlation might be explained by negative emotion arising when the individual is forced to engage in an activity that interferes with cognitive processes for decision making about using an otherwise-employed relaxation strategy. Further analyses are needed to determine why this group of teens preferred these strategies versus others.

Aspire consults with public schools in the Boston area to provide program design and development for students diagnosed with AS. One component of this consultation was the implementation of the *Science of Me* curriculum to enhance and increase social and emotional learning programming for students with AS. The curriculum was presented as a special education class to influence credibility among staff and students alike; thus the students have homework, take tests, and earn credit for the course. General education teachers were also trained to use the concepts and vocabulary of the *Science of Me* curriculum, leading to the generalization from one setting to another. Modifying the instruction based on the setting and

Table 11.2.   Perception of physiological signs of stress during negative events

		Teen reported: stomach discomfort	Teen reported: jaw/ neck discomfort	Teen reported: eye/ head discomfort
Teen reported: argued with peer	Pearson correlation	−.206*	−.191*	.784**
	Sig. (2-tailed)	.027	.041	.000
	N episodes	115	115	115
Teen reported: argued with adult	Pearson correlation	−.225*	−.171	.330**
	Sig. (2-tailed)	.015	.067	.000
	N episodes	115	115	115

* Correlation is significant at the .05 level (2-tailed); ** Correlation is significant at the .01 level (2-tailed).

Table 11.3.   Strategy for teens to use during negative events

		Unexpected change	Unmet expectation	Perseverative thinking	Forced to do activity
Used deep breathing	Pearson correlation	.295*	.404**	.314**	−.370**
	Sig. (2-tailed)	.036	.000	.004	.000
	N	57	105	77	105
Used visualization	Pearson correlation	.279*	.418**	.329**	−.431**
	Sig. (2-tailed)	.036	.000	.004	.000
	N	57	105	77	105

* Correlation is significant at the .05 level (2-tailed); ** Correlation is significant at the .01 level (2-tailed).

delivering it in a way that matched the environment maximized positive outcomes. Overall, individuals who participated at Aspire or at schools with Aspire consultation showed an increase in the skill set of SEI and a decrease in "meltdowns."

By combining technology with the *Science of Me* curriculum, Aspire and the participating schools saw demonstrable promise teaching individuals diagnosed with ASD or other social-cognitive challenges such as self-awareness, SEI, and self-regulation. The use of technology enhanced interest, participation, and understanding of psychophysiological states, self-awareness, self-regulation, and SEI. The behavioral data viewed and interpreted by participants themselves and others contributed greatly to this learning. The teens and preteens made links between their internal thinking and their physiological signs of stress and were willing to engage in stress management. Knowledge of the ASD perspective was expanded through the use of qualitative SymTrend visual representational data, stress management technology, and the *Science of Me* curriculum.

Future Directions

These promising results are based on clinical and teaching implementation of the curriculum, not a formal research trial. This chapter highlighted many specific research projects that could be conducted with students with and without ASD utilizing the HeartMath emWave Desktop stress reduction and other technologies, the *Science of Me* and other curricula, and SymTrend or other self-monitoring technologies. To our knowledge, at this time there is only one research paper on this topic, a dissertation studying the emWave and students with ASD (Aguinaga, 2006). Aguinaga (2006) studied the relationship between on-task behavior and biofeedback; of her three subjects, two showed very positive results. A larger study investigating the potential efficacy of the HeartMath emWave technology and the specific techniques for improving SEI, self-awareness, and self-regulation in individuals diagnosed with ASD described in this chapter should be explored. Further studies comparing individuals diagnosed with ASD using SymTrend technology versus data collection and paper-and-pencil analysis could also be explored. The use of SymTrend improved interest and participation in self-reporting in the studies presented in this chapter. Research conducted by Levine and colleagues using SymTrend for social skills, executive functioning, and emotion regulation is described in Chapter 12.

A number of broader research questions remain: Will instructing individuals with ASD in stress management or mindfulness techniques improve overall emotion regulation and SEI? Would linking ANS data with SymTrend provide richer data to compare subjective and objective impressions? How would the use of videotaping enhance the outcomes? Will persons diagnosed with ASD prefer specific stress management techniques over others? Which others? Ultimately, we believe that technology is an important teaching tool for individuals diagnosed with ASD and can greatly enhance learning and participation when used purposefully.

REFERENCES

Aguinaga, N. (2006). An investigation of the effectiveness of computer-assisted biofeedback for students diagnosed as having autism spectrum disorder: The relationship between the use of computer assisted biofeedback and on-task behavior. Retrieved from http://www.heart math.org/research

Allen, N.B., Chambers, R., & Knight, W. (2006). Mindfulness-based psychotherapies: A review of conceptual foundations, empirical evidence and practical considerations. *Australian and New Zealand Journal of Psychiatry, 40,* 285–294.

American Psychiatric Association (APA). (1994). *Diagnostic and statistical manual of mental disorders, fourth edition (DSM-IV).* Washington, D.C.: Author.

Amon, K.L., & Campbell, A. (2008). Can children with AD/HD learn relaxation and breathing techniques through biofeedback video games? *Australian Journal of Educational & Developmental Psychology, 8,* 72–84.

Appelhans, B.M., & Luecken, L.J. (2006). Heart rate as an index of regulated emotional responding. *Review of General Psychology, 10*(3), 229–240.

Armstrong, T. (2009). *Multiple intelligences in the classroom* (3rd ed.). Alexandria, VA: ASCD.

Armstrong, T. (2010). *The power of neurodiversity: Unleashing the advantages of your differently wired brain.* Philadelphia, PA: Da Capo Press.

Attwood, T. (2008). *The complete guide to Asperger's syndrome.* London, England: Jessica Kingsley.

Baron, M.G., Groden, J., Groden, G., & Lipsitt, L. (2006). *Stress and coping in autism.* London, England: Oxford University Press.

Baron-Cohen, S. (1995). *Mindblindness: An essay of autism and theory of mind.* London, England: Bradford.

Baron-Cohen, S. (2002). The extreme male brain theory of autism. *Trends in Cognitive Sciences, 6,* 248–254.

Beauchaine, T. (2001). Vagal tone, development and Gray's motivational theory: Toward an integrated model of autonomic nervous system functioning in psychopathology. *Developmental Psychopathology, 13*(2), 183–214.

Berthoz, S., & Hill, E.L. (2005). The validity of using self-reports to assess emotion regulation abilities in adults with autism spectrum disorder. *European Psychiatry, 20,* 291–298.

Bölte, S., Golan, O., Goodwin, M.S., & Zwaigenbaum, L. (2010). What can innovative technologies do for autism spectrum disorders? *Autism, 14*(3), 155–159.

Bradley, R.T., McCraty, R., Atkinson, M., & Tomasino, D. (2010). Emotion self-regulation, psychophysiological coherence, and test anxiety: Results from an experiment using electrophysiological measures. *Association of Applied Psychophysiological Biofeedback 35*(4), 261–283.

Cannon, L., Kenworthy, L., Alexander, K.C., Werner, M.A., Anthony, L.G., & Robinson, J.E. (2011). *Unstuck and on target!: An executive functioning curriculum to improve flexibility for children with autism spectrum disorders* (Research ed.). Baltimore, MD: Paul H. Brookes Publishing Co.

CASEL. (2003). Safe and sound: An educational leader's guide to evidence-based social and emotional learning (SEL) programs. Retrieved from http://www.casel. org/publications/safe-and-sound-an-educational-leaders-guide-to-evidence-based-sel-programs

CASEL. (2012). What is social and emotional learning (SEL)? Retrieved from http:// www.casel.org/why-it-matters/what-is-sel

Centers for Disease Control. (2012). Autism and Developmental Disabilities

Monitoring (ADDM) Network. http://www.cdc.gov/ncbddd/autism/addm.html

Cooper, P. (2007). Are some children unteachable? An approach to social, emotional, and behavioral difficulties. In R. Cigman (Ed.), *Included or excluded: The challenge of mainstream for some SEN children* (158–169). Abingdon, England: Routledge.

Damasio, H., Grabowski, T., Frank, R., Galaburda, A.M., & Damasio, A.R. (1994). The return of Phineas Gage: Clues about the brain from the skull of a famous patient. *Science, 264,* 1102–1105.

de Bruin, E.I., Ferdinand, R.F., Meester, S., de Nijs, P.F.A., & Verheij, F. (2007). High rates of psychiatric co-morbidity in PDD-NOS. *Journal of Autism Developmental Disorders, 37,* 877–886.

Dickerson, S.S., & Kemeny, M.E. (2004). Acute stressors and cortisol responses: A theoretical integration and synthesis of laboratory research. *Psychological Bulletin 130(3),* 355–391.

Durlak, J.A., Weissberg, R.P., Dymnicki, A.B., Taylor, R.D., & Schellinger, K.B. (2011). The impact of students' social and emotional learning: A meta-analysis of school-based universal interventions. *Child Development, 82(1),* 405–432.

Fein, D., Lucci, D., Braverman, M., & Waterhouse, L. (1992). Comprehension of affect in context on children with pervasive developmental disorders. *Journal of Child Psychology and Psychiatry, 33(7),* 1157–1167.

Fonagy, P., & Target, M. (2002). Early intervention and the development of self-regulation. *Psychoanalytic Inquiry, 22,* 307–335.

Frith, U. (2001). Mind blindness and the brain in autism. *Neuron, 32(6),* 969–979.

Frith, U. (2003). *Autism: Explaining the enigma* (2nd ed.). Oxford, England: Blackwell.

Gardner, H. (2011). *Frames of mind: The theory of multiple intelligences.* New York, NY: Basic Books.

Gaus, V.L. (2007). *Cognitive-behavioral therapy for adult Asperger syndrome.* New York, NY: Guilford Press.

Goleman, D. (1995). *Emotional intelligence.* New York, NY: Bantam Books.

Goleman, D. (2006). *Social intelligence: The new science of human relationships.* New York, NY: Bantam Books.

Goodwin, M.S., Groden, J., Velicer, W.F., Lipsitt, L.P., Baron, M.G., Hofmann, S.G., & Groden, G. (2006). Cardiovascular arousal in individuals with autism. *Focus on Autism and Other Developmental Disabilities, 21,* 100–123.

Greenberg, M.T., Weissberg, R.P., O'Brien, M.U., Zins, J.E., Fredericks, L., Resnick, H., & Elias, M.J. (2003). Enhancing school-based prevention and youth development through coordinated social, emotional, and academic learning. *American Psychologist, 58(6–7),* 466–474.

Groden, J., Kantor, A., Woodard, C.R., & Lipsitt, L. (2011). *How everyone on the autism spectrum, young and old, can...become resilient, be more optimistic, enjoy humor, be kind, and increase self-efficacy: A positive psychology approach.* Philadelphia, PA: Jessica Kinsley.

Grossman, P., Nieman, L., Schmidt, S., & Walach, H. (2004). Mindfulness-based stress reduction and health benefits: A meta-analysis. *Journal of Psychosomatic Research, 57,* 35–43.

Hanson, R. (2009). *Buddha's brain: The practical neuroscience of happiness, love and wisdom.* Oakland, CA: New Harbinger.

Happé, F. (1994). *Autism: An introduction to psychological theory.* Cambridge, MA: Harvard University Press.

HeartMath. (2002). *TestEdge Grades 6–8 and TestEdge Grades 9–12.* Boulder Creek, CA: Institute of HeartMath.

HeartMath. (2006). *The inside story booklet: Understanding the power of feelings.* Boulder Creek, CA: Institute of HeartMath.

Henry, D.A., Wheeler, T., & Sava, D.I. (2004). *Sensory integration tools for teens: Strategies to promote sensory processing.* Youngtown, AZ: Henry OT Services.

Higgins, K.K., Koch, L.C., Boughfman, E.M., & Vierstra, C. (2008). School-to-work transition and Asperger syndrome. *Work, 31,* 291–298.

Higgins, K., & Boone, R. (1996). Creating individualized computer-assisted instruction for students with autism using multimedia authoring software. *Focus on Autism and Developmental Disabilities, 11(2),* 69–78.

Hirstein, W., Iversen, P., & Ramachandran, V.S. (2001). Autonomic responses of autistic children to people and objects. *Proceedings Royal Society London B, 268,* 1883–1888.

Hölzel, B.K., Carmody, J., Vangel, M., Congleton, C., Yerramsetti, S.M., Gard, T., & Lazar, S.W. (2011). Mindfulness practice leads to increases in regional brain gray matter density. *Psychiatry Research: Neuroimaging, 191(1),* 36–43.

Hurley, R.S., Losh, M., Parlier, M., Reznick, J.S., & Piven, J. (2007). The broad autism phenotype questionnaire. *Journal of Autism and Developmental Disorders, 37*(9), 1679–1690.

Jackson, K., Skirrow, P., & Hare, D.J. (2012). Asperger through the looking glass: An explanatory study of self-understanding in people with Asperger's syndrome. *Journal of Autism and Developmental Disorders, 42*, 697–706.

Kabat-Zinn, J. (1982). An out-patient program in behavioral medicine for chronic pain patients based on the practice of mindfulness meditation: Theoretical considerations and preliminary results. *General Hospital Psychiatry, 4*, 33–47.

Kabat-Zinn, J. (1990). *Full catastrophe living: Using wisdom of your body and mind to face stress, pain and illness.* New York, NY: Bantam Dell.

King, N., Hamilton, D., & Ollendick, T. (1994). *Children's phobias: A behavioral perspective.* New York, NY: Wiley.

Kuypers, L.M. (2011). *Zones of regulation: A curriculum designed to foster self-regulation and emotional control.* San Jose, CA: Think Social.

Lantieri, L., & Goleman, D. (2008). *Building emotional intelligence: Techniques to cultivate inner strength in children.* Boulder: CO: Sounds True.

Lantieri, L., & Patti, J. (1996). *Waging peace in our schools.* Boston, MA: Beacon Press.

Laugeson, E.A., Frankel, F., Gantman, A., Dillon, A.R., & Mogil, C. (2012). Evidence-based social skills training for adolescents with autism spectrum disorders: The UCLA PEERS program. *Journal of Autism Developmental Disorders, 42*(6), 1025–1036.

Ledoux, J. (2002). *The synaptic self: How our brains become who we are.* New York, NY: Penguin.

Levine, M. (1993). *All kinds of minds: A young student's book about learning abilities and learning disorders.* Cambridge, MA: Educator's Publishers Service.

Leyfer, O.T., Folstein, S.E., Bacalman, S., Davis, N.O., Dinh, E., Morgan, J.,... Lainhart, J.E. (2006). Comorbid psychiatric disorders in children with autism: Interview development and rates of disorders. *Journal of Autism Developmental Disorders, 36*, 849–861.

Lloyd, A., Brett, D., & Wesnes, K. (2010). Coherence training in children with attention-deficit-hyperactivity disorder: Cognitive functions and behavioral changes. *Alternative Therapies in Health and Medicine, 16*(4), 34–42.

Lucci, D., & McLeod, D.S. (2008). *Pilot use of PDA technology to teach teens with ASD & NLD about flexibility, feelings, and sensory states at a therapeutic summer day camp.* Poster presented at the International Meeting for Autism Research, London, England.

Lucci, D., McLeod, D.S., & Challen-Wittmer, K. (2010). *Male teens with Asperger's syndrome and NLD learn about stress and its physiological signs.* Poster presented at the International Meeting for Autism Research, Philadelphia, PA.

McCarthy, B. (1990). Using the 4MAT system to bring learning styles to schools. *Educational Leadership, 48*, 31–36.

McCraty, R. (2005). Enhancing emotional, social, and academic learning with heart rhythm coherence feedback. *Biofeedback, 33*(4), 130–134.

McLeod, D.S., & Lucci, D. (2009). *PDA technology to improve self-awareness in teens with ASD.* Poster presented at International Meeting for Autism Research, Chicago, IL.

McLeod, D.S., Lucci, D., & Challen-Wittmer, K. (2010). *Asperger male teens' use of relaxation strategies and selection preferences: Which strategies for which stressors.* Poster presented at the International Meeting for Autism Research, Philadelphia, PA.

Meiklejohn, J., Phillips, C., Freedman, M.L., Griffin, M.L., Biegel, G., Roach, A.,...Pinger, L. (2012, March). Integrating mindfulness training into K–12 education: Fostering resilience of teachers and students. *Mindfulness* [Online publication].

Meyer, J.A., & Minshew, N.J. (2002). An update on neurocognitive profiles in Asperger syndrome and high-functioning autism. *Focus on Autism and Other Developmental Disabilities, 17*(3), 152–160.

Mitchell, C. (2009). *Asperger's syndrome and mindfulness: Taking refuge in the Buddha.* Philadelphia, PA: Jessica Kingsley.

Moore, D. (1998). Computers and people with autism/Asperger syndrome. *Communication* [magazine of the National Autism Society], Summer, 20–21.

Myers, I.B., McCaulley, M.H., Quenk, N.L., & Hammer, A.L. (1998). *MBTI manual: A guide to the development and use of the Myers-Briggs Type Indicator* (3rd ed.).

Palo Alto, CA: Consulting Psychologists Press.

Myles, B.S., & Southwick, J. (1999). *Asperger syndrome and difficult moments*. Shawnee Mission, KS: Autism Asperger.

Payton, J., Weissberg, R.P., Durlak, J.A., Dymnicki, A.B., Taylor, R.D., Schellinger, K.B., & Pachan, M. (2008). *The positive impact of social and emotional learning for kindergarten to eighth-grade students: Findings from three scientific reviews*. Chicago, IL: Collaborative for Academic, Social, and Emotional Learning.

Porges, S.W. (1992). Vagal tone: A physiological marker of stress vulnerability. *Pediatrics, 90*(3, Pt. 2), 498–504.

Samson, F., Mottron, L., Soulières, I., & Zeffiro, T.A. (2012). Enhanced visual functioning in autism: An ALE meta-analysis. *Human Brain Mapping, 33*, 1553–1581.

Segal, Z.V., Williams, J.M.G., & Teasdale, J.D. (2002). *Mindfulness-based cognitive therapy for depression: A new approach to preventing relapse*. New York, NY: Guilford Press.

Silver, M., & Oakes, P. (2001). Evaluation of a new computer intervention to teach people with autism or Asperger syndrome to recognize and predict emotions in others. *Autism, 5*(3), 299–316.

Siegel, D. (2007). *The mindful brain: Reflection and attunement in the cultivation of well-being*. New York, NY: Norton.

Singh, N.N., Lancioni, G.E., Singh, A.D.A., Winton, A.S.W., Singh, A.N.A., & Singh, J. (2011). Adolescents with Asperger's syndrome can use a mindfulness-based strategy to control their aggressive behavior. *Research in Autism Spectrum Disorders, 5*(3), 1103–1109.

Snyder, A.W., & Mitchell, D.J. (1999). Is integer arithmetic fundamental to mental processing? The mind's secret arithmetic. *Proceedings of the Royal Society B: Biological Sciences, 266*, 587–592.

Soulières, I., Dawson, M., Gernsbacher, M.A., & Mottron, L. (2011, September). The level and nature of autistic intelligence II: What about Asperger syndrome? *PLoS One. 6*, 1.

Spek, A.A., van Ham, N.C., & Nykliček, I. (2012). Mindfulness-based therapy in adults with autism spectrum disorder: A randomized controlled trial. *Research in Developmental Disabilities, 34*(1), 246–253.

Spencer, L.M., Jr., & Spencer, S. (1993). *Competence at work: Models for superior performance*. New York, NY: Wiley.

Sroufe, L.A. (1996). *Emotional development: The organization of emotional life in the early years*. New York, NY: Cambridge University Press.

Wilbarger, P., & Wilbarger, J.L. (1991). *Sensory defensiveness in children aged 2–12*. Denver, CO: Avanti Educational Programs.

Williams, M.S., & Shellenberger, S. (1994). *How does your engine run? A leader's guide to the Alert Program for self-regulation*. Albuquerque, NM: Therapy Works.

Winner, M.G. (2000). *Inside out: What makes a person with a social cognitive deficit tick?* San Jose, CA: Think Social.

Winner, M.G. (2005). *Think social! A social thinking curriculum for school-age students*. San Jose, CA: Think Social.

Winner, M.G. (2007). *Thinking about you thinking about me* (2nd ed.). San Jose, CA: Think Social.

Zins, J.E., Weissberg, R.P., Wang, M.C., & Walberg, H.J. (Eds.). (2004). *Building academic success on social and emotional learning: What does the research say?* New York, NY: Teachers College Press.

Data-Collection Tools

Matthew S. Goodwin

■ ■

Educational and other intervention programs are typically embedded in a larger individualized education program (IEP) that specifies individualized objectives and interventions to address specific challenges a child faces, and contain criteria for measuring how closely an intervention reached its targeted objectives. Thus, objective data are a critical component to the successful establishment and evaluation of an IEP. In this section, two chapters describe myriad innovative technologies being co-opted or developed specifically for use as data collection tools in classrooms and other natural environments where children with autism spectrum disorder (ASD) often reside and receive support.

The first chapter, "No More Clipboards! Mobile Electronic Solutions for Data Collection, Behavior Analysis, Program Evaluation, and Self-Management Interventions," by Minna Levine, reviews a host of methodological problems associated with traditional data collection tools used for data management, behavior analysis, and intervention optimization. Levine also details how a range of commercially available digital technologies can overcome these methodological problems by facilitating more efficient and effective data collection forms, observational recordings, charting to monitor progress and analyze patterns, and communication among teams who coordinate support. In addition to data collection, the chapter suggests, mobile recording of behavior can serve as a self-management intervention to monitor and improve emotion self-regulation, social pragmatics, and executive functioning. The chapter ends with a thoughtful discussion of the challenges associated with using mobile technologies and proposed solutions.

The second chapter, "Tools to Support Simplified Capture of Activities in Natural Environments," by Gregory D. Abowd, Julie A. Kientz, Gillian R. Hayes, Rosa I.

Arriaga, and Nazneen describes a number of multimodal technology platforms developed at the Georgia Institute of Technology to facilitate innovative educational and behavioral data collection in classroom and home environments. The first platform, Abaris, is a data capture and access system for recording instructional data during structured discrete-trial training sessions involving an educator and a student. The second platform, CareLog, is a selective archiving tool to enhance functional behavioral assessments in school settings. The third platform, CRAFT, is similar to CareLog but designed specifically for use in home settings. The fourth platform, smartCapture, still under development, is intended to be a simplified mobile data capture solution that enables parents to more easily collect and share samples of their child's behaviors in the home with remote assistance from clinicians and teachers. The fifth and final platform, comprising KidCam and Baby Steps, also under development, is a semimobile system designed to help parents collect and share with pediatricians information on their child's developmental progress. In addition to providing qualitative and quantitative evaluations of these various systems, including suggestions for future research, the authors offer a thoughtful list of design recommendations and privacy issues to be considered when developing behavior archiving and access technologies.

Taken together, this section highlights a number of commercially available and emerging technologies for the collection of a variety of educational and clinically relevant data from children with ASD in classroom, home, and community settings.

No More Clipboards! Mobile Electronic Solutions for Data Collection, Behavior Analysis, and Self-Management Interventions

■ ■

Minna Levine

An intervention for a child with autism spectrum disorder (ASD) is typically part of a larger individualized education program (IEP) that contains several child-specific objectives with corresponding strategies for meeting those objectives. The objectives commonly involve social pragmatics, emotion regulation, executive functioning, communication, self-care, and academics (Massachusetts Department of Education, 2001). The IEP also contains measurable criteria for determining whether interventions have been successful in enabling the child to reach the targeted objectives.

Unfortunately, translating objectives into individualized interventions that demonstrably achieve them is a difficult task. This intervention individualization produces methodological challenges for 1) behavioral analysis and outcome measurement and 2) optimizing the intervention itself. When paper is the medium for behavior analysis and outcome measurement, methodological challenges can be daunting. Inefficiencies abound that can compromise intervention effectiveness, slowing student progress.

This chapter describes how to improve interventions by incorporating the power of mobile electronic technologies. The first section describes the advantages of using

The author is the president of the company that produced SymTrend, a product mentioned in the text. She frequently lectures on the subject of data collection software, without indicating preference for her product. The author thanks the developers of eCOVE, Catalyst, and ABC Data Pro, for sharing information about the extensive feature set of their products, beyond what was available on their web sites and thanks the developers of AutismTrack and Autism Tracker Pro for assistance with screen shots. The author also wishes to acknowledge the National Institute of Mental Health that funded three research and development projects for SymTrend.

mobile technology for behavior analysis and outcomes measurement; it includes an outline of critical features of mobile applications for behavior analysis, outcomes measurement, and data management. The second section describes uses of mobile technology by the target student as a self-management intervention. The third and final section describes the drawbacks of using mobile technologies for both applications.

ADVANTAGES OF MOBILE TECHNOLOGY FOR ANALYSIS AND OUTCOMES MEASUREMENT

The management of IEP-related behavioral data proceeds in four steps as team members 1) create forms for behavioral data collection and charting; 2) record observations on the data collection forms; 3) display the data in charts to monitor progress, analyze patterns, and determine the next intervention step; and 4) communicate impressions of the charted progress and ongoing issues to the team. Although almost all team members do each step at least quarterly, the degree of their involvement in each of these four steps varies considerably. This section describes how, with currently available handheld technology, substantial increases in accuracy and efficiency may be gained at each step.

Mobile technology vendors claim that greater efficiency and accuracy, and hence cost savings, can ultimately be achieved in each of these four categories through their products. Although their claims make intuitive sense, little evidence in support of these claims of superior accuracy and efficiency for mobile technologies has been published in general or for particular professional disciplines. The advantages of the features included below have not been substantiated in terms of comparisons of time using paper and pencil versus technology or comparisons of the time to complete the step with one product versus another, but these advantages in terms of information and insights gained have prima facie support. Versatility, flexibility, and breadth and depth of features for each of the four areas are typically advantageous for groups with potential users of varying professions, measurement styles, and technical expertise. As randomized control trials are conducted in the next few years, the science is likely to bear this out.

Creating Data Collection Forms

Data collection forms, whether on paper or in an electronic medium, that are used in intervention individualization and evaluation require 1) indication of the specifics of the student's task behavior(s) to be observed and recorded, 2) task goals, and 3) specifics of the teacher's intervention. Additional information about the context in which the intervention occurs is optional but helpful in training for and assessing generalization of the skill. Once a task is mastered, the data collection form must be altered to accommodate a new level of difficulty or the switch to a new task. Form individualization must specify the instructions used to explain and start the task (e.g., presentation sequence, prompt level), the use of foreground and contextual stimuli (e.g., targets and distractors), the behavioral measure(s) to record (e.g., accuracy, frequency, prompt required), the response to inappropriate behavior (e.g., ignore, warnings, time out), and so on. Data collection forms vary in several stylistic ways: the use of +/- scoring, visual analog scales, choices to circle, spaces for numeric scores, and summary calculations. In addition, forms vary regarding how much narrative, if any, they permit. These variations allow for different scoring methods depending on the purpose at hand, enabling versatility in data collection and charting for documenting performance on an IEP.

Discrete Trial Training   Discrete trial training most often uses a percent correct score for a fixed number of trials (e.g., 10 trials) and prompt level (e.g., verbal, manual) compiled under different conditions (e.g., prompt and reinforcement levels). Figure 12.1A shows an example of a paper form for this type of data collection. Figure 12.1B shows the screen of the SymTrials iPad application (app) with pull-down menus for selecting the program, discriminative stimulus, target, step, and prompt level. The response is scored by tapping one of the four response buttons for each of the 10 trials (SymTrend, 2012b). Some behavior analysts just conduct one trial and score it correct or incorrect.

Interval Recording   Interval recording involves observing behavior during a specified time interval. Observers record whether a behavior is evident throughout an interval (whole interval), at some point during the interval (partial), or at the end of the interval (momentary sampling), or they record the frequency or duration

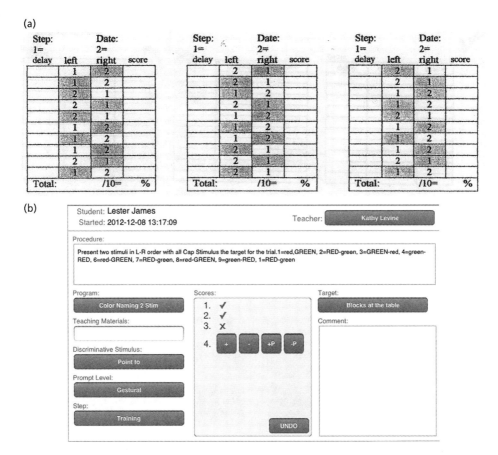

Figure 12.1. (a) Discrete trial training paper-based observation form. Observers grade performance with + or - and compute the percent correct, which is then transcribed to a chart. (b) SymTrend Trials data collection screen for the same protocol.

of the behavior during that interval. The type of scoring used dictates the type of form required: 1) a checklist or +/– to be circled to indicate whether or not the behavior was present, 2) a space for a number retrieved from a clicker (a device that an observer presses each time a behavior occurs that tallies the clicks) or a duration from a stopwatch, and 3) a tick mark in a box are just some of the variations. Figure 12.2A displays two types of paper forms for this type of recording. Figure 12.2B displays how similar forms look in two apps. On the left is the screen from eCOVE (eCOVE, 2012) and on the right is the screen from Autism Tracker Pro (Track & Share Apps, 2012).

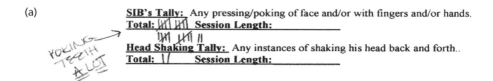

Figure 12.2. (a) Two paper-based observation forms for interval recording. Each time a behavior occurs, the observer makes a tick mark; the marks are then counted and transcribed to a chart. (b) eCOVE (left) and Autism Tracker Pro (right) iPhone app screens for the second protocol. The user just taps the behavior each time it occurs. The software tallies the taps and automatically plots on the device or online. (Images courtesy of eCOVE Software and Track & Share Apps.)

Task Analysis Task analysis involves breaking down a targeted task into a sequence of all the steps required and then recording which steps are completed independently or with a prompt. Professionals typically teach a child one step of a sequence at a time. Sometimes training starts at the beginning of the sequence (forward chaining), and sometimes at the last step, working backward (backward chaining). Sometimes the whole sequence is completed each session and sometimes only one step each practice session. Each step is graded in terms of accuracy and prompt level required. Figure 12.3A displays a sample paper form for grading a child putting on his pants. Figure 12.3B displays a screen from SymTrend for grading one of the steps. A variety of graphic and tabular methods are available for displaying the information for all steps. Figure 12.3C displays the performance on all steps of each trip to the bathroom on a given day using SymTrend's tabular format. This format permits the professional viewer to monitor progress over time for all steps at once. Figure 12.3D is a chart from Catalyst (Compass Solutions for Autism, 2012) for a similar task analysis protocol, showing the percentage of all steps done correctly and the percentage of days each step was completed.

ABC Recording Management of behavior is easier if one knows what triggers or diminishes the behavior. Professionals record the so-called ABCs of the behavior: antecedents, behaviors, and consequences. Getting information about antecedents (i.e., what happened before the behavior occurred) gives us clues as to what may have triggered it. Information about consequences (i.e., what happened after the behavior) sheds light on whether there is something rewarding about the behavior that keeps the child doing it. Many handheld apps enable an observer to record the ABCs as they happen or right after they occur. Figure 12.4 displays ABC recording screens from ABC Data Pro (CBTAonline, 2012) and SymTrend, respectively. The two products differ in how the ABC information is entered and in the ability to modify choices in the moment. Charts for both packages must be created online; SymTrend has more than one type of display for these data. SymTrend provides a wide range of graphical displays related to these data on its app-related web site. ABC Data Pro (not pictured) also enables creating an ABC matrix.

Many professionals do not do ABC recording on a regular basis; it is typically conducted only as needed, when progress is stalled and/or when challenging behaviors arise. Thus, in most products, ABC recording is done in a separate module from other data recording. Forms for interval recording, task analysis, and discrete trial training data collection often do not have fields for entering information about the context in which the teaching or observations occurred. For some products, the antecedents and consequences may need to be either described in comments or recorded as separate behaviors or events and then linked by the proximity of timing.

Recording Observations

Professionals who work with children with ASD have traditionally used paper-and-pencil methods to record information about behaviors and interventions, using the forms described above. They then summarize the data on the form, for example, by calculating a performance score such as frequency of behavior or percent correct (data reduction), and transcribe that score to a paper graph or table or enter it into computer software for charting (e.g., into an Excel spreadsheet for graphing). Data reduction and transcription takes time and may therefore contribute to the

(a)

+	Correct/unprompted	V	Verbal
GM	Gesture/model	P	Physically Prompted (shaped)

Step	Component Skill	Date	Date	Date	Date	Date	Date	Date
1	Grab waist of pants							
2	Pull pants down							
3	Sit down							
4	Cross midline and grab opposite pant leg							
5	Hold ankle of pants and pull leg out							
6	Cross midline and grab ankle of other pant leg							
7	Hold ankle of pants and pull leg out							

(b)

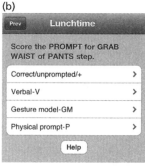

(c)

Date	Prompt Level Grab Waist of Pants Step	Prompt Level Pull Pants Down Step	Prompt Level for Sit Down Step	Prompt Level for Cross Midline/Grab Other Leg Step	Prompt Level for Hold Ankle of Pants/Pull Leg Out Step	Prompt Level for Cross Midline/Grab Ankle Other Pant Leg Step	Prompt Level for Hold Ankle of Pants/Pull 2nd Leg Out Step
2011-01-10 10:00 Mon	Physical prompt-P (1)	Physical prompt-P (1)	Physical prompt-P (1)	Physical prompt-P (1)	Physical prompt-P (1)	Physical prompt-P (1)	Physical prompt-P (1)
2011-01-10 14:30 Mon	Physical prompt-P (1)	Physical prompt-P (1)	Physical prompt-P (1)	Physical prompt-P (1)	Physical prompt-P (1)	Gesture model-GM (2)	Gesture model-GM (2)

(d)

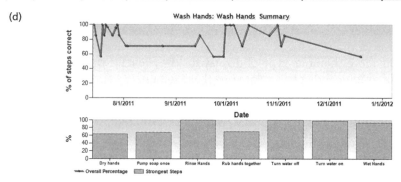

Figure 12.3. (a) Paper-based observation form for task analysis of taking off pants. The user grades each step with a letter or +. The number of + marks is tallied. (b) One of the series of SymTrend iPhone app screens for the same protocol, for someone grading each step. (c) One type of SymTrend table of data collected with this protocol. (d) Chart from Catalyst for a similar task analysis protocol (see text). (Catalyst image courtesy of Data-Finch Technologies.)

cost of special education interventions. Measurement of the contribution of this cost to overall special education is difficult because the time professionals spend doing data reduction and transcription differs. For some, an hour with the child includes therapy and data management, so there is no extra financial cost, but the child's actual therapy time is reduced by the time the professional spends on data management. For many professionals in schools who are salaried, data management takes place after hours during uncompensated time. For these professionals, the

(a)

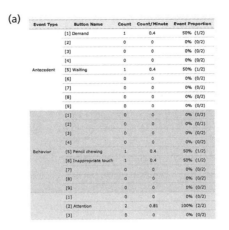

Event Type	Button Name	Count	Count/Minute	Event Proportion
	[1] Demand	1	0.4	50% (1/2)
	[2]	0	0	0% (0/2)
	[3]	0	0	0% (0/2)
	[4]	0	0	0% (0/2)
Antecedent	[5] Waiting	1	0.4	50% (1/2)
	[6]	0	0	0% (0/2)
	[7]	0	0	0% (0/2)
	[8]	0	0	0% (0/2)
	[9]	0	0	0% (0/2)
	[1]	0	0	0% (0/2)
	[2]	0	0	0% (0/2)
	[3]	0	0	0% (0/2)
	[4]	0	0	0% (0/2)
Behavior	[5] Pencil chewing	1	0.4	50% (1/2)
	[6] Inappropriate touch	1	0.4	50% (1/2)
	[7]	0	0	0% (0/2)
	[8]	0	0	0% (0/2)
	[9]	0	0	0% (0/2)
	[1]	0	0	0% (0/2)
	[2] Attention	2	0.81	100% (2/2)
	[3]	0	0	0% (0/2)

(b)

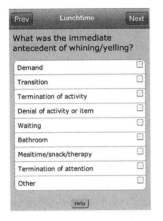

A-B-Cs of 9:30 - 10:30 Whining/Yelling [2010-10-12 to 2011-01-24]

Date	Antecedents for Whining/Yelling at School	Whining/Yelling Behaviors - 9:30-10:30 (Times)	Consequences for Whining/Yelling at School
2010-10-12 06:00 Tue	Waiting	1	Behavior plan implemented
2010-10-12 10:00 Tue	Other Transition Waiting	3	Behavior plan implemented
2010-10-13 11:45 Wed	Demand	4	Behavior plan implemented Maintained demand
2010-10-14 10:00 Thu	Other Waiting		Behavior plan implemented

Figure 12.4. Two apps for electronic antecedent, behavior, consequence (ABC) recording and charting. The figure presents one screen and one type of chart for the data entered. (a) ABC Data Pro. (b) SymTrend. (ABC Data Pro image courtesy of CBTAonline.)

cost is more limited data analysis and/or burnout (personal communications from the author's study participants, 2009).

One pilot study seeking to quantify potential time savings by using software for data recording rather than paper forms was conducted by Compass Solutions for Autism (2011) at the Keystone Center for Children with Autism in Alpharetta, Georgia. The time savings with most of the software mentioned here should be comparable. Students at Keystone receive 30 hours per week of intensive behavioral intervention. Before using Catalyst, the Board-Certified Behavior Analyst (BCBA) at Keystone spent an average of just over 1 hour per week per student, reentering and graphing hand-recorded data. Like the other software mentioned in this chapter, Catalyst automatically uploads student data to the portal and graphs the data according to user inputs, so that time was completely eliminated. The BCBA is also responsible for reviewing and analyzing each student's data at Keystone. Using Catalyst, this time was reduced from approximately 2.0 hours per week per student to just over 30 minutes. An analysis of accuracy also revealed that staff made an average of 15.7 errors per student per week when transcribing data, including not "opening" or "mastering" targets in a timely manner. Graphing errors, including premature, overdue, or otherwise incorrect mastery, occurred at a rate of approximately 3.3 errors per student per week. Using Catalyst, these errors were eliminated entirely. Finally, each BCBA at Keystone is responsible for generating data-based progress reports for each student. Before deploying Catalyst, these reports took an average of 4 hours per student per month to generate. Using Catalyst, Keystone was able to reduce this average to approximately 45 minutes per student per month.

Products differ in the versatility of their data collection features beyond the differences in types of data collection forms outlined above. Hardware options include data entry on the internet; on a handheld, portable tablet or phone (users will need to check which Apple, Android, and/or Windows mobile devices can run each module); or with a desktop or laptop computer. The applications differ in terms of how many versions of the software are available and in terms of which functions (data collection, charting, communication) are provided on each platform. Many vendors are working on increasing the range of options for data collection, so offerings on their web sites may have changed since this publication. Also variable is whether the handheld app needs constant connectivity to the internet during data collection or just for synching batches of data that have been saved during data collection.

Charting to Monitor Progress and Analyze Patterns

Progress charts are pictures of progress. The most commonly used chart types include line graphs (e.g., event magnitudes for frequencies plotted over time), bar or column charts (e.g., frequencies of different behaviors), and scatter plots (e.g., x–y graphs showing the values of two measures at a given time). Charts surpass words for ease and accuracy of communication. However, when this ease and accuracy is pursued by creating handmade paper charts, the time costs can be large. Because of these production costs, only a summary chart is typically produced and behavior scores are aggregated across a variety of intervention subtasks and conditions.

Behavioral charting can have greater utility than just providing a summarization of intervention outcomes. Charting behaviors can facilitate exploratory analysis of how behavior is influenced: Behavior can be depicted as a function of several features of the intervention and context. An exploratory chart is several graphs in one; thus, the time to make these charts increases exponentially as the number of features of an intervention and context increases. Consequently, such charts are rarely created and the information and insights are thus lost.

Charting Features   Products differ in their versatility in charting types and how the charts are generated. Some products have no output on the device and require synching of data to a web site where charts are generated. Having web-based graphics typically means that the charts are of a professional quality for copying and inserting into IEP reports and can be saved as pdf documents. Some allow annotation and insertion of condition lines (see Figure 12.5). Others have some limited reporting of summary data on the mobile device. Users should review the software's output versatility on the mobile device and web site. Some products produce the graphic directly with their software; others require export of the data into a

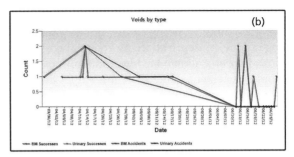

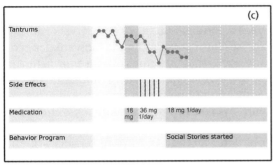

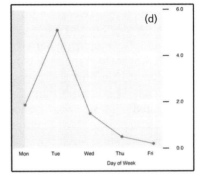

Figure 12.5. Variety of charting options in different apps. (a) Behavior frequency chart from AutismTrack (HandholdAdaptive, 2012) that is displayed on the device. (b) Voiding frequency data charted on DataFinch Technologies web site. (c) Behavior frequency data charted on SymTrend web site, with intervention changes reflected in background color changes. (d) Behavior frequency charted by day of the week on SymTrend web site, to see patterns not easily visible in day-to-day charts. (AutismTrack image courtesy of HandHold Adaptive. Catalyst image courtesy of DataFinch Technologies.)

spreadsheet for graphing. Other varied features include setting up custom reports and templates for later use and filtering by conditions or time.

Behavioral Data Analysis When data collection and behavioral analysis of a child's performance are done with electronic technology, a more comprehensive view of the child's abilities and an understanding of the impact of interventions are more readily available. Until now, using paper for recording and charting has meant that progress and protocols have been reevaluated less frequently, sometimes as infrequently as when preparing a quarterly progress report. Hand scoring of a paper form daily or weekly and then adding summary scores to a paper chart has been sufficient for determining when prompts or steps of multistep tasks or discrete trial training should be advanced (typically changes are made after "success" for 3 days in a row). The summary score (e.g., percent correct on labeling an object) alone is displayed in the charts. Contextual factors that likely affected performance are typically not scored, charted, examined, or discussed due to time constraints. Such oversights are unfortunate omissions because contextual factors are not only numerous but also potent. They include such influences as the impact of the success or failure of the previous task on the current task, the student's amount of sleep the night before, and the bullying on the bus. These influences may vary systematically according to the time of day or day of week, or they may produce incidental outliers, particularly bad or good days, that reveal clues to behaviors.

Mobile data collection turns these omissions into findings that can lead to insights. Since charting can be done instantaneously when electronic data recording is done, in-depth charting and analysis and assessment of the need for modifications in protocols can be done more often. By rescuing omissions and extending the available evidence, mobile technologies enable a better examination of the combinations of conditions that may optimize functioning or undermine it.

Digital behavioral recording with mobile devices may also enable a better measure of how behavior changes within a setting. Sometimes changes in behavior are subtle. Such gross measurements as "behavior occurred at least once during the interval" may hide slower improvements in self-regulation evidenced by a change in the rate of behavioral outbursts. Use of a handheld device to record as behaviors are happening can provide a picture of the ebbs and flows of self-control over time. For example, comparing behavior before a *sensory diet,* when the individual is given a period of more intense sensory stimulation such as jumping on a trampoline, to behavior after stimulation gives a view of the time course of the stimulation impact. This analysis over time can give an indication of how long the effect of a sensory diet lasted. Figure 12.6 was created with SymTrend software from a 5-minute continuous recording before and after a period of sensory stimulation. It depicts how an initial rapid reduction in stereotypy after a brief exposure to sensory stimulation was followed by a gradual return of the stereotypy in this child. From this type of observation, it is then possible to systematically test whether longer exposure, repeated brief exposures, or varied exposures to sensory diets have longer durations of effectiveness. Some software packages save a time-stamp for each tap of a behavior button, making it easy to look at the temporal pattern.

Digital behavioral recording also affords the opportunity to analyze how behavior changes as a function of the child's broader environment—something that is nearly impossible with paper-and-pencil recording and charting. It is a commonplace observation that what happens in a classroom setting is influenced by what happens outside that setting. "Outside" the classroom includes other settings at school, in the community, and at home. While this observation is a commonplace one, it is not common that information from these various settings is readily available in a common database to use as a part of a behavioral or intervention outcome analysis (as described in the section on team communication below). The utility of

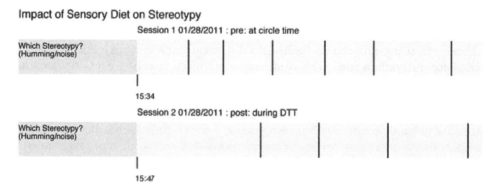

Figure 12.6. View of the time course of behavior during an observation interval on the SymTrend web site; intervention application for this type of chart is described in the text.

cross-setting data integration is that it enables a better understanding of the ways in which activities outside the classroom affect behavior in it. The integration of data into a common record provides a view of the antecedents of behavior (discussed above in the section on forms) in broader terms. One commonly used form for doing structured ABC data collection, developed by Iwata (Iwata, 2010), has space for recording both immediate antecedents (e.g., the child's having been asked to do a task) and distal antecedents (e.g., the setting of the event). With an integrated data approach, the notion of distal antecedents can be broadened even more to include the home and community and to include the child's inner arousal level and health, such as the sleep the child got the night before, the food eaten at breakfast, bowel movements, medications, and supplements, as well as activities in which the child participated prior to a training session or challenging behavior (e.g., occupational therapy, recess). Data collected when the child is in the other settings, either by the parents, professionals, or the individual, can be charted together on the same page as classroom data, making the impact of the broader environment easier to see. Each observer's data, from each context, is individually displayed on the same time line, providing a picture of the whole child.

Communicating Progress and Issues to the Team

A child with autism may see several therapists—behavioral, occupational, and speech—on the same day, in addition to special educators. Team members are often located in different buildings and thus may not meet regularly, if at all, or be able to access a colleague's records; as a result, they may have difficulty coordinating intervention changes. The time expended playing phone tag, making contacts, arranging meetings, and attending meetings is not always factored into special education costs. The therapeutic time lost not communicating progress in a timely fashion because of the delay in arranging a meeting is also not factored into assessments of intervention effectiveness. Although some of the products described in this chapter can be used to manage the care of individual children by individual clinicians or families, many of the vendors have built web portals for schools or clinical groups to enable sharing of information collected by all members of the child's team, putting everyone on the same page and enabling the integration benefits mentioned earlier.

How and what information may be shared by the team varies. Team portal features may include advanced data charting, messaging, personal health records, video storage, document management, training material, intervention program definitions, and/or web conferencing. These extra features come with a significant increase in cost per child; costs for site licenses typically vary with the number of students and staff members included.

Putting integration functionality on a portal facilitates integration, but actual use across settings does not happen automatically. As discussed in the last section of this chapter, adoption of the technology by all members of the child's team is a challenge. Whereas documentation of discrete trial training and related ABA observations often follow common formats across special education teachers and behavior analysts, data collected by occupational therapists, speech pathologists, non-ABA clinicians, and families are diverse in content, format, and frequency. These differences are not easily reconciled or cross-referenced with the rest of the team when made on paper, particularly when the data collected across disciplines do not follow consistent time lines, which is not uncommon. The same child may be scored by different disciplines using such varied measures as rating scales, checklists, number of items correct, and frequency or duration of behaviors. Digital data collection by the team may not have sufficient commonality to become integrated. Since some data may not be accommodated by all products, professionals may have to change their modus operandi to contribute to the integrated system.

MOBILE RECORDING AS A SELF-MANAGEMENT INTERVENTION

Thus far, the merits of mobile technologies have been described with regard to the roles they can play in data management, behavioral data analysis, and team communication. Mobile technologies are also a possible platform for self-management interventions with higher functioning students. Once again, the individualization that each student requires for self-monitoring, executive functioning, and self-regulation may be better met with mobile technologies than with paper. For example, a student can take a mobile device into more settings and use it unobtrusively, where in contrast, a clipboard would be cumbersome and possibly embarrassing. This section describes how mobile recording can be used with children with higher functioning ASD or attention-deficit/hyperactivity disorder (ADHD) for enhancing 1) emotion self-regulation, 2) social pragmatics guidance and monitoring, and 3) executive functioning.

Mobile Technology for Monitoring and Improving Emotion Self-Regulation

Portable electronic diaries were first used for self-monitoring and self-management in the late 1980s on Apple Newtons as part of cognitive behavior therapy (CBT) for anxiety with adults (Baer, Minichiello, Jenike, & Holland, 1988). Research conducted in the 1990s with Psion handheld computers demonstrated the effectiveness of self-monitoring in anxiety (Newman, 1999); adults needed fewer sessions of CBT for panic disorder if they used self-monitoring with a handheld device between sessions (Newman, Kennedy, Herman, & Taylor, 1997). Although this early work was not conducted with individuals on the autism spectrum, it paved the way to the use of handheld computers in the support of teens with ASD and emotion self-regulation issues, including anxiety comorbidity. A pilot study was conducted using a similar technology for CBT with 19 teens with ASD and anxiety (Blakeley-Smith et al., 2010); self-monitoring by the participants was brief (10–14 weeks), and feedback was not provided. Researchers found that CBT was an effective treatment for this population but suggested that the technology was not sufficiently incorporated in the treatment protocol to evaluate whether it contributed to that benefit. A similar pilot study was conducted with neurotypical teens with anxiety who used self-monitoring daily for up to 2 weeks, resulting in improved emotion self-regulation (Goldstein et al., 2004).

Initial studies have demonstrated that emotion self-regulation improves when teens self-monitor feelings, behaviors, and contextual triggers (Goldstein et al., 2004; Levine, O'Callaghan, Calvano, & Fishbein, 2008). A second, more extensive study gives additional evidence for the efficacy of this approach (Levine, Hearsey, Mesibov, & Calvano, 2010). The authors used simultaneous teen and observer monitoring on handhelds to improve self-management in a classroom setting. Participants were students with a high-functioning autism or Asperger syndrome diagnosis who were in inclusion classrooms in middle or high school; the waitlisted control group were similar students who were monitored by observers for 3 months prior to their participating in the simultaneous monitoring and feedback protocol. Among the 32 students in the intervention group, 15 (47%) improved to a level beyond the highest level of the control group. Of these 15 responders, 11 (73%) showed a strong response: three of five self-management behaviors improved; the remaining 4 students (27%) showed a weaker response, with one or two improvements out of five. Of the five self-rated behaviors, self-control and self-expression were the two most consistently improved behaviors. Chapter 11 describes the use of a similar simultaneous mobile self-reporting protocol as an intervention for social pragmatics, executive functioning, and stress management with teens on the autism spectrum in a camp setting.

Mobile Technology Use for In-the-Moment Monitoring and Guidance of Social Pragmatics

In SymTrend's Phase I Asperger Syndrome/High Functioning Autism (AS/HFA) grant research (NIMH 2R41MH75162-01), students monitored and evaluated their own class behavior—correct posture, hand raising, timely correct responses, and so on—on their personal digital assistants (PDAs) during a class discussion; teachers recorded student behavior simultaneously (Levine et al., 2007). Students compared their scores with those of the teacher after each class. Students and teachers reviewed trends in daily scores each week in charts that combined both teacher and student ratings. All students benefited from this intervention in both statistical and educational terms. Figure 12.7 illustrates this benefit for one such student, showing social pragmatics in two classes over 4 months. The student and teachers allocated points on the basis of the student's social pragmatics during discussions or questioning in class (e.g., staying on topic, raising one's hand, eye contact). In both classes the student (•) showed close agreement with teachers (o) and improvement after initial training and feedback was introduced (see Self Score interval). Besides producing improvement, this intervention revealed nuances of student responses to different curricular arrangements. For example, Figure 12.7 also shows an important between-class difference. The student showed more consistent behavior day to day in a current events class (top chart) than in a literature class (bottom chart), a difference likely explained by prior preparation being allowed in the current events class but questions having to be answered on the spot in the literature class. The electronic monitoring system had two particular features that contributed to its success as an intervention platform. First, the use of mobile technology for self-monitoring of social behavior simplifies the reporting task for students. In a one-to-one interpersonal exchange, when a professional asks a student to take stock of how things are going in terms of feelings or behavior, he or she often asks an open-ended question. For a teen with ASD, answering this question is an exercise in multitasking: maintaining eye contact, interpreting the question, formulating a response sequence, and making a judgment for each response. With the PDA report about how things are going, there are no eye contact demands and questions are asked in a specific sequence. To answer a question about a specific feeling the student rates his or her feelings on a 7-point scale and his or her behavior on a 5-point scale. Since the student rates him- or herself once or twice per day each day, how he or she is doing will be in a chart of those ratings, which can be printed out and discussed with a

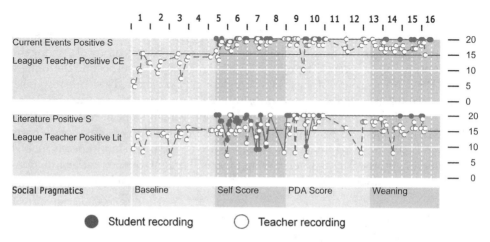

Figure 12.7. Feedback chart of tandem recording by teens with Asperger syndrome and their teachers. Teens view their own recordings but learn about another's perspective of the same events. (From Levine, M., & Mesibov, G. [2007, May]. *Personal guidance system [PGS] for school and vocational functioning.* Poster presented at the 6th Annual International Meeting for Autism Researchers, Seattle, WA.)

teacher. Students found discussing their feelings based on a chart they produced easier than talking about their feelings ad lib. In addition, mobile technology had a second clear intervention advantage. Preparations of each child's progress charts for weekly review took only seconds, requiring pressing a print chart button in the child's electronic account. In contrast, the information offered in Figure 12.7 would have taken hours to chart manually.

Mobile Technology Use for In-the-Moment Monitoring and Guidance of Executive Functioning

Parents and teachers are often frustrated by the difficulties students with ASD have managing their belongings and their schedule. Practitioners have considered the use of prompts and reminders as delivered by mobile electronic devices as a solution to these problems for students with higher functioning ASD.

In one study, my colleagues and I added both a self-monitoring feature and a feedback feature to the SymTrend software for improving executive functioning in scheduling and materials management (Levine et al., 2008). Students used a combination of SymTrend self-monitoring and Palm OS software to routinely set, then monitor class schedules, homework study, special school meetings, assignment turn-ins, material and gear checks, and computer usage (e.g., making data entries, uploading data, charging batteries). To test student proficiency using the system, we created a more demanding scheduling task, deliberately scheduling job-training sessions at different times of the day, on different days, for variable numbers of days per week, for a 4-week period. Students were responsible for programming their changing schedule. They were scored for showing up, for being on time (i.e., at most 5 minutes late), for bringing their handheld computers and work folders, and for not scheduling any conflicts between training sessions and other appointments, classes, or school functions. Students compared their data with a supervisor's records for feedback. The goal was 4 perfect days per week: 80% correct. Six students participated. Summary scores are displayed in Figure 12.8. Five of the six students reached criterion for on-time performance. Five of six students

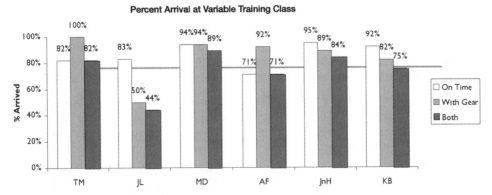

Figure 12.8. Success with following schedule to arrive at appropriate time and with necessary gear, using handheld computer reminders to drive performance. Chart is not created with software described here. (From Levine, M., & Mesibov, G. [2007, May]. *Personal guidance system [PGS] for school and vocational functioning.* Poster presented at the 6th Annual International Meeting for Autism Researchers, Seattle, WA.)

reached criterion for with-gear performance. JL, the only gear failure, had comorbid ADHD and required an additional "bring gear" reminder. Four of six students achieved the joint criteria of being on time with gear 80% of the time.

As another example, Myles, Ferguson, and Hagiwara (2007) trained a 17-year-old with Asperger syndrome to use a Hewlett-Packard Pocket PC device to use the calendar function for recording information about homework assignments in multiple classes. He recorded 1) the subject in which the homework was assigned, 2) the date the assignment was due, and 3) qualifying details of the assignment (e.g., problem numbers, chapter questions). The researchers used a multiple-baseline design to evaluate the effectiveness of the intervention. Their student was successful in increasing his rate of homework recording by using a handheld computer. Other studies have used handheld computers for prompting in vocational contexts for guiding completion of novel task boxes, for example, involving such tasks as lacing, assembling a plastic pipe, and packaging highlighter pens (Mechling & Savidge, 2011), and cooking recipes (Mechling, Gast, & Seid, 2009). Students performed better with the handheld device than with picture-based task schedules.

CHALLENGES OF USING MOBILE TECHNOLOGY AND PROPOSED SOLUTIONS

Although the adoption of technology has significant benefits for implementing, tracking, and evaluating the impact of interventions, it presents challenges as well (Adiguzel, 2008; Levine, Hearsey, Zekanovic, Barnwell, & Kozar, 2009). Many school districts and professionals have already purchased and used mobile devices for their educational software, videos, and games, so they have already had to devise policies and procedures for handling the equipment. Systematic adoption of mobile technologies for daily data collection requires extensive logistical planning because the equipment and software must be available at all times. Roles and responsibilities should be delineated ahead of time and back-up plans put in place. Listed below are some of the most common challenges and some ideas about how to manage them:

1. *Cost:* There is no getting around the cost of mobile devices and the data plans often required for use of mobile technology for data collection. Many programs are funding the purchase with grants from local organizations (charitable

foundations, businesses, state education grants). The purchase prices for portal and mobile software vary, but the hardware and connectivity costs are likely to dwarf the software costs. Although school systems are supposed to have allowance for adaptive technology for students with IEPs, their budgets often do not adequately cover the needs.

2. *Connectivity:* This is the most problematic issue in most buildings, but there are usually relatively inexpensive ways around them: Have a router installed in each classroom and do extensive testing. Some products require continuous contact with a server during data collection, so they would be bad choices if the signal is not dependable. Find the spot in the building where synching data to the server is most reliable. Have backup plans for when the systems go down. Specific recommendations for optimal connectivity are not included here because mobile technology and apps for the uses described here are continuously being developed and upgraded. The technologies may come with offers for free connect time or other solutions for connectivity as promotions. As new technologies come to market to address connectivity, make sure you do not sacrifice special education–related content in your search for this feature.

3. *Battery life:* Assign the responsibility of checking battery status to an individual and set up a safe and secure station for recharging devices. Older students often thrive on the responsibility of caring for technology, and it can be a small but helpful form of work experience for a student in transition.

4. *Theft:* Find a safe place for storage and create a system for checking devices in and out.

5. *Breakage and fragility:* Small devices, such as the iPod Touch can be worn in an armband, belt, or fanny pack to minimize risk of dropping. Heavy duty stands and cases are available for tablets, but add up to $50 per device or more.

6. *Technical knowledge required:* The primary technical expertise required is facility with managing connectivity when first setting things up. Each product also has a learning curve for translation of paper forms to the idiosyncratic way data collection is operationalized in the product. This issue requires 1) determination of roles and responsibilities of the staff in the program and 2) setting a timetable for conversion.

7. *Discontinuity of programs year to year:* If a local education agency does not adopt the technology throughout its schools, the transition from classrooms with the technology to those without or vice versa will be challenging at the start of a new school year.

8. *Requirements to upgrade:* The duration of backward compatibility of software by different vendors is an unknown, given the short life of some of these products. Behavior Tracker Pro and SymTrend have upgraded their products and remained backward compatible for at least one Apple operating system change, but the oldest iPod Touches cannot run the software anymore. The life span of the mobile devices, like mobile phones, is likely to be only a few years.

9. *Training time and turnover:* All products require intensive training for a complete transition of data collection, charting, and analysis. Professionals who

use fewer types of data collection formats may get going quickly. For example, translation of interval recording, which just requires entering a number from a clicker at the end of a recording interval, is easy to do. Setting up multistep task analysis is likely to take longer. The turnover of staff in special education classrooms, particularly of paraprofessionals, magnifies the training challenges because new staff need to focus on how to manage children and teach concepts. It may be months into the school year before they can learn new software. In addition, to optimize the benefits described above, senior professional staff (therapists and behavior analysts) would benefit from ongoing training in exploratory data analysis: relearning the scientific method, hypothesis testing, and single-case experimental designs. All professionals require continuing education credits, and educators in classrooms usually have skill development days scheduled during the year; administrators should find courses and provide incentives and support for allowing all staff to attend. They should reinforce in a concrete way that learning these skills sets the professionals up for advancement.

10. *Fixing data entry errors:* Not all products provide a means to revise saved data without deleting the data entirely and reentering it from paper. This is probably the feature most missed with the shift from paper to electronics. Users should check out this feature with each vendor.

11. *Privacy issues with video*: Some products have a place on their portal for sharing videos captured with mobile devices. Each school should have a policy in place for how these videos can be used and shared, including considering, for example, children in the background of the video that may be focused on a particular student.

12. *Incompatibility with IEP software:* The output from these products may not be easily incorporated into an IEP report without skilled use of pdf editors and/or word processors. This challenge can be overcome by merely placing the charts in an appendix.

SUMMARY

This chapter has provided examples of the benefits and challenges that mobile technologies can afford for behavioral data management, behavioral data analysis, and implementation of treatments for challenging behaviors, academics, emotion regulation, social pragmatics, and executive functioning. It has delineated important features to consider when evaluating these technologies and discussed ways in which use of these technologies may dramatically change and improve intervention efficacy.

REFERENCES

Adiguzel, T. (2008). Advantages of using handheld computers against other methodologies for data collection. *School Science and Mathematics, 108*, 224–226.

Baer, L., Minichiello, W.E., Jenike, M.A., & Holland, A. (1988). Use of a portable computer program to assist behavioral treatment in a case of obsessive compulsive disorder. *Journal of Behavior Therapy and Experimental Psychiatry, 19*(3), 237–240.

Blakeley-Smith, A., Reaven, J., Leuthe, E.M., Culhane-Shelburne, K., Moody, E.J., & Hepburn, S. (2010). *Incorporating* technology into a pilot cognitive behavioral therapy group treatment for adolescents with high functioning autism spectrum. Paper presented at the 9th Annual International Meeting of Autism Researchers, Philadelphia, PA.

CBTAonline. (2012). *ABC Data Pro.* Retrieved from http://www.cbtaonline.com

Compass Solutions for Autism. (2011). *Case study.* Retrieved from http://www.compassautism.com/Documents/keystone_case_study.pdf

Compass Solutions for Autism. (2012). *Catalyst.* Retrieved from http://www.compassautism.com

eCOVE Software LLC. (2012). *eCOVE Observation Software.* Retrieved from http://www.ecove.net

Goldstein, C.R., Choate, M.L., Ehrenreich, J.T., Micco, J.A., Landon, T.M., & Pincus, D.B. (2004, November). *Technology and the treatment of anxiety disorders in children: Using Palm Pilots to improve homework compliance.* Poster presentation at the annual meeting of the Association for Behavioral and Cognitive Therapies, New Orleans, LA.

HandholdAdaptive. (2012). *AutismTrack.* Retrieved from http://www.handholdadaptive.com/index.html

Iwata, B.A. (2010). *Functional behavior assessment in educational settings* (Unpublished presentation) University of Florida.

Levine, M., Hearsey, K., Mesibov, G.B., & Calvanio, R. (2010, May). *Self-monitoring with handheld computers by teens with high functioning autism/Asperger's syndrome in mainstream settings,* Poster presented at the 9th Annual International Meeting for Autism Researchers, Philadelphia, PA.

Levine, M., Hearsey, K., Zekanovic, L., Barnwell, J., & Kozar, L. (2009). *From the laboratory to the blackboard jungle: Conducting technology-based research in the inclusion setting.* Paper presented at the 8th Annual International Meeting for Autism Researchers, Chicago, IL.

Levine, M., & Mesibov, G. (2007, May). *Personal guidance system (PGS) for school and vocational functioning.* Poster presented at the 6th Annual International Meeting for Autism Researchers, Seattle, WA.

Levine, M., O'Callaghan, C., Calvanio, R., & Fishbein, H. (2008, May). *High functioning autism: The relationship among social skill execution, symptom expression, and feeling states.* Poster presented at the 7th Annual International Meeting for Autism Researchers, London, England.

Massachusetts Department of Education. (2001). *IEP process guide.* Malden, MA: Author.

Mechling, L.C., Gast, D.L., & Seid, N.H. (2009). Using a personal digital assistant to increase independent task completion by students with autism spectrum disorder. *Journal of Autism and Developmental Disorders, 39*(10), 1420–1434.

Mechling, L.C., & Savidge, E.J. (2011). Using a personal digital assistant to increase completion of novel tasks and independent transitioning by students with autism spectrum disorder. *Journal of Autism and Developmental Disorders, 41*(6), 687–704.

Myles, B.S., Ferguson, H., & Hagiwara, T. (2007). Using a personal digital assistant to improve the recording of homework assignments by an adolescent with Asperger syndrome. *Focus on Autism and Other Developmental Disabilities, 22,* 96–99.

Newman, M.G. (1999). The clinical use of palmtop computers in the treatment of generalized anxiety disorder. *Cognitive and Behavioral Practice, 6*(3), 222–234.

Newman, M.G., Kennedy, J., Herman, S., & Taylor, C.B. (1997). Comparison of palmtop- computer-assisted brief cognitive-behavioral treatment to cognitive-behavioral treatment for panic disorder. *Journal of Consulting & Clinical Psychology, 65*(1), 178–183.

SymTrend. (2012a). *SymTrend: Symptom tracking, charting & reminding.* Belmont, MA: SymTrend. Retrieved from https://www.symtrend.com/tw/public/index_standard

SymTrend. (2012b). *SymTrend trials.* Belmont, MA: SymTrend. Retrieved from https://www.symtrend.com/tw/public/public_docviewer?ltrans_doc=3141

Track & Share Apps, LLC. (2012). *Autism Tracker Pro.* Retrieved from http://www.trackandshareapps.com

Tools to Support Simplified Capture of Activities in Natural Environments

∎ ∎

Gregory D. Abowd, Julie A. Kientz, Gillian R. Hayes, Rosa I. Arriaga, and Nazneen

Autism is a lifelong condition, and thus care and support for people coping with autism is a complex, lifelong challenge. Families, care networks, and individuals with autism together face myriad options for therapies, doctors, educators, health specialists, drugs, and diet regimens. Although there are behaviors associated with people with autism, as indicated in the *DSM-IV-TR* (American Psychiatric Association, 2000), every individual is unique, and the particular set of behaviors are different in each person and sometimes different in the same person over time. The individual's unique behavioral and cognitive profile makes it difficult to predict which treatments will work. When the individual in question is young, the need for early intervention exacerbates this problem. In addition, individuals more severely affected by autism may not be able to communicate their internal states. This inability forces caregivers to rely on externally perceivable characteristics to determine the person's needs. Caregivers might try several interventions simultaneously, which makes it difficult to determine which work and which do not. Therefore, caregivers must communicate and collaborate with the individual's care network (i.e., educators, clinicians, nutritionists) to determine if an individual is receiving the best treatments possible. This collaboration requires that they sift through large amounts of data and also struggle with missing data.

Information technologies can play a vital role in the care and support of individuals with autism by addressing these challenges. In this chapter, we specifically focus on "capture and access" technologies (Abowd & Mynatt, 2000). These technologies serve to facilitate data collection and interpretation, which are crucial for both diagnosis and treatment monitoring. Specifically, they can increase the quantity and quality of collected data, make collection easier and more efficient, and help caregivers quickly scan through large amounts of data. The end goal is to allow the caregiver to make better decisions. For example, in a home setting, audio and video can be captured and linked to key data about a child's tantrums. The parent can then review these data at a later time with a clinician. Thus, capture and access technologies can help with decision making and lead to communication that is more effective and efficient (Kientz, 2012; Kientz, Hayes, Abowd, & Grinter, 2006; Kientz, Hayes, Westeyn, Starner, & Abowd, 2007) between parents and the care network. The challenge, then, is to enable caregivers to collect rich records in natural environments with minimal disruptions.

In this chapter, we present three types of tools that have been developed in our research lab at Georgia Tech for data collection in schools and homes. First, Abaris is a system for conducting one-to-one therapy in a structured setting where there is one educator and one student. Second, CareLog, CRAFT, and smartCapture support behavioral data collection in less controlled settings. Third, Baby Steps and KidCam support tracking developmental progress in children. We close the chapter with a reflection on our experiences and a vision for addressing future challenges in designing capture and access systems.

CAPTURE AND ACCESS FOR STRUCTURED, ONE-TO-ONE THERAPY

Multiple caregivers often conduct interventions for the same individual with autism across a long period of time. They may collect and review large amounts of both qualitative and quantitative data, which can help caregivers determine the effectiveness of these interventions and make adjustments as needed. Education sessions are often administered individually, and thus collaboration between the various clinicians is important in ensuring that sessions are administered consistently. Recorded data can serve as evidence to support decisions and help lead to more effective treatment. Making decisions based on the data is an important component of care, but collecting data can be burdensome, and teachers do not always have the time to collect data properly. Missing data points or unreliable data can result when the data are reported from a teacher's retrospective memory anywhere from minutes to hours or days after the session took place. When data are collected on paper, they can be difficult to synthesize, review, and share. Computing technologies that can help integrate different types of data and facilitate sharing for collaborative decision making can help alleviate some of these shortcomings.

In discrete trial training (DTT), teams of teachers and/or therapists teach basic skills, such as vocabulary or spoken words, intensively in one-to-one settings and assess the child's level of independence in completing new skills. After a therapy session, the teacher often calculates the percentage of times a skill was completed independently (by the child) and then manually plots corresponding data points on a paper graph. Teachers meet regularly to discuss the child's progress and make adjustments to the practice to improve the child's success. They commonly discuss skills the child has accomplished and clarify assessment of particular skills. DTT requires rigorous data collection and analysis to be effective, but it is unfortunately subject to inconsistencies and inaccuracies due to different skill sets of teachers and subjective interpretations of progress.

To address the real-life challenges of DTT therapy, we developed Abaris, a capture and access tool for recording instructional data during DTT sessions (Kientz at al., 2006). Abaris consists of a desktop application that enables customization of the child's daily therapy regimen and printing of data sheets. Data are recorded by writing on these special data sheets using an Anoto digital pen (Anoto Digital Pens, 2013). These written records are synchronized with audio and video recordings from a fixed environmental camera and microphone. After each session, the teacher docks the digital pen with the computer for automatic download and analysis. Phoneme spotting in the audio files and timestamps from the digital pen provide flags into videos of therapy sessions. This index allows for quick retrieval of moments of interest during team meetings, enabling teachers to easily use video evidence to review progress, find inconsistencies, and among the team discuss problem areas. Abaris also automatically generates graphs and links them with data sheets used during therapy (see Figure 13.1), which saves time for the therapy team.

We deployed Abaris for 4 months with a home-based DTT team and for 6 weeks with a school-based team. Abaris enabled home-based therapists to use evidence more frequently in discussions and decision making, including videos, graphs, and data sheets, than they did without the system. Prior to Abaris, therapists relied on their memories of events during therapy and only rarely consulted written data sheets, such as when there was a difficult decision to make. Furthermore, Abaris helped increase collaboration among the therapists during meetings with the home-based team (Kientz et al., 2006). School-based therapists used the video less frequently than did the home-based therapists due to time constraints and the logistics of having multiple videos concurrently in a classroom setting, but the digital pen and automatic graphing led teachers to review the data more frequently (Kientz, 2012; Kientz et al., 2006). Use of Abaris helped teachers to recognize when a child had mastered a skill more quickly because they had access to trending information more immediately, rather than only monthly with the paper-based system.

Mobile technology has been very useful in assisting with data collection and visualization and has shown much promise in educational settings. Our use of the digital pen and paper was crucial in developing a system that worked with teachers' existing practices. The latter is important because maintaining the teacher's work flow minimized the work load and distractions of introducing a

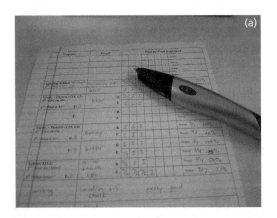

(continued)

Figure 13.1. Screen shots from Abaris data capture and analysis technology: (a) digital pen input, (b) video preview screen, and (c) data analysis graphs of a child's progress. (From Kientz, J.A. [2012]. Embedded capture and access: Encouraging recording and reviewing of data in the caregiving domain. *Personal and Ubiquitous Computing, 16*[2], 209–221 and Kientz, J.A., Boring, S., Abowd, G.D., & Hayes, G.R. [2005]. Abaris: Evaluating automated capture applied to structured autism interventions. In M. Beigl, S.S. Intille, J. Rekimoto, & H. Tokuda [Eds.], *UbiComp 2005* [pp. 323–339]. Berlin, Germany: Springer-Verlag; reprinted by kind permission of Springer Science and Business Media.)

Figure 13.1. *(continued)*

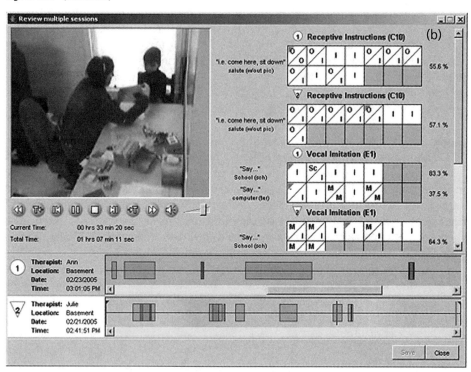

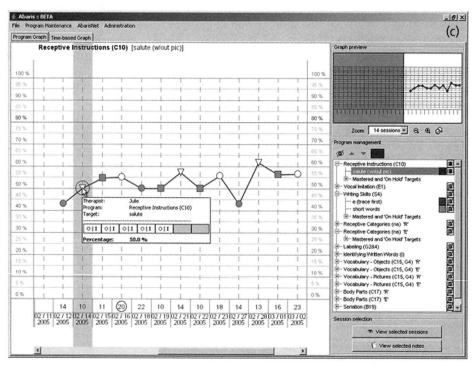

new input device into their sessions. In some cases, specialized digital pens may not be as desirable as other mobile input devices, such as smartphones or tablets. There have been efforts to use these for data collection and recording (as discussed in Chapter 12).

SUPPORTING SELECTIVE ARCHIVING OF CHILDREN'S BEHAVIORS

The Abaris project demonstrates how technologies can be used for data collection in predictable and structured settings. We have also explored the use of technology in less predictable situations, specifically the examination of severe behavior in schools and homes. Direct observation in clinics, homes, and schools is considered the gold standard for problem behavior assessment. However, it can be costly and intrusive, and it may cause behavior reactivity. In addition, it is common for families to be on long waiting lists to schedule appointments with specialists in the clinic or at school. Thus, we developed selective archiving as an approach to video capture that provides an alternative to direct observation for naturalistic data capture. In this section, we introduce the concept of *selective archiving,* or the ability to preserve a record of events for potential future use even after the events have passed (Hayes & Abowd, 2006; Hayes, Gardere, Abowd, & Truong, 2008). Selective archiving has been used to support functional behavior assessment in a special education setting (Hayes, 2006) and the collection of severe behaviorial data in homes (Nazneen, Rozga, et al., 2012).

Selective Archiving as a Tool for Behavioral Assessments in School Settings

Children with autism and other developmental disabilities exhibit behaviors that may be considered inappropriate and can even be disruptive or dangerous to themselves or others. Unfortunately, many of these children cannot explain what it is that leads them to perform this behavior (e.g., why they are hitting themselves and others). This can be the case because they are nonverbal or because they cannot reflect on their internal states. Addressing problem behaviors requires the collection of information about the underlying role and utility of these behaviors to the individuals who perform them. This data collection occurs through a variety of approaches. Functional behavior assessment (FBA) is commonly employed for understanding and addressing problem behavior (Horner & Carr, 1997). Often, FBA includes direct observation in the natural environment. Caregivers, seeing a behavioral incident, note the incident's context and what happened directly before (antecedent) and after it (consequence). Once a sufficient number of incidents have been recorded, a behavioral specialist analyzes the data to determine the behavior's function. For example, the child might be hitting to gain the teacher's attention. The FBA is a useful step in developing strategies to reduce the problem behavior. These strategies are frequently called behavioral intervention plans. Although there is evidence that lay caregivers can conduct these assessments with minimal training (Hayes & Abowd, 2006; Hayes et al., 2008), there is no evidence that their data can be used to do an FBA. One of the biggest problems is that incidents might occur at unexpected times and places, and caregivers might not be able to write down what happened before or after while simultaneously managing the behavior itself.

We developed an application to support FBA, called CareLog, which helps caregivers document and analyze specific, unplanned incidents of interest as part of an FBA. Because caregivers are good at recognizing events *after* they happen but less so at predicting them, the system uses audio and video buffering to allow selective archiving of these media after events have already occurred. Selective archiving (Hayes & Abowd, 2006; Hayes et al., 2008) includes the continual capture of streaming data but permanent storage only in response to an explicit trigger. A pre- and posttrigger window of data is stored, which effectively supports retroactive recording of context around the triggering point. This approach has several benefits. First, it puts the user in control of when data moves from being streamed to being stored. This is important because it simultaneously addresses privacy, control, and storage management concerns that arise from continuous data capture. Second, requiring an explicit indicator to save data whether through a human user or a sensor implicitly filters irrelevant data, saving resources both in the present (disk space) and in the future (time spent in viewing or analyzing relevant data). In the CareLog system, caregivers use a wireless button worn or carried to trigger archiving. They then use a standard desktop computer to watch the videos and tag them with metadata. Finally, CareLog provides graphs and other analytic tools for functional assessment (see Figure 13.2).

(continued)

Figure 13.2. Screen shots from the CareLog functional behavior assessment system: (a) video viewing and annotation screen with four camera angles, (b) automatically generated graphs showing when and how often a particular behavior occurs.

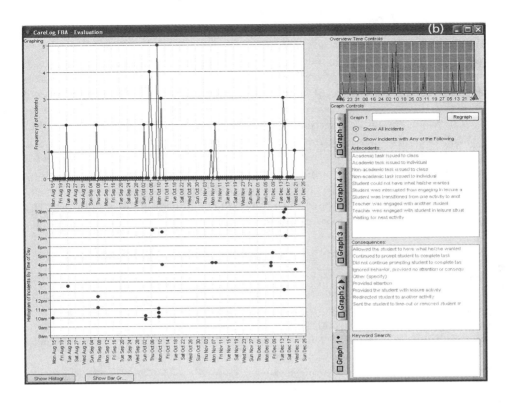

We deployed CareLog in four classrooms at a special education school for 5 months as part of a quasi-experimental study of its effectiveness. Four teachers conducted an FBA for each of their two students, one (randomly selected) using the traditional pen-and-paper method and one using CareLog. The ordering of the two methods was counterbalanced, and groups were randomly assigned to each condition. To establish ground truth data on the number of behavioral incidents, a member of the research staff recorded an average of 17 hours or 21.5% of time in study for each student with a handheld video camera. Independent coders then coded the videos for behavioral incidents using operational definitions created by the research team and teachers. We found with CareLog that teachers made an average of 43.37% fewer false negative errors (missed incidents) than they did with the traditional pen-and-paper method. There were almost no false positives (recorded incidents that were not appropriate for the operationally defined behavior) in either case. For this first attempt at using CareLog in classrooms, we measured only the accuracy with which teachers recorded behaviors and not the accuracy of their observation of antecedents or consequences. Our observations and interviews with teachers indicate that given the ability to go back to replay the video as often as they like, teachers also felt more confident in their notation of antecedent and consequence data in the CareLog condition.

To understand the work load differences between the traditional pen-and-paper method and CareLog, the NASA Task Load Index (NASA-TLX) was used. The NASA-TLX measures workload on six different dimensions that includes Mental Demands,

Physical Demands, Temporal Demands, Own Performance, Effort, and Frustration (Hart, 2006). Using CareLog was reported to be significantly easier in terms of work load than was the traditional method for recording basic behavioral information. In our discussion with teachers, we found that if teachers are to be in control of data capture, they must be able to do so in an incredibly simple and straightforward manner that blends almost seamlessly into their standard daily activities.

Overall, CareLog use significantly reduced errors and improved efficiency in data collection. Furthermore, the teachers reported enjoying the process more while feeling less burdened and more confident in the results of their assessments. This work in the educational setting demonstrates the potential for selective archiving to support contextual analysis of behavioral problems. CareLog has been licensed from Georgia Tech and commercialized as Behavior Imaging (BI) Capture by the company Behavior Imaging Solutions, Inc.

Selective Archiving as a Tool for Behavioral Assessments in Home Settings

Using FBA is not limited to school settings. Parents may be asked to use FBA or other related techniques for documenting and understanding incidents of problem behavior. However, some specialists found this practice dubious because there was no evidence that lay people could collect relevant data. Thus, to determine the quality of data collected by parents, we conducted a study with selective archiving technology similar to that used in CareLog.

We developed a robust, multicamera system, CRAFT (Continuous Recording and Flagging Technology), which collects continuous digital video and annotates it with problem behavior instances identified by parents through a button click on a remote control (Nazneen, Rozga, et al., 2012). Eight families, each with a child diagnosed with a developmental disorder, were recruited for the study. Parents were instructed how to use CRAFT and asked to gather instances of their child's problem behaviors at home. We installed (up to four) cameras that continuously recorded the activity in the areas of the home that parents had designated for the study. By the end of the study, we collected an average of 16 hours of video per family. This video was important because it provided the "ground truth" for the behavior instances that were flagged by parents as showing their child engaging in severe behaviors.

Behavior analysts coded the home videos in their entirety to identify all instances of problem behaviors and then compared them to the ones identified by parents. Results show that parents successfully identified (by clicking the remote) 55% of the problem behaviors that the clinical professionals would have identified had they been in the home. In addition, parents were able to provide at least one example of each different problem behavior their child has in a single day of deployment. By comparison, in the CareLog study, we found that teachers recorded 23.7% of observed incidences when using pen and paper and 58.25% when using CareLog. Although the sample size was small in this study, it indicates that parents are able to identify a comparable quality of behavioral incidents to satisfy the needs of a clinical professional.

Simplifying Selective Archiving for Home Use

Installing CRAFT in the home was a labor-intensive process. As a next step, to further simplify the data capture process, we are designing a smartphone-based video capture system, smartCapture, which can support parents in collecting samples of their child's behaviors in the home with remote assistance from such specialists as clinicians and teachers (Nazneen, Boujarwah, et al., 2012). This system can be used to 1) support the diagnosis process with evidence collected in the natural settings, 2) monitor a child's process during treatment, 3) follow up on a child's progress after a treatment is completed, and 4) train parents to implement a treatment protocol at home by reflecting on the sample they collected at home. Overall, this system is particularly useful for families living at a long distance from clinical specialists. There are other significant uses for cases outside clinical scenarios, such as when teachers want to analyze child behavior or progress in the home setting or when parents want to share home evidence with teachers or clinicians.

We conceptualize the smartCapture system as being analogous to specimen collection containers given to patients at a lab or clinic. In this case, the behavior clinic or school can mail a smartCapture device (installed with smartCapture mobile app), preset with a required list of behaviors, to parents to collect and share specimens of their child's behaviors. This approach is particularly useful for low-income families. However, if parents want to use their own smartphone for the purpose of data collection, they can download the smartCapture mobile app on their phone.

The smartCapture system facilitates behavior specimen capture via two components: the smartCapture web portal and the smartCapture mobile app (see Figure 13.3). Through the smartCapture web portal, the specialist presets the smartCapture device with a list of behaviors that parents should capture and mails the device to the parents. Parents can add additional custom behaviors to the list created by the specialist on the capture device. Parents can use the preset behaviors to annotate the behavior specimens they collect. The smartCapture mobile application allows parents to collect a behavior specimen with a single click either on the device or through a remote when the device is mounted on a cradle. It supports selective archiving so that parents can capture activity even after it has happened in the home. Parents can edit and upload recorded specimens, and specialists can analyze these behavior specimens through the smartCapture system. Specialists and parents can also communicate asynchronously through the smartCapture system. For example, specialists can alert parents when they have captured sufficient specimens or when they want to capture more specimens. Once the behavior specimens are collected, parents return the system to the clinic or school.

To further improve the quality of data collected in the home, smartCapture will support some automatic analysis of recorded specimens. Parents will receive automatic alerts of poor lighting conditions, excessive movement, poor framing of the shot (e.g., need to reposition the camera when no one is in view), and so on. The analysis of videos for these characteristics will be done automatically without human intervention.

Selective archiving of behavioral incidents allows for the collection of important video data that can be analyzed by parents, teachers, specialists, and other stakeholders without excessively burdening those doing the data collection. We have developed such systems for use in classrooms, homes, and mobile environments. Our pilot studies with these systems indicate that this approach shows promise in clinical, educational, and home data collection.

(continued)

Figure 13.3.   Behavior specimen collection process: (a) web-based system for experts to prescribe behaviors that parents should capture, (b) preconfigured smartphone for parent in-home behavior capture and sharing, (c) web-based system for expert analysis of in-home data collected by parents.

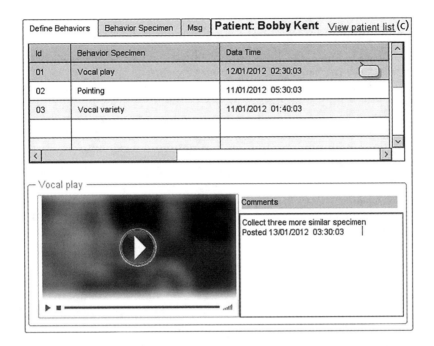

Using Mobile Technologies for Parents to Track Children's Developmental Progress

There is a general consensus that early diagnosis of autism might lead to improved intervention outcomes. Parent reporting and direct clinical observations are key to screening for developmental delays. In this project, we explored how parents of young children can be empowered and motivated to collect relevant evidence of their children's developmental progress that can be shared with other caregivers, such as their pediatrician. We conducted a field study with eight families in a single pediatric practice (Kientz, 2012; Kientz & Abowd, 2009). The results of this study inspired a new approach to the problem that addresses scaling to a much larger population by effective use of web and mobile phone technologies. Although the intended setting was largely clinical, we describe several implications for educational settings as well.

Detecting developmental delays, such as autism, as early as possible in young children is an important goal for public health. Earlier interventions are effective in helping children function better later in life (Shore, 1997). Unfortunately, these types of delays are often identified by parents, their pediatricians, or their teachers well after the earliest signs occur. The early identification of developmental delays has become the topic of a public health campaign sponsored by the Centers for Disease Control and Prevention (CDC) in the United States called Learn the Signs: Act Early (2013). This campaign aims to educate new parents, pediatricians, and secondary care providers on the warning signs of delays so that they may identify possible problems and seek early treatment. The CDC's web site (Learn the Signs) lists approximately 250 developmental milestones across a 5-year period that parents can use to assess their child's development. A child not meeting milestones by a certain age may be a sign of delay, as would a regression or plateau of previously obtained skills. However, manually tracking these data points over 5 years for possibly multiple children can be cumbersome and daunting.

Appropriately designed computing technology can help parents track and record their children's developmental progress over time. Different elements may motivate them to record milestones, proactively prompt parents to observe specific milestones, or facilitate communication with a health care professional. Video evidence of parental concerns can also help in diagnosing problems and identifying solutions. Thus, we developed a semimobile system, called KidCam, which helps parents capture video evidence to both archive their child's sentimental moments of interest, such as their first steps, or capture concerning events to share with their child's pediatrician. We prototyped KidCam on an ultra-mobile PC with a built-in camera and touchscreen. KidCam allows for semiautomatic capture of photos and videos of spontaneous events within the child's life by using selective archiving (Hayes & Abowd, 2006; Hayes et al., 2008). Photos and videos collected via KidCam can synchronize with another software application we have developed, called Baby Steps (Kientz, Arriaga, & Abowd, 2009). Baby Steps enables parents to record developmental milestones as well as personally meaningful records, such as pictures, videos, favorite toys, and favorite foods. Baby Steps allows parents to import pictures and videos from KidCam and other capture devices, generate keepsake newsletters for printing or e-mailing, and print reports of developmental progress to bring to their pediatrician (see Figure 13.4).

To evaluate KidCam and Baby Steps, we conducted a 3-month deployment study with eight families, in which we deployed two different versions of Baby Steps. Four families received KidCam and a full version of Baby Steps that included all the personal record-keeping features, and the remaining four families received a simplified version of Baby Steps that allowed them to record milestones only manually. We conducted surveys of parent confidence and collaboration with their pediatrician before and after the deployment; logged interaction with the system; and conducted interviews before, during, and after the deployment.

The results from this deployment showed that KidCam with the version of Baby Steps that included both personal and developmental record keeping was more successful than manually tracking milestones alone. Families using KidCam recorded more milestones over the 3-month period compared with the control group. Parents in both groups reported higher confidence at the end of the study than at the beginning. Parents using KidCam and the full version of Baby Steps accessed the data more often and had a statistically significant increase in their collaboration with their pediatricians for the patient–pediatrician interaction survey than did the other group. Similarly, pediatricians also rated collaboration with parents in the KidCam group higher at the end of the study.

Although there were positive results with this system overall, KidCam still required parents to manually indicate when events of interest they would like to save for later occurred. In practice, parents often did not have the time to manually trigger the recording, or they forgot to set up the device in the room where their child was playing. Future systems might employ the use of wearable or environmental sensors with computer vision to detect the presence of individuals and occasionally save pictures and videos while moments of interest are occurring. Accelerometers embedded in toys or special markers stitched onto children's clothing could assist with this automatic triggering. We are also working on future versions of Baby Steps that enhance

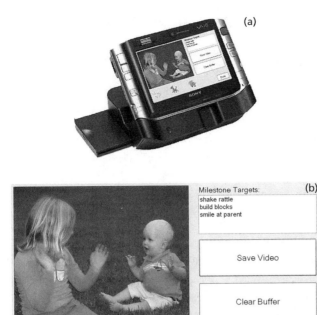

Figure 13.4. (a) View of KidCam prototype on a Sony VAIO and (b) a screen shot showing capture interface. (From Kientz, J.A., & Abowd, G.D. [2009]. KidCam: Toward an effective technology for the capture of children's moments of interest. In H. Tokuda, M. Biegl, A. Friday, A.J.B. Brush, & Y. Tobe [Eds.], *Lecture notes in computer science: Vol. 5538. Pervasive Computing: 7th International Conference, Pervasive 2009, Nara, Japan, May 11–14, 2009 Proceedings* [pp. 115–132]. Berlin, Germany: Springer Berlin Heidelberg; reprinted by kind permission of Springer Science and Business Media.)

the personally meaningful record-keeping aspects and provide additional ways of capturing data, such as through short message service (SMS), Facebook, and Twitter.

Although KidCam and Baby Steps were intended for use in a home setting and focused on health, there are many parallels to this work that relate to education. For example, parents may want to record information at home to share with a teacher as evidence of a child's abilities to perform a skill, which might be useful in developing an individualized education program (IEP). Likewise, teachers may want to use a system like KidCam to illustrate to parents a child's different behaviors or track fun things the child did that parents might be interested in seeing later. There is already a trend in a number of preschools to record this type of information to share with parents, and KidCam may be one way to help assist with these efforts.

DESIGN RECOMMENDATIONS

These projects, when considered collectively, reveal some key design recommendations for people working in this space.

1. *Capture as much* and *as little data as reasonably possible.*
   It can be difficult for users to know what information they need at the time of capture. At the same time, care of children with autism can involve the collection

of sensitive data. Therefore, it is useful to capture a wide variety of data but to limit this data collection to those areas and times that are most likely to be relevant. This objective was one of the strong motivations behind the use of selective archiving in much of the work presented in this chapter.

2. *Reduce the effort required to learn and use the system.*
   Caregivers of children with autism are already overloaded and often do not benefit directly from data collection. Thus, systems should carefully balance intervention and work required by caregivers with the benefits to them and other data consumers. Also, when possible, the task of keeping records should fade into the background.

3. *Provide access to data at a variety of levels.*
   Different users have varying requirements for accessing and understanding data. Thus, systems should allow access to both high-level data overviews and raw data as a backup. Likewise, allowing customization and providing various levels of views can alleviate concerns related to information overload.

4. *Provide controls for privacy and access to data.*
   The automatic or even semiautomatic capture of very rich and sensitive data, such as video, may raise concerns about privacy, control of data, reputation, and so on. In designing systems to support disparate groups of caregivers, designers must consider who determines what needs to be captured, how it is stored, when it is deleted, and who has access to it. In general, we found that if caregivers believe that data captured is relevant and useful to care, then they would be more willing to agree to recording the data. However, how to specify what happens to these data over the long term remains an open design question.

5. *Considerations must be balanced across all stakeholders.*
   Caring for children with autism typically involves a vast and varied team of family, friends, experts, and the children themselves. These highly varied stakeholder groups may have highly disparate needs and interests. Thus, applications must balance needs and tensions across them. In addition to using design methods that consider all these stakeholders at once, it can be useful to allow end users to pick which of the available features are most useful to them and thus customize their own application.

DISCUSSION

A central goal of our research agenda is to develop technology that can improve interventions children with autism receive. We have utilized capture and access capabilities to build systems that improve data collection and interpretation across a variety of natural environments. This has led us to design systems that are used by people who have minimal technical training. Our research indicates that the systems we have built are considered valuable by the parents, clinicians, therapists, and teachers who engaged with them. Although this result shows that we have been successful in meeting our research goals, there remain open questions to be addressed, particularly when considering how to transfer the lessons from this work to other domains. In this section, we reflect on our experiences and consider how lessons learned in designing and evaluating these systems might be taken into consideration for future research (Hayes et al., 2004; Kientz, 2012).

To design successful technology for individuals with autism, it is essential to have a good understanding of the goals, practices, and expectations of these individuals and their caregivers. A good understanding of existing work practices can help in determining how technology would best fit and integrate into user environments and daily practices. For example, in the case of the Abaris home study, the design of the application better suited the needs of therapists because the research team had acted as therapists and been trained by experts in DTT prior to beginning the design process. Working closely with clinicians, educators, and other professionals can be essential in gaining a deeper understanding of their needs.

Although recording audio, video, and photograph data can be of great benefit, it is still difficult to design a system to allow the capture of these data ethically and legally in all the spaces of interest. In our studies, we found that capturing rich media of children is particularly challenging. Legally, children are protected from being recorded in additional ways adults are not. For example, in schools, the Family Educational Rights and Privacy Act (PL 93-380), known as FERPA, regulates the capture and sharing of such media (FERPA, 1974), and additional local policies regulate recording in clinics, schools, and other environments. These regulations particularly affect the ability to capture data about multiple children at once. Thus, trade-offs must be made between what can be captured technologically and what can and should be captured legally and ethically.

Technologies and the social actors and relations surrounding them are interwoven and affect one another. For example, the deployment of a new technology can result in the shifting of power relations. Likewise, these power relations affect the ways in which the technologies are adopted and appropriated in use. For example, during the Baby Steps and KidCam deployments, we found that these systems affected parents' satisfaction with their pediatrician, as well as the pediatricians' perception about the parents in the study.

Capture systems are most easily accepted by their target users when they model current practices or at the very least complement them. For example, the manner in which DTT therapists who participated in our study conducted therapies mirrored their daily practices. Ensuring that their data capture practices did not change enabled them to adopt Abaris easily. On the other hand, in the CareLog deployment, although we made use of practices recommended by experts, the teachers in the study were not utilizing them. They required additional training in the clinical method and the system. However, with minimal training they were able to make use of the system. This kind of training, as well as adjustments to any caregiving practices, must be considered in the development and deployment of new technologies.

Finally, caring for an individual with autism is a costly endeavor. Caregivers in our studies highlighted that adoption of any system into their care routine would have to demonstrate significant benefit for the cost incurred. When designing systems, designers must consider not just the cost of a single installation but also the overall cost including the installation in every environment of interest and system maintenance costs.

CONCLUSION

Many of the decisions made concerning the diagnosis of developmental delay or the effectiveness of a given intervention are based on behavioral or academic data collected either first- or secondhand. One of our research goals has been to improve the collection of data in natural environments, such as schools and homes that support evidence-based decision practices. In this chapter, we have discussed research projects completed over the past decade. These projects all use information technologies integrated into existing practices to provide rich data collection and analysis capabilities for families, educators, and health professionals interested in diagnosis of and interventions for individuals with autism and related developmental disabilities. The use of such capture and access technologies shows much promise and can be extremely helpful for tracking behavioral activities, gathering evidence of learning or development, and illustrating examples between parents or teachers that are difficult to articulate otherwise.

REFERENCES

Abowd, G., & Mynatt, E. (2000). Charting past, present, and future research in ubiquitous computing. *ACM Transactions on Computer-Human Interaction, 7*(1), 29–58.

American Psychiatric Association. (2000). *Diagnostic and statistical manual of mental disorders, fourth edition, text revision (DSM-IV-TR).* Washington, D.C.: Author.

Anoto Digital Pens. (2013, January). Retrieved from Anoto Group AB, http://www.anoto.com

Family Educational Rights and Privacy Act (FERPA) of 1974, PL 93-380, 20 U.S.C., §§ 1232g *et seq.* Retrieved from U.S. Department of Education, http://www.all-acronyms.com/cat/8/FERPA

Hart, S.G. (2006). NASA–Task Load Index (NASA-TLX): 20 years later. *Proceedings of the Human Factors and Ergonomics Society Annual Meeting, 50*(9), 904–908.

Hayes, G.R., & Abowd, G.D. (2006). Tensions in designing capture technologies for an evidence-based care community. In R. Grinter, T. Rodden, P. Aoki, E. Cutrell, R. Jeffries, & G. Olson (Eds.), *Proceedings of the SIGCHI Conference on Human Factors in Computing Systems CHI,* 06, (pp. 937–946). New York, NY: ACM.

Hayes, G.R., Gardere, L.M., Abowd, G.D., & Truong, K.N. (2008). CareLog: A selective archiving tool for behavior management in schools. *Education,* 685–694.

Hayes, G.R., Kientz, J.A., Truong, K.N., White, D.R., Abowd, G.D., & Pering, T. (2004). Designing capture applications to support the education of children with autism. *Ubiquitous Computing, 3205,* 161–178.

Horner, R.H., & Carr, E.G. (1997). Behavioral support for students with severe disabilities: Functional assessment and comprehensive intervention. *Special Education, 31,* 84–104.

Kientz, J. (2012). Embedded capture and access: Encouraging recording and reviewing of data in the caregiving domain. *Personal Ubiquitous Computing, 16*(2), 209–221.

Kientz, J.A., & Abowd, G.D. (2009). KidCam: Toward an effective technology for the capture of children's moments of interest. In H. Tokuda, M. Biegl, A. Friday, A.J.B. Brush, & Y. Tobe (Eds.), *Lecture Notes in Computer Science: Vol. 5538. Pervasive Computing: 7th International Conference, Pervasive 2009, Nara, Japan, May 11–14, 2009 Proceedings* (pp. 115–132). Berlin, Germany: Springer Berlin Heidelberg.

Kientz, J.A., Arriaga, R.I., & Abowd, G.D. (2009). Baby steps: Evaluation of a system to support record-keeping for parents of young children. In D.R. Olsen, R.B. Arthur, K. Hinckley, M.R. Morris, S. Hudson, & S. Greenberg (Eds.), *Proceedings of the 27th International Conference on Human Factors in Computing Systems, 2001* (pp. 1713–1722). New York, NY: ACM.

Kientz, J.A., Boring, S., Abowd, G.D., & Hayes, G.R. (2005). Abaris: Evaluating automated capture applied to structured autism interventions. In M. Beigl, S.S. Intille, J. Rekimoto, & H. Tokuda (Eds.), *UbiComp 2005* (pp. 323–339). Berlin, Germany: Springer-Verlag.

Kientz, J.A., Hayes, G.R., Abowd, G.D., & Grinter, R.E. (2006). From the war room to the living room: Decision support for home-based therapy teams. In P. Hinds, D. Martin, S. Greenberg, G. Mark, S. Fussell, & K. Inkpen (Eds.), *Proceedings of the 2006*

20th Anniversary Conference on Computer Supported Cooperative Work (pp. 209–218). New York, NY: ACM.

Kientz, J., Hayes, G., Westeyn, T., Starner, T., & Abowd, G. (2007). Pervasive computing and autism: Assisting caregivers of children with special needs. *IEEE, Pervasive Computing, 6*(1), 28–35.

Learn the Signs, Act Early. (2013, January). Retrieved from Centers for Disease Control and Prevention (CDC), http://www.cdc.gov/ncbddd/actearly/index.html

Nazneen, N., Boujarwah, F.A., Rozga, A., Oberleitner, R., Pharkute, S., Abowd, G.D., & Arriaga, R.T. (2012, May). Towards in-home collection of behavior specimens: Within the cultural context of autism in Pakistan. In R. Arriaga, M. Tentori, A. Mihailidis, J. Bardram, & A. Matic (Eds.), *Proceedings of the 6th International Conference on Pervasive Computing Technologies for Healthcare, San Diego, CA.* New York, NY: IEEE.

Nazneen, N., Rozga, A., Romero, M., Findley, A., Call, N., Abowd, G.D., & Arriaga, R. (2012). Supporting parents for in-home capture of problem behaviors of children with developmental disabilities. *Personal Ubiquitous Computing, 16*(2), 193–207.

Shore, R. (1997). Rethinking the brain: New insights into early development. *Families and Work Institute,* 16–17.

Teacher Training and Practical Implementation

Sarah C. Wayland

■ ■

In this section, three chapters deal with the practical aspects of getting technology into the classroom. In the first chapter, "Racing Through the Professional-Development Obstacle Course," Christopher R. Bugaj, Melissa A. Hartman, and Mark E. Nichols describe the obstacle course leading to effective professional development in the area of technology. They begin with a review of research-based practices for delivering effective professional development, identify the common barriers, and describe the strategies used by Loudoun County Public Schools to ensure guided success for districts, schools, and teachers. They describe the status of digital learners within today's classrooms and emphasize the importance of a teacher's ability to effectively use technology, integrating it with the curriculum in the service of universal design for learning. For each type of training (district, school, and teacher), they describe a prerace checklist that lists important considerations as you plan your training, including money and materials. They then describe how to create a training plan that carefully considers how the material will be delivered, addressing issues of timing, location, and curriculum. The last consideration is how to maintain fitness by planning for follow-up so that teachers can follow through effectively.

The second chapter, "Using Distance Learning Technology to Increase Dissemination of Evidence-Based Practice in Autism Spectrum Disorder," by Brooke Ingersoll and Allison Wainer, describes how to effectively use distance learning to train parents and professionals to implement evidence-based interventions. These can include programs that use recorded lectures, slide presentations, written materials, and video examples to provide this training. The authors describe and evaluate the features of a variety of distance learning programs, including those that replace or supplement face-to-face instruction. They also describe how learners acquire knowledge and discuss whether the activities are synchronous or asynchronous. This approach has the potential to be far more cost effective than in-person training models and can increase access to evidence-based interventions for children with ASD.

The third chapter, "Bringing a School up to Speed: Experiences and Recommendations for Technology Implementation," by Monica Adler Werner, Kathryn Nagel, Chris Bendel, and Bonnie Beers, describes the process of selecting, evaluating, and implementing new technology in the Model Asperger Program at Ivymount, a nonpublic school in Rockville, Maryland, so as to prepare students for the real world. In the first part of this chapter, they describe how the school chose from the many available resources. They describe how they put together a working group, determined (and funded) the appropriate infrastructure, set priorities, and vetted their options. In the second part, they describe how they prepared for getting the technology into the classroom, including dealing with administrative issues; training teachers, parents, and students; pilot programs; and other implementation issues. The last part of their chapter describes how they developed acceptable use policies for staff and students, established internet safety policy, and taught students to self-monitor.

This section provides practical advice for teachers, clinicians, and parents, and it is our hope that it will help guide you through the critically important process of integrating technology into the school curriculum for students with ASD.

Racing Through the Professional-Development Obstacle Course

▪ ▪

Christopher R. Bugaj, Melissa A. Hartman, and Mark E. Nichols

Take a moment to reflect on the best professional development (PD) experience you have ever had. What made it so good, so memorable? Now take another moment to ponder the worst. Not hard to find one of those, was it? If you have never experienced bad PD, you need to give us a call so we can visit your school system! Even after years of research on effective PD, we all continue to sit through painful lectures and "sit & git" sessions that are all too soon forgotten. There is a better way!

In this chapter, we race through the PD obstacle course to demonstrate how effective PD can be provided related to serving students with autism spectrum disorders (ASDs) using technology. We leap time constraints in a single bound, dodge naysayers, jump the hurdles of learning preferences and variability of participants—you get the picture. Our goal is to provide you with ideas for creating your own high-quality PD that yields positive results for students with ASDs. After briefly reviewing what the scholarly literature has to say about preferred practices in PD, we focus on PD at the central office, building, and individual levels. Each part of this chapter reviews the prerace checklist, continues with a training plan, and ends with maintaining your fitness levels after the race.

PREFERRED PRACTICES IN A NUTSHELL

According to Reeves (2010), PD should focus on how teachers and leaders can affect student achievement. Student results must be analyzed within each classroom and high-impact professional learning should link student gains to strategies. Reeves believes that the analysis of teacher or leader decision making is as important as monitoring student gains, and effective, high-impact, professional development should focus on practices and people rather than on specific programs (Reeves, 2010). We agree.

When designing PD, it is extremely important that trainers focus on content and accessibility. By following the three basic principles of universal design for learning (UDL; i.e., multiple means of representation, action and expression, and engagement) in designing PD, trainers ensure access to the widest range of learners regardless of age. It is a well-known fact that everyone has learning preferences and each of us likes to do some things better than others. Research has shown that all learners need to engage in meaningful collaboration and be active participants in learning (National Staff Development Council [NSDC], 2010).

To begin the process, a needs assessment should be conducted to determine areas of student need (Bubb & Early, 2007; Reeves, 2010). Once the needs of the students have been prioritized and narrowed, trainers may utilize the principles of UDL (see Chapter 2) to determine how to design materials, produce meaningful products, and engage participants by making the learning relevant and interactive. For more information on UDL, visit the CAST web site (http://www.cast.org), which provides a wealth of resources and information. Utilizing the UDL principles will ensure accessibility for participants in PD and students.

Researchers in preferred practices support utilizing the UDL framework for PD when they state that participants must see immediate value in what they are doing and that learning should be collaborative, interactive, and multimodal (Bubb & Early, 2007). Adults and children alike need to be active learners. Participants love to walk away from PD with a product or strategy they can use right away. Many authors agree that another key piece of PD is ongoing support and follow-up (Bubb & Early, 2007; NSDC, 2010; Reeves, 2010; Robb, 2000; Sparks, 2002). There should be mechanisms in place to monitor and evaluate progress toward goals and evaluate products created during PD. Otherwise, why are we doing it?

PROFESSIONAL DEVELOPMENT
AT THE DISTRICT LEVEL: PRERACE CHECKLIST

District-level administrators are in essence the guiding beacons for the school division in aligning the focus of PD for training ASD-specific education to the division-level goals and priority projects. They carry the immense responsibility of determining how to provide efficient and effective staff development to those in need. So how are the needs determined? The item at the top of every administrative checklist should be a needs assessment that identifies the "competencies and needs of individual staff members" (Wald & Castleberry, 2000, p. 43). District administrators can use a variety of tools and data for conducting the needs assessment. These may include, but are not limited to, program surveys, suggestions from advisory committees, and reviews of student education plans and past performance indicators, as well as direct classroom observations. A mix of qualitative and quantitative data should be incorporated into developing the specifics of the training plan that will provide the best options for participants to engage and grow professionally. The checklist itself can be quite simple:

• Who will the audience be?

• Is attendance by certain populations required?

- Will remuneration be provided?

- When will the audience receive the training?

- Where will the professional development occur?

- Will make-up sessions be offered?

- Who will design and/or facilitate the training?

- Will follow-up be provided to support the implementation of the strategies or tools learned, and what amount of such follow-up is adequate?

- Will participants be evaluated on the use of the learned content?

All these questions should be considered in the prerace checklist so that the actual training plan can be appropriately designed to allow participants to navigate the PD obstacle course to reach the goals established.

PROFESSIONAL DEVELOPMENT
AT THE DISTRICT LEVEL: TRAINING PLAN

Although the PD obstacle course may appear impossible to navigate for some, there is always a path to success. Sometimes, a nontraditional approach is required to engage all adults regardless of the obstacle course's barriers. Finding the right balance to motivate and deliver the "big picture" during PD is vital to the completion of the course. Opportunities for customized training plans should be offered to all course participants. This involves building in choice and providing flexible options for staff to learn and obtain the information needed. Too often, PD is viewed as something that must occur prior to a teacher entering the classroom. The logic and evidence are certainly sound for this model, but the reality is that teachers (especially new teachers) frequently are thrown into the obstacle course with no sense of context. Prioritizing which PD teachers need prior to the start of school can often be a contentious subject among the various program administrators who support them. There are certainly peak times when PD should be provided throughout the school year. Finding the right balance to deliver continuous opportunities for PD is vital to success.

According to the national findings of the 2011 Speak Up survey by Project Tomorrow, a national education nonprofit group, 38% of the 36,477 surveyed teachers still prefer face-to-face PD on digital content usage and curriculum integration. However, as the roles and responsibilities of teachers are increasing while the time for face-to-face PD is decreasing, district administrators should leverage technology for providing sustainable and collaborative PD opportunities. Fifty-six percent of the surveyed teachers indicated that they would like to leverage technology to allow collaboration with other teachers within schools through an online collection of vetted, grade-level, content-specific resources. High-quality PD can occur on demand, any time, any day, from any device with internet access. Some tools that can be used to support this model include blogs, wikis, podcasts, video supports, asynchronous webinars, and online management systems and courses. Utilizing tools of this nature can greatly reduce some of the most common barriers to completion of the PD obstacle course, including location, time, and money. Using tools of this nature also provides multiple representations of the material and fosters increased opportunities for engagement at the leisure of each participant. In some instances, professional development must occur at a time or location that may not be convenient. In this case, why not seek permission to videotape the event and then share the information with colleagues? For example, Tori Saylor, an adult with ASD, recently provided an inspirational account of her life and the supports provided to help her reach her goals both within and beyond the K–12 environment. The session was videotaped (with her permission) and made available to all staff and parents who were unable to attend in person. Thus, this great opportunity could be viewed on demand from any computer with access to the school's network.

If the actual delivery of PD becomes a barrier, PD trainers can video document the model classrooms supporting students with ASD and share the content with teachers who are struggling to find the right supports and resources. Perhaps a classroom adoption model would work. For whatever reason, every district has classrooms where teachers are struggling to support students. A group of administrators and/or teachers could adopt one of these classrooms and video document the makeover process to share with other teachers—call it your Extreme Autism Classroom Makeover and make a big deal out of the selection process so that teachers feel enthusiastic about being selected, not terrified! There are various ways to capture and distribute the documents, pictures, and videos associated with this transition. One method that might captivate a greater number of staff involves the creation of instructional CDs or DVDs to provide a mobile and on-demand learning opportunity. Include a questionnaire for participants to complete once the CD or DVD has been viewed, and you now have a PD session that participants can complete in any environment with a computer or DVD player, at any preferred time, and for which quantitative data can be collected to ensure the media has been viewed.

Let us not forget the importance of including fellow administrators in the training plan; they should also have exposure to preferred practices and techniques for supporting students with ASD. Although scheduling administrators for training events can seem like an insurmountable obstacle, there is usually a common, overlapping time when PD can be delivered—something quick and simple that administrators can really sink their teeth into, like a lunch-and-learn series called Tech Bite Tuesdays. Any administrator who oversees student services could participate in the series. The idea would be to provide a 1-hour session when administrators can bring their lunch and engage with various techniques and technologies for supporting teachers and students. However, just providing the opportunity for the series to occur is not sufficient. One must find a way to attract attendance to these sessions. Perhaps it is a motivating colleague who is presenting, a technology support used by teachers and/or students that has been advertised to increase personal productivity levels, a certificate program offering recertification or time-compensation points, or simply an open and inviting delivery method that encourages all staff regardless of ability or current knowledge levels. Let's face it, PD can be intimidating for many adults, especially those unfamiliar or uncomfortable with certain practices, techniques, technologies, or, quite simply, change.

PROFESSIONAL DEVELOPMENT
AT THE DISTRICT LEVEL: MAINTAINING FITNESS

District- and school-based administrators can continue to foster a high level of mental fitness and engagement by frequently reviewing and adjusting the fitness plan, and encouraging teacher involvement. Administrators should require teacher participation in one or many of the various forms of PD offered within the district and include participation as part of a teacher's evaluation process toward relicensure. Administrators should identify and advertise specialized supports (technology or personnel based, or both) to further enhance and help integrate learned strategies and techniques for instructing students with autism. Remember, administrators should act as personal trainers to foster collaborative partnerships between other administrators, technology support staff, and teachers to provide a platform that allows the learning to continue.

PROFESSIONAL DEVELOPMENT
FOR TEACHERS: PRERACE CHECKLIST

The challenges of creating PD for teachers at the school level are much the same as they are at every other level—money, time, location, and type of training to conduct. Training at this level should be completed at the school site or in school clusters so that it is convenient for teachers and does not waste travel time. Training may be conducted by school staff who are on site, staff who are at another school, central office staff, or outside professionals. Teachers may obtain funding for PD and related materials through grants provided by local education agencies, business partners, parent–teacher organizations, and associations that support students with ASD and other disabilities.

Who do you train? When focusing on students with ASD, the answer would be everyone. All staff should be trained in the basic characteristics and needs of students with ASD. The bus drivers, cafeteria workers, and anyone in the school the student may interact with should be educated. If students have specific behavior plans that must be followed throughout the day, everyone involved with the student needs to be trained for consistency and data collection purposes. Small teams of teachers and paraprofessionals may need to be trained on specific techniques to utilize with students in class such as discrete trial training, applied behavior analysis (ABA), picture exchange communication system (PECS), creating visual schedules, designing workspace, or training how to conduct functional behaviorial assessments and develop behaviorial intervention plans.

Options for conducting training include providing time through designated staff development days, on teacher workdays, through independent learning outside of school via online modules, during regularly scheduled staff meetings, or during the school day. Some teachers appreciate PD when it is provided during the school day, whereas others prefer to use non–school hours. How do you find the time? Consider the following example of what Ms. GoodTeacher did in her school.

Based upon the needs assessment survey conducted at the beginning of the year, the principal asked Ms. GoodTeacher to conduct several training sessions throughout the year on utilizing interactive whiteboards to teach students with ASD in the content areas. Since she knew her fellow teachers did not want to come in before or after school, she decided to conduct mini trainings during teacher planning periods that would focus on one small topic at a time. Her first session focused on virtual sorting activities where students had to place items in the correct container. If the answer was correct, the item stayed in the container and the class heard applause; if not, it popped back out of the container and prompted the student to try again. During the session, teachers would adapt this activity utilizing their own content.

PROFESSIONAL DEVELOPMENT FOR TEACHERS: TRAINING PLAN

Establishing a plan that allows sufficient time for training and follow-up is crucial. Research indicates that single trainings with no follow-up or individual accountability tend to be ineffective (Reeves, 2010). Training for teachers who work with students with ASDs may occur at required monthly meetings or during extended staff development days for which teachers are paid to attend. These may be large-group trainings that focus on particular topics during each session. Teachers have the opportunity during these meetings to share what they are doing, troubleshoot issues, and learn new skills. Ongoing training may also occur at the school level with the assistance of consulting teachers (generally master teachers hired to provide support to schools in such areas as specific disability or specific content areas). Here is how Ms. GoodTeacher conducted PD for the staff at her school.

Ms. GoodTeacher knew that utilizing the whiteboard and computer with many students on the spectrum was effective, motivating, and engaging. She had created structured activities that could be geared toward students' special interests. The tool also allowed students (and teachers) the flexibility of using movement and tactile, auditory, and visual stimulation depending upon a student's needs and preferences. So, she decided to arrange for eight mini sessions (two per quarter). Teachers were given topics for the training ahead of time and asked to bring information with them to the training that suited the topic of the day. Trainings were conducted in the computer lab, so everyone had access to a device that would allow them to create his or her own activities. Teachers in the same content areas were encouraged to collaborate during the sessions. Ms. GoodTeacher would model a completed activity first, then demonstrate how it was created, allowing the teachers to follow along step by step. The teachers could either watch Ms. GoodTeacher on the board or work from printed directions.

You are probably thinking, how does this teacher keep up with her own classes? Well, at the high school level, Ms. GoodTeacher's school runs on a 4×4 block; she has another teacher trainer split the time with her. If the issue is coverage, she may have the consulting teacher and/or technology resource teacher work with her to create a schedule to ensure coverage during training days.

PROFESSIONAL DEVELOPMENT FOR TEACHERS: MAINTAINING FITNESS

Follow-up and accountability are key to ongoing development and learning. Teachers may be assigned homework, data collection, or mini projects to complete between meeting sessions. If teachers are participating in a one-shot training, it will be up to the staff at the school to design activities for follow-up practice and monitoring of new skills and/or techniques. Teachers may also focus on a particular student or group of students to implement a strategy and monitor progress. If teachers are working on behavior plans, submitting regular progress reports would be the follow-up plan.

Constructive and timely feedback must be a central part of follow-up activities. Teachers need to be able to submit their work and either have a peer review system or someone to review the work to provide feedback. Feedback could come in written form for a specific product, in the form of a classroom walk-through, face-to-face meetings, online collaborative environments such as Moodle or e-mail. If teachers are utilizing time outside of school for projects and meetings, it is important to provide them with recertification points or some other incentive to attend.

In the example of Ms. GoodTeacher's work, teachers create their own activities and utilize them with their students in the interim between trainings. During the next meeting time, teachers share the created activities and post them on the school web site so everyone can access them. To further motivate teachers to use the new technique, the principal has offered prizes for those who create and share additional activities throughout the year.

INDIVIDUAL PROFESSIONAL DEVELOPMENT: PRERACE CHECKLIST

Despite PD happening at the district and school levels, there is a continued need for PD to occur centering on the needs of individual students. However, a variety of challenges present themselves when attempting to provide PD based on specific individual student needs. These challenges include providing for time to conduct the training, targeting various competencies in relation to the content for each team member, establishing who will conduct the training, and developing a plan of action for implementing what is learned through the training.

The needs of individual students with autism may vary greatly; in turn, the needs of those educators working with each individual may vary. For example, at a district-level, workshops might be offered to instruct educators about behavioral intervention plans. Administrators at a school level might initiate trainings for the entire school staff to implement a schoolwide behavior plan. Educators working with a student with autism may require additional training to personalize, customize, and successfully implement a behavior plan for each individual student. Providing training to educators working with students with autism based on the needs of their specific situation increases the likelihood of meaningful implementation of interventions, tools, and strategies.

Once individual goals are established for a student and strategies are put in place, the professionals working with the student begin collecting data on whether or not the student is making progress. When data reflect a lack of achievement, additional or alternative strategies should be implemented. At times, the cadre of professionals working with a student might require training to establish and implement the new strategies.

For example, Tucker is a fifth-grade student with goals focusing on increasing length of utterance and increasing the number of communication interactions he has within a day. At the beginning of the school year, his teacher participated in district-wide training, presented by two district speech-language pathologists, where she learned strategies to facilitate communication. She then applied these strategies with Tucker during the first two quarters of the school year. After collecting data and documenting progress on his communication goals, his teacher realized that Tucker was communicating more frequently, but his length of utterance was still about the same. She got in touch with her colleagues on Tucker's team, and as a group they decided to consult with the speech-language pathologists who conducted the initial training to generate additional strategies specific to Tucker.

INDIVIDUAL PROFESSIONAL DEVELOPMENT: TRAINING PLAN

No educator working with a student with autism is an island. A team of professionals exists to provide the necessary supports to meet the unique needs of every student. In this way, no one educator is forced to decide alone on the best approach to take to help a student achieve. Instead, the group of professionals work together to gather and analyze evidence to guide the decision-making process. At times, these teams may require additional and ongoing trainings to help them make informed decisions; this is when individualized training plans pertaining to the specific needs of that team can be established.

Needs of individual students are dynamic, constantly shifting as students learn new skills. Likewise, a team's professional development needs will shift over time to match what is required to educate each student. In this way, PD initiatives based on the needs of an individual student cannot be provided as a one-time occurrence. Multiple means of representing information over time based on the ever-changing needs of the student will help to provide a consistent platform from which to grow. Furthermore, research indicates that PD that is provided over a span of time has a greater instructional impact than shorter, one-time, training episodes (Garet, Porter, Desimone, Birman, & Yoon, 2001). Therefore, providing content specific to student or situation in various ways over a span of time maximizes the chances that the content will be integrated successfully to cause change.

For example, the team of individuals working with Maggie decided that she would benefit from a communication device. The assistive technology trainer working with the team to implement the device presented the team with multiple modalities over a span of weeks to help with the successful integration of the device by providing video, audio, images, and text customized to Maggie's situation. Initially, the trainer established a semiflexible schedule to instruct the team regarding the device, starting by providing a podcast episode on the concept of augmentative communication that contained stories of students successfully implementing a device. The team listened to the audio to gain a basic understanding. Later, the trainer conducted face-to-face training where members of the team experienced the device firsthand, becoming familiar with its different features. Next, the trainer provided the team with a video of another student successfully using the software. Likewise, in the following weeks, the trainer shared blogs, research articles, charts, and graphics promoting use of the device. Once the team members initiated use of the device, they participated in online discussion forums about how implementation was working. Based on the feedback provided in the discussion, the trainer considered the next steps necessary to foster continued integration. When the team created specialized pages for Maggie to use on the devices, the trainer found that these pages would be beneficial to other students as well. In this way, the team generated products that were useful in training other educators. Using this collaborative and universally designed approach, the trainer provided every team member with the content over time using modalities that best matched their learning styles at a level of complexity suitable to meet their needs.

The role of the trainer changes over time to meet the needs of individual situations. At first, the trainer might be one of the core or extended team members who helps to formulate the decision about which tool, strategy, or intervention should be put in place. In this role, the trainer acts as an evaluator who helps to analyze the situation to make an informed decision. Once the decision is made regarding how to act, the role of the trainer changes to that of a content planner. In this role, the trainer is deciding the necessary content, the best formats for delivering the content, and how often the content should be delivered. In a sense, the trainer is devising a training plan, either formally or informally, to create a path of successful integration. Once the plan is established, the trainer's role shifts again to that of a content provider. When utilizing and maintaining different modes of communication, among them discussion forums, e-mail, and face-to-face interactions, the role of the trainer shifts from providing content to guiding or mentoring and continuing to facilitate change.

■ ■

PARENTS AND STUDENTS AS PARTNERS

Although not participating in a professional role, parents are an integral part of the decision-making process. In every situation, a student benefits when a synergistic partnership occurs across all learning environments, including the home, private therapies, and other environments. Although situations vary, the average student spends approximately 40 hours a week in a school environment and 128 hours a week in the home environment (Figure 14.1). With that amount at home, the greatest chance of successfully integrating a strategy at school is to implement it not just at school but everywhere outside of school as well. Therefore, it is often necessary to provide training to the parents, caregivers, and other family members who frequently interact with the student. This could be accomplished using social media, web-based PD delivery platforms (videos, podcasts, tweets, and webinars, etc.), or in-person trainings.

■ ■

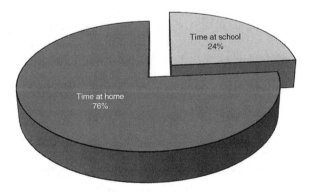

Figure 14.1   Student time per environment.

Depending on the strategy being implemented, as well as the student's age and abilities, the student should also be considered part of the team. In many situations, the student might be included in the training for the implementation of a strategy. In every case, it is important to consider the potential benefits of involving the student in the training.

Consider the implementation of a software program that provides auditory feedback for written text with a student named Marco. Marco was shown the software and asked if he thought it would help him write. Marco felt empowered that he was involved in the decision-making process. When it was decided that he would begin to use the software to help him achieve his written expression goal, training was conducted with Marco present, learning beside his teachers. Excited by the benefits, Marco told other students in his class about the software, effectively inviting his peers to begin using the software. Months later, after he had successfully integrated the software into his writing practice, Marco helped to demonstrate how he used the software in training videos for other classrooms by modeling its successful use.

Maintaining Fitness

After strategies stemming from PD are put in place for an individual, it is necessary to continue to monitor progress toward achieving the targeted goal. When data show that progress is being made, it is reasonable to assume that the PD trainers have done what they set out to do. Successful implementation should lead to measurably positive results, so measuring the outcomes becomes a key element in the ongoing education of the student (and teacher). Once team members successfully internalize and utilize a tool, strategy, intervention, or approach, they can begin to share what they have learned with other educators.

Educators who have practical implementation experience can share their successful methodologies with others at any level. These educators could conduct district-level trainings to provide an overview to other professionals working with students with autism throughout the district, provide schoolwide trainings discussing how best to serve the students with autism at their school or provide direct or indirect consultation services to other educators in the district who share students with similar needs. Likewise, educators can form personal learning communities around a central condition, tool, or strategy or collectively join a larger, existing community. Ultimately establishing, maintaining, or participating in a community helps to ensure continued successful implementation of the content while cultivating a sense of collaboration, which breeds success for individual students, every student in the school, and every student in the district.

Returning to the example of Ms. GoodTeacher, consider another student of hers, Ty, who has the accommodation of using graphic organizers for both reading and writing assignments. Ms. GoodTeacher has developed a number of different templates containing graphic organizers that Ty has successfully used to achieve his writing goals. Knowing other students could utilize these templates and knowing that it might save other teachers development time, she decided to share her templates online for others to download via her blog. Teachers began to download the templates; they left comments about how they used the templates and made suggestions, and so a community formed, centered around the varied uses of the templates. Ms. GoodTeacher and all the other users of her templates began to rely on each other to exchange ideas. Soon many users began sharing their own graphic organizing templates, and what started as a strategy used for one individual blossomed into a network of support.

CONCLUSION

After racing through the PD obstacle course with us, we hope you see that PD can be delivered at any and all levels in a school system to enable professionals to learn new techniques, strategies, and practices. Following preferred practices by providing various modalities for PD, including follow-up activities and accountability, is key to ongoing success and growth at all levels.

REFERENCES

Bubb, S., & Early, P. (2007). *Leading & managing continuing professional development: Developing people, developing schools* (2nd ed.). London, England: Paul Chapman.

Garet, M.S., Porter, A.C., Desimone, L., Birman, B., & Yoon, K.S. (2001). What makes professional development effective? Results from a national sample of teachers. *American Educational Research Journal, 38*(4), 915–945.

National Staff Development Council (NSDC). (2010). *National staff development council standards* (Rev. ed.). Retrieved from http://www.nsdc.org/standards/index.cfm

Project Tomorrow. (2011). *Personalizing the classroom experience: Teachers, librarians and administrators connect the dots with digital learning.* Retrieved from http://www.tomorrow.org/speakup/pdfs/SU11_PersonalizedLearning_Educators.pdf

Reeves, D. (2010). *Transforming professional development in student results.* Alexandria, VA: ASCD.

Robb, L. (2000). *Redifining staff development: A collaborative model for teachers and administrators.* Portsmouth, NH: Heinemann.

Sparks, D. (2002). *Designing powerful professional development for teachers and principals.* Oxford, OH: National Staff Development Council.

Wald, P.J., & Castleberry, M.S. (2000). *Educators as learners: Creating a professional learning community in your school.* Alexandria, VA: Association for Supervision and Career Development.

Using Distance Learning Technology to Increase Dissemination of Evidence-Based Practice in Autism Spectrum Disorder

■ ■

Brooke Ingersoll and Allison Wainer

Given the need for intensive early intervention in children with autism spectrum disorders (ASDs; Maglione, Gans, Das, Timbie, & Kasari, 2012; National Research Council [NRC], 2001) and the growing number of children requiring such services (Matson & Kozlowski, 2011), an expansion in the availability of, and access to, evidence-based treatments is essential. Unfortunately, there has not been a corresponding growth in the dissemination of evidenced-based interventions for children with autism. This, in turn, has engendered a service–need discrepancy for children with autism and their families (Sperry, Whaley, Shaw, & Brame, 1999; Stahmer & Gist, 2001; Symon, 2005). Indeed, the majority of families of children with autism in the United States report receiving substantially fewer hours of services than the 25 hours per week recommended by the National Research Council (2001; Hume, Bellini, & Pratt, 2005). Further, much of the intervention being provided to children with ASD is not considered evidence based (NRC, 2001). This is due, in part, to the fact that many individuals working with children with ASD do not receive sufficient instruction in evidence-based intervention techniques (NRC, 2001). Barriers associated with training therapists in evidence-based intervention techniques include limited monetary resources, significant time demands, and problems with the portability of intervention from the research laboratory to existing clinical settings (Kazdin, 2004). As such, it is necessary to consider training models in which these barriers can be overcome in time- and cost-effective ways.

One approach to increasing access to evidence-based interventions for children with ASD has been to train parents. Teaching parents to provide intervention themselves can increase the number of intervention hours that a child receives and improve long-term outcomes. A number of studies have demonstrated that parent training is an effective approach for improving social-communicative development and decreasing problem behavior in children with ASD (Brookman-Frazee, Vismara, Drahota, Stahmer, & Openden, 2009). Research indicates that parents can learn to use intervention strategies with fidelity (Alpert & Kaiser, 1992) and that parent use of these strategies results in increased language, social interaction, and play skills (Drew et al., 2002; Gillett & LeBlanc, 2007; Green et al., 2010; Kasari, Gulsrud, Wong, Kwon, & Locke, 2010; Laski, Charlop, & Schreibman, 1988), as well as decreased problem behaviors (Aman et al., 2009) in their child with ASD. Parent training also improves the quality of life for the family by reducing parental stress (Tonge et al., 2006) and increasing parental leisure and recreation time (Koegel, Schreibman, Britten, Burke, & O'Neill, 1982). This benefit is important, given the high rate of stress and depression in parents of children with ASD (Dumas, Wolf, Fisman, & Culligan, 1991).

Despite the benefits of training parents to provide evidence-based interventions to their children with ASD, formal parent-training programs are rare in community-based settings. In an Indiana survey, only 21% of parents of children with ASD under 8 years of age reported receiving parent training (Hume et al., 2005). A major obstacle to the provision of parent training in community settings is the lack of appropriately trained providers (Mahoney et al., 1999), underscoring the need for cost-effect dissemination efforts for providers. Further, most parent-training programs for children with ASD involve frequent parent coaching by a therapist. Thus, the absence of reliable transportation, lack of child care, cost of treatment, and limited flexibility in scheduling can significantly affect access to these services (Koegel, Symon, & Kern Koegel, 2002). These barriers are even more pronounced for families in rural areas, for whom long distances, poor roads, and climatic barriers also limit access to services (Horner et al., 1994). Thus, dissemination efforts, which can increase access to instruction in evidence-based interventions, are also needed for parents.

DISTANCE LEARNING TOOLS

Computerized distance learning programs have the potential to help address, and surmount, many of the challenges associated with traditional dissemination models by granting remote access to training in evidence-based practices. There are numerous benefits associated with using computer and internet-based technology to disseminate evidence-based practices, including the potential for intervention to be accessed from anywhere at any time and the ability to individualize training while keeping instruction standardized and maintaining fidelity of program implementation (Hollon et al., 2002; Mandel, Bigelow, & Lutzker, 1998). Computerized distance learning programs also favor an exciting and interactive learning experience, allowing for the combination of many instructional formats, including graphics, animation, video, and audio. This format makes it possible for the learner to directly interact with the instructional content; hypothetical situations, vignettes, and practice exercises can be transformed from words on a page into such rich media forms as video or animation, which then can be used to develop and test the participant's knowledge (Weingardt, 2004). Moreover, advances in computer and internet technology have made it possible for users to stream or upload video of themselves using intervention techniques and to receive remote feedback or coaching from an expert trainer via phone, e-mail, or web chat. Given the promise of such service delivery models, research has begun to explore the use of distance learning technology to supplement, or even replace, traditional training models that typically require both significant travel and time commitments.

This approach to disseminating evidence-based interventions is low cost and can surmount many barriers to participation in traditional training programs. Computer and internet-delivered programs have been utilized to train professionals in a variety of health- and education-related settings (Benjamin et al., 2008; Weingardt, Cucciare, Bellotti, & Lai, 2009). Moreover, distance learning technology has been utilized to train parents in evidence-based techniques for reducing disruptive child behaviors and increasing positive parenting behaviors (Feil et al., 2008; Kacir & Gordon, 1999; Taylor et al., 2008). The promise of disseminating evidence-based interventions to professionals and parents via distance learning technology has recently been recognized in the autism intervention field. Over the past few years, several online programs that require a paid subscription have become available, including RethinkAutism (http://www.rethinkautism.com), AutismPro (http://www.autismpro.com), Advanced Training Solutions (http://www.advancedtrainingsolutions.com), and Skills by the Center for Autism and Related Disorders (http://www.skillsforautism.com). In addition, several programs are also provided over the internet free of charge, including Autism Distance Education Parent Training (ADEPT), offered through University of California, Davis's MIND Institute (http://www.ucdmc.ucdavis.edu/ddcenter/CEDD_ourproducts.html), and the Autism Internet Modules (AIM), offered through the Ohio Center for Autism and Low Incidence (OCALI; http://www.autisminternetmodules.org).

Features of Distance Learning Programs

The U.S. Department of Education characterized distance learning activities in terms of three dimensions in their recent meta-analysis evaluating the effectiveness of online learning (U.S. Department of Education, 2010). The first dimension is whether the program is intended to replace face-to-face instruction or to supplement or augment face-to-face instruction. Programs whose aim is to replace face-to-face instruction should demonstrate learning outcomes that are at least equivalent to traditional forms of instruction. On the other hand, programs whose aim is to supplement face-to-face instructions should demonstrate outcomes that are better than face-to-face instruction alone. Although many online or distance learning courses use online components to supplement face-to-face instruction by encouraging learners to engage more with the material (e.g., learners attend a lecture and then complete online quizzes to test their comprehension of the material), distance learning programs aimed at disseminating autism interventions have focused primarily on the goal of replacing some or all components of face-to-face instruction.

The second dimension is the learning experience itself or how learners acquire knowledge. Distance learning experiences, like face-to-face learning, can be conceptualized as expository, active, or interactive. In expository learning, the content is transmitted to the learner by lecture, written material, or some other mechanism. For autism programs, this has primarily involved the presentation of written information, slide shows, or streaming or recorded lectures presented via DVD or internet technology. In active learning, the learner acquires knowledge through interaction with the instructional content in the form of self-check exercises or quizzes or interactive simulations. For autism programs, this type of learning has primarily involved the use of self-check exercises tapping the understanding of the instructional content and video ratings tapping the recognition of correct and incorrect examples of implementation.

In interactive learning, the learner builds knowledge through collaborative interaction with others. In most distance learning contexts, interactive learning is conducted between learners (e.g., students taking an online course participate in a guided discussion over an online message board). In distance learning programs aimed at disseminating autism interventions, it is more common to see interactive learning conducted through the use of technology to provide the learner with feedback or coaching regarding their use of the intervention with the children with ASD. In this way, the learner gains knowledge through interaction with an expert, rather than with other learners.

The third dimension used to characterize distance learning is whether the activity is *synchronous*, with instruction occurring in real time, or *asynchronous*, with a lag between the presentation of the material and the learner's response. Autism programs using synchronous instruction have used live webcasts or teleconferencing to present lectures or workshops, as well as live coaching via video chat programs, such as Skype or GoogleTalk. Autism programs using asynchronous instruction have utilized written information, recorded webcasts, or videotaped lectures presented via DVD or over the web, as well as video-based coaching in which an expert coach provides feedback to the learner based on a prerecorded video of the learner using the techniques at an earlier time.

IMPLEMENTATION

Although current research is sparse, there is growing support for the efficacy of such technology for disseminating training in evidence-based ASD intervention. At the writing of this chapter, 12 studies had been published in peer-reviewed journals that evaluated computerized distance learning programs for training providers or parents in ASD interventions. These programs vary across the U.S. Department of Education's three distance learning dimensions (see Figure 15.1). It is important to note that several of the programs were developed in order to enhance and streamline traditional face-to-face instruction, whereas others were developed with the potential to replace in-person training models all together. Although both uses of distance learning are beneficial for moving the ASD intervention field forward, the programs that replace face-to-face instruction hold the most promise for surmounting barriers associated with current service delivery models. Moreover, the relationship of the online program to face-to-face instruction should influence the types of activities utilized, the synchronicity of instruction, and important outcome measures. Thus, programs developed to augment in-person training are discussed first, followed by those programs with the potential to replace traditional face-to-face instruction.

Distance Learning Programs Designed to Supplement Face-to-Face Instruction

Of the 12 computerized distance learning programs for ASD interventions that have been assessed in the literature, 3 were evaluated as supplemental tools to augment in-person instruction. These programs typically have combined online distance

Article	Learners		Relationship to face-to-face instruction		Types of computerized learning activities			Synchronicity of instruction		Outcomes measured			
	Providers	Parents	Replace	Supplement	Expository	Active	Interactive	Synchronous	Asynchronous	Usability	Knowledge	Learner fidelity	Child behavior
Baharav and Reiser (2010)		X		X			D	X		X			X
Buzhardt and Heitzman-Powell (2005)	X			X	A, B, C	E			X	X	X		
Gibson et al. (2010)	X		X		B		D	X	X	X		X	X
Granpeesheh et al. (2010)	X			X	A, C				X		X		
Hamad et al. (2010)	X	X	X		A, B, C	E				X	X		
Howroyd and Peeters (2007)		X	X		B, C	E, F			X	X			
Machalicek, O'Reilly, Chan, Lang, et al. (2009); Machalicek, O'Reilly, Chan, Rispoli, et al. (2009); Machalicek et al. (2010)							D					X	X
Nefdt et al. (2009)		X	X		A, B, C	E			X	X		X	X
Wainer and Ingersoll (2013)	X	X	X		A, B, C	E			X	X	X	X	X
Vismara et al. (2009)	X	X	X		A, B, C		D	X	X	X	X	X	X

Note: X is used to indicate that the program included the specific attribute described above. The specific types of computerized activities used are denoted using the following letters:
A. Lectures, slideshows
B. Written information, manual
C. Video examples, animation
D. Video conferencing (teleconferencing, Skype)
E. Quizzes, self-check, application exercises
F. Behavior tracking

Figure 15.1. Distance learning programs for interventions for persons with autism spectrum disorders.

learning activities with traditional in-person training to disseminate ASD intervention techniques. For example, Granpeesheh and colleagues (2010) compared the effectiveness of an e-Learning program with traditional in-person didactic training to teach new behavioral therapists the principles and procedures involved with applied behavior analysis (ABA). The e-Learning program was asynchronous and consisted of several expository learning activities. In particular, this program utilized training modules with animated slides, audio recordings, and video demonstrations. After completing the modules, participants attended a 2-hour follow-up discussion with an expert therapist to address questions about the teaching techniques. Results from this study indicate that participants in both training groups significantly increased their knowledge about ABA principles and procedures, with those in the traditional training group demonstrating slightly more gains than those in the e-Learning condition (Granpeesheh et al., 2010). These results suggest that a computerized training program can be an effective supplemental information delivery system, yet it is unclear how these gains in knowledge translate to the ability to correctly implement the ABA techniques. It is important to note that support from expert trainers seemed to produce additional learning benefits.

Buzhardt and Heitzman-Powell (2005) also investigated a program to introduce ABA principles to behavioral aides working with children with ASD. The program instruction was delivered asynchronously and utilized expository as well as active learning activities. The online lessons included text, graphics, animation, and short quizzes to learn about the various ABA procedures. Participants had a week to work through each module; however, they reported that it took an average of 56 minutes to complete each tutorial and an average of 21 minutes to complete the associated quizzes. In order to bolster participants' ability to implement ABA techniques, a 3-hour-long, group face-to-face training session was held with the participants each week after they completed the corresponding module. During these sessions, the participants spent 2 hours practicing or observing ABA with two to three different children with ASD. The end of each session was spent summarizing the practice session and introducing the next week's topic. Participants increased their scores on a knowledge quiz of ABA from pre- to posttraining. Moreover, participants reported that the technology was easy to use and noted high levels of satisfaction with the training program. Although the live practice sessions were integrated into the program in order to help participants apply ABA techniques, the study investigators did not evaluate changes in participant fidelity of intervention implementation.

Baharav and Reiser (2010) explored the use of distance learning to supplement traditional face-to-face training for parents implementing in-home speech and language therapy. Participants attended weekly in-person clinic-based training sessions and then received weekly home-based remote coaching and feedback sessions. In this case, the remote coaching program was interactive and delivered synchronously. Moment-to-moment feedback was delivered using an internet-based video chat system and wireless Bluetooth headsets. Results from the pilot study with two parents and their children with ASD suggested that the remote coaching was both feasible and effective; they found that child gains achieved in traditional therapy settings could be maintained and improved when the parent received remote synchronous feedback and supervision from an expert therapist. Moreover, the parents found that the technology was useable and the distance coaching was valuable. Nonetheless, the parents indicated some challenges associated with the remote coaching including the difficulty of staying within the range of the webcam and the uncontrolled nature of training sessions conducted in the home (Baharav & Reiser, 2010).

The foregoing studies lend preliminary evidence to the suggestion that distance learning tools may be helpful supports to augment traditional face-to-face learning formats. The use of this technology to supplement in-person training may help to make a more interactive and effective training program and may reduce the overall number of hours of face-to-face instruction needed. However, such programs do not necessarily address the issue of increasing access to intervention for individuals without access to traditional face-to-face programs. Given that the need for increased access to ASD intervention is so great, research on distance learning in ASD intervention has also focused on programs with potential to replace more traditional in-person training models.

Distance Learning Programs Designed to Replace Face-to-Face Instruction

A number of distance learning programs have been developed with the potential to replace face-to-face instruction. These programs can be classified as either self-directed, in which the learner completes the training independently, or remote coaching, in which the learner receives active coaching from an expert at a distance.

Self-Directed Programs   Several studies have examined the potential of self-directed distance learning programs to provide total training in ASD intervention techniques. Such programs have been designed with the possibility of replacing traditional in-person face-to-face training models. These programs have primarily utilized expository and active learning activities with content that is delivered asynchronously. For example, Hamad, Serna, Morrison, and Fleming (2010) explored the feasibility and utility of an internet-based distance learning program to teach ASD service providers, educators, paraprofessionals, and parents behavioral intervention techniques. The online course consisted of three training modules that introduced the concepts of positive reinforcement, relationship building, and prompting. The modules included lecture, video examples across several different children, providers, and settings, self-check exercises, and links to other sources of information about the behavioral intervention techniques. In an initial evaluation of the program, approximately half of the users took from 1 to 4 hours to complete each of the modules and the other half from 5 to 8 hours to complete each module (Hamad et al., 2010). In this study, users significantly increased their scores on a knowledge quiz of behavioral intervention techniques from pre- to posttraining. Although individuals with bachelor's degrees and associate's degrees had mean pretests scores that were significantly lower than did individuals with master's degrees, all three groups performed comparably on the posttest measure. This finding is encouraging, given the dearth of research that has evaluated the effect of education level on distance learning program outcomes. In addition, the majority of participants rated the program very highly in terms of usability, quality, and appropriateness of the course materials (Hamad et al., 2010). Although this study suggests that this type of distance learning program is feasible and satisfactory for increasing knowledge, it remains unclear whether this program would be sufficient for training users to implement behavioral intervention. Furthermore, only 60% of individuals who were enrolled in the study completed the course, yet variables influencing course completion were not evaluated.

In another study, Howroyd and Peeters (2007) described a self-directed distance learning program, AutismPro, that is aimed at teaching parents strategies for building social-emotional, communication, academic, language, understanding, self-care, and motor skills in their young children with ASD. The program consists of an online software system that utilizes multimedia to teach various intervention techniques, including video demonstrations and step-by-step procedures for implementing the strategies with a given child. The software also provides the user with treatment recommendations and allows for child progress to be tracked. An initial evaluation of the program explored the feasibility, utility, and perceived value of this program for parents of children with ASD (Howroyd & Peeters, 2007). The results from this study suggest that parents were able to navigate the online program and felt that the instructional content was appropriate, easy to understand, and helpful. Finally, parents felt that this was a valuable program to help support, guide, and manage their child's intervention. It is important to note that this research did not evaluate parents' implementation of the content introduced in AutismPro. Although program usefulness was rated highly, it is unknown how well parents were actually learning and utilizing the information presented in the course. Moreover, only approximately half of families given access returned their ratings of the program. As such, the experiences and perceptions of the other half of program users are unknown. Nonetheless, this initial study suggests that distance learning programs may be ecologically valid ways to increase access to training and educational information for parents of children with ASD.

Acknowledging the lack of research evaluating procedural knowledge, Nefdt, Koegel, Singer, and Gerber (2010) examined the use of a self-directed distance learning program on parents' fidelity of intervention implementation. Parents of young children with autism were randomly assigned to a treatment or control group. Parents in the treatment group received a distance learning program that taught motivational techniques from pivotal response training (PRT), an intervention approach aimed at increasing children's social communication, primarily their verbal language, whereas parents in the control group were simply monitored. The program consisted of 14 training modules presented via DVD with an accompanying paper-based parent manual. Each module presented information via text and audio lecture and provided short video examples of each technique. Parents completed short quizzes to check for comprehension at the conclusion of each module. In addition, at the conclusion of the program, parents participated in an interactive learning task where they assessed others' abilities to implement PRT techniques. Results indicated that parents were generally willing to complete such a program and that those who completed it were able to implement PRT strategies with fidelity, provided more language opportunities for their children, and displayed greater confidence when interacting with their children. In addition, children of these parents showed an increase in their use of verbal language compared to the children in the control group (Nefdt et al., 2010). Thus, results suggest that such a training program has the potential to take the place of traditional in-person training models. However, since the distance learning program was not compared to a face-to-face training program, it is unclear whether gains in parent and child skills were commensurate with gains seen in traditional training models.

Most recently, Wainer and Ingersoll (2013) used a single-subject, multiple-baseline design to examine the ability of a self-directed distance learning program to train new research assistants and parents in reciprocal imitation training (RIT), a naturalistic behavioral imitation intervention for young children with ASD. The training program was administered using commercially available distance learning course management software. Course content was presented via narrated slide presentations augmented with video examples and written descriptions of the techniques. Each lesson concluded with a short comprehension quiz and several interactive learning tasks in which users rated others' abilities to implement RIT techniques. The program consisted of five training modules that took between 4 and 40 minutes to view, depending on lesson content and the number of embedded video examples. Research assistants took an average of 14 days to work through the entire program, whereas parents took an average of 22 days to do the same. Results from this initial study indicated that both sets of participants increased their knowledge of RIT and naturalistic intervention from pre- to posttraining. All participants increased their use of the intervention techniques during the treatment phase. Moreover, two thirds of the participants were able to achieve fidelity of RIT implementation based solely on their use of the self-directed program. The remaining participants were able to achieve fidelity of implementation after one 30-minute in-person coaching session consisting of demonstration, feedback, and discussion. In addition, participation in this training led to increases in child imitation rates during adult–child interactions. It is important to note that parents found that this program and service delivery model were effective, acceptable, and usable. Results suggest that this self-directed distance learning program may be effective for disseminating training in ASD intervention techniques. Whereas this program utilized face-to-face coaching for one third of the participants, future research is underway to evaluate the use of a synchronous remote coaching and feedback system in order to augment the asynchronous distance learning program.

Remote Coaching Programs   Advances in computer and internet technology have made it possible for individuals utilizing distance learning programs to receive remote coaching and feedback from expert trainers. Although feedback can be delivered via asynchronous programs (e.g., a user uploads video and a coach watches it at a later time), research has primarily focused on feedback provided via synchronous programs, such as videoconferencing or live video chat. The majority of this research has evaluated programs that utilize expository and/or interactive learning activities to replace traditional in-person face-to-face dissemination of evidence-based intervention techniques.

In a series of studies, Machalicek and colleagues (Machalicek, O'Reilly, Chan, Lang, et al., 2009; Machalicek, O'Reilly, Chan, Rispoli, et al., 2009; Machalicek et al., 2010) examined the use of videoconferencing to provide immediate feedback to teachers learning to implement several different behavior management strategies. In each study, a live internet-based, video-chat system was utilized so that trainers could observe the teachers in the classroom and provide moment-to-moment feedback using built-in computer microphones and speakers. Machalicek, O'Reilly, Chan, Lang, et al. (2009) evaluated the efficacy of this approach for training preservice teachers to implement preference assessments with individuals with ASD and developmental disabilities. Before engaging in the distance learning, teachers

were provided with a brief written description of the procedures involved with conducting preference assessments and told to practice these with their student. During
subsequent sessions, teachers implemented the task procedures while supervisors
watched the implementation via the videoconferencing technology. Supervisors
collected data on teacher performance and provided immediate feedback throughout the session. Teachers were able to implement the procedures with 100% accuracy during their supervised sessions. Because teachers were already implementing
the techniques correctly, it was impossible to evaluate the incremental utility of the
remote coaching on implementation. Nonetheless, these initial evaluations suggest
that videoconferencing is a feasible option for providing synchronous feedback and
coaching during implementation of a set protocol.

In a related study, this group evaluated the use of the same technology to train
preservice teachers to conduct a functional analysis for two children with ASD who
were exhibiting problem behavior (Machalicek, O'Reilly, Chan, Rispoli, et al., 2009).
Teachers were supervised implementing their first-ever functional behavior analysis via this distance learning technology. Advanced trainers instructed the teachers though the analysis procedures and provided corrective feedback if there were
errors in implementation. Classroom interventions based on the information provided by the functional analysis resulted in a decrease in problem behavior for the
two children, corroborating the validity of the functional analysis. In a follow-up
study, Machalicek et al. (2010) evaluated the efficacy of this synchronous distance
learning approach for training teachers to conduct a functional analysis for children
with ASD exhibiting problem behavior. Teachers initially learned about functional
analysis by reading a written description outlining the procedures involved in the
task delivered via e-mail. During subsequent sessions, teachers implemented the
procedures in the classroom while receiving supervision via video teleconferencing. Immediate corrective feedback (including modeling of a correct procedure) was
provided if the teacher made an error in implementation. Although the six teachers
implemented functional analysis with relatively high accuracy after only reading
the manual, performance was also quite variable across teachers and tasks. During
the video teleconferencing coaching condition, teachers improved their implementation and all teachers reached fidelity within 19 sessions. Teacher fidelity maintained for several weeks after performance feedback was discontinued; however,
fidelity declined significantly thereafter, suggesting that continued performance
feedback may have been necessary for maintaining teacher fidelity.

Taken together, the studies done by Machalicek and colleagues suggest that
distance learning technology can be feasibly and effectively used to provide immediate feedback and coaching to individuals learning to implement intervention
techniques. It is important to note that utilization of this technology did present
challenges to trainers and trainees. For example, when teachers were working with
children who had more frequent or severe disruptive behaviors, they were more
likely to experience technical difficulties (Machalicek et al., 2010).

Gibson, Pennington, Stenhoff, and Hopper (2010) explored the use of videoconferencing to provide consultation support to preschool staff learning to implement functional communication training, a procedure that involves implementing
functional behavioral assessments of problem behaviors and then replacing such
behaviors with more appropriate communicative responses. A live web-based, teleconferencing system (Skype) was utilized so that trainers could observe the staff in

the classroom and provide feedback using built-in computer microphones and ear buds. Before implementing the techniques directly with a child, the participants were e-mailed procedural instructions for the intervention and engaged a videoconference with an expert consultant. During this initial training videoconference, the consultants demonstrated the techniques and then coached the staff with moment-to-moment feedback as they practiced the procedures. The training lasted approximately 45 minutes, at which time the participants demonstrated 100% accuracy of the techniques and felt confident in their abilities to implement the intervention procedures. During the classroom intervention sessions, the consultants viewed the participants' implementation but waited until after the procedure concluded in order to give feedback on the intervention implementation to all participants at once. Once the staff began implementing the intervention, the target child's problem behaviors decreased. The results from this study suggest that classroom staff could be successfully trained to implement effective intervention techniques via an interactive synchronous distance learning program.

Blended Programs   To date, a limited amount of research has explored the integration of asynchronous self-directed programs using expository and active learning elements with synchronous interactive coaching components. Such blended models hold particular promise in that they provide both didactic instruction as well as live feedback, both of which are common elements in effective training programs. In one study, investigators compared the effectiveness of a DVD-delivered self-directed training program with either in-person didactic instruction and team supervision or remote didactic instruction and team supervision to train community-based therapists working with children with autism and their families (Vismara, Young, Stahmer, Griffith, & Rogers, 2009). This particular study evaluated both instructional format (e.g., self-directed vs. self-directed with didactic instruction and supervision) and service delivery model (e.g., live instruction vs. remote instruction) for improving fidelity of intervention implementation, as well as improving fidelity of parent coaching. The self-directed portion of the training utilized a DVD with the treatment manual, copies of data collection materials, and video examples of the techniques. The didactic portion of the training consisted of a 10-hour, 2-day seminar that presented information about the intervention and techniques via a slide show, video examples, group discussion, and role play. Finally, the team supervision component of the training consisted of a 2-hour small-group meeting where expert coaches answered questions and provided individual feedback based on previously submitted video of therapists implementing the intervention techniques. Each small group received a 1-hour telephone call at the end of training. All therapists utilized the same self-directed training program; half of them participated in the seminar and supervision in person; the other half participated in the seminar and supervision remotely via video teleconferencing (Vismara et al., 2009).

Results from this study indicated that after participating in the self-directed component, therapists significantly improved their implementation of intervention techniques and parent coaching. Moreover, these abilities improved even more after therapists received the didactic instruction and team supervision. The majority of therapists required these additional training components to achieve fidelity of implementation in the direct implementation of the intervention, and only one out of seven therapists was able to achieve fidelity of parent coaching by the end of all training components. It is important to note that there were no differences in fidelity of intervention or parent coaching between the in-person and remote didactic instruction and team supervision groups. Together, these findings suggest that asynchronous self-directed learning and synchronous interactive coaching can be effectively integrated into blended distance learning programs that are comparable to in-person training formats. Given the time, cost, and logistics associated with traditional in-person expert coaching, results from this study suggest that the potential for the replacement of such models with remote instruction and feedback is particularly promising.

IMPLICATIONS

Thus far, there is emerging evidence to suggest that computerized distance learning programs can effectively disseminate training in evidence-based interventions to parents and providers who work with children with ASD. A number of different distance learning programs that employ a variety of learning activities have been developed and evaluated. There is preliminary evidence to suggest that distance learning alone or in combination with face-to-face instruction can increase parent and provider knowledge of key intervention concepts (Buzhardt & Heitzman-Powell, 2005; Granpeeshah et al., 2010; Hamad et al., 2010), as well as correct implementation of intervention procedures for increasing appropriate social communication skills (Nefdt et al., 2010; Vismara et al., 2009; Wainer & Ingersoll, 2013) and decreasing problematic behaviors (Gibson et al., 2010; Machalicek, O'Reilly, Chan, Lang, et al., 2009; Machalicek, O'Reilly, Chan, Rispoli, et al., 2009; Machalicek et al., 2010). Although fewer studies have examined changes in child behaviors, those that have, have found that increases in adult fidelity of implementation are associated with improvements in child behavior (Machalicek, O'Reilly, Chan, Lang, et al., 2009; Vismara et al., 2009; Wainer & Ingersoll, 2013). Most studies have found high user satisfaction ratings for the distance learning components, though some have found that learners were less confident in the skills they learned through self-directed distance learning activities than through face-to-face or remote interactive activities (i.e., videoconferencing; Vismara et al., 2009; Wainer & Ingersoll, 2013). So far, no studies have examined the effect of distance learning on the maintenance of learner skill or child improvements after the training phase. Skill maintenance might be expected to wane over time, especially for programs that are completely self-directed. Thus, evaluating maintenance over time is an important next step for studies evaluating the efficacy of distance learning programs for training parents and providers in ASD interventions.

Although there is growing evidence for the efficacy of distance learning programs for teaching individuals to implement ASD interventions, it is unclear how this method of instruction compares to traditional training models. Although many of the programs reviewed above have the potential to replace in-person face-to-face instruction, research demonstrating that such programs are at least equivalent to traditional training models is lacking. Only two studies thus far have compared distance learning directly to traditional training models for teaching intervention strategies (Granpeesheh et al., 2010; Vismara et al., 2009). Vismara and colleagues (2009) did not find any differences in therapist fidelity or child outcomes for face-to-face training versus video conference training. Granpeesheh and colleagues (2010) found that participants in the face-to-face training condition made greater gains in knowledge than those in the distance learning condition. However, there were a number of differences between the two conditions in terms of the learning activities employed as well as the time involved. For example, the face-to-face condition included didactic instruction, group discussion, and role play and took learners 16 hours to complete; whereas the distance learning condition included slide shows with corresponding audio lectures and video examples and took roughly 10 hours to complete. Thus it is not clear whether differences in knowledge acquisition were due to differences in the method of presentation or in the learning activities employed. Given the conflicting results, additional research is needed that can compare distance learning to face-to-face instruction for ASD interventions. Such comparisons are challenging because computerized distance learning often lends itself to the use of different instructional strategies than face-to-face instruction. Since different learning activities may have a differential impact on knowledge or skill acquisition, it may be desirable to compare similar learning activities implemented in a face-to-face or distance learning format.

Clearly, more research is needed to determine which individual training activities are important for learner acquisition of evidence-based interventions for children with ASD and whether those activities are better implemented in a synchronous or asynchronous manner. Of course, this issue is not unique to distance learning. The effectiveness of different distance learning components or activities is likely to differ depending on the learning objective. For example, it might be expected that didactic and active learning activities may be most effective for increasing conceptual knowledge regarding the intervention, whereas interactive learning activities, particularly in the form of expert feedback or coaching conducted through videoconferencing, may be more important for increasing procedural knowledge (i.e., fidelity of implementation).

Despite limited data from autism interventions, there is substantial research on the comparative efficacy of distance learning programs for teaching a wide variety of concepts and skills to adults of varying backgrounds. Several recent meta-analyses of distance learning have been published (e.g., Allen et al., 2004; Bernard et al., 2004; Cavanaugh, 2001; U.S. Department of Education, 2010). These meta-analyses have found distance learning to be at least equivalent to live instruction for both declarative knowledge and procedural learning. A recent meta-analysis by the U.S. Department of Education (2010) that compared online learning to face-to-face instruction or blended online and face-to-face instruction found that learners that completed all or some of their learning online (blended instruction) outperformed those who completed all of their learning face to face. Blended learning programs that included online and face-to-face elements had a greater advantage than online-only programs. However, the report noted that across studies, learners engaged more with the material in online or blended courses than in face-to-face courses; thus it is unclear whether the time with the material or the delivery method is responsible for outcomes. Given these findings, research aimed at disseminating evidence-based treatments may wish to examine whether adding distance learning components to face-to-face training models can improve learning outcomes.

Finally, the potential reach of distance learning programs for disseminating autism interventions is wide, particularly for those programs that are self-directed and accessed over the internet. At the same time, little is known about how potential learners access and use such programs. The one study that looked at completion rates found that only 60% of learners who began the program completed it (Hamad et al., 2010). Since there was no comparison condition, it is unclear whether this rate is lower than would be expected for more traditional training approaches. However, it might be expected that the use of distance learning programs may differ from face-to-face training models, particularly for programs that are self-directed. It is also unknown what factors may affect whether or not learners use distance learning programs. For programs that use the internet, access to and familiarity with computer and internet technology might be expected to influence learners' willingness to engage in the program and may also affect learning outcomes. However, more research is needed in this area.

SUMMARY

The literature thus far is supportive of the role that distance learning programs can play in the dissemination of evidence-based interventions for children with ASD. The use of computerized technology has the potential to significantly increase access to services for children with ASD. Emerging research in this area as well as research on distance learning more broadly suggests that distance learning results in learning outcomes that are at least equivalent, if not superior, to traditional training approaches. More research is needed on ways to optimize the use of distance learning technology for disseminating ASD interventions and improving child and family outcomes.

REFERENCES

Allen, M., Mabry, E., Mattrey, M., Bourhis, J., Titsworth, S., & Burrell, N. (2004). Evaluating the effectiveness of distance learning: A comparison using meta-analysis. *Journal of Communication, 54,* 402–420.

Alpert, C.L., & Kaiser, A.P. (1992). Training parents as milieu language teachers. *Journal of Early Intervention, 16,* 31–52.

Aman, M.G., McDougle, C.J., Scahill, L., Handen, B., Arnold, L.E., Johnson, C.,... Wagner, A. (2009). Medication and parent training in children with pervasive developmental disorders and serious behavior problems: Results from a randomized clinical trial. *Journal of the American Academy of Child & Adolescent Psychiatry, 48,* 1143–1154.

Baharav, E., & Reiser, C. (2010). Using telepractice in parent training in early autism. *Telemedicine and e-Health, 16,* 727–731.

Benjamin, S.E., Tate, D.F., Bangdiwala, S.I., Neelon, B.H., Ammerman, A.S., Dodds, J.M., & Ward, D.S. (2008). Preparing child care health consultants to address childhood overweight: A randomized controlled trial comparing web to in-person training. *Maternal and Child Health Journal, 12,* 662–669.

Bernard, R.M., Abrami, P.C., Lou, Y., Borokhovski, E., Wade, A., Wozney, L.,... Huang, B. W. (2004). How does distance education compare with classroom instruction? A meta-analysis of the empirical literature. *Review of Educational Research, 74,* 379–439.

Brookman-Frazee, L., Vismara, L., Drahota, A., Stahmer, A., & Openden, D. (2009). Parent training interventions for children with autism spectrum disorders. *Applied behavior analysis for children with autism spectrum disorders* (pp. 237–257). New York, NY: Springer.

Buzhardt, J., & Heitzman-Powell, L. (2005). Training behavioral aides with a combination of online and face-to-face procedures. *Teaching Exceptional Children, 37,* 20–26.

Cavanaugh, C.S. (2001). The effectiveness of interactive distance education technologies in K–12 learning: A meta-analysis. *International Journal of Educational Telecommunications, 7,* 73–88.

Drew, A., Baird, G., Baron-Cohen, S., Cox, A.,

Slonims, V., Wheelwright, S.,...Charman, T. (2002). A pilot randomised control trial of a parent training intervention for preschool children with autism. *European Child & Adolescent Psychiatry, 11,* 266–272.

Dumas, J.E., Wolf, L.C., Fisman, S.N., & Culligan, A. (1991). Parenting stress, child behavior problems, and dysphoria in parents of children with autism, Down syndrome, behavior disorders, and normal development. *Exceptionality, 2,* 97–110.

Feil, E.G., Baggett, K.M., Davis, B., Sheeber, L., Landry, S., Carta, J.J., & Buzhardt, J. (2008). Expanding the reach of preventive interventions: Development of an internet-based training for parents of infants. *Child Maltreatment, 13,* 334–346.

Gibson, J.L., Pennington, R.C., Stenhoff, D.M., & Hopper, J.S. (2010). Using desktop videoconferencing to deliver interventions to a preschool student with autism. *Topics in Early Childhood Special Education, 29,* 214–225.

Gillett, J.N., & LeBlanc, L.A. (2007). Parent-implemented natural language paradigm to increase language and play in children with autism. *Research in Autism Spectrum Disorders, 1,* 247–255.

Granpeesheh, D., Tarbox, J., Dixon, D.R., Peters, C.A., Thompson, K., & Kenzer, A. (2010). Evaluation of an eLearning tool for training behavioral therapists in academic knowledge of applied behavior analysis. *Research in Autism Spectrum Disorders, 4,* 11–17.

Green, J., Charman, T., McConachie, H., Aldred, C., Slonims, V., Howlin, P.,...Pickles, A. (2010). Parent-mediated communication-focused treatment in children with autism (PACT): A randomised controlled trial. *Lancet, 375,* 2152–2160.

Hamad, C.D., Serna, R.W., Morrison, L., & Fleming, R. (2010). Extending the reach of early intervention training for practitioners. *Infants & Young Children, 23,* 195–208.

Hollon, S.D., Muñoz, R.F., Barlow, D.H., Beardslee, W.R., Bell, C.C., Bernal, G.,...Sommers, D. (2002). Psychosocial intervention development for the prevention and treatment of depression: Promoting innovation and increasing access. *Biological Psychiatry, 52,* 610–630.

Horner, S.D., Ambrogne, J., Coleman, M.A., Hanson, C., Hodnicki, D., Lopez, S.A., & Talmadge, M.C. (1994). Traveling for care: Factors influencing health care access for rural dwellers. *Public Health Nursing, 11,* 145–149.

Howroyd, C., & Peeters, T. (2007). Parent participation in early intervention with software-assisted guidance from Autism-Pro. *Good Autism Practice (GAP), 8,* 31–36.

Hume, K., Bellini, S., & Pratt, C. (2005). The usage and perceived outcomes of early intervention and early childhood programs for young children with autism spectrum disorder. *Topics for Early Childhood Special Education, 25,* 195–207.

Kacir, C.D., & Gordon, D.A. (1999). Parenting adolescents wisely: The effectiveness of an interactive videodisk parent training program in Appalachia. *Child and Family Behavior Therapy, 21,* 1–22.

Kasari, C., Gulsrud, A.C., Wong, C., Kwon, S., & Locke, J. (2010). Randomized controlled caregiver mediated joint engagement intervention for toddlers with autism. *Journal of Autism and Developmental Disorders, 40,* 1045–1056.

Kazdin, A.E. (2004). Evidence-based treatments: Challenges and priorities for practice and research. *Child and Adolescent Psychiatric Clinics of North America, 13,* 923–940.

Koegel, R.L., Schreibman, L., Britten, K.R., Burke, J.C., & O'Neill, R.E. (1982). A comparison of parent training to direct child treatment. In R.L. Koegel, A. Rincover, & A.L. Egel (Eds.), *Educating and understanding autistic children* (pp. 260–279). San Diego, CA: College-Hill Press.

Koegel, R.L., Symon, J.B., & Kern Koegel, L. (2002). Parent education for families of children with autism living in geographically distant areas. *Journal of Positive Behavior Interventions, 4,* 88–103.

Laski, K.E., Charlop, M.H., & Schreibman, L. (1988). Training parents to use the natural language paradigm to increase their autistic children's speech. *Journal of Applied Behavior Analysis, 21,* 391–400.

Machalicek, W., O'Reilly, M., Chan, J.M., Lang, R., Rispoli, M., Davis, T.,...Didden, R. (2009). Using videoconferencing to conduct functional analysis of challenging behavior and develop classroom behavioral support plans for students with autism. *Education and Training in Developmental Disabilities, 44,* 207–217.

Machalicek, W., O'Reilly, M., Chan, J.M., Rispoli, M., Lang, R., Davis, T.,...Langthorne, P. (2009). Using videoconferencing to support teachers to conduct preference assessments with students with autism and developmental disabilities. *Research in Autism Spectrum Disorders, 3*, 32–41.

Machalicek, W., O'Reilly, M.F., Rispoli, M., Davis, T., Lang, R., Franco, J.H., & Chan, J.M. (2010). Training teachers to assess the challenging behaviors of students with autism using video tele-conferencing. *Education and Training in Autism and Developmental Disabilities, 45*, 203–215

Maglione, M., Gans, G., Das, L., Timbie, J., & Kasari, C. (2012). Nonmedical interventions for children with ASD: Recommended guidelines and further research needs. *Pediatrics, 130*, S169 –S178.

Mahoney, G., Kaiser, A., Girolametto, L., MacDonald, J., Robinson, C., Safford, P., & Spiker, D. (1999). Parent education in early intervention: A call for a renewed focus. *Topics for Early Childhood Special Education, 19*, 131–140.

Mandel, U., Bigelow, K.M., & Lutzker, J.R. (1998). Using video to reduce home safety hazards with parents reported for child abuse and neglect. *Journal of Family Violence, 13*, 147–162.

Matson, J.L., & Kozlowski, A.M. (2011). The increasing prevalence of autism spectrum disorders. *Research in Autism Spectrum Disorders, 5*, 418–425.

National Research Council (NRC). (2001). *Educating children with autism.* Committee on Educational Interventions for Children with Autism. C. Lord and J.P. McGee (Eds.). Division of Behavioral and Social Sciences and Education. Washington, D.C.: National Academy Press.

Nefdt, N., Koegel, R., Singer, G., & Gerber, M. (2010). The use of a self-directed learning program to provide introductory training in pivotal response treatment to parents of children with autism. *Journal of Positive Behavior Interventions, 12*, 23–32.

Sperry, L.A., Whaley, K.T., Shaw, E., & Brame, K. (1999). Services for young children with autism spectrum disorder: Voices of parents and providers. *Infants & Young Children, 11*, 17–33.

Stahmer, A.C., & Gist, K. (2001). The effects of an accelerated parent education program

on technique mastery and child outcome. *Journal of Positive Behavior Interventions, 3*, 75–82.

Symon, J.B. (2005). Expanding interventions for children with autism. *Journal of Positive Behavior Interventions, 7*, 159–173.

Taylor, T.K., Webster-Stratton, C., Feil, E.G., Broadbent, B., Widdop, C.S., & Severson, H.H. (2008). Computer-based intervention with coaching: An example using the Incredible Years Program. *Cognitive Behaviour Therapy, 37*, 233–246.

Tonge, B., Brereton, A., Kiomall, M., Mackinnon, A., King, N., & Rinehart, N. (2006). Effects on parental mental health of an education and skills training program for parents of young children with autism: A randomized controlled trial. *Journal of the American Academy of Child & Adolescent Psychiatry, 45*, 561–569.

U.S. Department of Education. Office of Planning, Evaluation, and Policy Development. (2010). *Evaluation of evidence-based practices in online learning: A meta-analysis and review of online learning studies,* Washington, D.C.: U.S. Government Printing Office.

Vismara, L.A., Young, G.S., Stahmer, A.C., Griffith, E.M.M., & Rogers, S.J. (2009). Dissemination of evidence-based practice: Can we train therapists from a distance? *Journal of Autism and Developmental Disorders, 39*, 1636–1651.

Wainer, A., & Ingersoll, B. (2013). Using an internet-based training program to disseminate naturalistic behavioral techniques to individuals working with young children with autism. *Journal of Autism and Developmental Disorders, 43*, 11–24.

Weingardt, K.R. (2004). The role of instructional design and technology in the dssemination of empirically supported, manual-based therapies. *Clinical Psychology: Science and Practice, 11*, 313–331.

Weingardt, K.R., Cucciare, M.A., Bellotti, C., & Lai, W.P. (2009). A randomized trial comparing two models of web-based training in cognitive-behavioral therapy for substance abuse counselors. *Journal of Substance Abuse Treatment, 37*, 219–227.

Bringing a School up to Speed

*Experiences and Recommendations
for Technology Implementation*

∎∎∎∎∎∎∎∎∎∎∎∎∎∎∎∎∎∎∎∎∎∎∎∎∎∎∎∎∎∎

Monica Adler Werner, Kathryn Nagle, Chris Bendel, and Bonnie Beers

Although it is evident to most educators and intervention specialists that technology can support students with autism spectrum disorders (ASDs) in ways previously only dreamed, the task of implementing that technology in a classroom or therapeutic setting can be paralyzing. Many educators and therapists have little background in technology and even less in how to vet options, create integrated systems, and train students and staff on effective use. Resistance to change is not unique to people with ASDs: When it comes to shifting to new, promising technologies, teachers and therapists also require support and need help understanding the value of change.

This chapter presents a real-world perspective on some of the considerations, strategies, challenges, and benefits involved in implementing technology in a class or schoolwide, sharing our experiences from the Model Asperger Program (MAP) at the Ivymount School in Rockville, Maryland. Utilizing the existing talents of engaged staff, investing in workshops and trainings for the program's "thought leaders," and carefully assessing our needs, we are moving to robustly using cloud-based computing and free web tools for parent communication and student organization. In addition, laptop computers support students in writing and note taking, and a pilot classroom is exploring the advantages of switching from laptops to iPads for use as communication tools and educational resources. It has taken a lot of work to get to this point, but the result is an exciting and dynamic technology-supported environment in which students, teachers, and administrators work cooperatively to maximize resources and to explore developing new tools to meet our specific needs. The work involved in getting to this point, specifically for the two most recent initiatives of the cloud and iPads, is the focus of this chapter.

ABOUT THE MODEL ASPERGER PROGRAM

A 6-year-old program, MAP is designed to serve the special learning needs of students with ASDs with average to above-average cognitive skills and solid language skills. Ivymount is a nonpublic school certified by the state of Maryland Department of Education and focused on serving students with special needs; most of our students are placed at Ivymount by public school systems to provide their students with a free and appropriate public education (FAPE). Our students have challenges that the public schools were not able to manage, generally in the areas of executive functioning, anxiety, and behavior. Using a fully integrated social learning program directed toward core areas of challenge, MAP guides students to understand themselves so they can self-advocate and set goals for learning and life success. The challenges to integrating technology are compounded by the fact that MAP is one of two programs for students with autism at the Ivymount School, both with technology needs that compete for resources and server capacity because the number of devices has increased almost fivefold in 5 years.

Laptops have been an integral part of the program from the beginning. Students use them to type their notes and papers, demonstrate knowledge through PowerPoint, and surf the internet. Our students have always pushed the technology envelope for us. As our program grew from 12 students to 50, so did the technology demands, but without parallel growth in technology staff. We have developed some internal expertise, with two teachers—Chris Bendel and Kathryn Nagle, two coauthors of this chapter—emerging as technology leaders in the program and assuming many responsibilities that traditional information technology (IT) support staff perform. They have helped to channel our enthusiasm for innovation with practical support and understanding.

We encountered three key challenges as we moved beyond basic laptop functions to implement a new phase of integrating technology in our program:

- Creating a system for making decisions and determining needs

- Getting to rollout of the new systems and training the users

- Developing internet use policies and safe surfing procedures

Overcoming these challenges took careful planning combined with the willingness to take risks. We have had to persevere and maintain resilience as we have made mistakes at each juncture, requiring us after each setback to quickly regroup, learn the necessary lessons, and develop a Plan B—fittingly, the same themes we emphasize with our students to develop their flexibility and problem-solving skills. The process has not been the neat rollout for which we had hoped: We have had to make decisions before we felt completely ready, missed deadlines, and felt discouraged by the innumerable obstacles that even the best planning could not foresee. Although we have been able to maintain momentum and have made progress, we have had to adjust our criteria for success and maintain a sense of humor. In the face of yet another technology snafu our teachers joke, "Stay calm and pretend it's in the lesson plan."

CREATING A SYSTEM FOR MAKING DECISIONS AND DETERMINING NEEDS

The first and ongoing challenge we have faced was information overload. There are so many resources available and seemingly infinite variations on the same themes.

With so many choices, one would think perfect solutions could be found. However, enthusiasm for an application (app) or program was often quickly squelched by an overwhelming number of questions; concerns about the tension between individual needs, the needs of the classroom teachers, and the needs of the administrations; and the costs and benefits of any given options.

Putting Together a Working Group

To create a clearinghouse for our issues, we formed a small working committee composed of two administrators and two technology-savvy teachers. The committee members explored new technology options both during planning at school and on their own time. The two teachers met weekly; the whole group met once or twice a month. Flexibility in scheduling these meetings was integral in maintaining a positive attitude toward the project. Teacher buy-in at this level was key and it was important that the meetings never seemed frivolous. The composition of this group was an essential asset: The administrators contributed the global perspective and the ability to make decisions and secure resources, whereas the teachers brought an on-the-ground perspective as well as the technological knowledge to effectively assess options and answer the administrators' many questions. Defined roles quickly emerged, with one administrator representing the role of outside users (parents) and institutional concerns, the second administrator representing students and usability, and the teachers representing classroom teachers' needs, implementation feasibility, and technological expertise. We identified pressing needs (our needs assessment), set priorities, and then vetted solutions. As roles emerged and the administrative team realized how much time and effort teachers required to follow through with research and planning, the team worked to alleviate extra demands and give teachers the required space and time without asking them to make time and energy sacrifices outside their contractual agreements. Because MAP is an 11-month program, this objective was most easily accomplished by reducing the teachers' content and classroom involvement during the summer school session, thus giving them a month of time to dedicate almost exclusively to this process. Once the skeletal structure was developed and we moved into the regular school year, meetings were scheduled twice a week. The times and attendance for these meetings were flexible and regularity of meetings were faded to an as-needed basis once programs were underway.

Infrastructure Matters and Is Expensive

The needs assessment began with the identification of basic infrastructure requirements, including such essentials as access to hardware and reliable internet with sufficient bandwidth and stability. Building up the infrastructure to meet the needs of not only MAP but also the other programs at Ivymount took longer and cost more money than we would have predicted. Trying to move forward without adequate internet access, however, proved to be a disaster. Early on in our experimentation with web-based programs, before we attempted iPad implementation, we found that our limited infrastructure resulted in lost teaching time due to slow or intermittent access to the wireless network. Streaming video would constantly pause to buffer, wireless connections would drop in the middle of uploading to or downloading from cloud-based services, and web-based textbooks were simply unusable. Students who typically had challenges managing frustration were overwhelmed by despair over slow and inadequate technology. While administrators at MAP and Ivymount looked for the resources to upgrade our connectivity in the building, MAP reverted to more reliable ways, using the laptops as productivity devices and relying on network drives rather than cloud-based services for organization and sharing.

A year later, we had perfect wireless connectivity. However, word spread fast in the building, and the three other programs at Ivymount began to compete with MAP for bandwidth. A quick review revealed our bandwidth as inadequate, especially in a building where most teachers consider streaming media a fundamental part of learning, reinforcement, and self-regulation. Another year later (yes, we were now 2 years into our process), we acquired enough bandwidth to begin trying some of the technology solutions that our original needs assessment identified as possible.

Setting Priorities

While we worked to address our infrastructure needs, our technology committee continued the needs assessment process and determined that we were in fact working on two projects, one about our communications system and one about optimal use of iPads. The communication challenge was finding a web-based system that would facilitate communication among teachers, students, and parents. We needed a program that would allow individual students and families to access homework, grades, and classwork and provide an online document storage system to facilitate accessing work at home or school. Our choice in this area touched every member of our community. The iPad project was more limited, though important for us to explore future possibilities for both hardware and software choices. The iPads were a vector for the web-based systems and a seemingly appropriate replacement for heavier, more expensive, and less alluring laptops. For our students' needs, the greatest attraction of the iPad was the robust number of apps that support attention, executive function, and organization.

Vetting Options

The technology committee served as an excellent clearinghouse as teachers requested they vet apps and programs that claimed to solve all problems for all students. First, the teacher members of the technology committee looked for outside experts to help cull the options. Careful internet searches led to extraordinarily useful blogs, wikis, and web sites run by users and reviewers within the educational technology world. This was a more effective strategy than relying on vendors and random "app store" searches (see Useful Websites and Blogs sidebar for a list of the sites we found most useful). Second, the teachers on the technology committee educated themselves by attending the Maryland Society for Educational Technology's (MSET) Common Ground conference. There, they attended panel discussions directed to MAP's specific needs and collected materials from vendors. The teachers supplemented their conference experience with free, interactive webinars that could be scheduled at their convenience and targeted their specific questions about systems, apps, and programs.

USEFUL WEB SITES AND BLOGS

Computer Technology and Special Education Blogs
- Edutopia: http://www.edutopia.org
- TeachThought: http://www.teachthought.com
- Free Technology for Teachers: http://www.freetech4teachers.com
- Moving at the Speed of Creativity: http://www.speedofcreativity.org
- SpeechTechie: http://www.speechtechie.com
- OT's with Apps: http://www.otswithapps.com
- Teachers with Apps (both the reviews and blog): http://www.teacherswithapps.com

Sites We Check Weekly (General Education)
- Edshelf: http://www.edshelf.com
- Teaching Like It's 2999: http://www.teachinglikeits2999.blogspot.com
- EmergingEdTech: http://www.emergingedtech.com
- The Pursuit of Technology Integration Happiness: http://www.edutechintegration.blogspot.com
- Learning in Hand: http://www.learninginhand.squarespace.com/blog
- Discovery Education Blog: http://www.blog.discoveryeducation.com
- Teach42 (Steve Dembo from Discovery Ed.): http://www.teach42.com
- Several *Education Week* blogs (and *Education Week* itself), mainly:
  - Ed Tech Researcher: http://www.blogs.edweek.org/edweek/edtechresearcher
  - Digital Education: http://www.blogs.edweek.org/edweek/DigitalEducation
- Tech Savvy Educator: http://www.techsavvyed.net

Bookmarked Sites for Information on Our Current Systems
- Kathy Schrock's Guide to Everything: http://www.schrockguide.net (see Kathy's blog on Discovery Education and her "Kaffeeklatsch" blog)
- Google Apps Webinars: http://www.google.com/enterprise/apps/education/resources/recorded-webinars.html
- Google in Education Google+ page: https://plus.google.com/+GoogleinEducation/posts
- UDL Tech Toolkit: http://www.udltechtoolkit.wikispaces.com
- Eric Sheninger's Pinterest: http://www.pinterest.com/esheninger

The large number of options forced us to focus our energy. There were many applications that performed similar functions but did not cross-communicate, so we added interoperability as an important criterion for our organizational apps. For example, all programs that had calendar functions had to be able to sync to iCal so that students and teachers could maintain consolidated calendars. This one small requirement—an essential one for students struggling with executive function deficits—helped eliminate many options and highlighted the strengths of others.

Another example of this selection process was our response to students' struggle with basic study skills like note taking and studying for tests. We had observed that flashcards were a very useful tool for our students, but their function was diminished because students struggled to decide what to put on them, keep track of them, and sort them (categorizing flashcards into "know," "sort of know," and "don't know"). In addition, many of our students have poor handwriting skills, so handwritten flashcards were illegible or cryptic. To respond to these needs, we piloted a system of two-column note taking that could easily be transferred into a flashcard application. We found about 10 flashcard apps that looked reasonable. In the end, we selected Quizlet (http://www.quizlet.com) because it was easy to import to and from Excel (perfect for taking two-column notes), was useable both online and on the device after synching (so students could study outside internet range), and had a robust library of flashcards that students could use. Last, we liked Quizlet because it is free, meeting all our criteria: student needs, ease of use, compatibility with our other systems, and cost. When vetting options, we always kept cost in mind and explored free and inexpensive options first. Our assessments of paid programs always evaluated the value added when there was a paid version of an application rather than the trimmed down "lite" version. For the most part, we found that the free or inexpensive solutions met our most important needs.

MOVING TO ROLLOUT

Part of the technology committee's work was to determine how to best give access to iPads along with the ability to experiment with a wide variety of apps. As our technology teachers conspicuously "played" with the new technology resources and options, interest and enthusiasm for trying new technology spread to other staff. This enthusiasm was essential to combat the understandable apprehension that teachers had about its potential distraction from content. The technology teachers demonstrated iPad use in classroom settings, providing other teachers with a pre-view of the benefits. The technology committee shared its failures and frustrations, modeling a process that encouraged generating solutions rather than becoming sty-mied by obstacles. We also openly discussed the fact that while there might not be a perfect solution, "good enough" was worthwhile and could get us started.

Rolling out Edmodo

Our natural deadline, the start of the new school year, forced us to move forward, even as we struggled to make final decisions. We focused tightly on our most impor-tant priority as determined by the needs assessment: getting a programwide com-munication system in place. Our needs assessment phase had resulted in our using our systematic process to make a head-to-head comparison of our options. From four options, Google, Edline (bought by Blackboard), SchoolForce, and Edmodo, we decided to go with Edmodo. Our decision spreadsheet can be found in Figure 16.1.

As shown in the spreadsheet, the technology committee found that Edmodo best met our needs. A key selling point was the interoperability with Google Drive, which provides a cloud-based document storage system. In addition, there were several other options on Edmodo that appealed to the technology committee. The interface was accessible and user-friendly and felt familiar to Facebook users. In addition, a robust system of notices promised to help keep students and parents informed of new assign-ments. Edmodo's very basic gradebook required us to create a workaround through which we maintained the most basic subscription to Edline so that teachers could continue to use the online gradebook feature (Easy Grade Pro). Creating a transparent and easily navigable workaround (we had to teach parents and students to ignore the conspicuous "grades" tab on Edmodo) took hours of experimentation and discussion. In the end, our solution was not so elegant as we would like, but it is easy for parents to access once they have completed the multistep process the first time.

The rollout for Edmodo took detailed planning that was different for different stakeholders. Over the course of a month, we used enthusiastic summer interns to

Need	Issue to keep in mind when assessing software	Edline	Google	Edmodo	SchoolForce	Other comments
Cost		Several thousand dollars	Free	Free	Program too expensive, Model Autism Program is too small	
Central interface, connectivity	Need one interface	One portal	Separate from Edmodo	Can synch Google Docs	Eliminated	
Online grades	Easy for teachers, parents	Easy Grade Pro only	n/a	Gradebook inadequate.	Eliminated	Teachers like, used to Easy Grade Pro
Calendar synchronization	Good access for all	Can export to iCal, no import	Multiple calendars, synchronizes to iCal, push notifications	Calendar synch no iCal import, only exports	Eliminated	Query need to import and export
Notes storage	Can access at home and school	Student posting	Google Drive	Can link Google Drive folder to Edmodo	Eliminated	Student participation important
Clear assignments (calendar links to assignments)	Easy for parents to check, need due date and supporting docs	Clumsy, have to click around, poor linking	Complicated	Does it all	Eliminated	Essential this be easy
Push notification		No	n/a, but Google calendar reminders	Lots of notices	Eliminated	
Reminders synchronized to one calendar		Reminders hard to find, must force push, some e-mail notices	No	Reminder on Edmodo home page	Eliminated	Reminders important
Task list		No		No task list but can use calendar	Eliminated	
Parent communication		Grades only, update web pages	Parents have to set up Google accounts for under-13-year-olds	Sends e-mails and text messages	Eliminated	
Alternatives to hand writing (voice-to-text, keyboarding)			Easy taking notes in Google Docs, hard with Word	Templates can be uploaded	Eliminated	iPad can have DragonSpeak

Figure 16.1.   Decision spreadsheet for comparing options. We chose Edmodo.

set up all the pages we would need. They created the spreadsheets necessary to track usernames, passwords, and page codes. Students were enrolled on Edmodo in their class so that they had individualized pages reflecting their fall courses; teachers were linked to the courses and the students they were teaching, and parents were given access codes so they could track their child's account.

The training that the teachers received during our precious 3 days of orientation before school started took the form of three 1-hour workshops. Teachers came with their laptops and worked directly on their pages with support from the technology committee. Teachers were required to use Edmodo consistently for making assignments (on the calendar); storing class notes, with supporting information for studying for tests and basic information about the current unit; and posting grades (via Edline and Easy Grade Pro). By the time school started, all teachers were ready to go, though some more robustly than others.

Training was also essential for students and their parents, especially students with executive function challenges. We spent most of the first week of school working with students to learn Edmodo and navigate Google Drive. Students set up their Google Drive folders, created organization systems, and turned in fake assignments on Edmodo until they demonstrated fluency. Although the week was a lot of classtime to take up front, the teachers who did not go through this process slowly and systematically enough found that certain students were still struggling after 2 months into the school year. This confirmed what educators know to be preferred practice: One must spend time at the beginning of the year teaching routines and skills so that students can navigate them fluently. Doing so will free up time for substantive learning the rest of the year.

Parents also needed training, and we dedicated half of back-to-school night to technology walk-throughs. All parents were given a laptop (one per family) and an individualized packet with activation codes and basic instructions for using Edmodo. Parents navigated their child's pages while trainers went through the essential points on a projected "test student" (whose parent was "Helicopter Mom"). By the end of the evening, parents had completed basic competency tasks; perhaps more important, we were able to identify parents with challenges in managing the system. As a result, teachers focused on ensuring that their children, who would not have effective IT support at home, acquired independent mastery of the technology at school.

Rolling out the iPads

The iPad rollout involved training and supporting fewer players. To identify highly motivated teachers, we invited classroom teams to fill out applications (see Figure 16.2) to pilot our new technology in their classrooms. We focused on convincing teams to support the difficulties that might arise with students struggling with unforeseen issues or with staff frustrated by new systems, and we involved classroom teachers as a program "sales force" and as trainers for other staff. We purposefully did not move to a programwide rollout: We wanted highly motivated partners in the classrooms to help us work out the program kinks and create an atmosphere of privilege regarding access to these new resources. We hoped to spread the use of these technologies organically, from peer to peer (teacher to teacher), and foster a climate of exploration and expansion that had begun with the technology working committee. Four classrooms were targeted for the first phase of the rollout, with

Fill out ALL application sections with black type below. Examples of the white section are below the application in white type.

DUE Friday, JULY 13th

	Application 1	Application 2	Point Person
	What is one way you will you use the iPad/have students use the iPad for support in this area?	What is another way you will use the iPad/have students use the iPad for support in this area?	Who in your classroom will take responsibility for these applications?
Executive Function/ Organization			
Academics			
Arts			
Accessibility			
Other—This is your place to show why your classroom is a better fit than any of the other MAP classrooms			
In what ways will your classroom staff be available to support other staff members in transitioning to iPads?			
Where do you think your classroom would have the most trouble switching from laptops to iPads?			
Problem Solve! You come in and the internet is down. Unfortunately, everything you were going to do on the iPads today was on the internet. What is your Plan B?			

EXAMPLES	Application 1	Application 2	Point Person
Executive Function/Organization	Using iCal to organize due dates for student work.		Monica
Academics	Using GoogleDocs to create student note templates—students will fill in notes and save to their own folders.		Bonnie
Arts	Students can work in groups to create songs in GarageBand and then work as a class to produce their own radio show podcast.		Kevan
Accessibility	Teach a class where all the students go into Universal Access settings and try out different screen reader voices and speeds, rating them and deciding their personal preferences.		Erin
Other	Have students map out a route to Grub Club using the Maps app.		Erin

Figure 16.2. Classroom team application for pilot iPad set. Distributed to all classrooms in MAP via Google Drive.

some classrooms receiving a set of devices and others receiving devices for targeted students. One lower school classroom received a set of iPads loaded with apps that the teachers had requested and that had been vetted by the technology committee. Middle and high school classrooms received a set of iPads for use in designated instructional areas and to support specific students. Each iPad had easy-to-use

speech-to-text apps (Nuance's Dragon Dictation app and the iPad's built in Dictation feature) and text-to-speech apps (VoiceOver), which quickly won supporters.
In math, students used the iPad for IXL, a math fluency program, and the Rover
browser let students do web searches even on sites that use flash animation. By our
adding a ZAGG keyboard case, students found the iPads as useable in typing tasks
as a laptop.

In addition, we gave individual students iPads if their individualized education
programs (IEPs) called for text-to-speech or speech-to-text software. To augment
students' listening experience, we also included the Audible app on the iPad; this
allowed students to listen to beautifully narrated books while following along in
their hard copies. The iPad's VoiceOver feature that can read text on the screen
has helped many students, though some complain about the synthetic voice. Apps
that provide more user-friendly readers are a high priority for us. However, even
just using Audible, VoiceOver, and Dragon Dictation made the iPad worthwhile;
these apps gave students access to the curriculum in a way that would previously
have required extensive staff support as scribes or readers. In addition to the independence gained by students through the iPad, once mastered, the iPad allowed
instructional staff to support multiple students at once. We also found that though
not as robust as software like Dragon Naturally Speaking or Read&Write Gold, the
alternatives given to us by the iPad required less training to use and were a cost-
effective method of implementing the assistive technology services needed by our
students.

One of our biggest challenges was managing student distractibility with the
iPad; students wanted to fill the iPad with apps for games. We were forced to limit
iPad use, although we still allowed students to access the iPads as a reward for
appropriate behaviors and participation.

Student Use Issues: Evolving Policies

Confidentiality and user policies were a major area of challenge. We had to work
with Ivymount to completely revamp our acceptable use policies for staff and students. We were able to get pro bono services from a law firm to review Ivymount's
confidentiality requirements, highlighting the need for systematic policies to protect student confidentiality and promote safe use. This issue has been an evolving challenge, and we remain cautious about cloud-based computing. To ensure
compliance with the confidentiality standards required by our school, we had to
carefully vet applications that store data in the cloud. Doing so was often a time-
consuming process, but the assistance of our extraordinary technology teachers
and pro bono lawyers made it possible.

In addition to formulating an acceptable use policy, we implemented an internet safety policy. A new responsibility for schools using technology, as well as a
requirement for those taking part in the E-Rate program,[1] is teaching students
how to be safe on the internet and responsible in their use of that technology in
school and, in the future, work settings. Although we continue to use filters to block
sites considered dangerous or inappropriate (social media and pornography are

---

[1]The E-Rate program is a federal support program for schools in the United States that helps them obtain affordable telecommunications and internet access. It is funded by the Universal Service Fund based
on fees collected by companies that provide interstate and/or international telecommunications services.

two examples), these filters are not perfect. In fact, to determined teenagers, they can be seen as challenges to be circumvented. Here again, we did not reinvent the wheel; we found policies adopted by other educational institutions on the web and adapted them for our needs. We needed our lawyers and technology committee to merge the needs of the school with the legal requirements of school responsibilities in the technology setting. The results were documents that all teachers and students had to sign. For staff, this consisted of a Technology Policy and an Acceptable Use Policy. These outlined the staff's responsibility to follow any Ivymount, state, and federal guidelines (e.g., COMAR, FERPA, HIPAA) as they relate to technology use, and outlined the process of getting support for technology at Ivymount. Students have a modified version of the Acceptable Use Policy giving guidelines of what is appropriate to access at school and consequences for misuse. In addition, everyone was given an Internet Safety Policy that outlines the steps Ivymount takes to protect students from obscene material at Ivymount.

More important than that document, however, was the educating that administration and teachers did to support common sense use and safety. No policy covers every eventuality, and we worked actively to help teachers and students learn to see when they were straying into unethical or dangerous territory with the technology, whether by "borrowing" devices for personal use or using their personal devices during the school day to surf to inappropriate sites. With free access to the internet via cell phones, we had to expand our technology policies to include use of those devices by teachers and students during the day. For the most part, cell phone use was not allowed and enforcement was consistent across the school. This policy helped reduce teacher and student distraction and navigation to inappropriate sites.

Teaching Students to Self-Monitor

Embracing new technology gave us ample opportunities to teach an essential 21st century skill: learning to use the internet in a safe, appropriate way. We combined a robust internet education program with equally robust external monitoring. Whereas all schools should do some internet education, in the case of students with autism that education needs to be much more systematic, explicit, and frequent to ensure that rules and expectations are clear. At MAP, our students have unusual facility to circumvent filters, post to web sites, and enter potentially dangerous sites. Incidents of misuse result both from intentional access and innocent misunderstandings. Therefore, we put great emphasis on identifying school-appropriate web sites, described the details of safe internet use, and provided incentives to identify misuse. For example, we explicitly taught that pornography is ubiquitous on the internet and that students may stumble on sites when conducting research (the most famous example being http://www.whitehouse.gov vs. http://www.whitehouse.com). Students were taught to immediately navigate to a known site and get a teacher to help them clean out cookies and the history from the browser. As part of our behavior system, students were awarded bonus points for this honesty and for their help identifying inappropriate sites (these bonus points could be accumulated to purchase various rewards, including iPad and computer use). To monitor student use, we allowed laptops or iPads to be used only where these devices could be monitored; we turned all computer screens to face the classroom so that they could easily be seen by other students and teachers across the room. In addition, to further monitor use, we made sure students understood that teachers would check browser histories and that if their history has been erased, teachers would assume students had been surfing sites not allowed at school. Students who had consistent difficulty staying on safe sites made lists of sites that were appropriate and limited themselves to those sites, a strategy used with our more impulsive "clickers." The sites might contain recreational destinations, but none with adult sections so frequent in fan fiction and other sites where users upload content. These students were also not allowed to search the web during academic times without supervision. This strategy helped them learn to control what to click on.

In addition, we worked explicitly with students to help them learn how to vet web sites for academic integrity as well as social appropriateness. We openly discussed the difference between what students could access at school versus at home. Our standards at school are rigorous. This instruction allowed our students to articulate and practice different use patterns in different settings. For example, in school, we did not allow any games involving guns or blood, even though we knew that many students played such games at home with parental permission. We also encouraged and supported families to openly discuss what is appropriate in their home settings and to monitor that use through keystroke and monitoring software. We helped students determine legal versus illegal sites, as distinct from sites that are socially or morally acceptable and unacceptable (which can shift from family to family). It took a high level of vigilance, some luck, and many mistakes to arrive at a place where students had their own web pages, managed their electronic calendars, and could petition teachers and administrators to lift restrictions on blocked web sites.

CONCLUSION

Technology has been a big part of MAP since its inception in 2006, when we assigned each student a laptop to support written production and allowed each to do research on the internet. Many fiascos later, including multiple student melt-downs and teacher tantrums over the internet being inaccessible, presentations not projecting, folders and files lost or moved (sometimes for malicious reasons), and innumerable visits to unmentionable web sites, we are still learning. However, we continue to learn and grow and use each obstacle as a teaching opportunity to show our students how to manage frustration, temptation, and rage. Challenges will continue, and learning to use technology as the powerful tool it can be is a process that we must embrace to prepare our students for maximum options in the world outside of school, the real world. Although the road to implementation for many of these emerging technologies can be intimidating—and not entirely paved—the educational world, especially within the context of diverse student needs, is transforming. We have a responsibility as educators to lead our students into this new and exciting era. As we better understand these technologies, we can equip our students with the tools to master them and open doors to opportunities that were dismissed as impossible less than 10 years ago.

Adult Transition to the Workplace

Katharina I. Boser

■ ■

In this section, we highlight a study that investigates ways in which mobile technologies can enhance the transition from a school environment to the workplace for young adults with autism spectrum disorder (ASD).

Use of mobile technologies can support the difficult task of developing independent living and working skills for adolescents and adults with ASD. In this final chapter "Using Mobile Technologies to Support Students in Work-Transition Programs" by Gillian R. Hayes, Michael T. Yeganyan, Jed R. Brubaker, Linda J. O'Neal, and Stephen W. Hosaflook, the authors describe an intervention study that evaluated the impact of providing a program they developed for iOS mobile devices called Transition in the Workplace (TiW). Adolescents with ASD and supporting school staff used the software to develop action plans for training students how to do such activities as updating a resume, securing job applications, preparing for interview questions, enrolling in classes, completing homework, attending specialist appointments, and coordinating transportation. Etiquette reminders, destination check-in points, and hygiene were other areas addressed in the training.

Program participants improved their ability to learn socially from each other, gained confidence, and were highly motivated to make use of the mobile devices in their transition activities. Likewise, staff demonstrated both increased confidence and improved abilities in their use of the technologies and in application of these new skills to their own and their students' workplaces.

This study represents important work that is needed to help a growing group of people with ASD who are now young adults. In our increasingly technology-driven world, people with ASD draw a unique benefit from their affinity with machines. Developers and researchers should capitalize on this affinity when designing tools to be used in therapy and education to help young adults with ASD learn the skills necessary for independence and success in adulthood.

Using Mobile Technologies to Support Students in Work-Transition Programs

■ ■

Gillian R. Hayes, Michael T. Yeganyan, Jed R. Brubaker, Linda J. O'Neal, and Stephen W. Hosaflook

Supporting students with disabilities, particularly those with autism spectrum disorder (ASD), to transition from school into adulthood can be a difficult challenge (Schall & Wehman, 2008; Sitlington & Clark, 2006). The Individuals with Disabilities Education Act (IDEA) Amendments of 1997 (PL 105-17) requires schools to promote transition planning: movement from school to postschool activities (e.g., work, further education and training, independent living). However, even with IDEA, transition planning has been somewhat unsuccessful in the face of four substantial challenges (Tomas & Dykes, 2011). First, youth with disabilities are significantly more underemployed or unemployed when compared to their peers in the general population (Lindstrom, Doren, Metheny, Johnson, & Zance, 2007). Second, youth with disabilities are far more likely to drop out of school (both high school and postsecondary education). Third, people experiencing disabilities participate in fewer community activities and social relationships and report feeling more isolated (Stancliffe et al., 2007; Wehman, Inge, Revell, & Brooke, 2006). Fourth, the majority of these individuals do not expect their low quality of life to improve, and 40% of them expect life to get worse (Wehman et al., 2006).

We are grateful to the numerous sources of funding for this work, including an NSF CAREER Grant 0846063, support from the California Department of Rehabilitation, Orange County Department of Education, and the Regional Center of Orange County. In addition, we appreciate the in-kind donation of time from Tiwahe Technology to support this work. Meg Cramer, Lynn Dombrowski, Erick Custodio, Sen Hirano, and the numerous students, staff members, and parents who participated in this program were essential to the completion of this work. Finally, we thank Katharina I. Boser and Matthew S. Goodwin for their support, encouragement, and critique in the writing of this chapter.

There are many strategies proposed for addressing transition planning. These include starting at a young age (Tomas & Dykes, 2011) and maximizing personal freedom and self-sufficiency through self-determination (Skouge, Kelly, Roberts, Leake, & Stodden, 2007; Steer & Cavioulo, 2002). Assistive and educational technologies have also been touted as a response to the challenges of transition planning (Skouge et al., 2007; Tomas & Dykes, 2011). Computer-based instruction has been used to teach transition skills such as shopping (Hansen & Morgan, 2008), scheduling (Gentry, Wallace, Kvarfordt, & Lynch, 2010), and using public transportation (Mechling & O'Brien, 2010). In addition, some classroom-based technologies designed for academic learning have resulted in teaching the social skills needed for transition (Cramer, Hirano, Tentori, Yeganyan, & Hayes, 2011). Adopting simple off-the-shelf hardware (e.g., iPods, iPads, mobile phones) has been suggested by both the media and researchers (Blood, Johnson, Ridenour, Simmons, & Crouch, 2011) to teach transition skills. These systems can support work (e.g., scheduling, communication, task management) and life skills (e.g., way finding, socialization). In this chapter, we discuss our experiences with an intervention that introduces iOS devices and applications to students to support transition.

INTERVENTION

Technological interventions—such as computer-mediated communication (Burke, Kraut, & Williams, 2010), video modeling (Bellini & Akullian, 2007), and socially assistive robots (Feil-Seifer, 2008)—have been used to help students with ASD become more independent and better prepared for adulthood. Building on these approaches, we developed Technology in the Workplace (TiW), a program for students with ASD, school staff, and their parents to support the transition from school to the work force. The TiW program was designed in cooperation with five school districts and two county organizations using relatively low-cost, off-the-shelf technologies. Due to an overall interest in standardization, particularly going forward as new devices are purchased year after year, the school districts made a choice to use iOS as the platform for the mobile intervention, including iPod Touch, iPad, and iPhone devices. The iOS hardware involved in this intervention cost less than $500 per student (and typically less than $200), and all downloaded content and applications were free.

The TiW program includes the development of individualized action plans for student transition (see Figure 17.1); use of iOS mobile devices during school, work, and personal time; attendance at training workshops focused on using these devices; and in most cases, on-the-job use of iOS devices. To further motivate students, a variety of strategies were used, including signing contracts dealing with acceptable and regular use or incentive and token-based rewards programs. In general, such strategies as action plans and incentive structures are often used in transition programs. What is unique about the TiW program is its emphasis on engagement with and use of mobile technologies, in this case iOS devices.

Participants

Across five public school districts and two county organizations, 61 students and 27 staff participated in the first year of the intervention, and 61 students and 43 staff in the second year (Table 17.1). Staff included individuals working at the department of rehabilitation, regional centers, work transition specialists from individual schools,

| TECHNOLOGY IN THE WORKPLACE ACTION PLAN | Page 1of 2 |

| Last Name | First Name | ID #: | Employment Specialist | Agency |

Participant Employment Goal/IPE:_____

DOR/ARRA Project 1/2011 –6/2011

TECHNOLOGY BASICS COMPLETED

☐ Email Account   *_____
☐ Calendar   *_____
☐ Application Store Access *_____

☐ Task Manager Application *_____
☐ Map Application   *_____
☐ Weather Application   *_____

*Please indicate date completed   ☐ iPad   ☐ iPodTouch   ☐ iPhone   ☐ Other

TECHNOLOGY OBJECTIVE:	ACTION PLAN ACTIVITIES	SUPPORTS/ ACCOMMODATIONS	EXPECTED OUTCOME (Date)	AGENCY/PERSON PROVIDING SERVICE	OUTCOME PROGRESS* M/NM (Date)					
					M	NM	1	2	3	4

* (1) Beginner Skills   (2) Needs Consistent Staff Support   (3) Needs Minimal Staff Support   (4) 100% Independent

Figure 17.1.   Front page of an action plan.

and teachers. Parents at times attended workshops during the first year, but they are not heavily represented in our data (*n* = 9). Parents did not participate in the second year of the program.

Action Plans

Known as job coaches, work transition specialists from each school district who work hands-on with students to place them in jobs regularly prepare action plans for students in their programs. These plans include tasks and goals focused on work

Table 17.1.   Summary of program participants

Organization	Year one			Year two		
	Students	% ASD	Staff	Students	% ASD	Staff
School I	15	100	13	14	100	8
School C	15	100	1	16	75	6
School N	6	50	2	14	29	5
School S	10	30	2	6	33	2
School W	15	87	2	11	82	2
Regional Center and Dept. of Rehabilitation			7			20
Total participants	61	80	27	61	67	43

transition, academic education, and daily living challenges. Action plans are highly individualized, like other curricula for students with disabilities, and are matched to varied ability levels, work duties, and education plans. Common work-related duties include updating the student's resume, securing applications for work for the student, preparing the student for interview questions, providing etiquette reminders, and arranging destination check-in points. Common education goals include assisting the student in enrolling in classes and completing homework on a daily basis. Common daily living goals include helping the student with attending specialist appointments, transportation coordination, and hygiene care. During the first month of the intervention each year, job coaches developed action plans related to technology use alongside other skills.

iOS Devices

Each TiW student uses an iOS device provided by a variety of sources (e.g., schools, the department of rehabilitation, parents, private donors). Most students use an iPod Touch, but in special cases, a different platform may be substituted. For example, through the individual's involvement in the program, we learned that one student had a significant visual impairment (neither his parents nor any teacher had previously recognized the problem) and so in the second year we provided him with an iPad with a larger screen size. Staff in the program also used mobile devices, including iPhones, iPods, iPads, and Android phones. Nearly all the staff members were using personal devices.

Training

All TiW program participants also participated in monthly training workshops lasting approximately 2 hours (see Figure 17.2 for overall program time line). The first two workshops each year focused on administrative topics and staff training and included only staff. Students then joined staff during the following months. These workshops focused on two objectives: First, they established a core set of iOS applications and usability skills across all districts, and second, they served to motivate and interest participants while providing the support needed for individuals struggling to use and to understand the technology.

In the first 2 years of the program, we experimented with two different models of instruction. In the first year, each session typically started with a short classroom lecture covering the specific topics for that month (Table 17.2). Once the participants were familiar with the overall information, they were encouraged to use these skills at hands-on, topic-specific stations positioned around the room, each of which was staffed by a researcher. During this time, participants learned topic-specific application (app) functions and were encouraged to explore other applications with similar functionality. Participants moved between stations, spending as much or as little time as needed to feel competent.

In the second year, we took a lab model approach for the hands-on learning. In this model, we again began with a short lecture for each type of activity, but between these lectures, rather than allow open experimentation, participants practiced with specific activities. To facilitate these activities, participants completed monthly challenges leading up to the workshops (e.g., create a list of tasks needed for a job interview, collect e-mail addresses for three people). At the workshops,

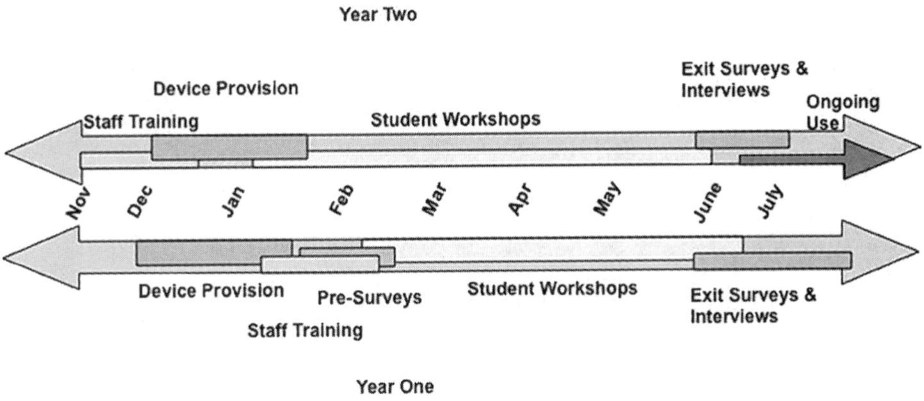

Year Two

Figure 17.2. Timeline of TiW program and evaluation activities.

participants discussed specifics regarding implementation of specific tasks using the information and materials prepared as part of the monthly challenges.

During both years, the workshops then concluded with small-group discussions (5–10 participants, including students and staff) of what was learned, strategies for using devices, and so on. Finally, in a large group, participants shared conversation highlights from their small-group discussions, with students being encouraged to speak on behalf of their groups.

EVALUATION

We used a mixed-methods approach to understand the effectiveness of this intervention, including participant observation, interviews, and surveys. Our observations during workshops focused on how the students and staff interacted with each other and with their devices during the training, as well as on specific challenges and successes during the hands-on work sessions.

We administered a repeated cross-sectional survey at the beginning and end of the first year to measure differences in attitudes, awareness, and perceptions of technology among participants. The majority of questions used a 5-point Likert scale for which pre- versus post-scores were analyzed using two-tailed t tests. This survey also queried participant demographics and overall views on transition activities.

At the end of the first year, we conducted phone interviews with 10 participants (5 students, 5 staff) for approximately 30 minutes each. Interview topics included reasons for joining the program, favorite topics, interesting experiences within and outside the workshops, and any issues and challenges. All interviews were audio-recorded and transcribed. The transcripts were then coded to uncover themes for understanding participant experiences, attitudes, perceptions, and challenges within the workshops. We noted which iOS applications participants explored and how useful they found these tools to be in their experiences outside of the workshops. These themes were used to inform the quantitative analysis of the survey data (and vice versa) as well as evidence from the field notes.

Table 17.2.   Summary of workshop activities

Year one		
Month	Activities	Participants
February	• District introductions	District staff and job coaches
	• Project overview	
	• Project implementation	
	• Overall scheduling	
March	• Acceptable use policies and cyber safety	District staff and job coaches
	• Device setup and account registration	
	• Calendar sharing	
April	• Google calendar	Students and staff
	• Google maps	
	• Gmail	
May	• Task management	Students and staff
	• Work etiquette and appropriateness	
June	• Hygiene	Students and staff
	• Nutrition and fitness	
	• Music and art	
Year two		
Month	Activities	Participants
September	• Results of workshops from previous year	Transition specialists only
	• Planning for upcoming year	
October	• Results of workshops from previous year	All staff
	• Overview of current year activities	
	• Device setup	
	• Action plans	
January	• Technology etiquette	Students and staff
	• Contact management	
	• Basic e-mail	
	• Basic calendaring	
	• Finding directions	
February	• E-mail etiquette	Students and staff
	• Advanced e-mail	
	• ToDo lists and task management	
	• Sharing calendars and calendar events	
March	• Alarms, reminders, and notifications	Students and staff
	• Shared ToDo lists	
	• Advanced mapping	

Table 17.2.

	Year two	
Month	Activities	Participants
April	• Social skills	Students and staff
	• Video modeling	
	• Social networking (for work and fun)	
May	• Hygiene	Students and staff
	• Health and fitness	

RESULTS

Our multipronged approach adapted to the various needs of program participants. It also drove motivation for participants to become and stay involved in the program. The intervention increased the participants' confidence and competence in their abilities. In this section, we present these results in more detail and describe the open challenges that remain for this and similar technology-based interventions.

Learning Through Workshops and Social Interaction

Students with ASD often struggle to develop social skills and engage in meaningful social interactions (Volkmar, Lord, Bailey, Schultz, & Klin, 2004; Wing, 1981). They report that they feel lonely and, as a result of their disabilities, have fewer friends than do their peers (Bauminger & Kasari, 2000). Much effort has gone into helping students with ASD build these highly needed social skills from an early age (Kamps, Leonard, Vernon, Dugan, & Delquandri, 1992; Laushey, Heflin, Shippen, Alberto, & Fredrick, 2009; Sasso, Peck, & Garrison-Harrell, 1998) to enable greater independence and social activity in adulthood (Matson, Dempsey, & Fodstad, 2009; Orsmond, Krauss, & Seltzer, 2004). Thus, social skills development is a core component in transition planning. In the intervention, we emphasized building social skills through use of collaborative iOS applications (e.g., calendar sharing) as well as by using a breakout-style model of instruction that emphasized small-group interaction.

Topic-Specific Work In the first year, we used a workstation approach for specific topics. In this model, a researcher led each topic-specific workstation to help participants learn to use features and functionality of various iOS applications. Participants moved from one station to the next in a self-organized fluid manner. At each station, the researcher provided participants with a set of tasks (e.g., creating a Google calendar and sharing that calendar with someone else). During these activities, participants would ask the researchers and other participants questions about setup, usage, and functionality. Participants were also encouraged to continue exploring features and functionality of the specific application being taught and to investigate similar types of applications they downloaded on their own.

In the second year, we used a similar approach in terms of having participants work hands-on in small groups. The primary difference, however, was greater use of a lab model and less freeform interactivity. In this model, an instructor explained a particular activity, and participants then practiced that activity in small groups. In both models, participants were encouraged to explore on their own and bring new apps they had found to the attention of their small groups.

> "I learned a lot more about the apps, the Apps Store; it got me exploring more than I did on my own... that's definitely one thing it [workshops] did." (RB, staff)

As participants explored applications they downloaded on their own, they shared ideas and daily life scenarios with each other, leading to searching and discovery of other useful apps. Some students were surprised and excited to find tools that they never thought existed. These apps included support for better shopping strategies, health awareness, and fitness training. Often, these apps were introduced to the students by other students, not by researchers or school staff. The desire to learn about more apps and to share with one another enabled students to overcome many of the barriers that might have prevented them from interacting socially in other contexts.

Collaborative Learning with Peers and Staff   Survey results indicate that participants felt more confident in their ability to "teach other people about apps [they] have used for mobile devices" (Pre M = 3.37, SD = 1.03; Post M = 3.74, SD = 1.18, p = 0.007). The small-group instruction model supported our goal of increased socialization and social learning. In this model, when students struggled, staff could either help them resolve issues or communicate with the research team for further assistance. In practice, however, we observed a surprising result. Not only did the support flow in this expected direction but also students helped each other and staff. Interviews also support this finding:

> "There's, like, other people like me, just like me who are curious and, like, need assistance with their future careers and stuff like that...it really made me feel comfortable that I get to be around students who are, kind of like, are on the same level and position as me." (AC, student)

> "The people were really nice there, and they were allowing us to share our inputs, and that's the main thing that stood out to me....It's not all just take, it's like give and take... and like communications." (JM, student)

Peer interaction among students is particularly important to develop due to the inherent challenges to socialization students with ASD experience (Cotugno 2009; Tse, Strulovitch, Tagalakis, Meng, & Fombonne, 2007; Williams, Koenig, & Scahill, 2007).

> "I liked that it actually allowed them to converse with one another,...sometimes that's hard...I was really excited to hear the knowledge that some of them had regarding the app and the tool and how they were able to share that knowledge...in a different role." (DD, staff)

> "My students, they go out on the weekends together, and so they're using their iPhones more and more. I watched a student in the workshop that actually shares his iPhone with another student for looking up bus routes and looking up movie times and organizing how to get there and what time they're going to meet and all of that...It's just phenomenal." (CH, staff)

Staff can also benefit from social interaction and social learning. In a relatively nonthreatening group setting, they explored apps with other participants, tried new methods to achieve work-related goals, and conversed with other staff about different techniques for supporting their students.

"I think when you get into the smaller groups or the breakout session, it gives people the ability to work with your knowledge and to help us learn more things to teach our students and to help us." (DD, staff)

Regular communication between job coaches and students is critical for supporting transition activities. Applications, such as e-mail or chat, introduced through the TiW program allowed job coaches and students to communicate more easily "through the cloud" than using previous strategies that relied heavily on phone calls and face-to-face meetings. As students became more comfortable with these tools, they began staying in contact with their peers through social network or instant messaging apps. These tools allowed students to increase social interaction among each other, potentially promoting social skills and reducing feelings of being alone.

No single learning style meets all the needs of individuals grappling with incorporating new technologies into their daily living. For students with ASD transitioning into adulthood, this need for multiple approaches to teaching and supporting exploration becomes even more important. The combination of topic-specific stations, small groups, large groups, and extended support at a distance enabled participants to build on basic skills and to improve confidence in their abilities to use mobile technologies and to teach others about them.

Motivation and Sustained Engagement

Often, interventions to support transition activities suffer from a lack of interest or motivation by staff and students. In particular, sustaining engagement following the initial novelty effects of technology-based interventions can be challenging (Bouxsein, Tiger, & Fisher, 2008; Lerner, Mikami, & Levine, 2011).

For students, key motivating factors for participating in the program included using technologies in and learning skills for the workplace. For individuals with disabilities, using assistive technologies can often be stigmatizing (Kaliouby & Goodwin, 2008; Mankoff, Hayes, & Kasnitz, 2010; Morris, Kirschbaum, & Picard, 2010). The opportunity to use iOS devices, however, which are not only mainstream but "cool," garnered interest in the program.

"I was really interested, because I get to use an iTouch, which I thought I would never get. So, it was a good chance to use it, and I know everyone uses it. I heard it was a good opportunity for me to use it in my work, work for the future stuff." (AC, student)

"I wanted to learn something new and how to make working in a work environment easier using technology." (KG, student)

Staff, likewise, were initially motivated by the novelty of the TiW program and the ability to learn more about how technologies can improve their own work practices and those of their students.

"I volunteered because it seemed like a really neat project that I wanted to be involved in. I sort of wanted to learn more about what was out there." (RB, staff)

Continued staff participation indicates that the workshops were meeting the initial goals of the staff as well as those of the students. However, sustained engagement appears also to be related to the staff's ability to see the effect the program had on their students.

"It surprised me probably how quickly and easily they [students] were able to do things on the device,...but it was fun to watch students, how quickly they adapted to using the iPod Touches, which they hadn't had prior use with." (CH, staff)

Throughout the program, both staff and students acquired domain knowledge and expertise. Participants reported significantly higher scores regarding their knowledge of "how to find answers to questions...about mobile technologies" (Pre M = 3.6, SD = 0.98; Post M = 3.9, SD = 0.75, p = 0.04) following the program. This understanding builds confidence and motivation to use these tools.

"I changed with my actual working knowledge of the device 'cause I had an idea of what it was [before the program], but I just didn't have it in my hands to play with it as much. I'm having the opportunity now through the workshops...just actually gaining that practical hands on knowledge." (RB, staff)

In survey responses, a general trend echoes the statements made during interviews. Even before beginning the intervention, participants agreed strongly with such statements as "I enjoy working with mobile devices and other technologies" (Pre M = 4.24, SD = 0.75). Even with participants' initial affinity toward technology, however, the program met the goal of teaching participants new information, as evidenced by sustained participation and changes in attitudes measured on the pre and post surveys. This same question, for example, indicated that participants enjoyed working with the devices more by the end of the program than they had before the program (Pre M = 4.24, SD = 0.75; Post M = 4.47, SD = 0.55, p = 0.02).

Despite the high levels of motivation and interest, as students and staff began to explore more advanced topics, substantial hurdles emerged around continued use. In particular, staff noted the need for extended training, a common problem in adoption of educational technologies in schools (Swallow, Petrie, & Power, 2010), and one that is incredibly expensive to overcome. For these kinds of interventions to be sustained long term, staff members need to be experts in not only their domain of special education and disabilities service but also information technologies.

"[Training] allowed me to assist [students] or kind of troubleshoot something or know what if a parent had a question about an app, or I could go to look for those kinds of things. I mean, you gave me that knowledge that would allow me to help the student with the limited amount that I have, but at least a stepping stone, if that makes sense, to help them." (DD, staff)

Growing Confidence in Use of Technological Tools

"I'm getting a lot more confident...with some of the different technology." (SN, student)

Barriers to learning how to use the technology and deploy it in new and creative ways to support specific needs and goals can challenge educators and their students (Hayes et al., 2010; Hirano et al., 2010). By building both confidence and knowledge, we hoped to improve the capacity of participants to solve problems creatively using the technologies provided. Following the program, participants reported agreeing more strongly with such statements as, "I have valuable ideas about using technology to transition to the workplace" (Pre M = 3.2, SD = 0.91; Post M = 3.5, SD = 0.88; p = 0.02). Likewise, participants described viewing technologies, including laptops and mobile phones they had used prior to the program, differently after their experiences with the intervention.

"I love it, once I started using the [iPhone] I was, like, 'How did we live so long without it? What were we doing before?'...It's amazing how there [are] so many functions to it and there [are] so many ways to connect with people and things to learn about and I think every day it's just, like, wow! ...It's so addicting." (RM, staff)

"Do I view technology differently? I always viewed it as helpful. I guess I view it as more beneficial and seeing how to implement it... in more settings... with more students." (RB, staff)

Through exposure to the tools in workshops and use of them in school, work, and personal activities, students with ASD and the staff who support them were able to explore iOS mobile devices and applications with greater ease. These approaches could be used in the deployment of other assistive and educational technology interventions to limit stress and anxiety for students and staff.

OPEN CHALLENGES FOR TECHNOLOGY ADOPTION AND USE

Several open challenges remain for use of mobile devices to support transition and for other types of assistive and educational technology interventions. These challenges include the struggle between the need for a comprehensive, individualized curriculum and the additional overhead of learning and understanding to use a wide variety of technologies. In addition, technology challenges require skills and resources that educators lack, even with additional training. Finally, concerns relating to personal data, privacy, and security are not yet well addressed for technology-based school interventions. In this section, we describe some of these open challenges.

Software systems built for a broad audience, such as those available for iOS devices, do not always match student goals and capabilities. Job coaches typically work with several students with individualized action plans, making it labor intensive to find applications that each student can use effectively.

"There's no way that you can hand someone or 10 people the same apps and expect all 10 to love them, so it's still going to be a matter of exploring... test and trial. It's kind of complicated!" (RM, staff)

"It's tough to figure out what would work well with or, like, what kinds of applications would work well with different students." (LM, staff)

Universal design for learning (UDL), a key tenet of much of the research work in technology use for individuals with disabilities, stresses the idea of designing for all people, not just persons with disabilities. The Higher Education Opportunity Act of 2008 (PL 110-315) notes that UDL should provide "flexibility in the ways information is presented" and "appropriate accommodation and supports" for students with disabilities. This emphasis on flexibility allows for designers of curricula and technology to develop solutions that work for all while supporting individualized needs. iOS tools are an excellent example of technologies that have been universally designed for all people while allowing for individualization and personalization through the choice of which apps to use, how to use them, and ways to personalize features on these devices. In practice, however, the variety of apps available with similar functionality and descriptions became challenging for participants for a variety of reasons. More "apps for autism" show up in the iTunes App Store every day, and almost none of them have any scientific testing of their efficacy. More research is needed to explore iOS devices as a flexible platform for substantial engagement and learning across a variety of students and contexts.

Second, limitations on devices and available infrastructure act as barriers for sustained use of mobile devices in schools, homes, and the workplace. For example, many participants found that most apps useful for transition activities (e.g., e-mail and mapping) require network connectivity. However, student participants rarely had the resources for mobile phone data plans and instead relied on wireless internet (WiFi) access, which was inconsistent and sometimes required remembering password information, which many students found challenging—an issue we describe in more detail below. Likewise, apps tended to work differently across the various platforms students had, leaving job coaches responsible for learning how to use the apps across multiple devices and troubleshooting issues for several students.

> *"Most surprising thing for me was just that even though the equipment was all made by the same maker, they all do something a little bit different." (DD, staff)*

This difference in functionality created confusion and frustration for both students and staff. Given the limited resources available in schools, rapid technological change is likely to continue to be a challenge.

Third, although security of school networks and student computational devices is a concern in most schools, current practices and policies are not comprehensive enough to address all the potential issues. In our observations, students and job coaches had difficulty remembering usernames and passwords for multiple applications and WiFi hotspots, which reduced app usability and usefulness. In response to this challenge, at each workshop, we set up a station in addition to the task- and topic-specific stations to handle password resets and other support issues.

> *"That's probably one of the things I had trouble with. I'm not too fond of having to create the usernames and passwords for everything." (RM, staff)*

Job coaches, attempting to support students with these issues, responded in a wide variety of ways. Some encouraged students to store login information in unencrypted to-do list apps on their devices, potentially exposing them to security vulnerability issues if someone else were to access their devices. Other job coaches, however, recognized the potential security risks of such a solution and expressed concerns about vulnerabilities. In particular, because of the personal information stored on the devices, they often worried about students losing their devices.

> *"It's so scary, because as much as and as useful as they are, to know that someone can get into your phone and have access to every single contact, messages, voicemails, personal anything, pictures, all of it." (RM, staff)*

In light of these concerns, some staff members described being eager to learn more about the underlying working of the technologies so that they can make knowledgeable decisions. In particular, the individual who expressed the most concerns during interviews also expressed the most interest in learning more about what could be done to keep students "safe":

"I would be probably interested in...safety and security and making sure that the students are and staff are being careful and learning the capabilities of locking passwords and all that kind of stuff so I'm still interested in that." (RM, staff)

Thus, in the second year, we developed modules on the topic of staying safe online, including appropriate presentation of self in social networks and protecting passwords. Although these lessons were well received, particularly by staff members, it is unclear how much of a difference the instruction actually made. Much as with the general population, students who could not remember their various passwords would write them on a piece of paper, often placed in the case with the iOS device. Likewise, rather than safely differentiating passwords among different systems, almost every workshop participant used the same or similar passwords across all apps.

These practices are not entirely surprising—after all, the general population tends to behave in the same way—but they are worrying, particularly for a group of people who may have an especially difficult time differentiating spammers and hackers from others in their social networks. These results indicate that strategies and solutions for securing personal data must be developed that are appropriate for individuals with cognitive disabilities. Thus, we leave as an open challenge the development of additional curricula focused on not only the appropriate behaviors to protect privacy and security online but also the underlying motivation and need for such protection. In addition, an expanded curriculum and more care in the creation and implementation of school-based acceptable use policies would help address some of the risk for schools associated with encouraging both staff and student use.

CONCLUSIONS

Participants in a technology-based transition program initially learned to use a standard suite of tools applicable to independent living and workplace support. As their confidence grew however, they began to explore other apps. These newly discovered apps included games and entertainment, social networking, and nutrition and fitness, as well as a variety of other topics. Many of these are not on the surface work- or transition-related but speak to a broad familiarity with and enjoyment of technology that can help foster successful use of other systems and improve social and life skills. Likewise, staff who were encouraged to take devices home with them, explore on their own, and use them for their own goals were thereby able to begin to learn about a variety of technologies that could be helpful for students. A curriculum that emphasizes hands-on, discussion-oriented, exploratory work can facilitate this type of self-directed learning. However, the sheer volume of available apps, as mentioned earlier, could be overwhelming.

The trend in this space is often to develop custom solutions for specific needs. This path raises barriers for schools trying to limit costs through standardization across particular platforms. Using low-cost, off-the-shelf components presents opportunities for apps that can be individualized at lower costs than using the more traditional custom hardware solutions. However, despite the numerous "apps for autism" in the Android Marketplace and iOS App Store, very few have empirical evidence of efficacy.

At the same time, although many schools have begun to standardize through single-provider platforms for a variety of basic services (e.g., Google for calendaring, e-mail, task and document management), the requirement to have network access on all devices and to enable access to these cloud services through otherwise restrictive school networks can be too high a barrier for usage in everyday school settings. At the same time, continuing the current trend of using only custom applications and one-off solutions is untenable in a digital schooling model. Thus, designers and developers of assistive and educational technologies should consider how to balance the benefits of low-cost, off-the-shelf solutions and those of custom, personalized systems to meet the individual needs of students, especially those with disabilities.

Technological interventions can help support students with ASD and other disabilities during transition planning and transition activities. However, incorporating such interventions requires a comprehensive approach that includes development of individualized plans for students and training for staff as well as students, as we did in the intervention we developed and evaluated in this work. Our experiences over 2 years of offering technology for transition workshops indicate that these kinds of comprehensive interventions can support students in transition and staff by engaging them in self-directed as well as social learning in the use of technologies. Through this model, confidence in the ability to use technologies in transition efforts can improve, and participants are likely to share knowledge, not only with each other, but also with individuals not participating in the program.

REFERENCES

Bauminger, N., & Kasari, C. (2000). Loneliness and friendship in high functioning children with autism. *Child Development, 71,* 447–456.

Bellini, S., & Akullian, J. (2007). A meta-analysis of video modeling and video self-modeling interventions for children and adolescents with autism spectrum disorders. *Exceptional Children, 73,* 261–284.

Blood, E., Johnson, J.W., Ridenour, L., Simmons, K., & Crouch, S. (2011). Using an iPod Touch to teach social and self-management skills to an elementary student with emotional/behavioral disorders. *Education and Treatment of Children, 34*(3), 299–321.

Bouxsein, K.J., Tiger, J.H., & Fisher, W.W. (2008). A comparison of general and specific instructions to promote task engagement and completion by a young man with Asperger's syndrome. *Journal of Applied Behavior Analysis, 41,* 113–116.

Burke, M., Kraut, R., & Williams, D. (2010). Social use of computer-mediated communication by adults on the autism spectrum. In *Proceedings of the 2010 ACM Conference on Computer Supported Cooperative Work* (pp. 425–434). New York, NY: ACM.

Cotugno, A.J. (2009). Social competence and social skills training and intervention for children with autism spectrum disorders. *Journal of Autism and Developmental Disorders, 39,* 1268–1277.

Cramer, M., Hirano, S.H., Tentori, M., Yeganyan, M.T., & Hayes, G.R. (2011, May). *Classroom-based assistive technology: Collective use of interactive visual schedules by students with autism.* Proceedings of CHI meeting, Vancouver, BC, Canada.

Feil-Seifer, D. (2008). *Socially assistive robot-based intervention for children with autism spectrum disorder.* Paper presented at the NEWHRI Workshop, Pasadena, CA.

Gentry, T., Wallace, J., Kvarfordt, C., & Lynch, K. (2010). Personal digital assistants as cognitive aids for high school students with autism: Results of a community-based trial. *Journal of Vocational Rehabilitation, 32,* 101–107.

Hansen, D.L., & Morgan, R.L. (2008). Teaching grocery store purchasing skills to students with intellectual disabilities using a computer based instruction program. *Education and Training in Developmental Disabilities, 43,* 431–442.

Hayes, G.R., Hirano, S., Marcu, G., Monibi, M., Nguyen, D.H., & Yeganyan, M. (2010). Interactive visual supports for children with autism. *Springer Personal and Ubiquitous Computing, 14*(7), 663–680.

The Higher Education Opportunity Act of 2008 (PL 110-315). 20 U.S.C.§§ 1001 *et seq.*

Hirano, S., Yeganyan, M., Marcu, G., Nguyen, D., Boyd, L.A., & Hayes, G.R. (2010). vSked: Evaluation of a system to support classroom activities for children with autism. In *Proceedings of the 2010 Conference on Human Factors in Computing Systems* (pp. 1633–1642). New York, NY: ACM.

Individuals with Disabilities Education Act (IDEA) Amendments of 1997, PL 105-17, 20 U.S.C. §§ 1401 *et seq.*

Kaliouby, R., & Goodwin, M.S. (2008). iSET: Interactive social-emotional toolkit for autism spectrum disorder. In *Proceedings of the 7th International Conference on Interaction Design and Children* (pp. 77–80). New York, NY: ACM. 77–80.

Kamps, D.M., Leonard, B.R., Vernon, S., Dugan, E.P., & Delquandri, J.C. (1992). Teaching social skills to students with autism to increase peer interaction in an integrated first grade classroom. *Journal of Applied Behavior Analysis, 25,* 281–288.

Laushey, K.M., Heflin, L.J., Shippen, M., Alberto, P., & Fredrick, L. (2009).Concept mastery routines to teach social skills to elementary school children with high functioning autism. *Journal of Autism and Developmental Disorders, 39,* 1435–1448.

Lerner, M.D., Mikami, A.Y., & Levine, K. (2011). Socio-dramatic affective-relational intervention for adolescents with Asperger syndrome and high functioning autism: Pilot study. *Autism, 15*(1), 21–42.

Lindstrom, L., Doren, B., Metheny, J., Johnson, P., & Zance, C. (2007). Transition to employment: Role of the family in career development. *Exceptional Children, 73,* 348–366.

Mankoff, J., Hayes, G.R., & Kasnitz, D. (2010). Disability studies as a source of critical inquiry for the field of assistive technology. In *ASSETS '10 Proceedings of the 12th SIGACCESS Conference on Computers and Accessibility* (pp. 3–10). New York, NY: AMC.

Matson, J.L., Dempsey, T., & Fodstad, J.C. (2009). The effect of autism spectrum disorders on adaptive independent living skills in adults with severe intellectual disability. *Research in Developmental Disabilities, 30,* 1203–1211.

Mechling, L., & O'Brien, E. (2010). Computer-based video instruction to teach students with intellectual disabilities to use public bus transportation. *Education and Training in Autism and Developmental Disabilities, 45*(2), 230–241.

Morris, R.R., Kirschbaum, C., & Picard, R.W. (2010, October). Broadening accessibility through special interests: A new approach for software customization. In *ASSETS 2010*, pp. 171–178.

National Organization on Disability. (2007). *The state of the union for people with disabilities, 2007.* Retrieved from http://www.nod.org/about_us/our_history/annual_reports/2007_annual_report

Orsmond, G.I., Krauss, M.W., & Seltzer, M.M. (2004). Peer relationships and social and recreational activities among adolescents and adults with autism. *Journal of Autism and Developmental Disorders, 34*(3), 245–256.

Sasso, M.G., Peck, J., & Garrison-Harrell, L. (1998). Social interaction setting events: Experimental analysis of contextual variables. *Behavioral Disorders, 24,* 34–43.

Schall, C., & Wehman, P. (2008). Understanding the transition from school to adulthood for students with autism. In P. Wehman, M.D. Smith, & C. Schall (Eds.), *Autism and the transition to adulthood: Success beyond the classroom* (pp. 1–14). Baltimore, MD: Paul H. Brookes Publishing Co.

Sitlington, P.L., & Clark, G.M. (2006). *Transition education and services for students with disabilities* (4th ed.). Boston, MA: Allyn & Bacon.

Skouge, J.R., Kelly, M.L., Roberts, K.D., Leake, D.W., & Stodden, R.A. (2007). Technologies for self-determination for youth with developmental disabilities. *Education and Training in Developmental Disabilities, 42,* 475–482.

Stancliffe, R.J., Lakin, C., Doljanace, R., Byun, S.Y., Taub, S., & Chiri, G. (2007). Loneliness and living arrangements. *Intellectual and Developmental Disabilities, 45,* 380–390.

Steer, D.E., & Cavioulo, D. (2002). Connecting outcomes, goals, and objectives in transition planning. *Teaching Exceptional Children, 34,* 54–59.

Swallow, D., Petrie, H., & Power, C. (2010). Understanding and supporting the needs of educational professionals working with students with disabilities and mature age students. *Computers Helping People with Special Needs, 6179,* 489–491.

Tomas, S.B., & Dykes, F. (2011). Promoting successful transitions: What can we learn from RTI to enhance outcomes for all students? *Preventing School Failure, 55*(1), 1–9.

Toppo, G. (2009). iPhone applications can help the autistic. *USA Today.* Retrieved from http://www.usatoday.com/news/health/2009-05-27-iphone-autism_N.htm

Tse, J., Strulovitch, J., Tagalakis, V., Meng, L., & Fombonne, E. (2007). Social skills training for adolescents with Asperger's syndrome and high functioning autism. *Journal of Autism and Developmental Disorders, 37,* 1960–1968.

Volkmar, F.R., Lord, C., Bailey, A., Schultz, R.T., & Klin, A. (2004). Autism and pervasive developmental disorders. *Journal of Child Psychology and Psychiatry, 45,* 135–170.

Wehman, P., Inge, K.J., Revell, W.G., & Brooke, V.A. (Eds.). (2006). Real work for real pay: Inclusive employment for people with disabilities. Baltimore, MD: Paul H. Brookes Publishing Co.

Williams, S.K., Koenig, K., & Scahill, L. (2007). Social skills development in children with autism spectrum disorders: A review of intervention research. *Journal of Autism and Developmental Disorders, 37*(10), 1858–1868.

Wing, L. (1981). Language, social and cognitive impairments in autism and severe mental retardation. *Journal of Autism and Developmental Disorders, 11,* 31–44.

Index

Tables, figures, and footnotes are indicated by *t*, *f*, and *n*, respectively.